MONASTIC WISDOM SI

Thomas Merton

Pre-Benedictine Monasticism

Initiation into the Monastic Tradition 2

MONASTIC WISDOM SERIES

MW1 Cassian and the Fathers:
Initiation into the Monastic Tradition
Thomas Merton, OCSO

MW2 Secret of the Heart: Spiritual Being
Jean-Marie Howe, OCSO

MW3 Inside the Psalms: Reflections for Novices
Maureen F. McCabe, OCSO

MW4 Thomas Merton: Prophet of Renewal
John Eudes Bamberger, OCSO

MW5 Centered on Christ: A Guide to Monastic Profession
Augustine Roberts, OCSO

MW6 Passing from Self to God: A Cistercian Retreat
Robert Thomas, OCSO

MW7 Dom Gabriel Sortais:
An Amazing Abbot in Turbulent Times
Guy Oury, OSB

MW8 A Monastic Vision for the 21st Century:
Where Do We Go from Here?
Patrick Hart, OCSO, editor

MW9 Pre-Benedictine Monasticism:
Initiation into the Monastic Tradition 2
Thomas Merton, OCSO

MONASTIC WISDOM SERIES: NUMBER NINE

Pre-Benedictine Monasticism

Initiation into the Monastic Tradition 2

by

Thomas Merton

Edited with an Introduction by

Patrick F. O'Connell

Preface by

Sidney H. Griffith

CISTERCIAN PUBLICATIONS
Kalamazoo, Michigan

Cistercian Publications
Editorial Offices
The Institute of Cistercian Studies
Western Michigan University
Kalamazoo, Michigan 49008-5415
cistpub@wmich.edu

The work of Cistercian Publications is made possible in part by support from Western Michigan University to The Institute of Cistercian Studies.

Library of Congress Cataloging-in-Publication Data

Merton, Thomas, 1915–1968.
Pre-benedictine monasticism : initiation into the monastic tradition / Thomas Merton.
p. cm. — (Monastic wisdom series ; no. 9)
Includes bibliographical references and index.
ISBN-13: 978-0-87907-073-1
ISBN-10: 0-87907-073-0
1. Monasticism and religious orders—History—Early church, ca. 30–600. I. Title. II. Series.

BR195.M65M47 2006
271.009'015—dc22 2006016013

Printed in the United States of America

TABLE OF CONTENTS

PREFACE

One of Thomas Merton's most enduring gifts to the Church sprang from his ability to read deeply in the abundant and multi-faceted literature of her spiritual and mystical heritage and to give expression to the wisdom he found there in communicable, modern American English. He had the talents to do it; his classical education gave him an enviable command of Latin as well as a smattering of Greek, while his training as a writer and his experience as a poet gave him a rare command of exact expression. His own spiritual journey awakened his critical eye, and always being a "quick-study" in any endeavor he undertook, he soon apprehended the heart of the matter in the principal ancient and medieval sources of Western spirituality. In his own work he then gave the traditional insights an apt wording which spoke directly to the needs of modern times. We still read the results with amazed attention in such classics as *The Sign of Jonas*, *No Man Is an Island*, *The Ascent to Truth*, *New Seeds of Contemplation*, and *Thoughts in Solitude*, just to mention some of the most popular of Merton's books. In terms of clarity, depth and fetching expression, they all stand in stark contrast to the stodgy, impenetrable prose of the translations from French, Italian or Spanish which in Merton's day were still the standard fare for most American Catholics who were interested in serious contemplative reading.

In addition to his interest in the sources of Western spirituality more generally, Merton had a thirst for monastic lore of all kinds, monasticism and the contemplative life being his twin passions. The same skills which made him such a popular writer for the Church at large served him well in his formal capacity as novice master within the Gethsemani community, for whom he prepared lectures and conferences which sometimes drew not just novices and juniors, but a community-wide audience in his own day. Some of the sessions were recorded on audio tape at the time of their delivery, and in this medium a selection of them can still be heard. But now, with Patrick O'Connell's patient editing, the texts of these classes, conferences and lectures on the sources of monastic thought are finally being published. The first response one has on opening this volume of novitiate conferences on pre-Benedictine monasticism borders on awe that Merton had time and energy enough to search out all the material he consulted, some of it still hard to find and most of it still available only in specialized libraries. One has the impression that in spite of the sensible outline of topics he set for his inquiries, he actually followed where the available material led him, and in at least one instance it led him to canvas material of which few in America were even aware of in the sixties of the last century.

One is not surprised that Merton's quest for pre-Benedictine monastic lore led him to the deserts of Egypt, to Anthony, Pachomius and Ammonas. It was to be expected also that he would find his way to the Celtic tradition, long before this material became widely popular. But it is startling to find in his novitiate conferences what one now realizes must have been the first general survey in America of several of the works of the major "monastic" thinkers among the Syriac-speaking Fathers of the Church. Beyond some fairly dense, nineteenth-century translations of the *Demonstrations* of Aphrahat, "the Persian Sage" (d. after 349), and of some of the works of St. Ephraem the Syrian (c. 306–373), just about the only available discussion of Syrian ascetical texts then available in America was to be found in the first two volumes of the late Arthur Vööbus' *History of Asceticism in the Syrian Orient*, a work which Merton used but which he soon seems to have sensed was out of step with the spirit of the sources themselves. Merton then sensibly took Theodoret of Cyrrhus' *Historia Religiosa* as his guide, a source which led him to the riches of Aphrahat, Ephraem and Philoxenus of Mabbūg (d. 523), from whose works in fact one learns the most about the distinctive modes of "monastic" and contemplative life in Syria in the early days of the first flourishing of monasticism in that far-flung, early Christian milieu, where the Aramaic family of languages carried the Gospel as far east as China.

Merton would certainly have appreciated the insight which scholars after his time have achieved as a result of their studies of the texts of Aphrahat and Ephraem, in particular about the etymology and the connotations of the Syriac word for "monk" (*îḥîdāyâ*), and its likely influence on the choice of the Greek term *monachos* to designate one who singlemindedly devotes his or her life to Christ. In the Syriac scriptures, the term is a title of Christ, "the single one" of the Father, found in passages in which the Greek text usually has the phrase, "only begotten" (*monogenēs*). In Syriac, the term also means "single" in the sense of "unmarried." And so in Syriac a "monk" is one who is a "single" in God's service, just like the Father's own "single one," Christ the Lord, whom alone the monk imitates and serves.

Ephraem was a "single" in this sense of the word, albeit not a monk in the modern understanding of the term. Nevertheless, in the Greek monastic tradition of the fifth and sixth centuries he was not infrequently listed along with Anthony and Basil as one of the fathers of monasticism. Works attributed to him in Greek were soon translated into the other languages of early Christianity, including Latin and Old Church Slavonic. Most monastic libraries in the West included at least one work attributed to Ephraem, a fact that makes it ironic that his name seems to have been forgotten in later monastic history in the West. Leave it to Merton to have discovered him in this connection!

In the same vein, Merton's appreciation of the riches to be found in the monastic letters of Philoxenus of Mabbūg anticipated any other American's published appreciation of them by several decades. Doubtless Merton recognized in these letters the influence of Evagrius of Pontus (d. 399), who was also a major influence on the work of Cassian, and hence on the thought of St. Benedict. In this way, perhaps unbeknownst to Merton, Philoxenus' letters did in fact fit the plan to survey pre-Benedictine monasticism. Philoxenus, who belonged to the Church which today we call the "Syrian Orthodox Church," and Isaac of Nineveh after him, who belonged to the "Church of the East," were voices from the Orient which for Merton seem to have spoken for the whole Church, even from beyond the boundaries of what the West would accept as confessional orthodoxy. It must have pleased Merton very much to have perceived this ecumenical potential of monasticism active already in Christian antiquity. As a matter of fact, even today in the university department where I work we still get queries about Isaac of Nineveh, whose work is included in the Orthodox *Philokalia*; people want to know if it is really true that he belonged to the ancient "Church of the East," often deemed to have been "Nestorian."

One wonders if Gethsemani's novices in Merton's day had any inkling of the pioneering character of the journey to the early sources of the monastic heritage which their novice master provided for them. Even now, what Merton wrote and spoke more that forty years ago provides a good introduction to material that is still too often unfamiliar to those interested in monastic history and spirituality. One hopes that the welcome publication of his novitiate conferences will awaken new interest in these sources. Here is the same old Merton; the quick-study monk who gets to the heart of the matter and sets it down in easily communicable, American English! It almost makes you forget that he is retailing ideas which were first expressed more than a millennium ago in Oriental languages, which he read in mostly Latin translations.

Sidney H. Griffith
Institute of Christian Oriental Research
The Catholic University of America
Washington, DC 20064

INTRODUCTION

At the beginning of 1963, two changes took place that significantly affected Thomas Merton's duties as master of novices at the Abbey of Gethsemani. The first was the merging of the novitiate of the choir monks, which Merton had directed since October 1955, with that of the brothers. While Merton was initially of two minds about the new arrangement, worrying that the unique charism of the brothers might get deemphasized or lost by joining them with the choir novices,[1] when the change actually came he was enthusiastic about the result, and experienced a renewal of sorts in his own role as instructor and guide of those newly arrived men testing their vocation. On October 13, 1962, he had expressed in his journal a certain weariness with his teaching that recurred periodically in the years since he began as master of students in 1951:

> What has been the use of all the things I have said, all the spiritual conferences I have given in the last eleven years? All the "monastic spirituality"? The books have been less bad. Perhaps the only thing that can be said for all my "teaching" is that it has been more interesting and has taken a broader view, covered more ground, perhaps gone a little

1. See Merton's comments in a December 20, 1962 letter to Sr. Thérèse Lentfoehr, in which he writes, "I do not know if I told you that we are merging the brothers and choir novitiates in January and I am going to have to try to get the two groups functioning together, without of course changing the nature of the brothers' life. This is going to be quite difficult I think, and I need your prayers." This is an omitted passage from a letter published in Thomas Merton, *The Road to Joy: Letters to New and Old Friends,* ed. Robert E. Daggy (New York: Farrar, Straus, Giroux, 1989), 242–43.

> deeper than was usual. But what does *that* amount to? Fortunately I have also, to some extent, tried to live, and pray, and read, and listen to the silence of the woods.[2]

Writing two weeks later to Tarcisius Conner, OCSO, his former undermaster, who was then studying in Rome, he comments sardonically, "Next year we will probably amalgamate the two novitiates. It would be a logical time to fire me, and I would be delighted. However we will see what comes. I think it is going to be a pretty delicate operation and it will have to be done slowly and carefully and without false optimism and easy clichés, or celebrations of Sunday-school euphoria."[3]

Yet there is something at least approaching euphoria in the journal entry for January 4, 1963, as Merton reflects on the initial phase of the new configuration:

> The merger of the two novitiates is proceeding well, mainly because all the novices are so good. I am happy with the Brother novices, one loves them immediately. They really have something, a special grace of simplicity and honesty and goodness. It is a great grace to have them there: choir and brothers seem happy with each other and everyone seems agreed that the plan is working well—in fact there seems to be all sorts of good things about it that one had not anticipated. The unifying of the novitiate is certainly important and salutary. I think it will mean a great deal—and further I have to admit that though I am carrying it out, it is not originally my idea but the Abbot's. However, I did take a certain initiative and he was pleased to let me do so. I think the grace the brothers have comes from their work, which keeps them perhaps (when properly done) from getting too obsessed with themselves and with their spirituality. It is wonderful how they will go into anything and get it done, not standing

2. Thomas Merton, *Turning toward the World: The Pivotal Years. Journals, vol. 4: 1960–1963*, ed. Victor A. Kramer (San Francisco: HarperCollins, 1996), 257.

3. Thomas Merton, *The School of Charity: Letters on Religious Renewal and Spiritual Direction*, ed. Patrick Hart (New York: Farrar, Straus, Giroux, 1990), 158 [November 27, 1962].

> around scratching their heads with the dubiousness of the choir, or wanting to be told each next move.[4]

The sense of weariness and disillusion with his conferences that he expressed in November has been swept away by a revived enthusiasm for preparing his classes, along with a humble awareness of his own limitations and an increased reliance on the power of God. He writes in his journal for January 15:

> The noise and concern about the novitiate and all those who come to the classes, are having a deep effect on me. The work is hard, though I am doing more than I probably should, in my concern to be well prepared. But also realize the limitations of anything short of prayer and abandonment, as preparation. The limitations of my own capacity. Hence in everything I have come to feel more than ever my need for grace, my total dependence on God, my helplessness without His special intervention, which I may need at any moment. Never has this been so clear to me. Perhaps it was never before as true as now. In consequence my attitude toward the monastery changes. They have need of me and I have need of them. As if without this obedience, and charity, my life would lack sense. It is an existential situation which God has willed for me, and it is part of His Providence—it is not to be questioned, no matter how difficult it may be. I must simply obey God, and this reaches out into everything.[5]

As already evident in his initial comment on January 4, his new responsibilities have even had a transforming (if not permanent) effect on his frequently conflicted attitude toward Dom James Fox, the Abbot of Gethsemani: "In this new condition my attitude toward the abbot is changing. Of course it is obvious that my complaints and discontent have been absurd. Though I can perhaps back them up with plausible arguments, they have no real meaning, they don't make sense. He is what he is, and he means well, and in fact does well. He is the superior destined for me in

4. *Turning toward the World*, 285.
5. *Turning toward the World*, 288.

God's Providence, and it is absurd for me to complain. No harm will ever come to me through him—it cannot. How could I have thought otherwise?"[6]

Of course the initial wave of optimism subsides—already by early February he is writing in his journal, "There is no *need* for me to write or teach. I do not know if I *want* to write or teach. The very questions themselves are irrelevant. I am really beginning to see this and also to see that the 'seeing' is no achievement! What a fool I am to be less simple than the trees, in my own way! It is enough to swing your branches when the wind blows and no one needs to be told about it."[7] But this is rather a warning not to attach too much importance to his activities as a source of self-definition and satisfaction, than a loss of interest in these activities as such. Part of his desire for solitude in this period is to provide a firm ground for his work in the novitiate by not neglecting his own life with God. He writes in June, "I am under pressure and deeply 'involved' in the silly business of keeping the place going—though I admit there is nothing silly about a novitiate as such, and I love the novices, want to help them to keep clear of foolishness and have their lives make sense. . . . I have a lot of reading and thinking, most of which goes into conferences and direction for the novices and juniors. The consequence of this is that I need to get away to the hermitage to try to recover some semblance of a personal life of meditation and prayer."[8] By August he is reflecting that it is not so much what is said but why and how it is said that is of utmost importance: "What is said to reassure my novices is perhaps 'nothing' but it has its meaning. They need not the words, but the voice, and the warmth of a heart in it. This is not nothing."[9]

The other change initiated with the beginning of 1963 was the inauguration of a monastic formation program at Gethsemani

6. *Turning toward the World*, 288–89.

7. *Turning toward the World*, 295 [February 4, 1963].

8. *Turning toward the World*, 329 [June 6, 1963].

9. Thomas Merton, *Dancing in the Water of Life: Seeking Peace in the Hermitage. Journals, vol. 5: 1963–1965*, ed. Robert E. Daggy (San Francisco: HarperCollins, 1997), 4.

that continued the focus of the novitiate by immersion of the recently professed monks in specifically monastic sources rather than immediately moving them along to a seminary-style clerical training. Merton explains the new program in a November 13, 1962 letter to Benedictine Father Ronald Roloff: "After the novitiate, all the choir monks, whether they will eventually go on to the priesthood or not, *continue their purely monastic formation*. This is what we all here consider to be the really important point. They will not begin clerical studies for at least three years after the novitiate."[10] The rationale, as Merton explains it to Archbishop Paul Philippe, OP, Secretary to the Congregation of Religious at the Vatican, is to deepen the young monks' specifically monastic vocation: "I think it is true that in the case of priests, the studies and the inappropriate priestly formation led to a loss of the true sense of their monastic vocation, among other causes. It is possible that the new course of monastic studies and the longer delay before clerical studies, introduced here at Gethsemani, may help to mitigate this problem. In effect, the monastic formation is now prolonged six years beyond the novitiate, before clerical studies are thought of. And it is hoped that many will not even want to be priests at all, but will be happier to remain monks."[11] While Merton was not in charge of this program,[12] it did directly affect him because it meant that his conferences would now be attended not only by the novices but by these newly professed monks.[13] Even

10. *School of Charity*, 155; see also the later letter to Fr. M. Placid, OCSO (August 5, 1964): *School of Charity*, 225–26.

11. *School of Charity*, 163 [April 4, 1963].

12. It was initially directed by Fr. Flavian Burns: see Merton's November 27, 1962 letter to Tarcisius Conner (*School of Charity*, 158).

13. See the January 11, 1963 letter to E. I. Watkin: "I have been landed with a merged novitiate, that is to say the brother novices and the choir novices are one group with one Fr. Master, and I am giving them the same training. It is working better than I at first expected, thanks be to God. In the long run it should prove very good for the whole house. But it requires thought and preparation, especially as all the young professed brothers are in on my conferences too, as a kind of refresher course, though that is absolutely the wrong kind of term" (Thomas Merton, *The Hidden Ground of Love: Letters on Religious Experience and*

solemnly professed brothers were apparently showing up for at least one of Merton's classes once the new program began; while he considered it "embarrassing, and quite foolish" that someone in authority was evidently requiring, or at least strongly encouraging, these mature monks to attend the conferences, and comments, "I would much prefer simply to have small and quiet classes with my novices—after all, that is supposed to be my job!" he reminds himself, "I have to take the assignment as it comes, from God, and treat them with sincerity and concern for their real needs," and concludes, "this will require prayer, more prayer, and perhaps more study and even more care, and honesty, because novices are ready for anything, but these men have been fooled and disappointed before and some are perhaps on the verge of leaving."[14] Thus the audience for Merton's conferences over the final two and a half years of his term as novice master was considerably more inclusive than the group of choir novices he had been primarily teaching up to that time. The Sunday afternoon conferences, in particular, seem to have been open to anyone who wished to attend—at one of these conferences (March 3, 1963) Merton directs a question to the Prior, who is in attendance! This is a pattern that would continue for these weekly conferences even after Merton left for the hermitage in August 1965.

* * * * * * *

Beginning in February 1963 and continuing almost without interruption until the end of his time as novice master, the Sunday afternoon conferences were focused on the topic of pre-Benedictine monasticism. The first series of these conferences begins on February 3 and lasts exactly a year, concluding on

---

Social Concerns, ed. William H. Shannon [New York: Farrar, Straus, Giroux, 1985], 581); also the November 25, 1963 letter to Mother M. L. Schroen: "My novices are a joy, really. About twenty in the novitiate, but I also have the juniors in classes with them most of the time. They have a real taste for Scripture and the Fathers. . . . I am almost exclusively busy with the Fathers and monastic tradition, as well as the normal classes on vows and so on" (*School of Charity*, 185).

14. *Turning toward the World*, 286 [January 5, 1963].

February 2, 1964, when it is followed immediately by four weeks of related conferences on "The Spiritual Doctrine of St. Ammonas," the successor to St. Anthony (February 16 through March 22, 1964). Then after a brief hiatus a second series of conferences begins on June 21, 1964 and continues through August 15, 1965, five days before Merton retires permanently to the hermitage. The conferences were given during the period before the monastic office of vespers.[15] The first series of conferences, through the Ammonas classes, generally lasted about 55 minutes; the second series were shorter, running on average about 35 minutes.[16] Because they took place on Sundays, these conferences were given somewhat more irregularly than weekday conferences. They were cancelled on days of recollection that generally took place once a month, and were sometimes preempted for other topics, as when Merton discusses the new Cistercian Directory during December 1963. Occasionally the conferences were given on major feast days, when the Sunday schedule was evidently followed (e.g., May 23, 1963—Ascension Thursday). For the first series, conferences were given on a little more than half the Sundays; for the second series, they are given closer to 60% of the time.

Both sets of conferences, the first especially, developed rather differently than Merton had originally intended. In mid-July 1962, Merton had written in his journal, "Lately discovered the *Regula Magistri* [Rule of the Master] and began to take an interest in the whole question about it. . . . Have read a little of the *Regula* and it is wonderful."[17] The same day, he wrote his English friend Etta Gullick, "Am also getting involved in the monastic tradition of Lérins, together with Caesarius of Arles, and the whole question of the *Regula Magistri.* This of course for my classes for the novices

15. Tape of conference for May 16, 1965.

16. Merton notes at the beginning of the conference on July 19, 1964, the fourth class of the second series, that some have requested that the classes start earlier and run longer, but that most would prefer the briefer class period, and he recommends they spend the additional time going outside and enjoying nature.

17. *Turning toward the World*, 230–31 [July 14, 1962].

and students, but also for my own interest."[18] The "whole question" about the *Rule of the Master* that Merton refers to is its textual relationship to the *Rule* of St. Benedict and which document has priority. Modern scholarship had largely rejected the traditional position that the *Rule of the Master* was subsequent to and dependent on the Benedictine *Rule*, and now considered it to be an important source for the *Rule*. Merton began to delve deeply into the issue, and also to research other monastic sources, especially from southern France, with the idea of developing them into a course for the novices. He had already written to Henry Miller on July 9, "I am thinking a lot of Provence because I am doing some work on the early monastic literature surrounding the Provençal monasteries, of the 5th century, particularly Lérins. It was a great movement."[19] In his journal for August 28 he comments on the "stoical tropes of St. Eucherius in his *contemptus mundi* [rejection of the world]: the beauty of his prose. How the heavens observe the laws of God when they have been once commanded and we, with volumes of laws, do not obey Him";[20] and on August 4 he says he "found much light and interest in the *Vita S. Honorati* by St. Hilary of Arles. His style, his manner of approaching his subject, his classical *topoi*, all might seem corny; actually it represents a real culture."[21] During this period he filled an entire reading notebook and a substantial part of another with extensive citations from primary and secondary sources on the *Rule of the Master* and various other pre-Benedictine rules and monastic writings, particularly those from Lérins, Arles and other parts of southern France.[22]

18. *Hidden Ground of Love*, 354.

19. Thomas Merton, *The Courage for Truth: Letters to Writers*, ed. Christine M. Bochen (New York: Farrar, Straus, Giroux, 1993), 275.

20. *Turning toward the World*, 234.

21. *Turning toward the World*, 235.

22. Reading Notebook #57 (undated), housed at the Thomas Merton Center at Bellarmine University, Louisville, KY, includes extensive notes on Gallic monastic rules, Julian Pomerius, Caesarius of Arles, Hilary of Arles, the *Rule* of Férreol, the *Rule* of Tarnat, the *Life of St. Honoratus*, writings of Eucherius, Gennadius, Claudianus Mamertus, Salvian, and Vincent of Lérins, and extensive notes from Adalbert de Vogüé's writings on the *Regula Magistri*. Notebook #59,

While on November 5 Merton writes in his journal, "I hope to finish conferences on Cistercian history (the Sunday ones) by the end of November. And end the year with one or two on the *Regula Magistri* and Lérins,"[23] when he began to write up the lecture notes for these conferences[24] it is evident that he was envisioning a considerably more extensive treatment of this milieu. After summarizing recent scholarly developments on the Benedictine *Rule*, he writes, "In particular, it is of great value to read in detail the controversial *Regula Magistri* (hereafter referred to as *RM*), which is now generally recognized to antedate the *RB* and to be a source of most of the material in the *RB*. One of the best ways of understanding the *RB* is to read it in the light of the *RM* and to study all the material in *RM* that fills out the picture for us. Hence these notes will concentrate on the study of the *RM* and a comparison of its main chapters with those of *RB*" (6). He then adds, "Before beginning this we will look at the monastic milieu of the Gallo-Roman world in the fifth century, at the time of the first Invasions. First, at the beginning of the fifth century, we have documents of spirituality like the important tracts of St. Eucherius and other writings that emanated from the monastic centers of southern Gaul. . . . In brief, we will study the *RB* against the background of a monastic milieu which may well have been the milieu in which the *RM* was written, namely southern Gaul" (7). This, then, was the initial plan for the *Pre-Benedictine Monasticism* conferences.

In the event, however, they developed in a rather different direction than Merton had originally intended, and over the

also undated, which despite its numbering seems to have preceded #57, includes notes on Faustus of Riez, the *Rule* of Férreol, John and Aurelian of Arles, and St. Fructuosus, as well as the Latin translations of St. Basil by Rufinus.

23. *Turning toward the World*, 263.

24. It is actually not clear whether this journal entry precedes or follows the composition of the lecture notes; it is possible that by early November Merton had already decided to scale back the extensive treatment of the *Rule of the Master* and early French monasticism, though it seems somewhat more likely that he would not have composed the beginning of the *Pre-Benedictine Monasticism* notes this far before the beginning of the course (even if he did intend to give the lectures before the new year).

course of the next two and a half years Merton never does manage to return to the *Rule of the Master*, Lérins, and the rest of the early French monastic literature. While the focus remains on monasticism before Benedict, much of what Merton will be discussing in the two series of conferences will not be "pre-Benedictine" as first described, that is, directly preceding and directly or indirectly influencing the formation of the Benedictine *Rule* and of Benedictine life in general. The reason for the shift is largely due to Merton's typical enthusiasm for whatever has most recently attracted his attention and interest.

The earliest sections of the conferences, on Paulinus of Nola (a native of Bordeaux) (10–13) and Martin of Tours (13–17), stick closely to the original plan. Drawing on the work of his (future) friend and correspondent Nora Chadwick,[25] Merton focuses both on the ascetic but non-monastic character of Paulinus' community at Nola in southern Italy, where he lived in retirement with his wife and a like-minded group of friends, and on the eschatological dimension of his writing, which Merton considers "very close to the spirituality of Lérins" (11). Merton quotes with obvious agreement Chadwick's assessment that Paulinus' "quiet dignity and reserve, and perhaps most of all his humour, still link him to the ancient world, and at the same time make him peculiarly modern and congenial to us today" (13).

With Paulinus' friend Martin of Tours, Merton's attention turns to monasticism proper, specifically the beginnings of monastic life in southern France. As a hermit turned bishop, Martin establishes a somewhat eclectic type of monastic community at Marmoutier, Merton notes: "Without foresight or plan, or perhaps without being aware of the situation at all, Martin combines two monastic forms: the canonical or *clerical monasticism*, a community around a bishop (St. Augustine) and the *lay monasticism* which is more properly 'monastic'" (14–15). He also calls attention to the opposition on the part of many of Martin's fellow

25. Nora K. Chadwick, *Poetry and Letters in Early Christian Gaul* (London: Bowes & Bowes, 1955); for Merton's correspondence with Chadwick, which begins with a letter of May 26, 1964, see *School of Charity*, 217 and *passim*.

bishops to monasticism and to Martin himself, who refused to go along with the emerging episcopal policy of punishment of those deemed heretics, and (again drawing on Chadwick) he highlights the way in which Sulpicius Severus, Martin's biographer, makes his subject "a hero of Gallo-Roman monasticism as opposed to that of Egypt, and of {the} monastic apostolate as opposed to Gallo-Roman clergy" (16).

Sulpicius, whose *Dialogues* treat not only Gallic but Egyptian monasticism, serves as a transitional figure leading to consideration of early monastic life in the East, from which, it turns out, the conferences will never completely return. Merton states, "Now we must briefly consider the Egyptian sources" (17), but what follows is neither brief nor is it limited to "sources" in the particular sense of background material influencing Western and especially Benedictine monasticism. The material on St. Anthony (17–24) is of course relevant to his announced program, as Anthony is the single most significant and paradigmatic figure in early monasticism, and St. Athanasius' *Life* of the saint had a tremendous effect on the spread of monastic life in the West as in the East. But Merton had already discussed the *Life* thoroughly in the course of his conferences on *Cassian and the Fathers*,[26] and rather than repeat himself he concentrates here particularly on the sayings of Anthony as recorded in the alphabetical collection of the *Apophthegmata* (extant only in Greek), perhaps more than would be warranted by a strict "pre-Benedictine" focus.

It is with the discussion that follows of the *Historia Monachorum in Aegypto* that a decided shift in emphasis, if not yet a complete shift in direction, first becomes evident. On January 26, 1963, about a week before beginning the new course, Merton wrote in his journal, "Reading Rufinus *Historia Monachorum* and also *Dialogues* of Sulpicius Severus. Utterly ashamed and annoyed that I have never read the *Hist. Monachorum* before. What have I been doing? I have been under a kind of delusion that I

26. Thomas Merton, *Cassian and the Fathers: Initiation into the Monastic Tradition*, ed. Patrick F. O'Connell, Monastic Wisdom [MW], vol. 1 (Kalamazoo, MI: Cistercian Publications, 2005), 31–39.

was living as a monk all these years—and that I knew what the monastic life was and had read a great deal of the traditional source material. I haven't even scratched the surface, and my heart has not been that of a monk. The story of John of {Lycopolis}, the urgency of his lessons, the sweetness and simplicity of the style move me very deeply."[27] Merton's excitement about this early monastic text leads him to devote considerably more attention to the material (24–40) than it would warrant simply as preliminary background for his ostensible main focus on the *Rule of the Master* and Benedict, etc.; it has clearly become a topic of interest in its own right. He begins by noting the signal importance of Rufinus, the translator (or adaptor) of the *Historia Monachorum*, for the transmission to the West of monastic texts (as well as earlier Eastern writings that will be important for monasticism, especially those of Origen). But he then explores the spirituality of the *Historia* in great detail, particularly the Prologue, which he calls "a kind of monastic manifesto" (28), and the opening chapter, on the famous hermit John of Lycopolis, which he calls the "longest and most interesting chapter" and "a tract in favor of the purely eremitical and contemplative life" (31), "a conference on purity of heart and prayer in solitude" (33) comparable in doctrine and in quality to key *Conferences* of Cassian. The remainder of the monastic travelogue is treated more summarily, though the work's consideration of cenobitic life, the comparison of the merits of Abba Paphnutius with those of three saintly laypeople, and the visitors' encounters at Nitria and Kellia, particularly with Evagrius (unique to Rufinus' Latin version) receive special attention.

It is probably from this point onward that Merton realizes that the course of lectures will be heading in a somewhat different direction than he had originally planned. When he gives the opening *Pre-Benedictine* conference on February 4, shortly after immersing himself in the *Historia Monachorum*, he actually mentions the *Rule of the Master* only in passing, with no indication

27. *Turning toward the World*, 294 (text reads "Lycopotis").

that this was to have been the centerpiece of the entire series.[28] Even though relatively late in the first series he will still refer to the "sermons of Faustus and Eucherius which we hope to discuss" (137), evidence for his interest in these and the other early Gallic sources is limited to his extensive, and unused, notes—with the signal exception of John Cassian.

Although he had written at the outset in his set of notes that "We will not go into detailed study of Cassian, here, as this is done by us in another course of lectures" (7),[29] when he actually begins his treatment of Cassian it proves to be almost as long as all that had preceded it (40–72). Merton does stress here more than he had in *Cassian and the Fathers* that the *Conferences* of Cassian "are a record not simply of the thought of Egypt, or even of the Greco-Roman monastic world, but especially of the thought of *Southern Gaul*, the monastic milieu of Provence and Lérins" (41), and that Cassian deserves primary credit for adapting Eastern ideas to a Western context, credit often given almost solely to Benedict. But his primary focus turns out not to be on situating Cassian's teaching in this Gallic environment, but on relating Cassian to his predecessor Evagrius and so indicating Cassian's role in transmitting Evagrian teaching to the West (40). The reason for this specific emphasis is that he has come upon a source, Salvatore Marsili's *Giovanni Cassiano ed Evagrio Pontico*,[30] which he had evidently not read before and which interested him enough to discuss it in considerable detail. Relying largely on Marsili, he focuses on two *Conferences* particularly influenced by Evagrius that he had not considered at length in the *Cassian and the Fathers* notes (as well as three—*Conferences* 1, 9 and 10—that he had): *Conference* 14, on *actualis scientia* and *spiritualis scientia* (knowledge oriented toward practice and toward contemplation), and *Conference* 3, on the three renunciations (of the attractions of the

28. Conference for February 4, 1963.

29. See *Cassian and the Fathers*, 97–259.

30. Salvatore Marsili, OSB, *Giovanni Cassiano ed Evagrio Pontico: Dottrina sulla Carità e Contemplazione*, *Studia Anselmiana*, 5 (Rome: Herder, 1936).

world, of the passions of flesh and soul, and of the transitory in favor of the eternal).

Toward the end of his discussion of Cassian, in the context of his teaching on prayer and contemplation, Merton considers the matter of "prayer without forms" and its compatibility with a recognition of the centrality of the humanity of Christ and the role of Christ as mediator in prayer: "If the most perfect prayer is prayer beyond all words, all forms, all 'objects,' then what happens to the Humanity of Christ the 'One Mediator' between the Christian and the Father? No one can come to the Father but by Him" (69). He points out that this issue would not have been a problem for Cassian and his contemporaries in the same way that it was later in the history of Christian spirituality, for at least two reasons: first, for Cassian it was not a question of "choosing" prayer without forms in preference to meditation on the humanity of Christ—this "*oratio ignita*" (fiery prayer) was a divine gift, not a method among other methods, one of a number of different practices for prayer to be selected according to the preference of the one praying; second, prayer without forms did not exclude Christ's humanity, but was a way of sharing in Christ's own prayerful intimacy with the Father, above all the intimacy of the resurrected and glorified Christ at the Father's right hand, "the Person of Christ, in His glorified humanity as a manifestation of the divinity . . . revealed by Christ Himself to those of pure heart, who no longer contemplate any form or image" (72). This conference material became the nucleus for one of Merton's more scholarly essays, "The Humanity of Christ in Monastic Prayer,"[31] in which he concludes the discussion of Cassian that constitutes the first section of the article by declaring, "There is no question whatever of 'excluding' the humanity of Christ from contemplative prayer, in order to contemplate His divinity! On the contrary, humanity and divinity are contemplated in inseparable unity in

31. Thomas Merton, "The Humanity of Christ in Monastic Prayer," in *The Monastic Journey*, ed. Brother Patrick Hart (Kansas City, MO: Sheed, Andrews and McMeel, 1977), 87–106 (originally published in October 1964 in *Monastic Studies*).

the Person of the glorified Son of God."[32] Merton was so stimulated by the question that on June 2, 1963, the conference following that in which Cassian on pure prayer was discussed, he tells his students that he has been exploring the teaching of various Fathers on the role of Christ in prayer, and recommends examining commentaries of the Fathers on a particular scripture verse as a method of tracing a theme through patristic writings. This process led to the material on St. Leo, St. Gregory, St. Bede and Ambrose Autpert that make up the rest of the article, in which Merton finds a continuous tradition consistent with the teaching of Cassian that "the Christ of monastic contemplation is neither the divinity alone nor the humanity alone, but the unity of the two natures in one Person."[33]

As he moves on to his discussion of St. Pachomius, the great founding figure of Egyptian cenobitic monasticism, Merton's original intention was evidently to limit himself principally to the Latin translations of Pachomian documents. He reminds his listeners—and himself: "we must remember our purpose in these conferences: to discover the influences on pre-Benedictine monachism, especially in France at the time of Cassian. Hence we will be concerned with St. Pachomius primarily in connection with the forces that contributed to the formation of Benedictine monachism" (72–73). But once again his discovery of previously unperused sources, in this case translations of the extensive Coptic Pachomian documents, broadened his original scope considerably. On July 23, 1965, he writes to his friend Dom Jean Leclercq, "I have been talking to the novices about St. Pachomius and reading some of the material translated from Coptic. He has been too little known: there is much in him that is of great interest."[34] He did not neglect the material available in Latin: five days earlier he had quoted in his journal a passage from the second chapter of the Latin *Life* about Pachomius' love for solitude and the desert and commented, "Charmed by the life of Pachomius . . . . Too

32. *Monastic Journey*, 94.

33. *Monastic Journey*, 106.

34. *School of Charity*, 179.

many generalizations have falsified our view of Pachomian Cenobitism."[35] But the fascination he describes here makes his discussion of Pachomius (72–119) a topic of intrinsic significance in itself, not just as it relates to the Western monastic tradition. He shows himself receptive to the positive reevaluation of Pachomius found in recent studies, particularly those of the Jesuit Heinrich Bacht,[36] while at the same time resisting the concomitant devaluation of the Antonian and Evagrian traditions that such studies often involve. Merton values the strongly scriptural foundation of Pachomian spirituality, the "strong belief that the words of Scripture are addressed directly and personally to each monk, who is now *living in the time of the fulfillment of the word of God*" (77). He is fair and objective but obviously less enthusiastic about the emphasis on institutional order in the Pachomian tradition, with "its *pessimism about the individual* and *relative optimism about the organization, the institution* . . . in contrast to the basic optimism of Antonian-Evagrian-Origenist spirituality and its belief in the perfectibility of the individual, its trust in the inherent value of the *personal life of the spirit*" (79–80). The dominant image of God as lawgiver, the spiritual life as eschatological combat, and a "visible separation between the 'holy *koinonia*' and the outside world" (88) follow from this pessimism about human nature, but Merton nonetheless finds at the heart of Pachomian ascesis a love that is "deeply real, based on a profound and humble esteem of all one's brothers (affection not encouraged), a respect for their rights, minding one's own business, pardoning all, being the servant of all and at peace with all" (93). He highlights the emphasis on discretion that is apparent in both the Pachomian *Rule* (101) and in the Latin *Life* of Pachomius (104–105), which he summarizes at some length toward the end of his discussion (107–14), thus returning finally if somewhat belatedly

35. *Turning toward the World*, 340.

36. Heinrich Bacht, SJ, "L'Importance d'Idéal Monastique de S. Pacôme," *Revue d'Ascétique et de Mystique*, 26 (1950), 308–26; Heinrich Bacht, SJ, "Pakhome et ses Disciples," *Théologie de la Vie Monastique: Études sur la Tradition Patristique* (Paris: Aubier, 1961), 39–71.

to his stated concern "with St. Pachomius primarily in connection with the forces that contributed to the formation of Benedictine monachism."

The specifically Pachomian material is complemented by briefer discussions of the *Doctrina* of his successor Orsiesius (Horsiesios), which was translated into Latin by Jerome (who also translated the Pachomian *Rule*) and therefore was available in the West (114–18), but also of Shenoute (120–23), the great Coptic monastic figure of the fifth century whom Merton calls "interesting because there are no Greek and Latin sources. Shenoute is completely Coptic and has never entered into the Western tradition at all" (120), and so can be considered "pre-Benedictine" only in the chronological sense. Merton concludes by suggesting that much of the reputation of Pachomian monasticism for rigidity is due more to Shenoute than to Pachomius, whose "*genius, sanctity,* and *discretion* . . . his great warmth of humanity and his breadth of view" (122) are his most characteristic qualities—though he also recognizes Shenoute's historical significance and his "compassion for the poor—the oppressed class from which he himself came" (123).

When Merton then turns to St. Basil (123–51), he once again offers the now familiar disclaimer: "We shall confine ourselves to a brief introduction to St. Basil and his background, and then look a little more closely at some of the *Basilian documents in Latin that were widely known in the West in the sixth century*" (123). This does in fact prove to be the case here, for the most part. Following a not-so-brief introduction to Basil, in which he considers the influence of the (eventually heretical) bishop Eustathius of Sebaste on Basil's asceticism, and explores at some length new research that clearly intrigued him, the work of Jean Gribomont, OSB, which suggested that the Basilian "Rules" were actually composed for communities of Christian ascetics living in the world rather than for monastics in the strict sense,[37] two of the three texts he selects for extended consideration did have a

37. Jean Gribomont, OSB, "Saint Basile," *Théologie de la Vie Monastique*, 99–113.

significant impact in the West. After examining Basil's *Letter* 2, to Gregory Nazianzen, which he sees as a preliminary articulation of the ascetic doctrine that will be developed in the *Rules*, he turns to the "*Sermo Asceticus*" and the "*Admonitio ad Filium Spiritualem*"[38] (the former probably and the latter almost certainly not by Basil), that did influence the tradition leading up to St. Benedict, particularly the "*Admonitio*," which contains "passages clearly echoed in the Benedictine *Rule*," and which "may have been a text well known at Lérins" (137). In completing his discussion of Basil with some consideration of the spirituality of the Basilian *Rules*, he largely restricts himself to Rufinus' Latin translation, or adaptation, which he had said earlier in the course was "without great value for the critic" but was nevertheless "very important as the *actual source of Western knowledge of Basil* in the crucial formative period of early monasticism" (27). Merton focuses particularly on what he calls the "*disciplina placendi Deo*," ascetic discipline as a process of formation in perceiving and carrying out God's will: "the spiritual education of the Christian and above all the monk is training in how to please God by loving Him in all things" (147), a formulation Merton himself clearly views as central to the monastic life as a "school of the Lord's service," as Benedict calls it at the end of the Prologue to the *Rule*, and which is certainly germane to his own efforts as novice master for "the spiritual education" of those directly entrusted to him, and even toward those whom he would encounter in a less immediate way through his writing.

The remainder of the first part of *Pre-Benedictine Monasticism* is concerned exclusively with Western monastic figures—but all are figures who are situated, at least for the relevant period, in the

38. On November 10, 1963, Merton wrote to Jean Leclercq, asking, "Do you know, or can you find out for me from Dom Gribomont par ex., who is the author of the *Admonitio ad Filium Spiritualem* attributed to St. Basil, in PL. 1032? The novices are translating it here, and it is a very good parallel to the Benedictine Rule. I would like to do a short introduction, and wonder if there are any studies on it. I have not seen any myself" (*School of Charity*, 184). The introduction was apparently never written and the translation, if completed, was never published.

East. He turns in the penultimate section to "Roman Monasticism in Palestine," (151–69) in the fourth century: after brief sections on the communities of St. Jerome and St. Paula in Bethlehem and of St. Melania the Elder (and Rufinus) on the Mount of Olives in Jerusalem, he discusses in some detail the *Life of St. Melania the Younger* (the elder Melania's granddaughter) by Gerontius (written in Greek rather than Latin, ironically), then returns to Jerome, considering his controversy with Vigilantius (he "argues like a Kentucky politician," Merton concludes [162]), and his monastic theology in general, noting, as customarily, his importance for the Benedictine *Rule*, where he is "quoted as often as St. Basil—after Cassian, St. Augustine, St. Pachomius and the *Historia Monachorum*" (162) (a summary statement that seems to be implying that he has remained largely on track in his series of conferences after all!).

But his paramount interest in these final conferences of Part 1 is clearly in a figure who is just "passing through" the East, the pilgrim nun Egeria (or Aetheria as Merton calls her [169–87]). In his journal for December 5, 1963, he writes,

> Another Spanish writer—fourth-century Egeria (Etheria, "Sylvia") and her amazing Pilgrimage to Jerusalem, Egypt, Sinai and Mesopotamia. . . . I love her. Simplicity, practicality, insatiable curiosity, and tremendous endurance as long as she is riding her mule (laments a little when she has to go "straight up" the side of Sinai—any influence on St. John of the Cross?). All the holy women she meets—they must have been delighted with her and overwhelmed. This is a really marvelous book, one of the greatest monuments of fourth-century literature, and too few know it. Two English translations, the most recent being 1919. I am tempted to do it—but better not! Is she Spanish? Sounds like a Spaniard, with the simplicity, mixture of hope, humor, idealism and endurance. Or maybe some day she will turn out to have been Irish![39]

On the following day he adds, "Etheria (Egeria, Eucheria)—is my delight! Have read and dug around: [Germaine] Morin in

39. *Dancing in the Water of Life*, 43.

{*Rev*} *Benedictine* on Jerome's Letter to {Furia} (a veiled allusion to Etheria?—not too nice) and another letter, that of the {seventh-century} Spanish monk Valerius, on the 'Blessed Etheria'—a beautiful document. She is one of 'my saints' from now on."[40] Though much modern interest in Egeria focuses on the details she provides about the ancient liturgy in Jerusalem and elsewhere in the East, Merton's principal focus is on her character, her visits to the holy places, and her encounters with monks. He sees her as "a person of unusual courage, independence, determination, and one who is completely set on fulfilling what she conceives to be a demand of grace," with "a holy and insatiable curiosity" (172), though he is a bit bemused by her indefatigable busyness: "This may have been due as much to her psychology as to grace. Was she perhaps 'acting out' deep interior obsessions? Or was she really a saint? Who can say? Perhaps both" (173). His enthusiasm seems to have cooled off somewhat, as typically happened so often, from the initial encounter recorded in the journal. He goes on to note that "her piety, though genuine, lacks interior depth" and that "one feels at times a certain aimlessness and haste" along with a certain "credulous, almost naïve" willingness to accept whatever stories she is told, though he declares that this "adds to the simple charm of her style, which is completely genuine, and colloquial" (173). One gets the impression that he is delighted and fascinated with her but a trifle embarrassed about spending so much time traveling about in her company (instead of returning to Lérins, the *Regula Magistri*, etc.?). He finds in her a "triumphant, optimistic concept of the world as belonging to the Risen Christ and filled with visible, tangible, present and real signs of His victory" (174) characteristic of the era between the emergence of Christianity from the catacombs and the barbarian invasions.

She sees monks as "living signs of the resurrection. . . . Through the monks . . . she is in contact with the Risen Savior.

40. *Dancing in the Water of Life*, 43 (text reads ". . . *The* . . . Fusia . . . seventeenth-century . . .").

Her visits to them, meals with them, etc. are also a kind of participation in the Resurrection life" (175). They are "custodians of the traditional narratives as well as of the Holy Places" (175) so it is through them and their guidance that she comes into contact with the concrete physical setting of the mysteries of faith, particularly at Mount Sinai but also in Mesopotamia and even in Jerusalem. Though she has only the most tenuous connection with the Benedictine *Rule*, Merton does point out that she "constantly speaks of the cordiality and hospitality with which the monks receive her, using the word '*humanitas*' which appears in {the} *RB* in the chapter on guests" (177). Her description of the "apotactites," the rather loosely organized form of monastic life in Syria and Asia Minor that was "the most common type of monk in the Near East in the fourth century" (187), is much more positive than in Jerome, who condemned them as "*remoboth*" ("*remnuoth*"), the rough equivalent of Benedict's sarabaites and gyrovagues, and he finds in Egeria "an essential witness giving us a living picture of Palestinian monasticism as she saw it" (187).

Egeria has an afterlife for Merton beyond her appearance in the journal and the *Pre-Benedictine Monasticism* lectures. His reading of her *Itinerarium* provided the initial spark for his essay "From Pilgrimage to Crusade,"[41] along with his growing interest in Celtic monasticism, particularly the tradition of "*Peregrinatio*, or 'going forth into strange countries'" as "a characteristically Irish form of asceticism."[42] In the essay he calls her book "[o]ne of the liveliest and most interesting of all written pilgrimages,"[43] and juxtaposes her literal ascent of Mount Sinai with Gregory of Nyssa's theological and mystical ascent of the same mountain in his *Life of Moses*, and suggests that the "geographical pilgrimage

41. Thomas Merton, "From Pilgrimage to Crusade," in *Mystics and Zen Masters* (New York: Farrar, Straus, Giroux, 1967), 91–112; the essay was first published in *Cithera* in November, 1964. Merton speaks of finishing the essay on August 2, 1964 (*Dancing in the Water of Life*, 132), though it is not until August 29 that he is "finishing off footnotes as an afterthought" (*Dancing in the Water of Life*, 139).

42. *Mystics and Zen Masters*, 94.

43. *Mystics and Zen Masters*, 92.

is the symbolic acting out of an inner journey," or at least that it should be: "History would show the fatality and doom that would attend on the external pilgrimage with no interior spiritual integration,"[44] above all in the second kind of journey to the East mentioned in the essay's title, the crusade. Thus the initial reflections on Egeria and her journey lead eventually to Merton's well-known and frequently quoted statements at the end of the essay that "Our task now is to learn that if we can voyage to the ends of the earth and there find *ourselves* in the aborigine who most differs from ourselves, we will have made a fruitful pilgrimage. That is why pilgrimage is necessary, in some shape or other" and "Our pilgrimage to the Holy Sepulchre is our pilgrimage to the stranger who is Christ our fellow-pilgrim and our brother."[45]

Except for a brief appendix on monastic chant, the material on Egeria brings *Pre-Benedictine Monasticism*, first series, to a close, at least as far as the mimeographed text distributed to the novices is concerned. But without a pause Merton backtracks to spend four classes looking at a neglected monastic figure from the Egyptian desert, St. Ammonas, the successor to St. Anthony as abbot of Pispir. On January 31, 1964 he writes in his journal, "I know I should equally well read Sartre and Ammonas or Theodoret on Julian Saba. *Both* are relevant to me at the same time. To pretend otherwise would be to lie";[46] two days later he speaks of the "religious depth of Ammonas," again in juxtaposition with Sartre (as well as Merleau-Ponty) as "[m]eetings of opposites, not carefully planned exclusions and mere inclusion of the familiar."[47] On February 13, he writes more extensively:

> One of the great discoveries and graces of this year has been Abbot Ammonas. A magnificent primitive spirituality, the best of the ancient Egyptians (with Anthony, whom he succeeded as Abbot of {Pispir}). We have him in the *Patrologia*

44. *Mystics and Zen Masters*, 92.
45. *Mystics and Zen Masters*, 112.
46. *Dancing in the Water of Life*, 68.
47. *Dancing in the Water of Life*, 69.

> *Orientalis*, printed in 1913—no one has done anything with it. Ammonas is not even in the dictionaries (except *Dictionnaire d'histoire et de géographie ecclésiastique* [Paris, 1912–]). Hausherr refers to him frequently, however. He should be translated and I might write an article on him. Grace of Lent. Thinking this morning of the meaning of *covenant* in my life. Ammonas on striving for the gift of the Spirit.[48]

Three days later (the Sunday of his first conference on Ammonas), he writes to Etta Gullick: "I am discovering new things, for instance Abbot Ammonas, the successor of St. Anthony at Pispir. He is marvelous and so far completely neglected. The best texts have been edited in the *Patrologia Orientalis* since before the First World War, but no one has done anything with them except Hausherr (who has been doing good stuff on Oriental spirituality)."[49] In his journal entry of the following Tuesday he goes so far as to rank the teaching of Ammonas ahead of that of far more familiar spiritual masters: "The wonderful power of the Letters of Ammonas and his mystical doctrine. It is to me impressive, beyond all the others, beyond John of the Cross and [Meister] Eckhart, not to say the lesser ones. It is the pure doctrine of Christian monastic mysticism."[50] In early April, he is still under the spell of Ammonas, writing to his Hasidic Jewish friend Zalman Schachter, "Actually, according to Abbot Ammonas, my latest discovery, the prayer of dread is prelude to the gift of the Holy Spirit, after a 'last purification' in which one seems to be in hell."[51]

In his conference notes, Merton's tone is much more restrained, but the extent of his summarizing and quotation from Ammonas' writings as they survived in both Greek and Syriac

48. *Dancing in the Water of Life*, 76 (the text reads "Pisgar"); the reference to Hausherr is probably to Irénée Hausherr, SJ, *Solitude et Vie Contemplative d'après l'Hésychasme: Étude de Spiritualité Orientale* (Etiolles: Monastère de la Croix, 1962), which includes a discussion of Ammonas (42–46) that may well have been where Merton's attention was first drawn to him.

49. *Hidden Ground of Love*, 365.

50. *Dancing in the Water of Life*, 77.

51. *Hidden Ground of Love*, 539.

testifies to his fascination with this previously unknown monastic forbear. A hint of what struck Merton so strongly is perhaps evident in his comments on Ammonas' "Letter to Solitaries," where he counsels them *"to keep their lives simple and deep, by compunction and avoiding controversy."* After quoting what sounds like a rather anti-intellectualist warning of Ammonas that "love for inquisitive study of Scripture engenders discord and argument, whereas weeping for one's sins brings peace," Merton adds the comment, "What he says of scripture applies equally well to liturgy, to monastic reform, spirituality etc."—i.e., to issues that were very much current in life at Gethsemani and in Merton's own life at the beginning of 1964. Apparently Ammonas made such an impact on Merton because he heard the fourth-century monk speaking to his own mid-twentieth-century situation. He continues his reflection: "the monk who sits alone in his cell *sins* if he 'curiously investigates' (*periergazesthai*) Scripture while neglecting his own sins. To be '*periergos*' is to be overcareful, officious, a busybody, prying into every little detail, with excessive and inopportune work. It is a way of *evading* the reality of our sins" (195). Merton certainly wasn't advocating a rejection of historical-critical analysis of scripture here, or an avoidance of difficult issues in liturgy, monastic reform and spirituality either, for that matter. But he was reminding himself and his students of the temptation to allow knowledge about these topics to substitute for genuine self-knowledge and humble awareness of the presence of God, to substitute *scientia* for *sapientia*, to use his familiar terms from this period. He was listening to Ammonas' warning to solitaries (and would-be solitaries?) not to succumb to a seemingly productive busyness that is actually "excessive and inopportune work" (the root of the Greek "*periergos*" and its derivatives). The alternative is to rely not on one's own strength but on the power—the "*virtus*"—"*dunamis*"—of the Holy Spirit, who enables one to carry one's cross in the footsteps of Christ and leads to "unity between active and contemplative lives in the one *virtus*!!"—to both "apostolic fruitfulness" and a revelation of "the *maxima divinitatis mysteria*" (201). Such "*virtus*" does not exclude trial and temptation,[52] but makes it possible to endure and overcome them with an underlying confidence and peace despite the anguish or dread they entail, the "'last purification' in which one seems to be in hell" of which he wrote to Rabbi Schachter: "The importance of Ammonas' doctrine here is the clarity with which he shows that the time of temptation is the time of choice and is decisive for further progress" (205).[53] Here as elsewhere throughout the writings of Ammonas, Merton discovers teaching that is "apparently obvious, but in fact {is} a very deep truth {which} must be understood in depth" (197), and that evidently moved him deeply when he encountered it.

* * * * * * *

It may be that discovering Ammonas' letters as preserved in Syriac, or perhaps reading about Egeria's travels to Syrian sites and her encounters with the monks there, prompted Merton to explore the early Syriac monastic tradition itself. In any case, this becomes the focus of the second series of conferences on *Pre-Benedictine Monasticism*, in which the modifier has become strictly chronological, as the figures discussed by Merton in these lectures could have had at best only the most tenuous and indirect influence on the development of the Benedictine *Rule* and life. In this series, too, though, there is somewhat of a change in plan, evident in this case not in the written notes themselves but in letters and in the tapes of the actual classes. As Merton was beginning this

52. See Thomas Merton, *The Climate of Monastic Prayer*, Cistercian Studies [CS], vol. 1 (Washington, DC: Cistercian Publications, 1969), 136: "We begin to realize, at least obscurely, the truth of what the Desert Father, St. Ammonas, said: 'If God did not love you he would not bring temptations upon you. . . . For the faithful, temptation is necessary, for all those who are free of temptation are not among the elect'" (also published as *Contemplative Prayer* [New York: Herder & Herder, 1969], 126).

53. See also *Climate of Monastic Prayer*, 137 (*Contemplative Prayer*, 127): "The fourth-century monk Ammonas describes the testing of the man of prayer by dereliction and dread, following the 'fruitful' and consoling experiences of the beginners. It is this dread that proves the real seriousness of our love of God and prayer, for those who simply fall into coldness and indifference show they have little real desire to know him."

second series of conferences, he had become deeply immersed in studies of Celtic monasticism, initially an offshoot of his interest in medieval recluses and prompted in large part by his reading of Nora Chadwick's book *The Age of Saints in the Early Celtic Church*.[54] In his journal for June 2, shortly before beginning the second part of his pre-Benedictine conferences, he calls Irish monasticism a "new world that has waited until this time to open up,"[55] and in letters and journal entries in the weeks and months that follow he comments repeatedly on the *Navigatio Brendani*, Adamnan's *Life of Columba*, and other more esoteric Celtic documents.[56] In his May 26 letter to Nora Chadwick he writes, "your book has come along just when I was about to start on Celtic monasticism with my novices and students at this Abbey,"[57] and two months later he tells Dame Hildelith Cumming of Stanbrook Abbey that he is "especially working up my notes on Celtic monasticism, which I am going to take with the novices soon, I hope";[58] two months after that, on September 27, he writes to Hans Urs Von Balthasar, "The documents of Celtic monasticism

54. See Merton's May 22, 1964 letter to Etta Gullick: "The book I have on my mind and like very much is Nora Chadwick's lectures on the Celtic Church. This is really first rate, and especially interesting to me as I really intend now to do something on recluses and the Irish started all that, or so it seems, at least in Europe . . ." (*Hidden Ground of Love*, 366); see also his first letter to Chadwick herself four days later: "Having just read, and greatly enjoyed, your book *The Age of Saints in the Early Celtic Church*, I am emboldened by my friend [Eleanor] S. Duckett to write you a note about it. Speaking as a monk, I can hardly say how much I have responded to your ideas and theses. As I am not enough of a scholar to find reasons why they might not be perfectly correct, I am happy to agree with you throughout" (*School of Charity*, 217).

55. *Dancing in the Water of Life*, 107.

56. See *Dancing in the Water of Life*, 114 (6/16), 121 (6/23), 124 (7/8), 126 (7/12), 128 (7/18), 130 (7/21), 131 (7/28), 133 (8/9), 135 (8/10), 138 (8/21); *Hidden Ground of Love*, 192 (8/23); *Road to Joy*, 62 (5/27), 287 (9/3), 64–65 (9/23); *School of Charity*, 222–23 (7/22), 228–29 (8/20); Thomas Merton, *Witness to Freedom: Letters in Times of Crisis*, ed. William H. Shannon (New York: Farrar, Straus, Giroux, 1994), 9 (8/5).

57. *School of Charity*, 217.

58. *School of Charity*, 222 [7/22].

have absorbed me too, as I have been preparing a course on this for the novices."[59] Thus it was evidently Merton's intention as he began the second part of the pre-Benedictine conferences in mid-June, and for some time thereafter, to move on quickly to a discussion of early Celtic (still of course pre-Benedictine, at least in its initial phases) monastic sources. In fact on June 21, the first day of these lectures, when he wrote on the blackboard the chart of monastic chronology in various sites that prefaces the written text of *Pre-Benedictine Monasticism* Part Two (210–11), he added an extra column for Irish monasticism, and a week later he told the students that they weren't going to be doing much with Syrian monasticism but would be moving on soon to Irish monasticism. Fourteen months later, as he gave the last conference before leaving for the hermitage, he was still talking about the Syrians! The reason is the usual one for Merton: the more he read of the Syrian material the more interested he became in it, and in fact his Irish studies are largely laid aside in late 1964 and picked up again only when he has settled into life as a hermit.[60]

Basically the second series of conferences consists of four sections. After an introductory overview, based largely on the studies of Arthur Vööbus (which he gradually comes to realize are not universally accepted by other Syriac scholars), he discusses in turn the *Historia Religiosa* of Theodoret of Cyrrhus, a fifth-century history of monastic life in Syria, written in Greek

59. *School of Charity*, 241.

60. See Merton's letters to Fr. Brendan Connolly, librarian at Boston College, of September 7, 1965, in which he speaks of "getting back to work on the Celtic monks and . . . preparing a series of talks on them," and adds, "Maybe some day a book will come out of it" (*School of Charity*, 291), and October 21, in which he writes, "I really think I had better dig into the Irish material seriously. I learn from our monasteries in Ireland that no one there is doing much work on Celtic monasticism, and that is a pity, because there is so much and it is so fascinating," and goes on to request various books from the Boston College collection (*School of Charity*, 294). Merton did finally get around to giving a couple of Sunday afternoon conferences on Irish monasticism—in March 1968 (tape ## 175–2, 175–3; published by Credence Communications: AA2268—*The Irish Tradition of Mysticism*; AA2268—*Irish Monks on Mysticism*).

(unlike the rest of the material he will discuss); the writings of Aphraat, one of the early ascetic figures who appears in Theodoret; of Ephrem the Syrian, the best known and most widely read of the Syriac Fathers; and of Philoxenos, the sixth-century hermit and Monophysite bishop who has almost certainly become better known, at least in name, to contemporary readers through Merton's writing than through any other source.

Merton's acquaintance with Theodoret evidently began with an article by Pierre Canivet in the collection *Théologie de la Vie Monastique*,[61] which he had already been reading in connection with the earlier series of conferences.[62] While he relies heavily on Canivet for an overview of the material, as with previous figures he also acquainted himself thoroughly with primary sources (in this case the Latin translation of the Greek original, available in the *Patrologia Graeca*) (219–31). He was already reading the *Historia Religiosa* in January when he mentioned "Theodoret on Julian Saba" along with Ammonas as being just as relevant to him as Sartre,[63] and was perhaps still reading him, or already preparing his class notes, on April 28 when he speaks of himself in his journal as "[s]urfeited with letters" and goes on to remark ruefully, "This is so bad that it amounts to a sickness, like the obsessive gluttony of the rich woman in Theodoret who was eating thirty chickens a day until some hermit cured her. The only hermit that can cure me is myself and so I have to become that solitary in order to qualify as my own physician."[64]

After pointing out, following Canivet, that the *Historia* is less history in the modern sense than panegyric, a celebration of the

61. Pierre Canivet, SJ, "Théodoret et le Monachisme Syrien avant le Concile de Chalcédoine," *Théologie de la Vie Monastique*, 315–22.

62. Already in June 1962 Merton had written in his journal, "Read a little of the new *Théologie Monastique* [*Monastic Theology*], which is perhaps in some ways slighter than I expected, but informative. It does not seem very often to reach the level of theology: a series of historical background notes for monastic theology perhaps" (*Turning toward the World*, 227); Merton had used the volume in his lecture notes on Pachomius (see page 74, n. 318) and Basil (page 76, n. 325).

63. *Dancing in the Water of Life*, 68.

64. *Dancing in the Water of Life*, 101.

ascetic "athletes of Christ" who succeeded to the mantle of the martyrs, he goes on to provide sketches of many (though not all) of the ascetics, hermits and cenobites whom Theodoret describes, some from personal acquaintance. Merton has an eye for the picturesque detail in these stories—such as, of course, the lady with the thirty chickens (228), or the monk (the same one who cured the woman) who went after a bishop with his cane when he realized the bishop had come to ordain him (228), or the solitary who was so hirsute he was almost shot one night as a wolf (228), or the hermit Salamanes, who was "twice kidnapped" (230), by villagers on either side of a river eager for the special blessing the holy man's presence would bring, and who, being dead to the world, allowed himself to be carried hither and yon without protest or even acknowledgement. But he is also responsive to the authentic monastic theology in Theodoret: the "language of mysticism" (223), in fact of intense love mysticism, used to describe the experience of Julian Saba, one of the earliest of the Syrian ascetics; the description of the initial stages of the development in Syria of "cenobitic life, which necessarily implies certain compromises and adjustments 'so that all may be saved'" (224), the sensible and realistic outlook of Aphraat, who "[i]n time of conflict and persecution . . . leaves his solitude to defend the Church," and when criticized for doing so "replies that when the house is on fire it is not right for a virgin to remain lying in her marriage bed" (226), and of Theodosius, who "declared that it was ridiculous for monks to sit with their hands folded and live on the work of others while men in the world had to work to support families, pay taxes and give alms to the poor" (227). While he calls attention to certain aberrant tendencies in these early monastic figures, he also emphasizes that for Theodoret the monastic ideal is "more a question of attaining *equilibrium* between body and soul, than simply dominating the body," a quest for "*symmetry* rather than *ammetry*," and "above all" a recognition that "Christ is the model—*especially in gentleness, refusal of violence, universal love, and {the} capacity to pardon*" (231). Merton seems to find in Theodoret a Syrian analogue to the *Historia Monachorum in Aegypto* that he so enjoyed reading and discussing at a comparable point early in the first series of pre-Benedictine conferences.

One of the major figures described by Theodoret was Aphraat (or Afrahat), who was of particular note, as Merton points out, because even though he was "a Persian and {thus} a member of a despicable race" he nevertheless became "a philosopher," proof, according to Theodoret, of the unity of the human race as well as of the power of God (226). He is unusual also because the record of his "philosophizing" (as Theodoret calls it) has survived. The second section of Merton's text (232–41) discusses some of the *Demonstrationes* of Aphraat, which are significant because they are among the earliest records of Christian spiritual teaching in Syriac, but also (ironically, given Theodoret's terminology) because they are reflective of "a Biblical spirituality unaffected by philosophy" (232) (especially since Aphraat as a Persian would have been brought up away from all contact with Hellenic thought). Aphraat is not only pre-Benedictine but pre-monastic, writing for groups of ascetics known as sons and daughters of the covenant (*Benai Quejama*). In his overview of Aphraat's spirituality he notes the low view of marriage typical of the Syrian tradition (to leave father and mother to cling to a wife is for Aphraat to leave God the Father and the maternal Spirit for a fleshly love) (232), but he also highlights the stress on humility as the "basis of peace with men" and of "radiant joy, and even laughter" (233), along with Aphraat's understanding of prayer as a way *"to give God rest,"* and by doing so "to give rest to the weary" as well through "good works for others" (233), an appealing and attractive perspective on the complementarity of Christian prayer and action. Merton summarizes Aphraat's teaching as marked by "Discretion, Optimism, Solidity" and focused on the evangelical virtues of "faith, humility, love," which make the true Christian *"the child of peace"* (234). Most of Merton's attention is given to the (misleadingly titled) *"De Monachis"* (*Demonstratio* 6), the early sections of which concentrate on the importance of virginity and the dangers of men and women ascetics living together, albeit in chastity, but which goes on to articulate a deeply Christocentric and incarnational spirituality: "*We remain in our nature* in order to receive (participation in) His nature" (239). Christ's unity with the human race is also perceived as the source of community: "*Christ being one dwells in many without there being many Christs*" (240). The resurrected Christ is the source of the Holy Spirit, and the indwelling Holy Spirit given in baptism and preserved by purity of life will bring the Christian to share in the resurrection: "the Holy Spirit will urge Christ to raise up that body by which it was kept in purity" (240). Here is that "Biblical spirituality unaffected by philosophy" that Merton finds the most notable characteristic of Aphraat's writings.

The third section, on Ephrem (242–74), is longer than all that has preceded it. Merton first mentions being impressed with Ephrem in his September 27, 1964 letter to Hans Urs Von Balthasar: "Recently I have made the discovery of St. Ephrem, who is magnificent. I hope soon that he will be all accessible to those of us who do not know Syriac, etc.";[65] a month later (October 29) he writes to Dame Marcella Van Bruyn at Stanbrook, "I have been reading St. Ephrem wherever I can get access to bits and pieces of his work, and he is very fine."[66] This proves to be a quite accurate description of his efforts,[67] as he scours *L'Orient Syrien* and other journals that are beginning to publish particular works by Ephrem in French and/or Latin translation, and incorporates them into his expanding notes on Ephrem, at times in a fashion in which enthusiasm is more evident than logical organization. Merton uses the article in the *Dictionnaire de Spiritualité* by Dom Edmund Beck,[68] the most distinguished Ephrem scholar

65. *School of Charity*, 241.

66. *School of Charity*, 250.

67. Yet somewhat surprisingly Merton does not draw on the material by Ephrem available in volume 13 of *A Select Library of Nicene and Post-Nicene Fathers of the Christian Church*, second series, ed. Philip Schaff and Henry Wace (New York: Christian Literature Co., 1898), which also includes select *Demonstrations* of Aphraat; perhaps, published under non-Catholic auspices, it was not available at the time at Gethsemani.

68. Edmund Beck, "Éphrem," *Dictionnaire de Spiritualité Ascétique et Mystique* [*DS*], ed. F. Cavallera et al., 17 vols. (Paris: Beauchesne, 1932–95), 4:788–800.

of the day, for his basic framework and many of his citations from Ephrem's works, but inserts material from his "Hymns on Paradise," "Hymns on Virginity," and even material thought to be by Ephrem from medieval Latin and from Ethiopian sources into his discussion.

Ephrem is primarily a poet, the greatest hymnodist in the Syrian Church, and it is above all the vivid images and striking use of language that draw Merton's attention. While he usefully provides what amounts to an abbreviated summary in English of Beck's article, with its treatment of key topics in Ephrem's spiritual teaching such as faith, which "both finds the truth and *is found by* the truth," the God who constantly "seeks us in faith" (251); prayer, which is valid only in and through Christ, but "in order to pray in Christ we must *strip ourselves of self-love and of all that separates us from our brother*" (251); fasting, which "gives beauty to the soul and to the body together," a beauty that "is the sign of a supernatural transformation of nature, and prepares for the life of the risen body" (253); and virginity, which "makes the monk in a sense superior to the angels for he has to gain by bitter struggle what the angels possess without effort" (254)—it is in his exploration of the various primary sources that he was able to locate, mainly sequences of hymns, that Merton's fascination with Ephrem is most evident.

A spirit of celebration and gratitude pervades the "Hymns for the Table," which are "without any indication of a pessimistic and rigorist attitude toward the use of creatures" (245) and therefore contradict traditional presentations of Ephrem (such as that found in Vööbus, for example) as dour and life-denying. For one who has the eyes to see and the ears to hear, the entire creation, according to Ephrem, is a lyre, an instrument of praise with which the human voice and heart are called to sing in harmony (249). Merton's long-standing fascination with the theme of the spiritual journey as a return to paradise gave Ephrem's "Hymns on Paradise" a particular attraction. Ephrem's image of paradise as a mountain with various levels for those who have been banished from Eden is reminiscent of Dante's "seven-storey mountain" with Eden at its summit, but has its own unique Syrian strangeness. In being "pierced" on the cross, Ephrem sings in the refrain to the second hymn, Christ removes the sword from the gate of paradise, but to pass through the gate, Merton suggests, "*We spend our lives making our own key* to the door of paradise. Each one has to have his own key" (261), his (or her) own unique way of being restored to true identity, to that reflection of the divine image that no one else can be. What Merton finds above all in these hymns (strangely enough in a passage about hell) is that "[t]he cosmos remains *an integrated spiritual unity* for Ephrem. Nothing in it is lost or forgotten" (261). The "Hymns on Virginity" recognize both the necessity of marriage and the contributions of married people to the history of salvation, and indeed in the versified debates between virginity and "holy matrimony" give many of the good lines to the latter, but there is a sense in which marriage relies on logic but virginity on wonder, soaring above the world in the chariot of Elias (272), being joined to no human spouse but to Christ himself (273) (though the more practical elements of a celibate life are not neglected either: "Contrasted with the sufferings of childbirth, the sorrows of marriage, is the *freedom of the virgin life*, subjected directly to Christ" [273]). After ranging over this wide variety of disparate texts that he has managed to track down, Merton concludes his discussion of Ephrem (274) by returning to home ground, as it were, quoting, in Latin, a text attributed to Ephrem by Alcuin (with what degree of plausibility he does not say), as if to suggest that this interest in the Syrian poet and theologian is not a new one in the West, even if his authentic works are now becoming (somewhat) more available than they were to the Church in Carolingian times (and are certainly more widely available today than they were forty years ago, when Merton would have been one of the relatively few who were beginning to recognize the significance of Syriac texts for the development of early Christianity).

After a brief look (275–79) at Syrian monastic rules (particularly a set attributed to Ephrem), Merton turns to the last of his Syriac writers, Philoxenos of Mabbug, to whom he devotes more attention than he gave even to Ephrem (279–325). This is initially rather surprising, both because of Philoxenos' relative obscurity and because of his heterodox Christology, but Merton points out that his Monophysitism seems to be prompted by a fear of Nestorian undermining of the unitary personhood of Christ rather than by a denial of Christ's full humanity, and that in any case his ascetic writings are perfectly compatible with orthodoxy; and his obscurity, Merton clearly believes, needs to be dispelled. Also, unlike Ephrem, a volume of Philoxenos' homilies in French translation was included in the Sources Chrétiennes series, so a considerable collection of primary source material was readily available for discussion, though Merton also hunts through journals as he did for Ephrem to find further texts (including one that would subsequently be assigned to a later Syriac writer[69]). Philoxenos was actually a contemporary of St. Benedict, pre-Benedictine only in that he died in 523, earlier than the traditional date of Benedict's death in 547, and his principal writings may (or may not) have antedated the *Rule*, on which of course they had absolutely no influence. With Philoxenos Merton has moved as far away as he could from his original intent in projecting a series of pre-Benedictine conferences while still being able to call them pre-Benedictine. On the other hand, Philoxenos is clearly a witness to monasticism as it had developed in Syria, more so than the less organized asceticism found in Aphraat or even Ephrem, whose tradition "he combined . . . with the Greco-Egyptian philosophical thought of Evagrius and Origen" (280), making him one of the great synthesizers of late antique Christian spirituality in the East. Philoxenos was so congenial to Merton above all because his perspective is that of the desert, of emptiness and desolation and silence which is nevertheless the place of encounter with God.

Of the thirteen homilies of Philoxenos (an organized series consisting of an introductory homily followed by six pairs of homilies on faith, simplicity, fear of God, renunciation of the

69. See below, page 280, n. 401.

world, gluttony, and fornication), Merton discusses seven in detail, together with a number of letters that he has found elsewhere. He discovers in the introductory homily a recognition that the life of monastic discipleship is one of existential commitment, "learning Christ *in the heart* (by deep assimilation and experience) and not only 'in the ear'" (282). As for Evagrius and his tradition (including Cassian), so for Philoxenos the initial stages of spiritual growth are marked by the struggle against the passions, which is detailed by Philoxenos in what Merton calls "a study of great psychological subtlety" (286). Merton's detailed consideration of the homilies on gluttony (309–17) and fornication (320–25) provide evidence of this acuteness of psychological analysis, in which Philoxenos ruthlessly exposes the bad faith and unacknowledged motivations that lead even monks to deal only with surface manifestations of passion rather than excavating and pulling up its roots deep in the soul (though Merton does not endorse all of Philoxenos' advice, for example, striving to exercise control over the passions by only eating enough "barely to keep oneself alive" [316], or by "*arous*[*ing*] *impure desires and quiet*[*ing*] *them again by an act of will*" [323]). The same psychological and spiritual insightfulness, exercised in a more personal way, is evident in Philoxenos' letters to a novice, to a Jewish convert, to Patricius of Edessa (cf. "So too the mystical contemplation which you, O man of God, desire *is revealed to the intellect after the soul recovered its health*. But to seek to learn it by study and inspection of such mysteries is mere folly" [305–306]), which Merton also looks at in detail (along with the "Letter on Monastic Life," no longer considered to have been written by Philoxenos).

But Merton's interest in Philoxenos is most evident in his discussion of the pair of homilies (4-5) on simplicity, and of *Homily* 9 on renunciation, the "desert" homily par excellence. True simplicity according to Philoxenos is preserved in the desert but lost in the city. Indeed Philoxenos as Merton presents his teaching on simplicity sounds almost like a fifth-century Rousseau (or, to use his own perhaps more apt comparison, Mencius [292]) in his attack on the corruptive power of artificial worldly culture to distort human nature as created in the divine image: "Man is made *simple by nature*. He comes simple from the hand of God. *Society endows him with craftiness and duplicity*. If a man were to remain in the desert, untouched by social influences, he would remain simple" (289). Simplicity for Philoxenos is integrity, inner unity, the wholeness possessed by Adam in the garden, and the fall is a descent into duplicity, both double-mindedness and deceitfulness, an illusory autonomy predicated on presumed independence of the divine will, an "erroneous concept of liberty—*the presumption that liberty consists in judging reality and deciding not to conform to it!*" (291). Merton concludes that "Simplicity in Philoxenos has the same function as Purity of Heart in Cassian" (294).

Homily 9, on vocation to the desert, is perhaps the most Christocentric of the homilies: "Christ going out into the desert is the model of monastic renunciation. The monk, like Christ, goes into the desert to engage in combat with the spiritual enemy. *He must not take anything of the world with him. He leaves the world in the 'Jordan' or the 'Red Sea' on his way into the desert*. The Holy Spirit accompanies those who go out into the desert, but only if they rely on *no other source of strength*" (298). This passage into the desert with Christ after his baptism in the Jordan is a new birth, an emergence from the womb of worldly existence and growth into full spiritual adulthood. For Philoxenos, "true maturity of the Christian is in that knowledge of God that is granted only in the desert" (300), because only in the desert does one rely on God alone. As with Ammonas, this journey is one of existential dread, since it is a way of sharing in the confrontation of Jesus with the Tempter, but there is no way to the Promised Land but through the desert: "let the cry of anguish go up to God from the depths of our heart, thoughts or no thoughts, and then the sea will be parted and we will go through. 'Then the light of salvation [like the pillar of fire] will go before you and the darkness will be behind you between you and the Egyptians'" (304).

It is this deeply scriptural theology of the desert, which is also an equally scriptural theology of paradise, that made Philoxenos so congenial to Merton, and led him to mention the Syrian abbot as forming part of the "mental ecology" of his hermitage, the "living balance of spirits in this corner of the woods," in his essay *Day of a Stranger*,[70] and to incorporate his teaching into one of his most powerful and widely read essays, "Rain and the Rhinoceros,"[71] written as he was preparing his conferences on Philoxenos.[72] Here, Merton's initial reflection on technology, as exemplified in his Coleman lantern ("*Stretches days to give more hours of fun*"[73]) and more ominously in the SAC plane with its nuclear cargo, "brings me to Philoxenos, a Syrian who had fun in the sixth century, without benefit of appliances, still less of nuclear deterrents."[74] Philoxenos' reflections on the solitude of the desert in his ninth homily had become for Merton a sign of contradiction to all efforts, ancient or modern, to make personal identity dependent on social acceptance or acceptability. To be born spiritually is to emerge from the womb of social conformity, to be "liberated from the enclosing womb of myth and prejudice" through an active life of service to others (more Merton than Philoxenos here) or through "an advance into solitude and the desert, a confrontation with poverty and the void, a renunciation of the empirical self, in the presence of death, and nothingness, in order to overcome the ignorance and error that spring from the fear of 'being nothing.'"[75] Here is Merton's powerful restatement of the insights of Philoxenos for a contemporary audience. The desert of the authentic contemplative is not a way to avoid the common human condition but a vocation "to assume the

70. Thomas Merton, *Day of a Stranger* (Salt Lake City: Gibbs M. Smith, 1981), 35; the essay was written in May 1965 for publication in a South American journal, and first appeared in English in *The Hudson Review* in 1967.

71. Thomas Merton, "Rain and the Rhinoceros," in *Raids on the Unspeakable* (New York: New Directions, 1966), 9–23.

72. For references to the writing and publication of "Rain and the Rhinoceros," which first appeared in *Holiday* magazine in May 1965, see *Dancing in the Water of Life*, 180–81 (12/20/64), 197 (1/30/65), 204 (2/11), 214 (3/4); *Road to Joy*, 49 (12/19/64 letter to Mark Van Doren).

73. *Raids on the Unspeakable*, 13.

74. *Raids on the Unspeakable*, 14.

75. *Raids on the Unspeakable*, 17–18.

universal anguish and the inescapable condition of mortal man," as Jesus himself did: "It is in this sense that the hermit, according to Philoxenos, imitates Christ. For in Christ, God takes to Himself the solitude and dereliction of man: every man. From the moment Christ went out into the desert to be tempted, the loneliness, the temptation and the hunger of every man became the loneliness, temptation and hunger of Christ. But in return, the gift of truth with which Christ dispelled the three kinds of illusion offered him in his temptation (security, reputation and power) can become also our own truth, if we can only accept it."[76] This is the wisdom of Philoxenos as Merton understands and rearticulates it; and as he wrote in his journal of bringing together Ammonas and Sartre, so in his essay he juxtaposes the Syrian abbot with Ionesco: "Today the insights of a Philoxenos are to be sought less in the tracts of theologians than in the meditations of the existentialists and in the Theater of the Absurd."[77] It is in his marvelous ability to find and express convincingly such a connection between ancient monastic tradition and contemporary cultural critique that the power of this essay and of so much of Merton's work in general is rooted. It is in this unexpected yet surprisingly apt partnership with a twentieth-century playwright that Philoxenos makes what is surely his most vivid and significant appearance before a modern audience.

Philoxenos is also the focus of the Merton's May 3, 1965 letter to D. T. Suzuki, evidently the last letter he wrote to Suzuki before the Zen scholar's death on July 12, 1966.[78] Merton is moved to write about Philoxenos because he is reminded of the dialogue "Wisdom in Emptiness"[79] that he had written with Suzuki about the desert fathers, which focused largely on the meaning of the fall and the recovery of paradise. He begins his letter, "I have been reading a remarkable passage in a Syrian Christian thinker of the

76. *Raids on the Unspeakable*, 18.

77. *Raids on the Unspeakable*, 19.

78. *Hidden Ground of Love*, 570–71.

79. Thomas Merton, *Zen and the Birds of Appetite* (New York: New Directions, 1968), 99–138.

fifth century, Philoxenos. In fact I think *Holiday* magazine sent you an issue in which I had an article which refers to him. I think you will especially like this passage which discusses the *simplicity* which is a prime essential of spiritual life, and which was 'normal' to Adam and Eve in paradise. Hence it is a description of the 'paradise life' of prajna and emptiness." As he had focused in "Rain and the Rhinoceros" on Philoxenos' ninth homily, here he draws on the other texts that he had shown to be particularly meaningful to him in the pre-Benedictine conferences, the pair of homilies on simplicity. He quotes from the fourth homily:

> Here is what he says. After saying that God was with them and "showed them everything": "They received no thought about Him into their spirit. They never asked: Where does He live, who shows us these things? How long has He existed? If He created all, was He Himself created? By whom? And we, why has He created us? Why has He placed us in this paradise? Why has He given us this law? All these things were far from their minds, because simplicity does not think such thoughts. Simplicity is completely absorbed in listening to what it hears. All its thought is mingled with the word of him who speaks. It is like the little child, completely absorbed in the person speaking to it."[80]

As in "Rain and the Rhinoceros" Merton had brought Philoxenos into conversation with Ionesco, here he allows him to resonate with Zen Buddhism:[81]

> The mention of "law" here is actually no law other than that simplicity should be itself—namely, simplicity. That is

80. See page 292 below—Merton's translation is revised slightly in the letter.

81. Merton had already compared Philoxenos in rather similar fashion with Zen evidently as early as 1959, in the original draft of *The Inner Experience*: "One of the Fathers of the oriental Church, Philoxenus of Mabbugh, has an original and rather subtle view of original sin as a perversion of faith in which a false belief was superadded to the 'simple' and unspoiled view of truth, so that direct knowledge became distorted by a false affirmation and negation. . . . In any case the

> to say, absorbed in what is said to it, and not aware of itself as existing outside of what is spoken to it. Is this not paradise? I think that Buddhism is very aware of this, and it is therefore aware of that which is the intimate ground of all knowledge and all faith. And to the extent that Christian faith is unaware of this, it lacks some of the reality which it ought to have. However, I think it is there in the depths both of Christianity and Buddhism. Let us hope it is not being lost. In any event, there is only one meeting place for all religions, and it is paradise. How nice to be there and wander about looking at the flowers. Or being the flowers.

With these reflections on authentic simplicity—"one-pointedness" as Zen would call it—and on paradise as the place of encounter of all religious traditions, Merton concludes his conversation with the old Japanese master who had been instrumental in opening his mind and heart to Eastern spirituality. The words of Philoxenos become his last gift to his friend.

It is with Philoxenos that Merton brings his conferences on *Pre-Benedictine Monasticism* to an end on August 15, five days before leaving for the hermitage. (The five brief appendices that follow in the written text were not discussed in the conferences.) But back in January he had written in his journal, "what I like is to read Isaac of Nineveh in the hermitage,"[82] in reference to one of the greatest masters of the spiritual life in the Syriac tradition (fl. late seventh century), which suggests that if he had remained as novice master and continued the pre-Benedictine conferences, the Syrians would have kept the Celts "on hold" for at least a

---

idea of Philoxenus presents a striking affinity with the epistemological bases of Zen Buddhism, which seeks above all to clear away the clouds of self-deception which we cast over external reality when we set ourselves to thinking about it" (Thomas Merton, *The Inner Experience: Notes on Contemplation*, ed. William H. Shannon [San Francisco: HarperCollins, 2003], 20).

82. *Dancing in the Water of Life*, 192 (1/11/65).

while longer, and the title of the conferences would no longer have been accurate even in a chronological sense![83]

* * * * * * *

Since Merton's conferences had begun to be taped in April 1962, some ten months before the beginning of the pre-Benedictine classes, there is a virtually complete set of sound recordings for the entire series of these conferences.[84] It is therefore possible to compare the text of Merton's notes as edited in this volume with the actual class presentations. It is clear from a comparison of written and oral materials that Merton freely adapted, abridged, expanded and often spontaneously reworked his written text in order to make his class presentations as attractive and instructive as possible for his audience, so that the pertinence of the material for their own monastic formation would be highlighted, and Merton's own interest in and insights on particular authors and texts would be effectively conveyed.

As was his usual practice, Merton regularly began his conferences with various announcements. Some of these were of the domestic, "housekeeping" variety, as when he mentions leaving bars of soap in the shower on February 17, 1963—though these are kept to a minimum in these conferences since his audience was not limited to the novices; at one point he tells the young professed monks not to laugh as he gives the novices his standard instructions on the proper use of towels (April 12, 1963). He also uses the opening minutes to fill his audience in on upcoming events at the abbey, such as the first visit of Presbyterian

83. See also his journal entry for June 11, 1965: "I turned to read a bit of Youssef Yousnaya on Humility (Syrian—ninth century). It had extraordinary depth and resonance" (*Dancing in the Water of Life*, 255).

84. The conference for April 28, 1963 was inadvertently taped over the recording of the previous class (held either April 14 or April 21); only about a minute from the end of this earlier conference remains. Aside from this material, recordings of all the other conferences (now remastered on compact disc) are part of the archives at the Merton Center. Some of these recordings have been made available commercially. For a complete table of correspondences between the written text and the recordings, see Appendix B., 359–62.

seminarians to the abbey on February 17, 1963, or the death of one of the monks, "a very lively and humorous former Jesuit," Fr. Bellarmine, on March 3, 1963, or even seeing a muskrat in one of the lakes on April 21, 1963 or three deer when a visiting abbot was up at "the cottage" on October 11, 1964. He would also try to keep them somewhat abreast of what was happening in the wider world, since they had no access to newspapers or radios to let them know about current events. For example he tells them of the growing rift between Russia and China (July 28, 1963), and the surgeon general's initial report that smoking causes cancer (March 22, 1964); he often refers to events in the civil rights movement, as on June 23, 1963 when he announces that an NAACP leader (Medgar Evers) had been shot, and on August 9, 1964 when he tells his audience that the bodies of three slain civil rights workers have been found in Mississippi; and the growing conflict in Vietnam, as with the mention of the Tonkin Gulf resolution on August 16, 1964; while his comments on the war are initially rather low-key and circumspect, by August 8, 1965 he is calling it the stupidest war America has ever been involved in. Ecclesial events are also brought up, as he notes the passage of the Ecumenism decree at the Vatican Council, mentioned on October 18, 1964, and the trip of Pope Paul VI to India the following week. Not all the "news" is serious—on February 16, 1964 he announces that the New Zealand rugby team, composed mainly of Maoris, is beating all opposition on its world tour. At times these initial announcements can take up a good deal of the conference period, as on May 12, 1963, when he mentions a manuscript he had just received from the theologian Leslie Dewart, and then proceeds to discuss its contents for the next half hour, or on June 16, 1963 when he spends twenty minutes digressing on an article he has recently read on the cathedral at Bourges, or on August 25, 1963 when, after a visit by Fr. Bede Griffiths, he spends a half hour discussing the Hindu experience of God.

In comparing written and oral versions of the conferences, it is soon apparent that Merton often radically abridges his material. At times this is done simply by presenting only highlights of a particular section, as when he mentions only selected chapters of the *Vita Pachomii*, or omits a number of figures discussed by Theodoret; at other times he will select specific passages to discuss in detail and not discuss others, as he analyzes only the first part of the *Admonitio Filii Spiritualis*; sometimes whole sections are omitted, as with the introductory material on Cassian, or the spirituality of the Basilian *Rules*, or the sections on the Church and on fasting and watching in St. Ephrem, or the *Rules of Rabbula*; he tends to omit material that is of more scholarly than practical interest, as with the brief discussion of the relative merits of Pachomius and Evagrius, or the influence of Eustathius of Sebaste on St. Basil's ascetical teaching. The result is a more streamlined version of the material than is found in the written notes. Occasionally, the abridgement will result in a minor inaccuracy, as when a statement made about one monastery in the *Historia Monachorum* is applied to another (March 24, 1963). It is interesting to recognize, however, that his criteria for inclusion or exclusion do not uniformly correspond to his ostensible main focus, the background of the Benedictine *Rule*: for example the *Doctrina Orsiesii*, which had been translated into Latin by Jerome and was therefore available in the West, is passed over in silence in the classes, whereas the more picturesque material on Shenoute, who was completely unknown in the West until modern times, is discussed in some detail. It should also be noted that Merton does not reach the end of the written notes before entering the hermitage: not only the five appendices to the second series of conferences but material on Philoxenos' ninth *Homily*, which it is clear both from the written text and from his references in "Rain and the Rhinoceros" was deeply meaningful to him personally, were not discussed in class.

Material is also occasionally shifted around in the oral presentation. For example, when Merton is discussing Jerome on December 1, 1963, he incorporates material from the first appendix in Part I on Jerome's negative attitude toward chant (the only material from this appendix that is actually mentioned in the classes). Later, when discussing Philoxenos, he moves forward the material on fornication, from *Homilies* 12 and 13, evidently because he was at that point discussing the vow of chastity in the conferences on the vows being given concurrently.[85]

There are also a few instances in which Merton adds significant material that is not found in the written text. For example, on February 17, 1963, in discussing St. Anthony's move to a tomb, he adds the story about Macarius spending the night in a tomb and using a mummy for a pillow, and refusing to be dislodged by the demonic spirits who try to drive him out. In beginning his discussion of Ammonas on February 16, 1964, he considers the handful of apothegms about him found in the same volume of the *Patrologia Orientalis* that included the letters which he summarized in his written text.

Since the writing of the notes preceded their delivery by a considerable period of time, it is not surprising that Merton's conception of the material and of the overall shape of the course would have undergone some alteration in the meantime. In particular, it is evident from the very first lecture (February 3, 1963) that the focus of the course has already undergone considerable evolution. While Merton still talks of providing background for the Benedictine *Rule*, he gives the *Rule of the Master* considerably less attention than in the opening pages of the written text, and in fact is somewhat dismissive of it, calling it so long that evidently monks wouldn't copy it, as well as being somewhat tendentious; he points out for example that it "gets carried away" and spends three pages talking about gyrovagues, wandering

85. He mentions this in his opening announcements for the August 8 class. In the mimeographed version of the text this material has been inserted at the point where it was used in the classes, presumably because Merton had left the handwritten pages on these homilies at the point where he had used them; it is clear from the end of the text on the homilies on gluttony, however (see pages 317–18), that originally Merton had not yet written and perhaps was not intending to write about the fornication material, so that these pages clearly came later in the course of composition, just as the homilies on fornication follow those on gluttony in the text of Philoxenos itself. In this edition, the fornication material has been restored to its proper sequence at the end of the Philoxenos section.

monks, far more than is needed and far more than is found in the corresponding passage in Benedict. He also suggests at the very outset that he is just as interested in how the Holy Spirit worked in the lives of the people he will be discussing as he is in their possible relevance to and influence on the *Rule*, and goes on to demonstrate this focus in his discussion of St. Paulinus of Nola, whom he praises as a "real person—someone you can like and sympathize with" and concludes his discussion of Paulinus by noting that as human beings we learn from other human beings—not just by following a rule but by being inspired and instructed by the lives and words of other people. He can also modify his opinions in the course of the series, as when on June 2, 1963 he first mentions Shenoute as a "horrible man" and even calls him "disgusting," though when he actually discusses him in detail later he presents a more balanced view, admitting his positive qualities as well as his rigidity and violence.

Merton's main emphasis in the actual classes is to highlight the applicability of the material to his students. For example, on February 17, 1963, he uses the story of St. Anthony's struggles with demons to point out the necessity for perseverance in the monastic life, to remind his audience that Christ is present in consolations but even more present in desolations, and that too much clarity and certainty may be a sign of spiritual immaturity. In discussing on March 17, 1963 the statement in the *Historia Monachorum in Aegypto* that the world continues by the merits of monks, he cautions that this is to be understood not from the perspective of doing, an "accumulation of merits" in some quantitative sense, but from the perspective of being—that the primary job of the monk is to be real, and to allow the inner truth of one's being to emerge through both trials and graces. The following week, he points out that it is often the despised or undervalued aspects of a person that are actually the most powerful signs of God's presence, and refers both to the medieval legend of the juggler of Our Lady and to the Cinderella story to illustrate the beauty and power of "the true, simple, humble self." In discussing Cassian on April 21, 1963, he emphasizes the danger of confusing the voice of conscience with self-assertion, and points out that the same outward action can be the result of quite divergent and even incompatible motivations. In discussing the Pachomian model of monastic community, he stresses that it is not a matter of mere togetherness but first and foremost a mystery, a "*sacramentum*," an outward sign of the spiritual unity brought by Christ. While recognizing the extremism of the early Syrian tradition, he points out that in Theodoret there is an underlying emphasis on "symmetry," on keeping the passions in balance, which is ultimately a broader and more helpful concept than Evagrian *apatheia*.

While he is always on the alert to highlight the contemporary pertinence of the sources, he is also aware of the danger of discovering in these sources what one is predisposed to find and so distorting the original intent of the author, as when modern writers use Pachomius to assert the superiority of cenobitic to eremitic monastic life, when this was not the focus of Pachomius himself at all (July 21, 1963). He also emphasizes the need to read the sources critically, as when on August 18, 1963 he points out that the anti-Origenist polemic in the *Vita Pachomii* probably comes from his biographer rather than from Pachomius himself, who lived before the outbreak of the Origenist conflict at the end of the fourth century. He also warns against applying too rigidly norms instituted in a different age and for a different sensibility, as when in discussing regulations on food in a Basilian ascetic treatise on October 20, 1963 he cautions his listeners not to get obsessed with trivial things—better just to eat the cookie, he remarks—but don't take the bourbon set aside for the fruitcakes!

At times he also provides more insight into his own personal interest in a topic. For example, the written version of the Ammonas material, with its extensive quotations and summaries and relatively little commentary, resembles sections of Merton's reading notebooks. But in discussing Ammonas with his students, he emphasizes why he was so impressed with his new discovery that he called him "the best" (adding "right at the moment") (February 16, 1964). He highlights the existential immediacy he found in the desert father's letters. He speaks of the need for dialogue for the purpose of discernment, declares that nobody's version of the truth is sufficient in itself, and warns not to use ideas as weapons (February 23, 1964). Later in the same conference he points to Ammonas' profoundly paschal spirit, which finds the cross as the only true source of hope and takes a holistic view of the passage through death to resurrection and the gift of the Holy Spirit as a single process. A month later, in the last of the Ammonas conferences, he finds himself getting to the root of things by facing the radical challenge of death, and suggests that what the monastic life as Ammonas lives and describes it is intended to do is to make one's meeting with death a meeting with Christ.

His own abiding interest in the theme of the return to paradise is piqued by Ephrem's hymns on this topic, and he finds in the fifth hymn's suggestion that the right use of nature reconstructs paradise a basis for a positive theology of work and a vision of redeeming creation through proper use of created things (February 14, 1965).

He is at his most "Mertonian" in discussing simplicity in Philoxenos (May 16 and 23, 1965), noting that the assumption of individual autonomy that people associate with freedom is in fact the loss of freedom, because it sets oneself outside the Word and therefore apart from genuine reality. The whole purpose of monastic life, as Merton interprets Philoxenos, is to restore simplicity, which happens not through effort, or through self-consciously reflecting on simplicity in Cartesian fashion, but through the cross, through dying to self-consciousness and its complications—at which point, he concludes, Buber "goes out the window" because there is no longer an I-thou relationship but only Thou, no separate I—to be simple is to know God alone.

The "live" version occasionally also includes analogies not found in the written text. For example, in the first conference, Merton compares looking at pre-Benedictine monastic sources to looking at the Kentucky knobs surrounding the monastery. He suggests that viewing the knobs from a fire tower provides a different perspective than seeing them from ground level, and that just as it is good to know what is behind the knobs so it is helpful to find out what is "behind" the *Rule*. On April 21, 1963, in discussing the difference between means and ends, he refers to jumping up and down on a diving board, noting that the point is not to keep bouncing but to use the force generated to actually dive into the water. On May 12, 1963 he compares monastic formation to the life cycle of the bee, developing from a larva to a nymph in its cocoon to a working bee, first extracting jelly from the larvae while still unable to fly, then making wax and taking trial flights (like the juniors, he says), and finally leaving the hive to gather nectar and pollen.

There are also occasional references to his own experience, as on March 3, 1963 when in discussing the real and the ideal in monastic life he reminisces about his own first visit to the abbey during Holy Week of 1941—and how different monastic life looks from outside and from within—yet he points out that the ideal and the real are not mutually exclusive alternatives but coexist at the same time—providing two different perspectives on the same reality, and he adds that when people see Christ in them more clearly than they see Christ in themselves it is a grace to both. He talks on June 30, 1963 about teaching many students at St. Bonaventure who would later be killed in the Second World War, mentioning one, the football player Red McDonald, by name and calling him a great guy. In discussing some of the pointless conversations that go on in secular society on February 21, 1965, he mentions an argument that he and his brother John Paul got into one afternoon in Douglaston about whether Newark, New Jersey was part of "greater New York" or "the New York area," a dispute that eventually involved his uncle and grandparents as well.[86] In discussing the importance of living tradition on March 14, 1965, he provokes good-natured laughter by saying "look at me today," but goes on to point out that he could trace his experience of the monastery back to Dom Frederic's abbacy and Dom Robert's

86. He had mentioned this argument as probably occurring in 1934 in a journal entry for May 14, 1941: see Thomas Merton, *Run to the Mountain: The Story of a Vocation. Journals, vol. 1: 1939–1941*, ed. Patrick Hart (San Francisco: HarperCollins, 1995), 366.

mastership in the novitiate, and so was a link between this earlier era and the students who embodied the abbey's future.

He also frequently makes comparisons with later figures, not only the monastic and Cistercian figures frequently mentioned in the written text but others as well. For instance he compares Paulinus of Nola and his wife Therasia, who lived in married chastity, to Jacques and Raïssa Maritain, who did likewise and whom he calls two twentieth-century saints. In discussing apothegms on St. Anthony he compares him to Padre Pio, and says he became "sold" on Padre Pio by hearing stories about how he would flick his knotted handkerchief at the crowds of old ladies who would besiege him as he tried to cross the plaza from the church to the friary. On April 28, 1963, he moves from the vespers reading for the feast of St. Robert on the rejection of empty pomp to Cassian's similar teaching in his fourteenth *Conference* to contemporary witness to this same basic truth by Dorothy Day and the Catholic Worker movement. In discussing the distinction between Christian hope and worldly optimism on June 30, 1963, he mentions not only the followers of Teilhard de Chardin, who he thinks may tend to blur the two, but also Julian of Norwich's conviction that "all shall be well, and all manner of thing shall be well," which he finds rooted in trust in the redemptive love of Christ. He also makes occasional comparisons to Zen and other Eastern traditions, as when on May 19, 1963 he parallels Cassian's treatment of pure prayer as letting go and allowing God to act with Yoga and Zen teaching on self-surrender, and on March 15, 1964 he sees the teaching of Ammonas on radical confrontation with despair to be similar to Zen. On July 12, 1964, he relates the extreme asceticism of the early Syrian ascetics to a similar strain in Shia Islam, and on August 26, 1964 he finds a parallel to the idea in Theodoret that when one is ready, anything can put one over the edge into mystical reality, in the Persian Sufi mystic and poet Rumi.

Not all his comparisons are religious, or even serious. On February 16, 1964, discussing one of the apothegms of Ammonas, in which the *abba* sees a woman of rather shady reputation entering the hut of another monk and follows her in, then deliberately sits on a barrel where he knows she is hidden, and without indicating he has seen her, advises the monk to be careful and leaves, Merton remarks first that the story's effectiveness is in the extremely understated way in which it's told, and then compares the incident to the scene in a Marx Brothers movie (*Monkey Business*) in which the brothers are stowaways on board a ship and jump into barrels after being discovered, at which point Groucho, as though one of the officers, issues orders to disregard the barrels—from inside one of them!

As this example indicates, Merton frequently leavens his presentations with humor. Sometimes they are in-jokes, as when on June 16, 1963 he implies that the A. Boon who edited the Latin Pachomian material must be the abbey's neighbor Andy Boone, turning out translations in his spare time; in other cases they are prompted by details in the texts themselves, as when Merton himself becomes almost giddy describing the legendary outfitting of Shenoute, whose underwear is said to have belonged originally to the three young men in the fiery furnace from the Book of Daniel (August 18, 1963); on December 1, 1963 he speculates that Jerome's opposition to chant may have been because he had a voice like that of Cardinal Cushing of Boston. Punctuating his presentations with laughter, both his listeners' and his own, is not only a way of changing the tone and pace of the discussion, but a way of exemplifying what he says on February 17, 1963 about taking the monastic life seriously, but not taking themselves too seriously; for example, during this same conference, when he compares the miraculous flowering of the dry stick in Sulpicius Severus' version of the story with the ending of the same story in Cassian, where the *abba* finally kicks the dry stick over after the novice has obediently watered it for a year, he provokes laughter when he says of Sulpicius, "he's a great writer—you can't believe a word he says," but he then goes on to point out that for Cassian the story is a way of recognizing one's own uselessness and so of getting rid of the nonsense of a false sense of one's own importance. He makes a similar point in his discussion of Aphraat (August 16, 1964), where he finds an intrinsic connection between laughter and humility, in which only God, not even one's most cherished ideas, is to be taken with utter seriousness.

Opening the conference on August 15, 1965, after mentioning that Fr. Lawrence (Ernesto Cardenal) was being ordained that day, Merton announces that there will be a conference on Friday (August 20), but that there would be no conference on the following Sunday—crepe armbands and large handkerchiefs would be in order—but that after that there may be conferences again. While there had been no official announcement as yet, it is evident that word of Merton's impending move to the hermitage had begun to circulate. In this final pre-Benedictine conference he then went on to discuss Philoxenos' view of the monastic vocation as a call out of the world into the desert, a life of complete dependence upon God, of spiritual poverty that surrendered all human sources of strength, even the consolation of help from the community. The key word, Merton suggests, is "care"—for freedom from "the world" is freedom from care, freedom from anxiety that springs from fruitless, useless, meaningless responsibility, freedom from the organized futility of a world that measures success by achievement. "We may or may not talk about this again some time," he concludes—in fact this becomes the focus of his very last conference as novice master on the following Friday, given the title "A Life Free from Care,"[87] which thus became both the coda to his two and a half years of conferences on the monastic tradition before Benedict, and more generally to the decade and a half of instructing young monks and novices in authentic monastic life, and the prelude to the three and a half years that would follow in which Merton would try to be faithful to that tradition in a new and challenging solitary setting.

87. See Thomas Merton, "A Life Free from Care," *Cistercian Studies*, 5.3 (1970), 217–26.

****

The text of *Pre-Benedictine Monasticism* consists of three related sections, all of which are included in Volume 18 of Merton's "Collected Essays," the 24-volume compendium of published and unpublished materials assembled and bound at the Abbey of Gethsemani some time after Merton's death and now available both at the abbey and at the Merton Center in Louisville. A title page headed "PRE-BENEDICTINE MONASTICISM / Series I / & / Series II // ABBEY OF GETHSEMANI / NOVITIATE / 1963–64"[88] is followed by mimeographed texts of the two parts of Merton's *Pre-Benedictine* notes that were distributed to his students before the conclusion of each course, and were also circulated beyond the abbey (usually, if not always, separately), to friends and to other monastic communities. The mimeograph version of Part I is headed "GALLO ROMAN MONASTICISM / CASSIAN / THE REGULA MAGISTRI / AND THE BACKGROUND / to the RULE of / ST BENEDICT" with the added notation "Notes for conferences—Choir Novitiate—Gethsemani—1963." It consists of 96 pages of single-spaced text. The mimeographed text of Part II consists of a title page headed "PRE-BENEDICTINE MONACHISM / Series II / Syria, Persia, and Palestine // Abbey of Gethsemani / Novitiate / 1964" followed by 89 pages of typed, single-spaced text, beginning with an unnumbered chart headed "PRE-BENEDICTINE MONACHISM / Monastic Chronology" succeeded by pages numbered 1-87, with two successive pages numbered "23".

Also in Volume 18 is a mimeographed text headed "THE SPIRITUAL DOCTRINE OF ST AMMONAS" on the top of the first page and consisting of 17 pages of typed double-spaced text (the numbering is centered in the lower margin for the first six pages and switches to the center of the upper margin for the re-

88. The decision to use the title *Pre-Benedictine Monasticism* for this volume, rather than *Pre-Benedictine Monachism*, which is the heading used for the second series and at times in references within the text, is based on this general heading in the "Collected Essays" volume.

maining pages).[89] Since this material was presented to the class directly after the conclusion of the first series of pre-Benedictine conferences, it is included in the present edition as Appendix 2 to Part 1 (there already being a brief Appendix 1 on "Chant and the Monastic Life").

Since the mimeographed text of "The Spiritual Doctrine of St. Ammonas" is the only version of this material that has been located, it serves as the copy text for this section. For the two parts of the pre-Benedictine conferences themselves, however, the mimeographed texts are superceded in part or in whole by Merton's own typescripts, heavily modified by handwritten additions, which he had in front of him while teaching and which were the basis for the retyped versions that were mimeographed and distributed to the novices and other students.[90] The typescript for *Pre-Benedictine Monasticism*, Part I is only partially extant. An extensive fragment survives in the Merton archives at the Friedsam Memorial Library at St. Bonaventure University, Olean, New York. It was apparently given by Merton to his friend Fr. Irenaeus Herscher, OFM, the St. Bonaventure Librarian, perhaps when Fr. Irenaeus had come to Gethsemani on retreat in

89. It is accompanied by a thirty-five page translation of the sixteen letters of Ammonas preserved in Syriac, headed "THE LETTERS OF BLESSED AMMONAS / Successor of St Antony as Superior / of the anchoritic colony at Pispir. / (Literally translated according to the Syriac text of / the edition of Michael Kmosko published in P. O. 10)." While it is possible that the translation was made by Merton from the Latin version of the text included in the *Patrologia Orientalis*, passages included in "The Spiritual Doctrine of St. Ammonas" do not correspond in wording to the same passages in the translation, and the notation "translated according to the Syriac text" seems to suggest that the translation was made directly from the Syriac, which Merton did not know (though "according to" is less unambiguous than "from" would have been); it is clear from the tape of the February 23, 1964 conference on Ammonas that one of the students did know Syriac, so that he may have been the translator of the letters.

90. In the typescript of the second part of the conferences, and at least once in the first part, there are occasional inserted markings indicating the page numbers of the mimeographed version at the corresponding point in the typescript, presumably made in order to note where the typist had ended his work on a particular day.

August, 1964,[91] or it may have been sent to him some time afterward. The first fourteen pages of the typescript are missing, page 15 is extant, pages 16 through 24 are missing, and then the rest of the text, consisting of 55 pages of typed and handwritten material,[92] is extant. For those sections of the material for which the typescript is extant, it serves as the copy text, since it consists of Merton's own typed and handwritten text. This includes the material on pages 44–45 from: "f) THE SPIRITUAL DOCTRINE OF CASSIAN and Evagrius" through "discipline for attaining it." along with the two sentences: "4. In either case . . . (see esp. *Conf.* 8)." on page 47, which is a handwritten addition on the verso of this sheet marked for insertion on the no longer extant page 16 of the typescript; and the material from page 68 ("This is also to be completed . . .") to the conclusion of the text, the end of Appendix 1 of the first part (page 190). For the remaining material in Part 1, the mimeographed text serves as copy text. The entire text of Merton's typescript for the second part of the pre-Benedictine material, consisting of 80 pages of text,[93] of which 28

91. See *Dancing in the Water of Life*, 136 [Sunday, August 16, 1964]: "And on Thursday Father Irenaeus [Herscher, O.F.M.] of St. Bonaventure [University] was here with a group of Franciscans and Capuchins. I had not seen him in twenty-three years."

92. The pagination of these pages is inconsistent and occasionally confusing: the extant portions of the typescript consist of the typed page 15; fourteen typed pages headed 25–37 (two successive pages numbered 37); an unnumbered handwritten page; a typed page numbered 38a; three handwritten pages on the *Vita Pachomii* numbered 39–41; two typed pages on the *Doctrina Orsiesii* numbered 42–43; three handwritten pages on the "Two Weeks" and Shenoute numbered 44, 44a, 44b; twelve typed pages on St. Basil numbered 45–56 (the numbers 48 through 54 and 56 typed, the rest handwritten); ten handwritten pages on Roman Monasticism in Palestine, numbered 57–66; seven typed pages on Aetheria numbered 67–70, [unnumbered page], 72, [unnumbered page] by hand (along with separate typed pagination numbered Aetheria 2–7); two handwritten pages entitled "Appendix I" numbered 74–75.

93. There are also six cancelled or omitted pages: a page headed "Latin Texts of Ephrem in High Middle Ages." cancelled and marked "Do not copy." (with material for insertion on its verso side); a page with seven lines on Manichaeism, evidently unrelated to the surrounding material, and the heading "ST EPHREM" lower down on the recto side and with extensive material on Ephrem

pages are typed and 52 handwritten,[94] survives in the archives of the Thomas Merton Center at Bellarmine University, Louisville, KY, and it therefore serves as copy text for this section of the material.[95]

The editorial text of this edition follows the copy text for each section, with the following modifications. All substantive addi-

---

on the verso, marked for insertion on the following page; three pages of introductory material on Ephrem headed "Voobus. Syrian monasticism."; one page of material headed "St Ephrem—Moine et Pasteur—(306–373)" drawn from Louis Leloir's article of the same title in *Théologie de la Vie Monastique*. The three pages drawn largely from Vööbus were apparently intended to be the original beginning of the Ephrem section but were replaced by new introductory pages dependent largely on the article on Ephrem in the *Dictionnaire de Spiritualité* by Edmund Beck, whose judgements are sometimes incompatible with those of Vööbus. All the omitted material is transcribed in Appendix A of the present edition (352–55).

94. The high proportion of handwritten material in Part II, and to a lesser extent in Part I, is probably due at least in part to Merton's physical condition: his cervical disk problems, for which he was hospitalized in August–September 1963, made it difficult at times to type, especially with his left hand: see his October 3, 1963 letter to Sr. Thérèse Lentfoehr: "The reason I have not written is that I just got out of the hospital a few days ago. I have had and still have a cervical disc along with arthritis and other unpleasant things. I am trying to get this disc fixed up without an operation & am therefore still a bit cramped. My left hand is not much good for typing" (*Road to Joy*, 246); see also *Hidden Ground of Love*, 55 [October 18, 1963], 189 [August 22, 1963], 277 [October 19, 1963], 362 [October 18, 1963], 554 [October 2, 1963]; *Road to Joy*, 46 [February 11, 1964]; *School of Charity*, 243–44 [October, 1964], 273 [April 7, 1965]; *Dancing in the Water of Life*, 18 [September 20, 1963], 20 [September 28, 1963], 75 [February 11, 1964]. Further problems developed with the rash on his hands that began in August 1964: see his September 10, 1964 letter to Sr. M. Emmanuel: "This will have to be short. Poison ivy has taken the skin off my hands and if I type long my fingers start bleeding" (*Hidden Ground of Love*, 193); see also *Hidden Ground of Love*, 367 [September 12, 1964]; *Road to Joy*, 64 [September 23, 1964]; *Dancing in the Water of Life*, 135 [August 12, 1964].

95. Despite the high proportion of handwritten pages, this version will be referred to as "typescript" to be consistent with the principal copy text of Part I. The text consists of an unnumbered title page in Merton's hand, an unnumbered handwritten chronology page; two typed pages, the second numbered 2; a page numbered 3 on which the first two lines are typed and the rest is handwritten; seven pages of handwritten material, on Theodoret and Aphraat, the first two of

tions made to the text, in order to turn elliptical or fragmentary statements into complete sentences, are included in braces, as are the few emendations incorporated directly into the text, so that the reader can always determine exactly what Merton himself wrote (or at least, where the mimeograph serves as copy text, what his typist typed). No effort is made to reproduce Merton's rather inconsistent punctuation, paragraphing, abbreviations and typographical features; a standardized format for these features is established that in the judgement of the editor best represents a synthesis of Merton's own practice and contemporary usage: e.g., all Latin passages are italicized unless specific parts of a longer passage are underlined by Merton, in which case the under-

---

which are numbered 4–5 in the right-hand corner by Merton, others numbered 6, 8–10 in the left-hand corner in another hand, probably that of the mimeograph typist, with the last of these pages numbered "Afrahat 2" in Merton's hand; three typed pages on Aphraat, the first two numbered 11–12 by the unknown hand in the left-hand corner, with "Aphraat 4" typed in the right-hand corner of the page numbered 12; one handwritten page on Aphraat numbered 14 in the left-hand corner by the unknown hand; six typed pages on Ephrem numbered 1, 1a, 1b, 2, 3, 4 in the right-hand corner, and 15, 17, 18 found in the left-hand corner of the first, third and fourth pages; one handwritten page numbered 5 in the right-hand corner and 21 in the left-hand corner (this is the last of the pages where the consecutive numbering by the second hand is attempted); three typed pages numbered 5a, 5b, 5c; three handwritten pages, the last two of which are numbered 5d, 5e; two typed pages, the first numbered 6 by hand, the second numbered 7 typed; three handwritten pages, the first of which is numbered 8, the last two unnumbered; six omitted pages, the fourth of which is numbered "Ephrem 2"; two typed pages on Syrian Monastic Rules, the second of which is headed "Syrian Rules 2"; one handwritten page on Syrian Monastic Rules; three handwritten pages headed "Philox[enos]" 1–3; three typed pages, the first two headed "Philox" 3a and 3b, the third unnumbered; three handwritten pages, the first unnumbered, the latter two headed "P. simplicity 2," and "Philox. Simplic. 3."; two unnumbered handwritten pages on Philoxenos' "Letter to a Converted Jew"; two handwritten pages on Philoxenos' "Letter to a Novice" numbered "Philox." 3c. and 3d.; six typewritten pages, the first five headed "Philox." 4–8; a cover page and six handwritten pages on Philoxenos on Gluttony, the last five of which are numbered "[Philox.] Glutt[ony]" 2–6; one typewritten page headed "Appendix to Philoxenos on Gluttony"; four handwritten pages on Philoxenos on Fornication, the last three of which are headed "Forn." 2–4; twelve handwritten pages consisting of the five appendices.

lined section of the passage is in roman type; all other passages underlined by Merton are italicized; words in upper case in the text are printed in small caps (unless the capitalization in handwritten passages is considered to be for purposes of orthographical clarity—i.e., for unfamiliar proper names); periods and commas are uniformly included within quotation marks; patterns of abbreviation and capitalization, very inconsistent in the copy text, are regularized. Latin passages in the original text are left in Latin but translated by the editor in the notes. All references to primary and secondary sources are cited in the notes. All identified errors in Merton's text are noted and if possible corrected. All instances where subsequent research and expanded knowledge affect Merton's accuracy are discussed in the notes.

The textual apparatus does not attempt to record every variation between the different versions of the text. Errors, whether of omission or of mistranscription, in the mimeograph versions of the text where these are not being used as copy text, are not recorded since they have no independent authority vis-à-vis the copy text. No attempt is made to record on-line corrections Merton made in the process of typing (i.e., crossing out one word or phrase and immediately substituting another); changes in handwritten additions are recorded, however.

Notes on the text record:

a) all cases in which a reading from the mimeograph version is substituted for the copy text—generally limited to the typist following Merton's own instructions for expanding the text; in those cases where Merton's direction to expand the text is not followed, the text is left as it is, the direction is recorded in the textual apparatus, and the addition is included in the explanatory notes;
b) all handwritten additions or alterations to the original text.

Thus the textual notes allow the interested reader to distinguish between the preliminary draft of Merton's notes and the additions that he made before actually delivering the conference lectures. Since these conferences were given only once, the additions were made during the same general period as the original drafting of the text, but they do serve to indicate how Merton continued to rework his material as he prepared the conferences.

Also included as a second appendix is a table correlating the written text and the taped lectures, which facilitates comparison of Merton's version of the material as published in this edition with the conferences as actually delivered to the novices.

Finally, a list of suggestions for further reading is included as a third appendix, consisting first of other sources in Merton's published works where figures and topics from this volume are discussed, followed by a list of important recent studies on the major figures and topics of this volume, that will provide helpful updating on material discussed by Merton.

****

In conclusion I would like to express my gratitude to all those who have made this volume possible:

- to the Trustees of the Merton Legacy Trust, Robert Giroux, Anne McCormick and Tommie O'Callaghan, for permission to publish the *Pre-Benedictine Monasticism* conferences;
- to the late Robert E. Daggy, former director of the Thomas Merton Center, Bellarmine College (now University), Louisville, KY, for first alerting me to the project of editing the novitiate conferences, and for his encouragement in this and other efforts in Merton studies;
- to E. Rozanne Elder, director of Cistercian Publications, for continued support for the project of publishing Merton's novitiate conferences;
- to Brother Patrick Hart, ocso, for his friendship, for continued encouragement in the publication of the volumes of the novitiate conferences in the Monastic Wisdom series, for which he serves as editor, and for facilitating my research visits to the library at the Abbey of Gethsemani;

- to Sidney H. Griffith of the Catholic University of America, for graciously accepting an invitation to provide the Preface for this volume;
- to Paul M. Pearson, director and archivist of the Merton Center, and Mark C. Meade, assistant archivist, for their gracious hospitality and valued assistance during my visits to the Center, and especially to Dr. Pearson for locating and making available the original typescript of the second series of *Pre-Benedictine Monasticism* conferences;
- to Fr. Elias Dietz, ocso, for graciously assisting my research at the Gethsemani library by locating hard-to-find materials;
- to Paul Spaeth, director of the Friedsam Memorial Library of St. Bonaventure University, and Lorraine Welch, formerly assistant archivist of the library, for making available the original typescript of the first series of *Pre-Benedictine Monasticism* conferences;
- to the Gannon University Research Committee, which provided a grant that allowed me to pursue research on this project at the Merton Center and at the Abbey of Gethsemani;
- to Mary Beth Earll of the interlibrary loan department of the Nash Library, Gannon University, for her tireless efforts in locating and acquiring various obscure volumes; to library staff of the Geisel Library of St. Anselm College, of the Burr Shelving Facility of the University of Michigan Library, of the Hesburgh Library of the University of Notre Dame, and of the Divinity School Library, the Sterling Memorial Library and the Mudd Library of Yale University, for assistance in locating important materials in their collections;
- again and always to my wife Suzanne and our children for their continual love, support and encouragement in this and other projects.

PRE-BENEDICTINE MONASTICISM

Series I
&
Series II

ABBEY OF GETHSEMANI
NOVITIATE
1963–64

GALLO-ROMAN MONASTICISM

CASSIAN

THE *REGULA MAGISTRI*

and the BACKGROUND

to the *RULE* of

ST. BENEDICT

Notes for Conferences—Choir Novitiate—Gethsemani—1963

Prologue

The *Rule* of St. Benedict, the "Patriarch of Western Monasticism," is thought to have been composed somewhere around 530 to 540 A.D. St. Benedict himself is thought to have died around 547. Hitherto the picture we have had of St. Benedict, in monasteries since the nineteenth-century revival of monasticism, has been rather oversimplified. We have taken it for granted that St. Benedict, single-handed, introduced a really organized and regular form of monastic life to the West, as if before him there had been no rules, no systematic organization of community life, and even no sane asceticism, in the West. True, the fact of Cassian was there for all to see. Cassian had come from the East a century before St. Benedict flourished, and had written his great works, the *Institutes* and *Conferences*, in France in the early fifth century. And it also had to be recognized, though in a very confused way, that there were monks of a sort in France, as well as Italy. Perhaps the tendency was, however, to regard them either as worthy ascetes, on the pattern of St. Paulinus of Nola, or exceptional vocations, hermit types; but the rest, it is assumed, were gyrovagues and sarabaites. St. Benedict was, we supposed, "the first" to react against a condition of general anarchy.

Add to this the mythical idea of "St. Benedict the Roman," a picture that has been fancifully elaborated by Cardinal Ildefons Schuster.[1] But at any rate, the image of St. Benedict that has been

1. While Cardinal Schuster frequently does emphasize the Roman connections of St. Benedict (see Ildefonso Schuster, *Saint Benedict and His Times*, trans. Gregory J. Roettger [St. Louis: B. Herder, 1951], 208–210, 221–25, 299, 384), the title "St. Benedict the Roman" actually is found in Ildefons Herwegen, OSB, *St. Benedict, A Character Study*, trans. P. Nugent (St. Louis: Herder, 1924), 67: "It was

built up, notably by the Benedictine commentators on the *Rule* at the turn of the twentieth century,[2] has been of Benedict the practical, prudent, legal-minded Roman, with his feet on the ground, a profoundly original yet prudent mind, who in a synthesis of genius knew how to preserve the fundamental values of Eastern monasticism in a framework that made them livable and "practical" for men of the West. This of course is basically a just estimate, but Benedict must not be seen as the *only* prudent legislator or spiritual guide of the West.

Without minimizing the greatness of the *Rule* of St. Benedict as a legislative document, and without entering into controversies about the life and work of St. Benedict himself, it is necessary first of all to get a more exact perspective. This, with {the} aid of more recent studies, we are now able to do. The following notes are intended to make our monks aware of these recent developments, at least some of the fruits of a few studies, and to enable them to gain a deeper and more just appreciation and understanding of the *Rule*.

Elements in this readjustment of perspective must include the following:

1) While there is no denying the *practicality* of the *Rule* of St. Benedict as a very "workable" rule for monasteries, clear, concise and realistic, we must recognize that it is only *one of many* Rules written at the beginning of the sixth century.

2) Not only is it one of many, and therefore not unique and quasi-miraculous, but it is *not the first* of the relatively numerous Western rules. Setting aside the *Rule* of St. Augustine (with which we will not be at all concerned here) in North Africa (not strictly a monastic rule in any case, though it had an influence in mo-

---

reserved for St. Benedict the Roman to erect the whole structure of his monastic community clearly and distinctly on the principle of paternity."

2. See for example Dom John Chapman, *Saint Benedict and the Sixth Century* (New York: Longmans, Green, 1929), 204: "He produced a Rule which was so practical and moderate that it could be enforced as a minimum, and so wise and holy that it could lead saints to perfection."

nastic circles) there are at least half a dozen Western rules prior to the *Rule* of St. Benedict or contemporaneous with it.

3) Not only is the *Rule* of St. Benedict *not unique*, and *not the first* among these Western rules, but also a great deal of the material in the *Rule* of St. Benedict (hereafter it will be referred to as *RB*) is taken from *earlier Western Rules*.

4) Hence the *Rule* is neither unique, nor the first, nor entirely original in its material. It is original in the sense of being a new redaction and editing of already known material, with significant additions and a viewpoint of its own. The *Rule* certainly has a character of its own impressed on it by a redactor of great wisdom and experience. The *Rule* has certainly a very real originality—as a work of genius in *making use of* previously existing matter and giving it a *new and definitive form*.

5) It must be said that the value of the *Rule* lies primarily in the fact that it is an *eminently practical digest of a body of traditional material*, a compilation rather than an original creation. Doubtless it is the best and most practical single rule among those found in France and Italy at the time (the Spanish rules come later than *RB*), but it is a resumé of the most practical points in the other rules, giving them a new form and orientation.

6) At the same time, in "digesting" the material from the other rules, *RB* tends often to leave out material of exceptional historical interest, as well as passages of deep spiritual value. These things are secondary to the purpose of the *RB*, and its practicality comes in part from the way in which they were edited out of the text. But for us these elements are very interesting, and *study of them is essential* for a full understanding of the *RB*, the rule according to which we have vowed to live.

7) The unique and authoritative character of the *RB* goes back to the times of Charlemagne and the Council of Aix (817).[3] In treating of the *Rule* as the "only" rule and the "original" creation

3. The Council of Aix-la-Chapelle (or Aachen), called by Emperor Louis the Pious and held under the direction of Benedict of Aniane, established the Benedictine *Rule* as the norm for all monasteries in the Carolingian Empire (see Hubert Van Zeller, *The Benedictine Idea* [Springfield, IL: Templegate, 1959], 85–89).

of a great monastic genius, we are really making a wrong interpretation of this historical fact.

8) It is important, then, to study the *RB* in the light of these new perspectives, that is to say, against the background of fifth-century monasticism and fifth-century monastic documents, as well as the spirituality of such monastic centers in France as Lérins, Marseilles, and Arles.

9) In particular, it is of great value to read in detail the controversial *Regula Magistri* (hereafter referred to as *RM*),[4] which is now generally recognized to antedate the *RB* and to be a source of most of the material in the *RB*.[5] One of the best ways of understanding the *RB* is to read it in the light of the *RM* and to study all the material in *RM* that fills out the picture for us. Hence these notes will concentrate on the study of the *RM* and a comparison of its main chapters with those of *RB*.

4. The *Regula Magistri* is found in J. P. Migne, ed., *Patrologiae Cursus Completus, Series Latina*, 221 vols. (Paris: Garnier, 1844–1865), vol. 88, cols. 943–1052 (subsequently referred to as *PL* in text and notes).

5. This is somewhat of an overstatement. In his preface to the English translation of *RM* (based on his own French edition and translation: *La Règle du Maître*, ed. and trans. Adalbert de Vogüé, Sources Chrétiennes [SC], vols. 105–107 [Paris: Éditions du Cerf, 1964–65]), Adalbert de Vogüé writes, "From the prologue to the treatise on humility, these two texts often correspond verbatim. After that each rule follows its own course, though some correspondence may still be observed in the sequence of material and, at times, in the substance of the regulations" (*The Rule of the Master*, trans. Luke Eberle with an Introduction by Adalbert de Vogüé, Cistercian Studies [CS], vol. 6 [Kalamazoo, MI: Cistercian Publications, 1977], 80). A complete listing of studies on the relationship between *RM* and *RB* is found in G. Penco's edition of *RB*, *S. Benedicti Regula* (Florence: La Nuova Italia, 1958), xi–xvii. The precedence of *RM* has not gone unchallenged: see Marilyn Dunn, "Mastering Benedict: Monastic Rules and Their Authors in the Early Medieval West," *Ecclesiastical History Review*, 105 (1990), 567–94; Adalbert de Vogüé, "The Master and Benedict: A Reply to Marilyn Dunn," *Ecclesiastical History Review*, 107 (1992), 95–103; Marilyn Dunn, "The Master and St Benedict: A Rejoinder," *Ecclesiastical History Review*, 107 (1992), 104–11; Dunn summarizes her arguments for Benedict's priority in *The Emergence of Monasticism: From the Desert Fathers to the Middle Ages* (Oxford: Blackwell, 2000), 128–29, 182–86.

Gallo-Roman Monachism

Before beginning this we will look at the monastic milieu of the Gallo-Roman world in the fifth century, at the time of the first Invasions. First, at the beginning of the fifth century, we have documents of spirituality like the important tracts of St. Eucherius[6] and other writings that emanated from the monastic centers of southern Gaul. We will not go into detailed study of Cassian, here, as this is done by us in another course of lectures.[7]

In brief, we will study the *RB* against the background of a monastic milieu which may well have been the milieu in which the *RM* was written, namely southern Gaul.[8] Whether or not the *RM* was written in southern Gaul, it was certainly known there and it is filled with a spirituality and an outlook which we find in the other monastic writings of that area, as well as in St. Benedict. The chief importance of this study is that it concentrates on the time and way in which Western monasticism *developed into an institution* and took on a form which it has more or less retained ever since.

In a cursory glance, we can look over the area to be considered:

6. Eucherius' works are found in *PL* 50, cols. 685–894. Merton is probably thinking particularly of the *De Laude Eremi* and the *De Contemptu Mundi*. Eucherius is discussed by Nora K. Chadwick in *Poetry and Letters in Early Christian Gaul* (London: Bowes & Bowes, 1955), 151–60, a work that Merton uses as a source for these conferences.

7. Thomas Merton, *Cassian and the Fathers: Initiation into the Monastic Tradition*, ed. Patrick F. O'Connell, Monastic Wisdom [MW], vol. 1 (Kalamazoo, MI: Cistercian Publications, 2005), 97–259.

8. De Vogüé considers other locations, including southern Gaul (particularly Lérins), but concludes "with maximum probability" that "the RM was written in the first quarter of the sixth century in a region near Rome, to the southeast, where it would be open to the dominating influence of the Eternal City, and more tenuously, to that of certain churches of Campania" (*Rule of the Master*, 78–79). Dunn thinks it was "a product of a more northerly region" because "the content of the night office is modulated to take into account a very noticeable variation between the length of winter and summer nights" (*Emergence of Monasticism*, 128).

1) John Cassian, and his monastery and nunnery at Marseilles.

2) The island monastery of Lérins, a great center of learning and monasticism, very much influenced by Cassian. Between them, the centers of Marseilles and Lérins tend to develop the same kind of spirituality: with roots in Oriental tradition, and with a tendency to semi-pelagianism.

3) Later, the monastic center at Arles (an offshoot of Lérins), where St. Caesarius, combining the monastic ideas of Lérins with the theology and spirituality of St. Augustine, corrects the semi-pelagian tendencies. St. Caesarius is one of those who precedes St. Benedict in organizing and systematizing monastic life.[9] The problem of mutual influence between St. Caesarius and *RB* is however not easy, as they are contemporaries. Other *Rules* at Arles: St. Aurelian, John of Arles.[10]

4) There were other monastic centers in France, in the southern Alps, in the Jura and in the Auvergne. These centers are to some extent represented in other monastic rules which we have, from this period, like the *Rule* of St. Férreol, the *Rule* of Tarnat, etc.[11] We will consider in passing the so-called "Oriental Rules,"[12] which were more probably collections of statutes enacted by abbatial and episcopal synods in the early sixth century.[13]

It must be remembered that these monastic documents have their source in Oriental teachings and practice. Let us recall the existence of Oriental centers of monasticism:

9. The *Rule* of St. Caesarius found in *PL* 67, cols. 1097–1104.

10. The *Rule* of Aurelian is found in *PL* 68, cols. 385–98; the *Epistola ad Virgines Monasterii Sanctae Mariae* of John of Arles is found in *PL* 72, cols. 859–60.

11. The *Rule* of St. Férreol is found in *PL* 66, cols. 959–76; the *Rule* of Tarnat (Tarn) is found in *PL* 66, cols. 977–86.

12. These "Oriental Rules" are found in *PL* 103, cols. 423–554; for an English version see *Early Monastic Rules: The Rules of the Fathers and the Regula Orientalis*, trans. Carmela Vircillo Franklin, Ivan Havener and J. Alcuin Francis (Collegeville, MN: Liturgical Press, 1982).

13. See A. Mundó, "Les anciens synods abbatiaux et les *Regulae SS. Patrum*," *Studia Anselmiana*, 44 (1959), 107–25.

1) Origen, through Evagrius and Cassian: the monasticism of Nitria, Scete and the Nile Delta. This is a monasticism which in many pages of Cassian is colored by hellenizing tendencies. There is a lofty mysticism, with a neo-Platonic character at least in the way it is sometimes expressed.

2) Syrian and Palestinian monasticism: again through Cassian. This influence has not yet been sufficiently studied. Cassian knew St. John Chrysostom.

3) St. Basil, and Cappadocian asceticism. St. Honoratus of Lérins had been to Greece. To what extent had he come in contact with Basilian spirituality?[14]

4) St. Pachomius and Egyptian cenobitism. {This is} a very important source: {do we} know how? through St. Jerome and Rufinus, as well as Cassian. But Cassian has little to say that gives us a real idea of the cenobitism of the Thebaid, though he does talk of Egyptian cenobites. To what extent are the (Coptic) Pachomian documents which are known to us, known in the fifth century {in} Gaul?

5) What had St. Martin and St. Hilary contributed to the fund of monastic doctrine in Gaul, and imported from where? Note: St. Victricius of Rouen describes early French monasticism (*PL* 20, col. 445).[15]

6) The monks of Lérins were in contact with St. Paulinus of Nola and with his Italian associates.

7) Were there African (Carthage, etc.) influences in southern Gaul? Were they operative at Lérins and in the other monastic centers? Julian Pomerius, a refugee from the Invasions in Africa, brings a spirituality which is entirely different from that of Cassian and Lérins, a clerical idea of the "contemplative life" which

14. See N. Chadwick, 149: "Honoratus may himself have . . . hoped to put himself under the discipline of some Greek institution where St Basil's rule had been adopted. It is tempting to see in early Greek influence on Lérins the shaping force which gave to the monastery its 'Golden Age', the phase which was primarily intellectual."

15. See the *De Laude Sanctorum* (*PL* 20, cols. 443–58); see also N. Chadwick, 72.

does not fit in with the rest of the writings we find in southern Gaul.[16]

Note: from the very beginning in the West {there has been} a distinction between a "clerical" or "canonical" common life (St. Augustine) and the monastic (largely non-clerical) life. The relationship between these two trends is very important in the history of Western monasticism. The triumph of the "clerical" formula in the thirteenth century meant the eclipse of monasticism thereafter. Cîteaux was deeply involved in this: {cf.} the apostolic failure of Cîteaux in the Albigensian struggle.[17]

Monastic Sources and Traditions in Fourth-Century Gaul

1. *St. Paulinus of Nola*[18] (see Migne, *PL* 61).[19]

{He was} born at Bordeaux {in} 353–354, {became} bishop of Nola in 410 {and} died {in} 431. {He owned} rich estates {and} married a noble Spanish lady, Therasia. {He was} related to *St. Melania*.[20] {He was a} pupil of Ausonius, {and} became a poet and man of letters. {He was also a} friend of St. Martin. {The} spiritual influence of his wife and friends leads to retirement, against the wishes of Ausonius, but strongly urged by Jerome (*Ep.* 53 & 58; *PL* 22).[21]

16. See Julianus Pomerius, *De Vita Contemplativa* (*PL* 59, cols. 411–520).

17. For the Cistercian role in the Albigensian crusade, see Louis Lekai, *The Cistercians: Ideals and Reality* (Kent, OH: Kent State University Press, 1977), 54–56, 78–79.

18. Merton relies for his information on Paulinus on Nora Chadwick's chapter on the saint in *Poetry and Letters*, 63–88.

19. *PL* 61, cols. 153–438 (letters); cols. 437–710 (poems).

20. This relationship, based on a phrase in Paulinus' *Letter* 29:5 (*PL* 61, col. 315A), is possible but not certain; see N. Chadwick, *Poetry and Letters*, 64; for possible relationships see the first of the "Notes Complémentaires" in Gerontius, *Vie de Sainte Mélanie*, ed. and trans. Denys Gorce, SC 90 (Paris: Éditions du Cerf, 1962), 110–11; in his translation of *The Letters of Paulinus of Nola*, 2 vols., Ancient Christian Writers [ACW], vols. 35–36 (Westminster, MD: Newman Press, 1966, 1967), P. G. Walsh suggests the relationship might be with Paulinus' wife Therasia (2:324, n. 23).

21. Cols. 540–49 (*Ep.* 53); 579–86 (*Ep.* 58).

> In the knowledge of His coming my heart trembles and is shaken to its depths; my soul is full of longing, even now full of apprehension for the future, for fear lest, being fettered by painful cares about my body and burdened with the weight of worldly things, when the Heavens open and the fearful trumpet resounds, it may be unable to rise to the skies on light pinions to the assembly of our King, to fly to Heaven among the glorious thousands of the saints who raise to the sublime stars their winged feet freed from earth's fetters. Borne by the light clouds, they will pass through the constellations in the airy spaces, to pay homage to the King of Heaven, and join their bright ranks to the adored Christ. This is my fear, this my agony, lest the last day may come upon me slumbering in thick darkness . . . and wasting my time in futile activities and submerged in empty cares. For what would become of me if I should be dozing in dilatory homage and the Christ should reveal himself to me, flashing in glory from his citadel in the skies; and if, blinded by the sudden radiance of the Lord approaching when the Heavens open, I must seek to hide myself, dazzled by the violence of the light, in the darkness and the joyless night? (*Carmen* X, lines 304 ff. [in *Poetry and Letters in Early Christian Gaul*, by N. K. Chadwick][22]).

Eschatology! This is very close to the spirituality of Lérins. Paulinus was ordained against his will at Barcelona {in} 393. {He then} went to Italy, visited Ambrose {and} went on to {the} shrine of St. Felix of Nola (Felix {was} a Syrian "exile"). Simplicity {was central to his life; he} lived in simplicity and poverty, conducting a hospice for pilgrims. {He lived in} married chastity {with his wife and} a small community of friends, {a life of} "Idyllic simplicity and freedom before the era of rules." (READ Chadwick, p. 72.[23])

22. N. Chadwick, 67; the quotation is of lines 302–23 (*PL* 61, cols. 460B–461A).

23. Chadwick is quoting F. J. E. Raby, *A History of Christian Latin Poetry* (Oxford: Oxford University Press, 1953), 102; the quotation actually reads: "the monasticism of Nola bears that idyllic impress of freedom and simplicity which preceded the era of organization and rules." Chadwick goes on to describe the community as

St. Martin pointed to St. Paulinus as a shining example.[24] {He was} praised also by St. Ambrose (*Ep.* 58).[25] Rufinus and Melania spent some time at Nola after {the} sack of Rome (412).[26] Paulinus corresponded with Augustine.[27] Vigilantius, against whom Jerome wrote, carried letters from Paulinus to Jerome.[28] (Note: *Letter* 51 to Eucherius,[29] living on {the} island of Léro, {was} written because some monks of Lérins had visited Paulinus and hence there was an occasion to have a letter carried back {from}[30] Paulinus [about 410]).

Poems: {Note} especially poems on St. Felix, to be read aloud at the festival (see Chadwick, p. 83).[31]

"just a little group of relatives and friends, withdrawn from society, living and working together in mutual goodwill, devoting their lives and their wealth to the service of God and to the help of the sick and suffering," and adds that it is "perhaps austere rather than ascetic," with simple rather than coarse food.

24. Sulpicius Severus, *Vita Martini*, c. 25 (*PL* 20, cols. 174D–175B).

25. *PL* 16, cols. 1178–82.

26. Merton is mistaken here. Though the chronology of both Melania the Elder and her granddaughter Melania the Younger is somewhat hazy, neither seems to have stayed with Paulinus after the sack of Rome. According to Gorce (SC 90:39), Melania the Elder had visited Paulinus when she returned from the East in 397 (see Paulinus, *Letter* 29:12-13; *PL* 61, cols. 319C–321C), but she had returned to Jerusalem and was dead in 409 before the sack of Rome (40, and n. 2—somewhat conjectural). Melania the Younger and her husband Pinianus had spent time with Paulinus earlier, at the start of their life of asceticism (41); at the time of the sack of Rome they fled, bringing Rufinus with them, to Sicily (where he later died); from Sicily they tried to get to Paulinus but were blown off course by a storm and eventually went to Africa (167).

27. *Letters* 4, 6, 45, 50 (*PL* 61, cols. 164B–167B, 178A–179B, 391C–396D, 408B–417A).

28. See *Epistle* 61 of Jerome (*PL* 22, cols. 602–606).

29. *PL* 61, cols. 417B–418C.

30. Mimeograph reads "to".

31. Chadwick notes that thirty-three poems of Paulinus are extant, "including narrative historical poems; personal letters in verse; a charmingly sympathetic elegy on a dead child; an epithalamium; the inscriptions for the wall of Sulpicius Severus's new church and baptistery . . . ; above all, the annual birthday odes which he composed for St Felix," which describe both the life of the saint and the festivals which celebrate his patronage.

Summary of Paulinus:

> The pioneer work of Paulinus and Therasia in religious community life is to be regarded not as contempt for the world, but as a constructive renunciation. Theirs was a spiritual ideal fulfilled in daily life. Paulinus, the Christian devotee, with his background of classical culture, is typical of all that is best in the early Church in the West. Fanaticism is entirely absent, superstition as yet little developed. Persecution, force, quarrelling are utterly distasteful to this gentle spirit. In his tolerance and his close sympathy and observation of nature he foreshadows the Celtic Christian anchorites. His quiet dignity and reserve, and perhaps most of all his humour, still link him to the ancient world, and at the same time make him peculiarly modern and congenial to us today. He is perhaps the most beautiful personality among the great figures of the transition from the ancient world to the Christian world which was rapidly taking its place in the late fourth and early fifth centuries (Chadwick, p. 88).

2. *St. Martin of Tours and Sulpicius Severus.*[32]

Was St. Martin the very first to bring monasticism to Gaul? St. Athanasius was exiled to Gaul in 336, some thirty years before his composition of the *Vita Antonii*. He may have made eremitism known in Trier long before the *Vita* was read there (see below).[33] At this time Anthony was still alive.

St. Martin {was} born in Hungary, son of a Roman soldier stationed there. He becomes a catechumen when a child, at Pavia. The incident with the beggar occurs at Amiens when he is 17 (*Vita Martini*, c. 3).[34] His refusal {was} of military *action* (of violence in action) but not of military *service* (at first) (*Vita Martini*, c. 4). {He} quits {the} army in 356 and goes to St. Hilary at Poitiers.

32. Merton relies principally but not exclusively on Nora Chadwick's chapter on Sulpicius and Martin in *Poetry and Letters*, 89–121.

33. For the influence of the *Vita Antonii* in the West, see pages 19–20.

34. The *Vita Martini* by Sulpicius Severus is found in *PL* 20, cols. 159A–176C.

For the relations of St. Hilary and St. Martin, see N. Chadwick, pp. 116–117: "Martin was not only Hilary's disciple; he was virtually his creation."[35] {We see} how Martin followed Hilary's policies—opposition to state intervention in religion and especially to use of force by {the} state against heretics. Did Hilary's contact with monks in his exile in Asia Minor influence Martin's monasticism? After minor orders he goes to Hungary where he converts his mother. {He} embraces {the} solitary life, first near Milan, then on Gallinaria Island (off {the} Ligurian coast). Note: {the} island monasticism in {the} Mediterranean {was} criticized by the pagan Rutilius Namatianus: "*Ipsi se {monachos} Graio nomine dicunt / Quod soli nullo vivere teste volunt.*"[36] {In} 363 {he} establishes his hermitage at Ligugé. {By} 371 {he} is Bishop of Tours {and} works for {the} Christianization of rural areas of Gaul. {In} 397 {he} dies, on November 9th, just a few years before {the} arrival of Cassian at Marseilles.

Marmoutier[37] {had a} mixed form of monasticism: clerical and lay. Without foresight or plan, or perhaps without being aware of the situation at all, Martin combines two monastic forms: the canonical or *clerical monasticism*, a community around a bishop (St. Augustine) and the *lay monasticism* which is more

35. Chadwick notes (relying on the *Vita Martini*, cc. 5 and 7 [*PL* 20, cols. 163BD, 165A]), that Hilary made Martin an exorcist when he refused to be ordained deacon, and that after Hilary returned from exile (for his anti-Arian activities) and Martin from his mission to his homeland of Illyria and a period as a solitary in Milan and on the island of Gallinaria, they reunited at Poitiers, and Martin then established his monastic foundation at nearby Ligugé.

36. Rutilius Namatianus, *De Reditu Suo*, ll. 441–42 (mimeograph reads "*monachi*" for "*monachos*"): "They call themselves by the Greek name monks / Because they wish to live alone with no witness." The lines are referred to but not quoted by Nora Chadwick, 132–33, but are quoted in Pierre Courcelle, *Les Lettres Grecques en Occident de Macrobe à Cassiodore*, 2nd ed. (Paris: Éditions E. de Boccard, 1948), 212, n. 5 (ET: *Late Latin Writers and Their Greek Sources*, trans. Harry E. Wedeck [Cambridge: Harvard University Press, 1969], 227–28, n. 14); Merton refers to Courcelle's book below, page 26.

37. This was the monastery Martin established just outside Tours after he became bishop there; see N. Chadwick, 99: "The monastic settlement came to be known later as *magnum monasterium*, or in modern French *Marmoutier*."

properly "monastic." The lay monks work with their hands, copy manuscripts. The clerical monks *help in the apostolate,* which was urgent and important. Martin confronted political powers to defend spiritual liberty. This formula did not survive. READ *Vita Martini,* c. 10.[38]

{The main} source for information on St. Martin {is} *Sulpicius Severus* (363-420): *Vita Martini* (*PL* 20, col. 159 ff.; see {the} Office of St. Martin in {the} *Cistercian Breviary*[39]). Severus probably met Martin about 390. {In the} three {books of the} *Dialogues* (*PL* 20, col. 183 ff.) Sulpicius' friend Postumianus returns from a visit to the monks of Egypt and narrates his experiences. He was in Egypt in {the} thick of the Origenist controversy, about the same time as Cassian. {He} follows {the} prejudgement of Jerome against Origen.[40] {He has} great admiration for Jerome whom he visits in Bethlehem (1.8-9).[41] Then {he goes} to the cenobites of the Thebaid *quibus summum jus est, sub abbatis imperio vivere.*[42] Even hermits remain subject to {the} abbot of the cenobium. *Dialogues* 2 and 3 {are} about St. Martin, whose fame is to be spread over the whole world and who shows in his own life a sanctity greater than that of all the Egyptian saints put together.

The most important historical lesson in the writings of Sulpicius Severus is the evidence of the *opposition to early monasticism in Gaul on the part of the secular clergy and bishops,* as also at Rome. Sulpicius and Martin had many clerical enemies, as well as

38. Col. 166AC: this chapter describes Martin's life after becoming bishop, uniting the dignity of a bishop with the humility of a monk; after attempting to live a solitary life in a cell attached to his church, he established a monastic community (Marmoutier) some two miles outside the city in an isolated spot, with about eighty disciples living, eating and praying in common, many of whom came from the nobility and some of whom later became bishops themselves.

39. *Breviarium Cisterciense,* 4 vols. (Westmalle, 1935), *Autumnalis,* 460–68.

40. Actually Postumianus describes himself as somewhat disturbed by Jerome's wholesale condemnation of Origen's works, and definitely opposed to the harsh reaction of the bishops to the Origenists (c. 7; cols. 188B-189A).

41. Cols. 189A-190A.

42. Col. 190B (c. 10): "for whom the most important law is to live under the rule of an abbot."

enemies among the pagans (see *Vita Martini*, c. 22).[43] The episcopal party hated Martin also because he refused to approve of the condemnation of Priscillianist heretics to death.[44] The bishops of Gaul often represented an aristocratic and power-loving class, opposed to the poverty and asceticism of the monks. But there were saints among them.[45] See {the} opposition between Martin and Brictio (*Dial*. 3.{15})[46] (Chadwick, p. 114).[47]

Sulpicius makes a charismatic hero out of Martin and emphasizes the miraculous and extraordinary elements in his life. {He} makes him also a hero of Gallo-Roman monasticism as opposed to that of Egypt, and of {the} monastic apostolate as opposed to Gallo-Roman clergy. In his *Dialogues* however Sulpicius brings to the West material about Egyptian monasticism {that is even} earlier than Cassian: {the} *Dialogues* {were} written about 403. Note: to understand Sulpicius in relation to Cassian, it is interesting to compare the *Dialogues* and the *Institutes*.[48] *Instituta* 4.23 {contains} the story of the monk obediently watering the dry stick. *Dialogues* 1.19[49] {has the same story, but} in Sulpicius the stick flowers and grows into a tree which is "seen" by Postumianus in the courtyard of the monastery. In Cassian, it just rots. Cassian avoided the miraculous and concentrated on what was

43. This appears to be miscopied by Merton or his typist, as there is no mention in this chapter of opposition by pagans (discussed in chapters 11–15 [cols. 167C-169A]) or by bishops (discussed in chapter 27 [col. 176AC], probably the chapter intended).

44. See N. Chadwick, 107–108, *Dialogues*, 3.11-13 (cols. 217C-219C), and Sulpicius Severus, *Historia Sacra*, 2.50 (cols. 157D-158B).

45. Nora Chadwick notes that many of the Gaulish bishops "are among the finest men of the time" and provides a list, though many of these are later than Sulpicius and themselves come from a monastic environment (112–13).

46. Cols. 220C-221B (mimeograph reads 3.9).

47. Brictio was a disciple of Martin who was incited by demons to revile Martin, who had upbraided him for his lavish lifestyle. Brictio later repented and apologized, but represents the opposition to asceticism current at the time. According to Chadwick he is probably to be identified with a successor of Martin as bishop of Tours.

48. The comparison is made by Nora Chadwick, 231–32.

49. Cols. 195D-196B.

practical and useful for the spiritual life of the average man. {This is} more realistic than the dramatic presentation we find in Sulpicius, who often goes beyond the bounds of credibility.

Now we must briefly consider the Egyptian sources. We may reduce them to two, which, in the time of Cassian, may well have amounted to one tradition. First we must distinguish the *actual* monasticism of Egypt from the spirituality of those who transmitted it to the rest of the world. The spirituality of St. Anthony comes to us highly colored by Evagrius and St. Athanasius. The spirituality of Pachomius came to the West in a very impoverished form, mainly through Jerome and Rufinus or writers of the Evagrian tradition, who distorted it. For practical purposes, there was really but one current of monastic tradition from Egypt: both Anthony and Pachomius came via Evagrian channels, and Jerome. However, we should distinguish between real Antonian and Pachomian monasticism. And in doing so we will take due account of the way in which they were transmitted to the West.

3. *St. Anthony and Antonian Monasticism.*

We can only briefly treat of St. Anthony here; {we have provided a} more detailed study elsewhere.[50] Anthony furnished the classic example of the monastic vocation and the eremitical life. He lives first as an *ascete*. This is his novitiate for the hermit life. {The} essence of his life {is} conversion, {a} total gift of self to God, {in} struggle with the demons who wish to prevent this victory of Christ in Anthony. This struggle makes the *monk* the follower of the *martyrs*. (Compare the martyrdom of St. Stephen, with Christ watching at the right hand of God, and Anthony's realization that Christ had been present in him during the struggle with the demon. READ *Vita Antonii*, c. 10.[51]) Having vanquished

50. See *Cassian and the Fathers*, 31–39.

51. In this chapter Anthony, beset by demons, has a vision of the roof opening and a ray of light descending and driving away the demons; when he asks why the Lord had not come earlier, the reply is that he was watching the struggle and that because Anthony remained faithful he would always be with him. See the *Life of St. Anthony*, trans. Sr. Mary Emily Keenan, SCN, in *Early Christian Biographies*, ed.

the demons and passions (they are the same) Anthony attains to *apatheia* and then becomes worthy to be a spiritual father to countless souls. (Compare *Life of St. Benedict* by St. Gregory.[52]) He has returned to "man's natural state," i.e. the Paradisal state. He is therefore at peace with animals etc., which do not harm him. A body of doctrine is ascribed to him (*Vita Antonii*, c. 16 ff.[53]). READ c. 16.[54] "Perfection is within our reach."[55] "The soul is naturally good" because it is the image of God.[56] Hence perfection consists in recovering the primitive likeness to God, by what the Greeks later called "synergy," working together with God. The crux of the matter {is} control of the two great groups of passions: the aggressive passions {and} the appetite for pleasure.

Demonology: the demons, by inciting us to passion, try to keep us from recovering our likeness to God. The ascetic life is then not just a quiet moral progress, but a bitter struggle against preternatural forces. They must be understood. *Discretion* is the power to identify forces that work in us and resist them intelligently and consciously. We must therefore be on our guard

---

Roy J. Deferrari, Fathers of the Church [FC], vol. 15 (New York: Fathers of the Church, 1952), 145 (this is the translation of the *Life* that Merton used in *Cassian and the Fathers*).

52. See Gregory the Great, *Dialogues*, trans. Odo Zimmerman, OSB, FC 39 (New York: Fathers of the Church, 1959), Book 2, c. 3: "As Benedict's influence spread over the surrounding countryside because of his signs and wonders, a great number of men gathered around him to devote themselves to God's service. Christ blessed his work and before long he had established twelve monasteries there" (66). Merton makes the same comparison in *Cassian and the Fathers*, 34.

53. The discourse runs from chapter 16 through chapter 43 (*Life*, 150–75); Merton discusses this discourse in detail in *Cassian and the Fathers*, 34–37.

54. In the opening section of his discourse, Anthony begins by stating that while the scriptures should be sufficient for learning the faith, providing mutual encouragement and instruction is also advantageous for monks. He then urges his listeners to persevere in the life of asceticism they have undertaken, and not lose heart, for the time of testing is short compared to eternity, when the corruptible body will be made incorruptible (*Life*, 160).

55. Chapter 20 (*Life*, 153).

56. See chapter 20: "The soul is in its natural state when it remains as it was created, and it was created beautifully and exceedingly good" (*Life*, 154).

against false visions, etc. We must fear God alone and not fear the devil. The main weapons against the devil are the Holy Name of Jesus and the sign of the Cross. For the victor in the ascetic struggle the desert becomes a paradise. He also becomes a charismatic source of grace and sanctification to thousands. It is easy to see that this tradition persisted in its primitive form down through Eastern monasticism and especially in Russia (through St. Nilus Sorsky, the *Philokalia*, etc.,[57] it reached Russia via Sinai and Athos).

Channels of the Antonian tradition. What concerns us most is the transmission of the Egyptian traditions of monastic spirituality to the West, and the documents in which this tradition was embodied in Western tradition. First and most important {is} the *Antonian* tradition:

1) St. Athanasius: the *Vita Antonii*. Two early Latin translations make the life of Anthony by Athanasius known in the West. One translation is ascribed to a certain Evagrius (not Ponticus) (*PL* 73).[58] St. Augustine (*Confessions* VIII.15—{a} famous episode) bears witness to the diffusion of the *Vita Antonii* and to the effect it had in the West.[59] {It was} certainly the greatest single influence

57. For Nilus (1433–1508), who spent thirteen years at Constantinople, in the Holy Land and at Mount Athos and brought the teachings of hesychasm back to Russia when he returned there, see Sergius Bolshakoff, *Russian Mystics*, with a Preface by Thomas Merton, CS 26 (Kalamazoo, MI: Cistercian Publications, 1977), 18–38; a version of the *Philokalia*, an anthology of texts on prayer from Eastern patristic and monastic authors compiled in the late eighteenth century, was translated into Slavonic by Paisius Velichkovsky (1722–94) (Bolshakoff, 88–90) and later into Russian by Bishop Theophane the Recluse (1815–94) (Bolshakoff, 221). For a translation of the original Greek text of the *Philokalia*, see *The Philokalia: The Complete Text*, compiled by St. Nikodemos of the Holy Mountain and St. Makarios of Corinth, ed. and trans. G. F. H. Palmer, Philip Sherrard and Kallistos Ware, 4 vols. to date (London: Faber & Faber, 1979–95).

58. Cols. 115-94.

59. In this episode Augustine's fellow North African Ponticianus tells the story of two friends, government officials, who were out walking and happened upon a house of monastics in which they found a copy of the *Vita Antonii*. Both were immediately converted and decided to stay at the house and become monks. The story had a profound effect on Augustine, who was himself moving toward

in starting Western monasticism. The *Vita Antonii* was the model of Sulpicius Severus' *Life of St. Martin*, presented with all the traits of Anthony. The *Vita Antonii* was certainly widely read in the West before 384. Note: the so-called REGULA ANTONII[60] is a late compilation, based on the *Vita* and *Apothegmata*. Seven Letters are ascribed by Jerome to Anthony (*PG* 40).[61] Note also, the *Vita Antonii* reflects a great deal of the spirituality and the dogmatic concerns of Athanasius himself. It is a strongly anti-Arian tract. The Antonian monastic tradition tends to be closely identified with the Alexandrian theological tradition, both in its more acceptable form (Athanasius) and in its Origenist form (Evagrius and Cassian).

2) *Apothegmata*: {This is} the best, simplest, most authentic resumé of Antonian spirituality. The sayings of Anthony were widely read in the *Apothegmata* and *Verba Seniorum*. {The} *Apothegmata* {is} the Greek collection of the sayings of the Fathers, arranged alphabetically according to their names (*PG* 45 [?]); in our edition (Latin only) vol. 35.[62] {The} *Verba Seniorum* {consists of} two Latin collections, edited by Rosweyde in *PL* 73:

a. Books V and VI of the *Vitae Patrum*:[63] selections arranged according to *virtues*; {this is} perhaps contemporaneous with St. Benedict;

b. Book VII of {the} *Vitae Patrum*,[64] another collection about the same; {this is} earlier than Benedict, about 500.

---

conversion at the time (see Augustine, *Confessions*, trans. Henry Chadwick [New York: Oxford University Press, 1991], 143–44).

60. See *PL* 103, cols. 423-28.

61. J. P. Migne, ed., *Patrologiae Cursus Completus, Series Graeca*, 161 vols. (Paris: Garnier, 1857–1866), vol. 40, cols. 978-1000 (subsequently referred to as *PG* in text and notes). These letters are now generally considered to be authentic: see *The Letters of St. Antony the Great*, trans. Derwas J. Chitty (Oxford: SLG Press, 1975), and Samuel Rubenson, *The Letters of St. Antony: Monasticism and the Making of a Saint* (Minneapolis: Fortress Press, 1995).

62. Cols. 53–224; in the standard edition of *PG*, with both the original Greek and a Latin translation, the *Apophthegmata* is found in vol. 65, cols. 71-440.

63. Book V (cols. 851-992); Book VI (cols. 991-1024).

64. Cols. 1025-66. Merton does not mention the two hundred twenty paragraphs (not grouped into chapters) in Book III (cols. 739–814).

These Latin collections were obviously in circulation, as far as their *material* goes, early in the fifth century. It is thought that they were edited and arranged according to virtues, and in their present shape, at the end of the fifth century. These collections are easily accessible, in easy Latin, and should be read by every monk. {There is a} selection in *The Wisdom of the Desert*,[65] based on Rosweyde's text; see also *Western Asceticism* (ed. Chadwick).[66]

Both the Latin and Greek collections are essentially Antonian. That is to say they represent the Antonian monasticism of Nitria and Scete. This monasticism (Nitria, founded by Ammon, a contemporary of Anthony, is the "model" hermit community, and Scete is the type of the pure solitude) is imitated all over Middle and Lower Egypt as well as in Palestine and Syria. Characteristics: {it is} basically eremitical {but with a} flexible structure: {there are} some community elements. Monks {are} living in villages of cells around a church, or in separate cells alone in the desert. {There is} no emphasis on organization, no institutionalism, no written rule or code. The authority is that of the charismatic "abbas." The life is lived according to a practical spiritual doctrine, which is not studied in books but learned as it is lived, and complete docility to the Spiritual Father is the necessary condition. Note: in the twelfth century Peter the Cantor looks back to Anthony and praises him for not multiplying rules and observances, but for following only the Gospel: "Anthony the hermit, when some monks asked him for a rule and for a form of monastic life, gave the books of the Gospel. In the Lateran Council (1179) . . . John of Salisbury said: 'Let us not make new decrees or renew too many of the old ones! We are overburdened with a multitude of new statutes . . . even some good things should be {set}[67] aside lest we be weighed down by the sheer quantity of them. Indeed it would be better if we labored to observe the Gospel, which few

65. Thomas Merton, *The Wisdom of the Desert: Sayings from the Desert Fathers of the Fourth Century* (New York: New Directions, 1960).

66. Owen Chadwick, ed. and trans., *Western Asceticism*, Library of Christian Classics [LCC], vol. 12 (Philadelphia: Westminster, 1958), 33–189.

67. Mimeograph reads "let" (possibly for "left" rather then "set").

now obey. Let us therefore not leave the life-giving spirit of the letter for traditions and interpretations and someone's farfetched explanations!'" (see *PL* 205:233-239).[68]

Apothegmata of St. Anthony (*PG* {65:75-87}).

(1) {It is} curious that the very first is about the apparition of the angel showing Anthony how to alternate work and prayer and thus combat *acedia*. (READ and comment;[69] cf. 13, the archer.[70])

(2) On minding your own business and not worrying about {the} dispositions of Providence.[71]

(3) On expecting temptations until our last breath[72]—on helping others who are tempted (21; 29).[73]

(4) Other characteristic points: only the tempted and tried can be saved; they only have a realistic view of life (4; 5),[74] but the weak are less tempted (23);[75] humility {is} the only way to escape {the} snares of the enemy (7);[76] austerity without intelligence (discretion) separates {one} from God (8; 35);[77] {a} monk out of his cell

68. The passage is from the *Verbum Abbreviatum*, c. 79 (col. 235BC).

69. Col. 75AB: this first saying tells of Anthony praying about being beset by *acedia* and sinful thoughts, and then seeing someone like himself working, then praying, then working, then praying again; he realizes it is an angel, who tells him that if he does likewise he will be saved. This message renews Anthony's commitment, and the story concludes by affirming that he was indeed saved.

70. The story of the archer (cols. 78D-79A) tells of a hunter who sees Anthony and his companions at recreation and is scandalized; when he is instructed by Anthony to repeatedly shoot arrows from his bow he protests that the bow will break, and Anthony says that the brothers too will break if stretched too far.

71. #2 (col. 73BC).

72. #4 (col. 78A).

73. #21 (cols. 82D-83A) tells how Anthony intervened to get a monk readmitted to a monastery he had been dismissed from; #29 (col. 86AB) tells how Abba Paphnutius defends a brother falsely accused of fornication and is praised by Anthony for doing so.

74. Col. 78A.

75. Col. 83B: Anthony's point here is that the present generation is weaker than earlier generations and is therefore tempted less.

76. Col. 78AB.

77. Cols. 78B, 87A.

is like a fish out of water (10; 11; 31);[78] importance of "self-custody" (interior control of thoughts) (10); visions are from the demons (12);[79] miracles are no guarantee of sanctity (14);[80] {the} supreme importance of charity (9; 15; 21; 29);[81] {the} uselessness of passive dependence on others in {the} spiritual life (16);[82] silence and "nescience" (17; 18);[83] meekness and non-violence (19);[84] poverty and detachment (20);[85] three sources of impure temptations: nature, too much food, demons (22);[86] a time will come when all will be crazy and will attack those who are unlike themselves (25);[87] *caritas foras mittit timorem* (32);[88] austerity (33);[89] need for a spiritual father (37; 38).[90] {Note the} *realism* of this spirituality.

Thus Antonian monasticism stands in direct contrast to Pachomian, which is more highly organized, with a hierarchical structure of superiors, with a written rule, and a detailed code. However, the contrast has often been too crudely drawn. It has

78. Cols. 78BC, 78C, 86B: the first of these has the fish-out-of-water image.

79. Col. 78CD: the donkey of some brothers coming to Anthony to ask if their visions are demonically inspired dies on the way; Anthony tells them he knows of the donkey's death because demons revealed it.

80. Col. 79AC: a young monk who performs a miracle (ordering wild asses to carry tired monks) becomes proud and dies.

81. Cols. 78B, 79C, 82D-83A, 86AB.

82. Col. 79C: Anthony tells a monk who asked him to pray for him that it will do no good if he doesn't pray himself.

83. Cols. 79D, 82AB: Anthony approves Abba Joseph's response that he doesn't know the answer to a question about scripture; an elder reproves younger monks to Anthony for speaking without thinking.

84. Col. 82BC: when monks say they cannot turn the other cheek Anthony tells them they need prayers.

85. Col. 82CD: Anthony tells a monk who wants to retain some of his property for himself to tie meat to his naked body, and dogs and birds attack him; so, Anthony teaches, do the demons attack those who cling to wealth.

86. Col. 83AB.

87. Col. 83C.

88. Col. 86C: "love casts out fear."

89. Col. 86C.

90. Col. 87B.

often been assumed that Pachomian monasticism is "nothing but" a regular institutional life without any special doctrine (except that of obedience to the *Rule* and the Superior). But actually there was a deep biblical spirituality in the Pachomian communities.

3) *Rufinus and Palladius*. Two important and widely read collections, covering much the same ground, and disseminating Antonian monastic spirituality all over the West, are the *Historia Monachorum* of Rufinus, and the *Historia Lausiaca* of Palladius. The *Historia Lausiaca* is in *PL* 73,[91] by Palladius, a disciple of St. John Chrysostom. {It was} written before Cassian's *Conferences* (edited by Dom Cuthbert Butler).[92] {It} takes its name from the fact that it was dedicated to Lausus, chamberlain of Theodosius II. Butler defended the *Historia Lausiaca* against the attacks of the critic Reitzenstein,[93] and defended the authenticity of the Greek text. Since that time Draguet has been working on a more critical text which he thinks was based on a Coptic original.[94] As far as the controversies about the *Historia Lausiaca* go, they do not concern us here. What we need to know about the *HL* is that it is a kind of primer of Antonian monachism distilled through Evagrian

91. This is the Latin translation, included in Rosweyde's *Vitae Patrum* as the eighth book (cols. 1065-1234); the Greek version, superseded by Butler's edition, is found in *PG* 34, cols. 991-1278.

92. Cuthbert Butler, OSB, *The Lausiac History of Palladius*, 2 vols.: vol. 1: Prolegomena; vol. 2: The Greek Text with Introduction and Notes (Cambridge: Cambridge University Press, 1898, 1904).

93. Richard Reitzenstein, *Historia Monachorum und Historia Lausiaca: Eine Studie sur Geschichte des Mönchtums und der frühchristlichen Begriffe Gnostiker und Pneumatiker* (Göttingen: Vandenhoeck und Ruprecht, 1916).

94. Merton is mistaken in the idea that Draguet thinks the entire original text was Coptic; he does propose Coptic sources for two chapters: see R. Draguet, "Le chapitre de l'*Histoire Lausiaque* sur les Tabennésiotes dérive-t-il d'une source copte?" *La Muséon: Revue d'Études Orientales*, 57 (1944), 53–145; 58 (1945), 15–95; "Une nouvelle source copte de Pallade: le ch. VIII (Amoun)," *La Muséon*, 60 (1947), 227–55. Draguet published an edition and translation of material from the *Lausiac History* in Syriac: *Les Formes Syriaques de la matière de l'Histoire Lausiaque, Corpus Scriptorum Christianorum Orientalium* [CSCO], vols. 389–90 (Louvain: Secretariat du Corpus SCO, 1978).

channels.[95] It is therefore somewhat more typical of the popular Evagrian slant which we also find to some extent in Cassian.

The *Historia Monachorum*. Rufinus is an interesting and important figure and we may dwell on him more at length. It is important to restore to Rufinus his good name, of which he was robbed by the tirades of Jerome. {He was} born {in} 340, {and} he met Jerome while they were students at Rome. {He} went to visit the solitaries of Egypt with St. Melania, studied under Didymus the Blind at Alexandria, and became an Origenist. {He} suffered persecution from the Arians and was a confessor of the faith. {In} 377 {he} joined St. Melania in her community on {the} Mount of Olives; {in} 390 {he was} ordained priest. {In} 392 {the} Origenist controversy breaks out. {There is} conflict between Bishop Epiphanius of Salamina (Cyprus) and John of Jerusalem. The friends, Jerome and Rufinus, split up. Jerome {sides} with Epiphanius, Rufinus with John. {In} 397, Rufinus, in Italy, translates Origen's *De Principiis* and to protect himself, without any malice, refers to the fact that Jerome had been a translator of Origen. Jerome replies with a strong attack, tears apart Rufinus' treatment of Origen and shows how Rufinus has covered up some of Origen's errors, to make him more acceptable. {In} 400, Rufinus defends himself with his *Apologia ad Anastasium* ({*CCSL*} 20).[96] This is interesting; it shows Rufinus' attitude. He is in favor of peaceful discussion and settlement, and against violence and noisy conflict. He refers to the fact that the devil is the one who is the "accuser of the brethren."[97] He deplores schisms and quarrels in the Church. *Ubi enim simplicitas erit tuta et innocentia, si hic non erit?*[98] Finally he says that if he is to be blamed for translating Origen, let others who

95. See R. Draguet, "L''Histoire Lausiaque', une Oeuvre Écrite dans l'Esprit d'Évagre," *Revue d'Histoire Ecclésiastique*, 41 (1946), 321–64; 42 (1947), 5–49.

96. *Apologia ad Anastasium Romanae Urbis Episcopum*, in *Tyrannii Rufini Opera*, ed. Manlius Simonetti, *Corpus Christianorum Series Latina* [*CCSL*], vol. 20 (Turnholt: Brepols, 1961), 19–28; mimeograph reads *CSEL* (for *Corpus Scriptorum Ecclesiasticorum Latinum*, a different series) for *CCSL*.

97. Rufinus, *Apologia ad Anastasium*, 5 (26).

98. C. 7, ll. 16–17 (28), which reads ". . . *tuta erit* . . .": "For where will simplicity and innocence be secure, if not here?"

translated him first be blamed also. Jerome counters with three violent attacks to which Rufinus makes no reply.[99] It would seem at least that Rufinus acted as a monk should, and was basically reasonable. {In} 407, Rufinus fled the Barbarians and went to Sicily where he spent his last years in prayer and study, dying in 410. He continued to the last to work on Origen. G. Bardy sums up Rufinus: "He had solid qualities of character, was faithful to his friends as long as they did not betray him. He defends himself without passion, he knows how to keep silence and not feed the flames of bitterness and revenge. {. . .} He is not a genius and he never makes any effort to convey the impression that he is one. He never seeks for himself the first place and voluntarily confined himself to the humble role of a translator. . . . The case of Rufinus has often been argued by the advocates of St. Jerome. It would seem to be about time that it should be argued, once and for all, by an advocate of Rufinus" (*DTC* {14:1}; co1. 160).[100]

Rufinus disseminated monastic texts in the West in translations. Courcelle (*Lettres Grecques en Occident*, p. 313[101]) says that the two channels by which St. Benedict received monastic doctrines from the East were Cassian and Rufinus. It was through Rufinus that St. Benedict got the *Vitae Patrum* and *St. Basil*. However, Books V and VI of the *Vitae Patrum* were translated by Roman deacons from Greek mss.[102]

99. Merton evidently refers to the three books of the *Contra Rufinum*, although the first two books were written together, while the third, even more full of invective, was added as a response to a private letter from Rufinus to Jerome, which has not survived, in response to Jerome's attack in the first two books. Rufinus had, however, written a temperate *Apologia* to Jerome before the appearance of the *Contra Rufinum* (*CCSL* 20:29-123). For a helpful summary of the entire controversy, see John Hritzu's Introduction to his translation of the *Contra Rufinum* in St. Jerome, *Dogmatic and Polemical Works*, FC 53 (Washington: Catholic University of America Press, 1965), 47–58.

100. G. Bardy, "Rufin," *Dictionnaire de Théologie Catholique* [*DTC*], 15 vols. (Paris: Letouzey et Ané, 1908–1950), 14:1, cols. 153-60; Merton's translation.

101. ET: 331.

102. Book V was traditionally considered to have been translated by Pelagius, Book VI by John (see *PL* 73, cols. 49A-50A).

a) The "*Rule* of St. Basil." Rufinus combined the two "*Rules*" into one Latin version which is given in Holstenius,[103] and though this text is without great value for the critic, it is very important as the *actual source of Western knowledge of Basil* in the crucial formative period of early monasticism.

b) He translated some aphorisms of Evagrius, *Ad Virgines*. This was another important and influential text widely read in southern Gaul. (One of Jerome's hottest accusations of Rufinus was that he translated Evagrius and disseminated him in the West.[104]) Actually Wilmart has shown that there were two traditional translations of Evagrius *Ad Virgines* ({he} edits an alternative version in *Revue Bénédictine*, 1911, p. 143[105]). {The} spirituality of Evagrius *Ad Virgines*: {there is an} emphasis on charity, resisting anger, {and on} avoidance of contact with men and with the world, for "if you talk with men you will have idols in your mind at the time of prayer."[106] Hence the usual Evagrian concern (typical) with purity of heart and avoidance of distracting images and passionate thoughts. For the same reason {he} reproves laughter, dissipation, the *concupiscentia deambulandi*.[107] Virginity of body is allied to virginity of heart, that is, purity of *faith*. Heresy corrupts this virginity of heart, hence much space is given to warning against false doctrine. Speaking of these precepts of Evagrius and other such collections such as the *Monita Porcarii*, Wilmart says: "These collections of precepts for a long time took the place of Rules and they give us the best idea of the monastic life prior to the reform of St. Benedict. . . . They make us understand the

103. This edition is found in *PL* 103, cols. 475-554.

104. *Ep*. 133 (*PL* 22, col. 1151): "*Hujus libros . . . interpretante discipulo ejus Rufino, Latinos plerique in Occidente lecutant*" ("Many in the West read the books of this man in Latin, translated by his disciple Rufinus").

105. André Wilmart, OSB, "Les Versions Latines des Sentences d'Évagre pour les Vierges," *Revue Bénédictine*, 28 (1911), 143–53: text and notes on pages 148–51; according to Wilmart (152) it is uncertain which version is the work of Rufinus. The other version is found in *PL* 20, cols. 1185-88; *PG* 40, cols. 1283-86.

106. Wilmart, "Versions Latines," 148, ll. 9–10.

107. "desire for wandering about" (Wilmart, "Versions Latines," 149, l. 39).

famous chapter on the Instruments of Good Works," etc.[108] Rufinus in translating these materials contributed to the *second stage of monasticism*, the passage from the *authority of the spiritual master* to the *authority of the book of traditional sayings and teachings of the masters* (used and interpreted of course by the actual "*seniors*") and finally to the *authority of the Rule*, first interpreted and then enforced by the Abbot. (The *Regula Magistri* will be one of the chief links between the second and third stages.)

c) The *Historia Monachorum* ({a} translation of an unknown original account of {a} journey to the desert[109]). This is a great book, and one of the main sources of Antonian spirituality. It merits to be studied in some detail.

{The} *Prologue* to the *Historia Monachorum* {is} important because it contains the standard "tropes" which were to become classical in monastic tradition. {It is} a kind of monastic manifesto. (Note: how are we to handle this *ideal* image?)

(1) The holy monks of the desert are signs of Christ in the world. In frail vessels they contain the treasure of Christ (cf. 2 Cor. 4:7 in its whole context—a typical Pauline passage: the light of Christ in the vessel of clay, subject to all kinds of danger).

108. Wilmart, "Versions Latines," 152–53.

109. In *Cassian and the Fathers* Merton mistakenly wrote that the original Greek version had been lost (71), and he appears to continue to have this misconception. The Greek text has been edited by A. J. Festugière: *Historia Monachorum in Aegypto, Subsidia Hagiographica* 34 (Brussels: Société des Bollandistes, 1961); the Latin translation (or adaptation) is found in *PL* 21, cols. 387-462. In her Introduction to the English translation from the Greek of the *Historia Monachorum* (*The Lives of the Desert Fathers*, trans. Norman Russell, CS 34 [Kalamazoo, MI: Cistercian Publications, 1980]), Benedicta Ward identifies the anonymous author as "a monk from the monastery at Jerusalem on the Mount of Olives which was founded by Rufinus" (7), who writes of a journey to Egypt made by himself and six other monks from Palestine in 394. Given the date of the journey, this original version could not have been by Rufinus himself, who made a Latin translation sometime between 400 and his death in 410 that included additions and alterations, some based on his own earlier trip to Nitria in 375 (6–7). The English translation includes as an appendix a translation of all the major additions and changes in Rufinus' Latin version (139–55).

Rufinus {writes} *Vere vidi thesaurum Christi in humanis absconditum vasculis* (col. 388).[110] It is the triumph of Christ's grace that makes the virtues of the Desert Fathers possible. (Note {the} emphasis on grace in an atmosphere sometimes exaggeratedly called Pelagian.) In making this treasure known to others the writer brings them salvation and also saves his own soul. This implies a very clear notion of the monastic vocation and {its} charismatic place in the Church. The monks are a source of salvation to the rest of Christendom: "*. . . ut dubitari non debeat,* IPSORUM MERITIS ADHUC STARE MUNDUM" (390).[111]

(2) General information about the monastic life and virtues:

a. *Caelestem vitam in terra positos agentes.*[112] {This is} the *Bios angelikos,*[113] the life of heaven.

b. *Novos prophetas, tam virtutibus animi, quam vaticinandi officio suscitatos . . .*[114] {Note the} trope of the "prophetic" life of the monk: a living witness to the truth of God's word, of His promises, and of His demand for penance. The monk is the man who has taken the word of the Lord literally.

c. *The peacemakers,* the meek men, the non-violent: these are the monks. The innocence and purity of heart have entirely delivered them from the knowledge of evil. Note this other aspect of purity of heart—{the} connection with gentleness, meekness. Their thoughts are purified of all evil (an Evagrian theme): "Purified from all thought and suspicion of evil . . . as if they no longer remembered if some evil were yet done in the world."[115] (Note {the story in the} *Verba Seniorum* {of the} two old monks and the

110. "I have truly seen the treasure of Christ hidden in human vessels." (This statement is identical to the Greek original.)

111. "It should not be doubted that the world continues to exist up to the present because of their merits" (slightly different in the Greek).

112. Cols. 389-90: "living a heavenly life while still on earth."

113. "Angelic life"—the Greek equivalent of "*Caelestem vitam*" in this passage.

114. Cols. 389-90 (which reads "*novos . . . prophetas*"): "new prophets, raised up by the virtues of their souls as much as by the function of prophesying"; the phrasing is different in the Greek.

115. Cols. 389-90.

brick.[116]) Note: this is of course an idealized picture, but it is nevertheless what the monk himself claims to seek and what the world expects of him. {It relates to the} problem of monastic pugnacity.

d. Solitude and charity: the fact that they live scattered about the desert in separate cells does not prevent them from being united by warm charity.[117] He will take this theme up again when he discusses Nitria and Scete, the ideal monastic settlements.

e. Solitude and eschatology: *Intentis ergo suo quisque loco animis, velut boni Patris Christi exspectant adventum.*[118] Note {the} unusual expression, "the coming of Christ as a kind Father." Note also, the monastic note of "minding one's own business." READ in this connection the interesting passage from St. John of the Cross (*Living Flame*[119]).

f. Total freedom from care about food and clothing.

116. Book V, c. xvii.22 (*PL* 73, col. 977C): this story, which Merton translates in *Wisdom of the Desert* (#112 [67]), tells of two elders who had lived together for many years without quarreling, when one of them suggests they quarrel like people in the world. The other says he doesn't know how to quarrel, and the first says he will put a brick between them and each should claim it for himself, but after each says it is his, one agrees that it belongs to the other and they fail to create an argument.

117. These comments are found only in the Latin (cols. 389-90).

118. Cols. 389-90: "Therefore each in his own place awaits with attentive mind the coming of Christ as a good Father."

119. The reference is apparently to *The Living Flame of Love*, stanza 3:56 (first recension), stanza 3:65 (second recension): "Oh souls! Since God is showing you such sovereign mercies as to lead you through this state of solitude and recollection, withdrawing you from your labours of sense, return not to sense again. . . . If you are careful to set your faculties upon naught soever, withdrawing them from everything and in no way hindering them, which is the proper part for you to play in this state, and if you only wait upon God with loving and pure attentiveness, as I said above, in the way which I there described (working no violence to the soul save to detach it from everything and set it free, lest you disturb and spoil its peace or tranquillity), God will feed your soul for you with heavenly food, since you are not hindering Him" (St. John of the Cross, *Complete Works*, trans. E. Allison Peers, 3 vols., revised ed. [Westminster, MD: Newman, 1953], 3:84 [the second recension (3:177-78) is substantially the same]).

g. They are the *soldiers* of Christ, the *army of Christ*. Note that in the Alexandrian milieu and in the early Christian milieu generally, the "soldier of Christ" is distinguished by the fact that he is gentle and meek, and not hostile or aggressive. "*Ornati moribus, lenes, tranquilli,*"[120] etc.—rivalling in clemency, kindness, humility, patience (significant choice of virtues to emphasize!) but above all they are soldiers of Christ because in all things they OBEY GOD, and fight with weapons of prayer: *AD OBEDIENTIAM PRAECEPTORUM REGIS SEMPER INTENTUS, ARMIS ORATIONUM PUGNANS* (390)[121] (cf. St. Benedict[122]).

The Contents of the Historia Monachorum:

Chapter 1—The longest and most interesting chapter is a tract in favor of the purely eremitical and contemplative life. John of Lycopolis, living in an almost inaccessible cave on the side of the cliff, walled in, speaks to them through the window. In this chapter there is more monastic doctrine.[123] The rest is interesting for anecdotes and travel details.

120. Cols. 389-90: "equipped with morals, gentle, calm."

121. Cols. 389-90: "always intent upon obedience to the king's commands, fighting with the weapons of prayer"; the text actually reads "*regi*" rather than "*regis*"—which may be an error, as Merton apparently thought, but is probably correct, as "*intentus*" takes a dative: "attentive to the king to obey his commands, . . ."

122. In the Prologue to his *Rule*, Benedict says he is addressing himself to "whosoever thou mayest be that renouncing thine own will to fight for the true King, Christ, dost take up the strong and glorious weapons of obedience" (*The Rule of Benedict in Latin and English*, ed. and trans. Justin McCann, OSB [London: Burns, Oates, 1952], 7; Merton explicitly refers to this edition of the *Rule* in *Cassian and the Fathers* [112]); see also "our hearts and bodies must be made ready to fight under the holy obedience of his commands" (11); likewise in chapter 2, on the abbot, he writes: "we are all one in Christ, and have to serve alike in the army of the same Lord" (19), and in chapter 61, on receiving monks from other monasteries, he notes, "wherever we are we serve the same Lord and fight for the same King" (139).

123. The Latin version of this chapter is quite different from the Greek: "Considerable material is added to the chapter on John of Lycopolis, mostly in the form of a sermon on pride, which contains some interesting teaching on

The value of the purely solitary life:

a. It keeps one free from sins;

b. It leads to a more pure and intimate knowledge of God. *Plurimum prodest secretior conversatio, et eremi interioris habitatio* (401).[124] John says: "Therefore, my sons, love quiet [*quies, hesychia*] and silence and devote yourselves to knowledge [*scientia, gnosis, theoria*] UT FREQUENTI COLLATIONE MENTEM VESTRAM EXHIBEATIS DEO."[125] {Note the} difficulty of translating "*collatio*" here; {it} implies *direct* experience. He admits that the works of mercy are good, but they are still "*terrenos actus*"[126] and not appropriate to the fully heavenly life. "*Qui vero in exercitio mentis desudat, et spiritales intra semetipsum excolit sensus, longe illis superior judicandus est. Locum enim intra semetipsum praeparat, ubi Spiritus Sanctus habitet, et oblivionem quodammodo capiens terrenorum, sollicitudinem gerit de caelestibus et aeternis. . . .*"[127] Note: the spiritual senses (Origen[128]); the "*locus Dei*" in the spirit (Evagrius[129]); the contrast between

prayer and the monastic life" (*Lives of the Desert Fathers*, 141); the additional material from the Latin is translated on pages 142–47 of this edition.

124. Col. 401C: "A more hidden encounter, and a dwelling in the interior desert, is much more beneficial."

125. Col. 404B: ". . . so that you might open your mind to God in frequent encounter"; the parenthetical words link the Latin terms with their Greek equivalents.

126. Col. 404C: "earthly actions."

127. Col. 404C (the text reads "*namque*" for "*enim*"): "One who exerts himself in spiritual exercises, and cultivates the spiritual senses within himself, should be judged far superior to those others. For he prepares within himself a place where the Holy Spirit may dwell, and becoming in a sense forgetful of earthly matters, becomes concerned for the heavenly and eternal."

128. For Origen on the spiritual senses, see *Cassian and the Fathers*, 29, which quotes from *Contra Celsum*, I:48.

129. See the discussion of this term in John Eudes Bamberger's Introduction to his translation of Evagrius Ponticus, *The Praktikos; Chapters on Prayer*, CS 4 (Spencer, MA: Cistercian Publications, 1970), in which he points out that while the passage including this phrase, "his most renowned description of the light-mystique," is included as part of the *Praktikos* in the *Patrologia Graeca* text (*PG* 40, col. 1244A), it is not actually part of that work: "When the spirit has put off the old man to replace him with the new man, created by charity, then he will see

"earthly" (material) and "heavenly" (spiritual)—this is basically Platonic; the *oblivio terrenorum* (cf. Cassian's third renunciation[130]). This chapter is comparable to the first *Conference* of Cassian, or the conferences of Abbot Isaac on Prayer (*Conf.* 9 and 10). It is in fact a conference on purity of heart and prayer in solitude. {This is} the most developed *"collatio"* in the *Historia Monachorum*. It is called *"doctrina mystica."*[131]

After a description of some miracles attributed to Abbot John, then {comes} the account of their arrival, his greeting and hospitality. NOTE: {in} col. 394 he identifies one of them who is a deacon, who is trying to keep his sacred orders a secret. He asks them why they have come so far to ask about spiritual things when at home they have the Epistles and Gospels. The "conference" proper begins with warnings against vanity: *jactantiae vitium* (col. 395).[132] Then he immediately goes on to a detailed discussion of the importance of watching our thoughts, specifically *voluntas prava et desiderium vanum.*[133] (This struggle is the *exercitium mentis*[134] referred to above.) These are the roots of all our troubles, faults and miseries and as long as these roots are present in the heart we can never have peace. Hence the spiritual life consists first of all in the extirpation of these roots. Exterior renunciation is not enough. We are not fully free of the devil until we have renounced *"desideria vana et nociva"* ({I} Tim. 6).[135] The mind that has these roots in it, constantly oscillates between *vain*

---

that his own state at the time of prayer resembles that of a sapphire; it is as clear and bright as the very sky. The Scriptures refer to this experience as the place of God which was seen by our ancestors, the elders, at Mount Sinai" (xci).

130. See below, pages 52–53.

131. Col. 394D: "mystical teaching."

132. Col. 395D: "the vice of boastfulness" (also col. 396A).

133. Col. 396A: "the depraved will and vain desire."

134. Col. 404C: "exercise of the spirit."

135. Col. 396B: "vain and harmful desires" (I Tim. 6:9; mimeograph reads "II Tim. 6").

joy and *useless sorrow*. This is classic doctrine all the way through {the} tradition: see St. John of the Cross, *Ascent of Mt. Carmel*.[136]

True renunciation of the world means: control of anger, falsehood, envy, detraction and suspicion (again note the significance of the vices here selected). It means *making the joys and sorrows of {the} brethren our own*. This opens the way to the *locus Sancti Spiritus*,[137] Who when present fills the heart with joy, charity etc. and all the fruits of the Spirit. Hence the essence of monastic asceticism and renunciation is the control of these roots of evil, and *munditia cordis* (397).[138] False monks go about gathering up sayings from venerable Fathers, and desiring to be made priests (397). They try to get into the clerical state by hook or crook. They want above all to teach others when they have not yet learned themselves by practice. Conclusion: on the monastic priesthood: *neque fugiendum omnimodis dicimus clericatum neque rursus omnimodis expetendum*, *SED DANDA OPERA EST, UT VITIA QUIDEM A NOBIS DEPELLANTUR, ET VIRTUTES ANIMI CONQUIRANTUR*.[139] The rest is to be left to the judgement of God, to select those whom He wishes to make priests. For only those chosen by God are approved.

The Aim of the Monastic Life. MONACHI AUTEM ILLUD OPUS EST PRAECIPUUM, UT ORATIONEM PURAM OFFERAT DEO *nihil habens in conscientia reprehensibile* (397B).[140] {The} emphasis {is} on what is *given*, not what is *received*! If we have pure hearts, then the eye of the

136. See *Ascent* I.8.4 (Peers, I:40–41), where John laments the ignorance of those who concentrate on external penances but fail to mortify inner desires; for the sorrow caused by desire and attachment, see *Ascent* I.6–7 (Peers, I:33–39); for false joys coming from lack of detachment, see *Ascent* III:17–32 (Peers, I:245–89).

137. Col. 396D: "place of the Holy Spirit" (the text reads: "*Spiritui Sancti aperit in se locum*" ["he opens within himself a place for the Holy Spirit"]).

138. Col. 397A: "purity of heart."

139. Col. 397B (which reads: "*clericatum vel sacerdotium*" ["clerical or priestly state"] and "*animae*" rather than "*animi*"): "we do not say that the clerical state should be fled in all circumstances nor sought in all circumstances, but that we should certainly strive so that vices are driven from us and virtues of the soul are attained."

140. "The principal work of the monk is to offer pure prayer to God, having nothing blameworthy on his conscience."

heart will see the invisible (397). However, this does not mean visions or the perception of any form: *Nulla forma in Deo cogitetur, nulla circumscriptio, sed sensus, et {mens} quae {sentiri} quidem possit, et* PERSTRINGERE MENTIS AFFECTUM, NON TAMEN COMPREHENDI, AUT DESCRIBI AUT ENARR{AR}I VALET (397D).[141] This is the language taken up by the Cistercian Fathers and a very likely source for St. Bernard, among others.[142] They become the *friends of God* and therefore He reveals to them His secrets about His plan in the world, etc. (398A). Bodily pleasures must be renounced, not only worldly ones, but inordinate pleasure even in the simplest things—bread and water. It is here that the solitary life is especially to be recommended (398D). {He tells} the story of a vain monk, proud of his ascetic prowess, deceived by a devil appearing under the form of a woman (399). On the other hand, {there is the} victory of a converted sinner over the demons, resisting them even apparently unto death. With this and other stories he reaches the conclusion: love the life of prayer, prepare a place for the Holy Spirit in your hearts (see above). This is the content of chapter 1—John of Lycopolis.

Rufinus then goes on to treat more briefly of Cenobites. These are evidently the great cenobitic communities of the Thebaid, including Tabenna, where *Abbot Ammon* is father of 3000 monks.[143] Note

141. "No form, no limited concept, should be imagined in God, but there is an awareness, an impression, which can truly be perceived, and which can touch the disposition of the soul, but which cannot be grasped or described or communicated" (mimeograph omits "*mens*" and reads "*sentire*" for "*sentiri*").

142. On the vision of God in St. Bernard, see Étienne Gilson, *The Mystical Theology of St. Bernard*, trans. A. H. C. Downes (New York: Sheed & Ward, 1940), 91–92 and 235, n. 114. Bernard stresses the difference between seeing God as He is, impossible in this life, and as He wishes to be seen: "Even now he appears to whom he pleases, but as he pleases, not as he is. Neither sage nor saint nor prophet can or could ever see him as he is, while still in this mortal body; but whoever is found worthy will be able to do so when the body becomes immortal. Hence, though he is seen here below, it is in the form that seems good to him, not as he is" (*On the Song of Songs*, 31:2, in Bernard of Clairvaux, *On the Song of Songs* II, trans. Kilian Walsh, OCSO, Cistercian Fathers [CF], vol. 7 [Kalamazoo, MI: Cistercian Publications, 1976], 125).

143. Ammon is the abbot of a Pachomian, or Tabennisiot, monastery, but not the abbot of Tabenna (or Tabennisi) itself, which the travelers did not visit;

the different tone in talking of cenobites. What he remarks here is that they all eat with their eyes covered by their hoods so they do not see how much their neighbors are fasting . . . a different spiritual climate altogether from chapter 1. In describing cenobites he dwells briefly on the fact that their silence makes the cenobium *like* a solitude. The ideal cenobium is that of Abbot Isidore (c. 17; 439–440), a "most famous monastery"[144]—very spacious, surrounded by a wall, with "large buildings" (large individual cells, *larga habitacula*[145]) for the monks (more probably large cottages for groups of monks?). Within the enclosure {are} several wells, well-watered gardens, which were "paradises of all kinds of fruit-bearing and other trees" (or perhaps better, "filled with all the trees of paradise"[146]). "For this reason there was no need of the monks dwelling within to go out to satisfy any necessity"[147] ({note the} background of {the} *Rule* of St. Benedict[148]). {This is an} ideal image of the cenobium as a little paradisiacal and self-sufficient world, a microcosm and a restored primitive creation. "At the gate a grave old man elected from among the foremost [*de primis electus*] had the duty of receiving postulants only on condition that they should never again leave. If therefore one has once entered, the law [that he must stay] is irrevocable. But what is more admirable is that those who have entered are *kept there not by the compulsion of the law, but by the*

---

see the note in *Lives of the Desert Fathers*, 128: "Cenobitic monks who followed the Pachomian Rule were called Tabennisiots after St Pachomius's first monastery at Tabennisi nearly two hundred miles upstream from Lycopolis. There were two Pachomian monasteries near Hermopolis Magna (Eshmunên). One of these is likely to have been the monastery of Ammon."

144. Col. 439C.

145. Col. 439C.

146. Col. 439C.

147. Col. 439C.

148. See *Rule*, c. 66: "The monastery should, if possible, be so arranged that all necessary things, such as water, mill, garden, and various crafts may be within the enclosure, so that the monks may not be compelled to wander outside it, for that is not at all expedient for their souls" (McCann, 153).

perfection and blessedness of the life."[149] Rufinus[150] and companions are received in a cell next to the gate, but are not allowed to enter the monastery (since they could not leave again). But they are told about the life. Two seniors have the permission to go out to take care of needs of the community, especially to sell the products of the community's work. "But the rest of the monks are so established in silence and peace [*quies*], apply themselves to prayer and religious occupations, and so well provided with virtues of the soul that they all work wonders [*signa faciunt*], and what is a truly remarkable wonder among all the others, not one of them ever incurs any bodily infirmity, but when each one reaches the end of his life, knowing all about it beforehand, he tells his brethren he is about to die and bids them farewell, then lies down and joyfully breathes forth his soul."[151] {This is a} picture of the ideal cenobitic life.

The Monk and the Layman: A long and important chapter of Rufinus, *Historia Monachorum* (chapter 16)[152] deals with Paphnutius and three laymen who are saints:

1. When Paphnutius had reached an angelic degree of life, he asked God to show him which of the saints he had equalled. An angel tells him to go and see a minstrel who makes his living begging and singing through the villages. Paphnutius goes, finds the minstrel and questions him. {He} learns the minstrel is a great sinner and until recently lived as a brigand. But once he defended the purity of a nun who had been captured by the robbers. {He} also gives a poor woman money with which to ransom her husband, imprisoned and tortured for debt. Then Paphnutius announces that "he has done nothing like that himself"[153] and that

149. Col. 439CD.

150. Merton makes a slip here in supposing that Rufinus is the author rather than the translator of the *Historia Monachorum*.

151. Col. 440AB (which reads "*signa faciant*").

152. Chapter 14 of the original Greek text; see *Lives of the Desert Fathers*, 140, for a comparative table of chapters in the two versions.

153. Col. 436C.

the minstrel and he are of "equal merit."[154] However {he} counsels {the} minstrel to become a monk, which he does.

2. Later, Paphnutius, having worked harder than ever to purify his soul, prays again to know "what saint he has equalled."[155] A voice from heaven sends him to see the mayor of a nearby village, who has sanctified himself by married continency, hospitality, almsgiving, justice in exercise of his duty, peacemaking, mercy and protection of the weak.

3. After further efforts, he is shown a business man, as equal to himself. The business man is bringing three shiploads of merchandise to give to the monks. Alleluia. Great saint!

Conclusions: the fact that these three all become monks obscures the real meaning of the story, which is "that in no state of life are there lacking men who please God by acts of virtue, and no one is to be despised, even if he is a robber, or an actor, or a peasant," or if he "*appears* to be married."[156] (The narrator cannot quite bring himself to admit that ordinary married life can lead to high sanctity.) In spite of the way in which the perspectives are altered, the essence of the story remains intact: that a layman who lives well according to his state can attain just as high a degree of holiness as a hermit, fasting in the desert. Obviously the story had to be told in such a way that it did not make it seem altogether indifferent which state one chose, because the monastic state is in itself higher.

Nitria and Scete: {At} Nitria (c. 21)[157] the monks {are} living in separate cells, but he emphasizes their union in charity. *Mansione aliqui divisi animo autem et fide et caritate conjuncti et inseparabiles manent.*[158] He speaks of them coming out of their cells to

154. Col. 436C.

155. Col. 437A.

156. Col. 439B.

157. Chapter 20 in the original Greek text, which is considerably less detailed than Rufinus' version, and which also includes material found in the Latin chapters 23–25, 27; see *Lives of the Desert Fathers*, 140.

158. Col. 443B (which reads "*Mansione quidem aliqui . . .*"): "They remain apart in their dwellings but inseparably united in spirit and faith and love."

meet the visitors, bringing food and water (like bees out of a hive). They immediately wash the feet of the traveller "as though taking away the stains of earthly toil, but *in reality washing away the sorrows of human life by mystical and symbolic actions.*"[159]

Two characteristics of Nitria:

a) Nowhere had he found such *humanitas* and hospitality (cf. *Rule* of St. Benedict, c. 53[160]).

b) Nowhere had he found such zeal for *lectio divina*.[161] This combination is doubtless not fortuitous. Perhaps it has a certain importance.

c) He also adds that they have "diverse graces by one doctrine."[162] {Here is} a good picture of the spirit of a monastic group.

The desert of the cells: Cellia (Cellia, c. 22).[163] This is ten miles from Nitria—a place for those who have already been formed at Nitria, and who, having set aside their garments (*depositis indumentis*)[164] wish to lead a more hidden life (*secretiorem vitam*).[165] *Depositis indumentis* may have echoes from Greek spirituality and mysticism ("garments of skins"—{a} return to paradisiacal innocence and contemplation:[166] {it} refers more to the mind than to the body, though they also practiced ascetic nakedness and

159. Col. 444A.

160. This is the chapter on the reception of guests with its famous opening line, "Let all guests that come be received like Christ, . . ." (McCann, 119).

161. Col. 444B, which does not in fact use this term for spiritual reading but speaks of "*Scripturarum vero divinarum meditationes et intellectus*" ("meditations and penetration of the divine Scriptures").

162. Col. 444B.

163. The material in this chapter is found only in the Latin of Rufinus.

164. Col. 444C.

165. Col. 444BC.

166. See for example Gregory of Nyssa, *Life of Moses*, II.22: "The dead and earthly covering of skins, which was placed around our nature at the beginning when we were found naked because of disobedience to the divine will, must be removed from the feet of the soul. When we do this, the knowledge of the truth will result and manifest itself" (Gregory of Nyssa, *The Life of Moses*, trans. Abraham J. Malherbe and Everett Ferguson [New York: Paulist, 1978], 59–60); for extensive

poverty). They live out of sight of each other in great silence, coming together only on Sundays, bound together in great charity, speaking only when necessary to help a brother in need.

Chapter 27[167] {focuses on} *Evagrius*, {described as} *sapientissimum virum, et per omnia mirabilem.*[168] His characteristic grace {is} discernment of spirits and purifying of thoughts. No other of the brethren had attained to such subtle knowledge of spiritual things. {He} had been instructed by St. Macarius ({the narrator} does not say which). A man of "incredible abstinence,"[169] he advised the brethren not to be too free in drinking water if they want to control their thoughts! Thus, in Rufinus, Evagrius is still getting a good press! Rufinus and Evagrius were friends. But Cassian, while transmitting his doctrine, does not mention him by name.

4. John Cassian.

As we have a whole course on Cassian, it is sufficient at this point to show in outline the doctrine of Evagrius as transmitted by Cassian to the West. Cassian's life: {he was} born about 360 "*natione scytha*" (Gennadius)[170] in the Balkans (?); {he} received a classical education, and later lamented this as a source of distraction (*Con.* {14:12}).[171] {He} entered a monastery in Bethlehem. Cassian's monastery at Bethlehem was a Greek cenobium and had nothing to do with Jerome's community. Cassian may have left Bethlehem before Jerome's arrival. He went from there to Egypt about 380, having made a vow to return. Later he received

primary and secondary references for this image (based on Gen. 3:21), see 160, n. 29.

167. There is a brief mention of Evagrius in chapter 20:15-16 of the Greek version, but it is replaced by Rufinus' own chapter here (see *Lives of the Desert Fathers*, 150).

168. Cols. 448B-449A (which reads ". . . *virum, ac per* . . ."): "the wisest man, and remarkable in all things."

169. Col. 449A.

170. Gennadius, *De Scriptoribus Ecclesiasticis*, c. 61 (*PL* 58, col. 1094A): "of the Sythian nation."

171. Cols. 974B-979A (improperly assigned to Germanus in the Migne text) (mimeograph reads "2:14").

permission to settle definitely in Egypt, but was driven out in the Origenist conflict. {He then} went to Constantinople where he was ordained by Chrysostom about 400 (deacon), then to Rome about 405 on a mission on behalf of Chrysostom. After that {he goes} to Marseilles, where he founds two communities, one of men, one of women. *Lérins* was already in existence. Marseilles {was} more a center of asceticism, Lérins, of *learning*. {In} 419 (about) {he} writes {the} *Instituta* ({on} cenobitic life, monastic observances) for Bishop Castor of Apt, who is interested in monastic foundations. {In} 426–428 {he writes the} *Conferences* on mystical and solitary life with its various problems. {In} 430 {he writes the} *Contra Nestorium*. He dies about 433.

Concerning the works of Cassian, in general:

a) We must not take them purely and simply at their face value as personal records of experiences in Egypt. Actually they are much dependent on *written* sources, and not simply reports of the teachings and ideas of the monks who are "interviewed."

b) They are a record not simply of the thought of Egypt, or even of the Greco-Roman monastic world, but especially of the thought of *southern Gaul*, the monastic milieu of Provence and Lérins. They are "concerned with the most important subjects and questions which are exercising the minds of thinking men in southern Gaul at this period" (N. Chadwick).[172]

c) With great sense of balance and prudence, Cassian *adapts* Eastern ideas to Gaul. As a matter of fact, the credit for this adaptation of Eastern ideas to the West, which is so often given exclusively to St. Benedict, belongs perhaps more to Cassian than to any other single writer, but there were others who were quite well aware of the same need, for instance S. Severus. Note: Cassian does not, like S. Severus, exalt the monks of Gaul.[173] Cassian tends to suggest that Egypt is in every way superior.

172. Nora Chadwick, *Poetry and Letters*, 233.

173. See N. Chadwick, 232: "It is tempting to believe that Cassian wished deliberately to deny Severus's high claims for the prestige of the local national saint, and to insist on the superiority of the saints of Egypt to all others."

d) Special qualities of Cassian—he is:

(1) Comprehensive: {he} covers the whole field, cenobitism and eremitism, more fully than any other single writer. {He} goes into details of observance, but also discusses the deep problems of the spiritual life. {He treats both} asceticism and mysticism. {He} has a *spirituality*, a synthetic *doctrine* of the spiritual life (which is that of Evagrius). The *breadth of his experience* is very notable.

(2) {He is} judicious and objective: he resists the trend to multiply miraculous and marvelous tales (linked with {the} vogue for {the} Greek novel). {He} is not credulous, but realistic. READ {the} *Preface to the Instituta here*.[174] N. Chadwick regards this as in some measure a protest against the *Vita Antonii*, and its content of marvels.[175]

(3) {He is} moderate and prudent. READ N. Chadwick, p. 230.[176] He is not in favor of extreme rigor. He takes account of individual differences. He praises eremitism, but judiciously

174. Cols. 53A-60A: in his Preface to Bishop Castor of Apt, after professing his insufficiency to provide the information about the monastic way of life in the East that Castor had requested as a basis for founding monasteries in his diocese, Cassian says that his purpose is not to present stories of miraculous events, though he has seen some and heard about many more, but to provide instruction rather than astonishment, by explaining the rules and institutions of the monastic life and by discussing the eight principal faults and their remedies—to focus not on miracles but on ways to improve character.

175. See N. Chadwick, 218: "We cannot help suspecting that it is in some measure a protest against the popularity of stories of marvels which, first in the *Life of St Antony*, and later in that of St Martin, had brought the fashion to the West, partly as the heir, partly as the rival to the growth of fiction which had developed in the late Greek novel."

176. Chadwick emphasizes Cassian's focus on spiritual growth and communal harmony: "A quiet dignity of bearing and decorum of conduct go hand in hand with personal simplicity and high endeavour, and with mutual cooperation and loving-kindness. Renunciation and ascetic practices are only means to an end, and their object is a heightened and purified realization of divine perfection." She notes how Cassian includes the monks' failings and shortcomings without dwelling on them. "They fall into their natural place as the simple human frailties which men take with them into the religious life, but which they outgrow

prefers cenobitism for the majority. {He} has a deep understanding of psychology and human nature. {He shows a} *democratic* spirit, in the institutional setup of monasticism. {There is an} emphasis on humility, obedience, purity of heart (see N. Chadwick, p. 223[177]). {He} represents the Desert Fathers as solicitous for the old, the sick, the weak. {He} recognizes the importance of a relaxed and supple attitude (*Conf.* {24:21}).[178]

e) On {the} importance of studying Cassian:

> John Cassian has not received adequate study from ecclesiastical historians. Not only was he the teacher of Benedict and one of the principal architects of the western monastic system; through the charge of the Benedictine Rule that his writings should be read in religious communities, his teaching upon the ascetic life and the road to perfection dominated the origins and affected the spiritual ethos of medieval and modern monasticism. His work has permanently influenced the Christian life and culture of Europe through its effect upon the form and diffusion of the western ascetic movement. St Benedict was the master-builder; but Cassian provided for him much of the material and a number of the tools. Yet to many who are intimate with Benedict his great predecessor has remained unknown (O. Chadwick, *John Cassian*, p. 5).[179]

---

with the help and the kindly sympathy and wise counsel of the men who have grown old in the experience of temptation and self conquest."

177. Chadwick quotes passages from the final chapters of Book 12 of the *Institutes* warning against pride and emphasizing that "its only remedy is humility."

178. Cols. 1312B–1315A; see N. Chadwick, 228: "The value set on relaxation is delightfully illustrated by the well-known apocryphal story of St John who, when reproved by a passing huntsman for amusing himself by stroking a partridge, replied that his mind would lose its vigour unless relaxed from tension by recreation" (the mimeograph reads "3:24"—based on a misinterpretation of Chadwick's footnote reference, which reads: "III, xxiv, 21"—the first numeral refers to the third part of the *Conferences*).

179. Owen Chadwick, *John Cassian: A Study in Primitive Monasticism* (Cambridge: Cambridge University Press, 1950).

Between 425 and 430 "Cassian became one of the two principal figures in the Latin Church, second only to St Augustine" (Chadwick, p. 7).

f) The Spiritual Doctrine of Cassian and Evagrius. Let us outline the doctrine of Cassian, which we treat in detail elsewhere.

(1) Christian Philosophy—Cassian and Evagrius oppose the false philosophy of the world (i.e., of the classical Greek philosophers) with the "true philosophy" of the monks. Yet in so doing they borrow much from classical (especially neo-Platonic) philosophy. Cassian begins *Conference* 4 with the statement that Abbot Daniel stood out among all the "other men of Christian philosophy who were at Scete"[180] by his *humility*. {This is} a Christian trope: it is humility, meekness, selflessness, pure love, that distinguish the Christian philosopher (following the Gospel of Christ) from the pagan philosopher, led by self-seeking and spiritual ambition. A mark of the "Christian philosophy" of Abbot Daniel {is that} he was advanced to the diaconate under obedience to Paphnutius, then to the priesthood, but he refused to offer the holy sacrifice as long as Paphnutius was present, and though he had been designated as Paphnutius' successor, he died before Paphnutius did. Another instance of Christian philosophy {is found in} *Collatio* 5, chapter 21. One of the Desert Fathers, disputing with philosophers (pagans) who think him stupid and uneducated, remarking on gluttony, tells them a parable: "My Father left me indebted to many creditors: I have paid them all off but one, but this last one, though I pay him every day, I cannot get free of my debt."[181] This was a reference to gluttony. The philosophers then stated that this *abbas primas philosophiae partes, id est ethicam disciplinam, apprime comprehendisse*.[182] And they add that he has done so without labor, while they have worked for

180. Cols. 583C-584C.

181. Col. 637AB.

182. Col. 638A: "had especially grasped the first part of philosophy, that is, ethical discipline" ("*abbas*" is not part of the quotation).

years to acquire their knowledge. This theme will reappear in Cassian: {it is} sufficient to start with this as {an} introduction. Another Christian trope {is that} the true philosophy is a gift to the humble, and is acquired without learning. (Discuss this!)

THE DIVISION OF PHILOSOPHY. Evagrius (*Pract.* I:1) {writes that} the Christian teaching of Our Savior Jesus Christ consists of three parts: *PRAKTIKE*, *PHYSIKE*, *THEORETIKE*.[183] This is the classical division of (Greek) philosophy: *Praktike*—which Cassian calls *Scientia actualis*, or *ethica*;[184] *Physike*—true knowledge of nature such as Adam had before the fall, and which was passed on even after the fall until corrupted by magic and idolatry (see *Coll.* 5, c. 21);[185] *Theoretike*—*Scientia spiritualis*; *Theologia*; *solius Dei intuitus*.[186]

ACTUALIS SCIENTIA (*PRAKTIKE*) is not merely the knowledge of the passions, and how to control them, but also the knowledge and illumination that comes when the passions are brought under control. Here it is well to consider Cassian's own text (first chapters of *Coll.* 14, "*De Spirituali scientia*"[187]). Abbot Nesteros begins by saying that there are "many sciences"[188] in this world, most of which are useless. However they all have their disciplines which must be followed. So too, in the "science" of the monastic life, there must be a definite objective and a precise discipline for attaining it. What is the objective? *Spiritualis scientia: QUAE AD CONTEMPLANDA INVISIBILIUM SACRAMENTORUM TENDIT ARCANA* (col. 954).[189]

183. Merton relies here on Salvatore Marsili, OSB, *Giovanni Cassiano ed Evagrio Pontico: Dottrina sulla Carità e Contemplazione*, *Studia Anselmiana*, 5 (Rome: Herder, 1936), 106.

184. Practical knowledge is equated with ethics in *Conference* 14:9 (col. 966A).

185. Cols. 637A-638B: this is a reference back to the Desert Father story just told, which does not however mention corruption through magic or idolatry.

186. "intuitive awareness of God alone" (this precise term is not found in Cassian, though he does use the phrase "*contemplatio Dei solius*": see *Conf.* 9.18 [col. 788B]).

187. "On Spiritual Knowledge" (Merton regularly writes "*spiritualis*" where the text has the alternative spelling "*spiritalis*").

188. Col. 953B.

189. [spiritual knowledge] "which aims toward contemplating the secrets of invisible mysteries."

What is the way? *actualis scientia*.[190] Here Cassian divides philosophy into parts, simply: *PRIMA PRACTICE: id est actualis, quae emendatione morum et vitiorum purgatione perficitur. ALTERA THEORICE: id est QUAE IN CONTEMPLATIONE DIVINARUM RERUM ET SACRATISSIMORUM SENSUUM COGNITIONE CONSISTIT* (col. 955).[191] Chapters 2–7 are then about various aspects of the active life, *actualis scientia*:

Chapter 2: "Whoever wishes to attain to the *theorica* must perforce with all attention and effort labor first to acquire the *actualis scientia*."[192] The "*praktike*" can be had without the *theorike* but not vice versa. {The} basis {for this is} Wisdom 1:4.[193] This verse alone is quoted, but it should be seen in its context. (Note Alexandrian milieu.[194])

Chapter 3: Two aspects of the *actualis scientia*: (a) knowledge of the *nature and cure* of every vice; (b) *ordo virtutum*.[195]

1. In neither case is the knowledge merely speculative. It must be known by being lived. The knowledge of the vices is attained by recognizing them, discerning the "spirits" which prompt them. The knowledge of their cure is acquired by the wise struggle against them, aided by the grace of God.

2. The knowledge of the virtues is not speculative. It is, as St. Thomas would say, "connatural"[196]—that is to say it is ac-

190. "practical knowledge."

191. "First, practical, that is, active, which is accomplished in the correction of habits and the expulsion of vices; the other, contemplative, which consists in the contemplation of divine things and the comprehension of the most sacred meanings of things."

192. Col. 955A.

193. Col. 955B; the verse reads, "For wisdom will not enter into a malicious soul, nor dwell in a body subject to sins."

194. Merton refers to the fact that the Book of Wisdom is thought to have been written in Alexandria, and shares the sapiential focus of much Jewish and Christian writing emerging from that milieu (Philo, Clement, Origen).

195. Col. 955B: "the ordering of the virtues."

196. See Ralph McInerny, "Ethics," in *The Cambridge Companion to Aquinas*, ed. Norman Kretzmann and Eleanore Stump (Cambridge: Cambridge University Press, 1993), 206: "Sometimes Aquinas contrasts general knowledge and the kind of knowledge prudence is by describing the former as rational knowledge (*per*

quired when the virtues nourish the soul "AS A KIND OF NATURAL GOOD," that is to say when the soul takes spontaneous delight in virtue which can only be done when the practice of virtue has become habitual and pleasant (col. 956).

3. This delight in virtue, and this "taste" for the good, prepares us, he suggests (col. 956; c. 3) for a similar kind of understanding (by love) of "the heavenly sacraments and spiritual things" (*id.*).

4. In either case the *whole man* is involved in a *total experience* of either good or evil. This is due to the fact that the man in whom *Christ does not reign* is under the sway of the devil, in his whole life. But the devil is a heavenly spirit plunged in material things and concerns, and he does the same to us, according to Cassian (see esp. *Conf.* 8).[197]

Chapter 4: Various approaches to the *actualis scientia* {are presented}, according to different vocations and attractions.

a) Some find that the active life is most successful when they concentrate on solitude and purity of heart: *eremi secreta et cordis puritatem.*[198] They follow Elias and Eliseus as well as St. Anthony who "*familiarissime Deo per silentium solitudinis cohaesisse cognoscimus.*"[199] (This shows how different is the terminology of the early

---

modum rationis) and the latter as connatural knowledge (*per modum inclinationis* or *per modum connaturalitatis*). This connatural knowledge of prudence is tantamount to virtue." See *Summa Theologiae*, I-I, Q. 6, ad. 3 for the distinction between wisdom arrived at by intellectual judgement apart from personal virtue, and wisdom gained "from a bent that way [*per modum inclinationis*], as when a person who possesses a habit of a virtue rightly commits himself to what should be done in consonance with it, because he is already in sympathy with it [*ad illa inclinantur*]" (*Summa Theologiae*, ed. Thomas Gilby, OP, 61 vols. [New York: McGraw-Hill, 1964–80], 1:22/23-24/25); see also I-II, Q. 23, art. 4, where the good is said to cause in the appetitive faculty a certain "inclination towards [the good], a sense of affinity towards [the good], a sense that [the good] and itself are naturally fitted for each other" ("*quemdam inclinationem seu aptitudinem seu connaturalitatem ad bonum*"); this attraction to participation in the good is identified with love (Gilby, 19:28/29).

197. "*De Principatibus seu Potestatibus*" ("On the Principalities and Powers") (cols. 719-770).

198. Col. 957A: "the secrets of the desert and purity of heart."

199. Col. 957A: "we know have adhered to God most intimately through the silence of solitude."

Fathers from our own. Solitude and purity of heart would be for us *contemplative* life. This shows that actually for us the term contemplative life refers rather to a *means* than to an end. For Cassian, all means, however solitary and eremitical, are an *activity*, therefore "active life." The end of all active life is one: contemplation. We on the contrary regard active life and contemplative life together as two different kinds of means, doubtless to two different kinds of spiritual perfection. Note: Evagrius speaks of psalmody and liturgical prayer as works of the "active life"—*De Oratione*.[200])

b) Some find the most effective means to be in the teaching of other monks and the supervision of the community, as "Abbot John of Thmuis." He was distinguished by "apostolic signs"[201] (i.e., miracles).

c) Others perform other works of mercy such as feeding the poor, caring for the sick, etc. (959).

d) Others practice active works of mercy and hospitality. {He} mentions St. Macarius exercising hospitality in a house at Alexandria and attaining to equal perfection with monks of the desert. This is just another form of "*actualis scientia*" (col. 959; c. 5). What is important, Abba Nesteros continues, is that *each one persevere in the mode of active life which he has embraced. Summo studio ac diligentia ad operis arrepti perfectionem pervenire festinet* (959).[202] Each should praise the virtues of others who have chosen other ways, but each should stay in his own path. This is explained by reference to St. Paul's doctrine of the Mystical Body, especially Romans 12. The weak, on the contrary (c. 6), are not able to understand this, and they are moved to change from one

200. See the two-fold division of prayer into active and contemplative in the Prologue to the *De Oratione*, as well as the distinction between psalmody and prayer in *De Oratione*, 83–87 (see Evagrius, *Praktikos; Chapters on Prayer*, 53, 69); see also Marsili, 112–13, with its focus on spiritual exercises (vigils, fasting, *lectio divina*, etc.) as works of the active life.

201. Col. 958A.

202. "Let him hasten with the greatest eagerness and diligence to reach the perfection of the work he has chosen."

way to another when they hear of the virtues of other methods. Each should stay in his own way, because precisely *MOBILITAS MENTIS*[203] (c. 7) is a great obstacle to *actualis scientia*. Hence the importance of stability in {the} "active" way.

Chapter 9: {This is} a clear and important chapter, indicating the close relation between *actualis scientia* and *spiritualis scientia*:

a) Dispositions with which *spiritalis scientia* is to be sought {include the} *desire for beatitude of purity of heart, and not for knowledge or reputation*. {He} quotes *Beati mundo corde*,[204] also Daniel 12 on the learned and Osee 10: "*Illuminate vobis lumen scientiae dum tempus est*."[205]

b) {One must} combine *diligentia lectionis*[206] with *actualis scientia*: how? principally by *silence*—because it is by practicing what one learns that he attains to *spiritalis scientia*, not by talking about it. Talking about it generates only vanity. The fruit of reading is then killed (cf. St. John of the Cross, *Letter* 6[207]). Crucial in the active life are *humility* and *discretion*. Both are regarded as the "mother of all virtues," and are almost identified (see *Conf.* 2[208]

203. Col. 960B (which reads "*mobilitate*"): "unsteadiness of mind."

204. Col. 965C: "Blessed are the pure of heart."

205. Col. 966A: "Light for yourselves the light of knowledge while there is time."

206. Col. 966A (which reads "*diligentiam*"): "diligence in reading."

207. Here John writes to a convent of Carmelite nuns, emphasizing the importance of putting spiritual instruction into practice: "Enough has already been said and written for the accomplishment of what is needful; . . . what is lacking (if anything be lacking) is not writing or speaking, for of this there is generally too much, but silence and work. And, apart from this, speaking is a distraction, whereas silence and work bring to the spirit recollection and strength. And therefore, when a person once understands what has been said to him for his profit, he needs neither to hear nor to say more, but rather to practise what has been said to him silently and carefully, in humility and charity and self-contempt" (Peers, 3:247-49).

208. See especially chapter 10 (col. 537AB): "*discretio non nisi vera humilitate acquiritur*" ("discretion is acquired only through true humility").

and *Conf.* 19[209]). (READ c. 9.[210]) Note especially: "*Omni studio festinate actualem, id est, ethicam, quam primum ad integrum comprehendere disciplinam*" (col. 966).[211] {Note the} reference to the psalms: when the passions are "cooked out" one knows by experience the meaning of the psalms, in verses such as "*Psallam et intelligam in via immaculata.*"[212] To understand the psalms two things are necessary: (a) getting rid of vices; (b) getting rid of worldly cares. "It is impossible for a soul that is even slightly occupied in worldly distraction to earn the gift of knowledge, or to become a mother of spiritual meanings, and a tenacious devotee of holy reading."[213] {He} reiterates {the} importance of silence: to store away the words of the Fathers in our hearts and meditate on them, rather than talking about our reading to show off our knowledge: "It is impossible [cf. above] for one who devotes himself to reading with the idea of gaining human praise, to earn the gift of knowledge" (967). They must beware of thinking that brilliancy and facility of speech are a sign of real understanding, which can only be gained through purity of heart and docility to the Holy Spirit. "It is one thing to have a quick tongue and to use brilliant words, and another to contemplate with the most pure eye of the heart the deep and hidden mysteries, by entering into the secret veins and marrow of the heavenly sayings: for this is

209. This conference is given by Abba John, who is presented as an example of humility for having returned from a hermit life to the cenobium because it represented a less dangerous path to holiness.

210. In addition to what Merton quotes above and below, this chapter (cols. 965B-969B) emphasizes attaining knowledge in silence in order to guard against pride (addressing Cassian directly, as "*Joannes*," the only time in the *Conferences* he is called by that name: see Boniface Ramsey, OP, ed. and trans., John Cassian, *The Conferences*, ACW 57 [New York: Paulist, 1997], 530), and not teaching what one has not already put into practice—directives particularly relevant to the author.

211. "With all eagerness hasten to grasp completely, as soon as possible, the active, that is ethical, instruction."

212. Col. 966B: "I shall sing and understand in a spotless way" (Ps. 100 [101]:1-2).

213. Col. 966B.

not granted to human learning or to secular erudition, but only to purity of heart through the illumination of the Holy Spirit" (col. 969). The distinction between the two is then: secular science inflates with vanity; spiritual science edifies with charity (c. 10; col. 970); cf. St. Paul.[214]

{(2)} THE THREE RENUNCIATIONS—Essential for the understanding of the active life in Cassian is the Third *Conference* on the Three Renunciations. This is based on the *Centuries* of Evagrius on the Practical Life,[215] and is reminiscent of Origen (cf. Origen: *Prol. in Cant.*[216]). Abbot Paphnutius {teaches} there are "three vocations" or three ways of being called to the monastic life. That is to say there are three *ways of beginning* the monastic life and to these beginnings ought to correspond the whole of the rest of one's life. The higher and more supernatural "vocation" implies higher graces because a higher and more perfect origin. Hence one who has been called in a more special way, must correspond with a greater fidelity, worthy of the origin of his vocation.

The Three Vocations (c. 3) {are}: *from God*—a very special call, in a dream or vision (as in the case of Abraham), or as in the case of St. Anthony, a special grace recognized as such, received during the liturgy (col. 562): "*cum summa compunctione cordis suscepit, confestim qui renuntians cunctis, secutus est Christum, nulla doctrina neque exhortatione hominum provocatus*";[217] *from man*—by the example of the saints, by the advice of certain ones, we are aroused to the desire of salvation, *desiderium salutis*;[218] it is understood that those who inspire or advise us are acting as instruments of God; in this way the Israelites were called out of Egypt through Moses; *from necessity*—events themselves, placing us in danger of death or material ruin or when confronted by death of

214. 1 Cor. 8:1.

215. See Marsili, 94, 116 (referring to *Cent.* 1:78-80).

216. See Marsili, 103–104, n. 6, and 151–52.

217. C. 4 (col. 562B, which reads ". . . *cordis compunctione . . . confestimque . . . neque doctrina . . .*"): "with the deepest piercing of the heart he undertook [the directive of the Lord], and immediately renouncing all things, followed Christ, moved to do so by no teaching or encouragement of men."

218. Col. 562B.

friends, etc.: *ad Dominum quem sequi in rerum prosperitate contempsimus, saltem inviti properare compellimur* (col. 563).[219] He quotes several examples, including Psalm 106: "*Et clamaverunt ad Dominum cum {tribularentur}, et de necessitatibus eorum liberavit eos.*"[220] Their trial is itself a grace.

Chapters 4–5—The difference in beginning does not necessarily imply a difference throughout the whole life of the monk. Those who have begun in the third vocation can be just as perfect as those who have started by a special grace. And those who have started with a special grace may get tepid and end badly (*ad vituperabilem finem saepissime recedisse*) (col. 563).[221] Abbot Moses, who fled to {the} desert to escape punishment for murder, nevertheless became a saint (col. 564). Judas, he says, was called personally by Christ and responded willingly, only to fall into avarice and betray the Lord. Paul was blinded and drawn to Christ as it were unwillingly, yet became a great saint. The comparison is a bit forced. But the conclusion is the same: *TOTUM IN FINE CONSISTIT* (564).[222]

The Three Renunciations (c. 6). He now turns to the three renunciations, which of course are essential to all spiritual life, no matter what its beginning may have been. *Prima*: *qua corporaliter universas divitias mundi facultatesque contemnimus*. *Secunda*: *qua mores ac vitia affectusque pristinos animi carnisque respuimus*. *Tertia*: *qua MENTEM NOSTRAM DE PRESENTIBUS UNIVERSIS AC VISIBILIBUS evocantes, FUTURA TANTUMMODO ET EA QUAE SUNT INVISIBILIA CONCUPISCIMUS*.[223] {The prime} example {is} Abraham (always the model of renunciation

219. "We are compelled to hasten at least involuntarily to the Lord whom we scorned to follow in prosperous circumstances."

220. Col. 563B (mimeograph reads "*tribularemur*"): "And they cried out to the Lord when they were in trouble, and he freed them from their difficulties."

221. C. 5 (which reads "*recidisse*"): "very often descended to a disastrous end."

222. The text reads "*totum ergo* . . .": "What really matters, then, is the end."

223. Col. 564C (which reads *Prima est* . . . *tantummodo contemplamur*, . . ."): "The first is that in which we scorn through our bodies all the riches and opportunities of the world; the second, in which we reject the former habits and vices and affections of soul and flesh; the third, in which we summon our mind from

and following God, as well as of faith and justification). *Exi de terra tua* (first renunciation); *de cognatione tua*[224] (second) (our "ways" are "connatural"—*a nostra nativitate cohaerentia velut affinitate quodam et consanguinitate cognata sunt*[225]); *de domo patris*—ID EST, OMNI MEMORIA MUNDI HUJUS QUI OCULORUM OBTUTIBUS[226] in order to dwell "in that house where we will dwell forever"—that is in the house of God.

To these three renunciations correspond three books of Solomon: first—Proverbs (*vitia resecantur*);[227] second—Ecclesiastes (*universa quae aguntur sub sole vanitas {pronuntiantur}*);[228] third—*Cantica Canticorum*: IN QUO MENS VISIBILIA CUNCTA TRANSCENDENS VERBO DEI CAELESTIUM RERUM CONTEMPLATIONE CONJUNGITUR (566).[229] They must be seen as expressing the perfect *conversatio morum*[230] of the monk. Note the scripture texts with which he supports his "three renunciations" in a general way (col. 567): 2 Cor. 4:10—not the things which are seen (temporal) but the things not seen (eternal); Phil. 3:20—our conversation is in heaven; Ps. 38:13—*Incola ego sum in terris*;[231] Ps. 118; John 17:16—*Non sunt de hoc mundo*;[232] John 15:19—Because you are not of this world the world hates you.

---

all present and visible things and [contemplate] only future realities and desire that which is invisible."

224. Col. 565A: "Go forth from your land, from your kin."

225. Col. 565A (which reads: "*quadam*): "clinging to us from our birth as if they are related by some kinship or by blood."

226. Col. 565A (which reads: ". . . *oculorum occurrit* . . ."): "from your father's house—that is from all memory of this world which [comes before] the gaze of the eyes."

227. Col. 566A: "vices are cut away."

228. Col. 566A (mimeograph reads "*pronuntiatur*"): "everything which is done under the sun is declared to be vanity."

229. "in which the soul, going beyond all visible things, is united to the Word of God in contemplation of heavenly realities."

230. "conversion of manners" (the second monastic vow).

231. Col. 567B (which reads "*terra*"): "for I am a sojourner upon the earth."

232. Col. 567B (which reads "*De mundo hoc non sunt*"): "They are not of this world."

Then {he gives} further details on the *tertia renuntiatio* (567):

a) the mind loses the "fatness of flesh" (this affects his whole concept of asceticism as a kind of "reducing" regime for the "soul." *Mens nostra, nullo carneae pinguedinis hebetata contagio.*[233])

b) *Peritissimis eliminationibus expolita ab omni {affectu} et qualitate terrena.*[234]

c) *PER INDESINENTEM DIVINARUM MEDITATIONEM SCRIPTURARUM SPIRITUALESQUE THEORIAS.*[235] Note the positive effect of Scripture in ascetic life.

d) No longer is {it} aware of the fragility of the flesh, or of its bodily location *supernis et incorporeis intenta* [*ista*] *non sentiat* (567).[236] *In hujusmodi RAPIATUR EXCESSUS*[237] that it hears no voices (of bodies) and does not see even very large material objects (!) such as trees, etc.

e) This is learned only by experience (*experientia magistrante*).[238] It happens to those whose eyes have been *turned by the Lord* to supernal things (cf. Enoch [Gen. 5:{21-24}[239] and Hebrews 11:5]).

Some further remarks:

a) The Israelites who left Egypt with Moses still longed for Egypt with their hearts. So we who have left the world by the first and second renunciations, *must also aspire to the third renunciation*—otherwise our monastic life is truncated and incomplete (568). We will not "enter the Promised Land."[240] "It will be of no avail to us to have made a bodily renunciation and to have left

233. "Our soul, dulled by no contamination of fleshly grossness."

234. The text reads ". . . *elimationibus*"; mimeograph reads "*affecto* . . .": "through a very skillful filing process refined from every earthly disposition and quality."

235. The text reads "*spiritales*": "through continual meditation on the divine Scriptures and through contemplation of spiritual things."

236. "intent on the celestial and incorporeal, it is unaware of those other things" ("*ista*" added to text).

237. Col. 567C: "it is rapt into such ecstasies."

238. Col. 568A: "taught by experience."

239. Blank space left for verse numbers in mimeograph.

240. Cols. 568D-569A.

Egypt by a migration from place to place, if we have not likewise managed to obtain that third renunciation, that of the heart, which is so much more sublime and profitable."[241] But this third renunciation is purely and simply the PERFECTION OF CHARITY. Here he quotes 1 Cor. 13:{3}[242] and explains: it is of no avail to have given away all we have and still to be impatient or uncharitable, irascible, proud, self-seeking etc. Again {he} quotes 1 Cor. 13:{4-7}.[243] But the perfection of charity is not without contemplation, and therefore, according to Marsili, the third renunciation identifies perfect *charity with contemplation. "La perfetta carita e possibile solo nella contemplazione"* (Marsili, p. 68).[244] *Puritas cordis = perfecta charitas = contemplatio.*[245] *Secundum mensuram puritatis suae,* {. . .} *unaquaeque mens in oratione sua vel erigitur vel formatur* (*Coll.* 10.6).[246] Note how in *Collatio* 10:8-10 the "formula" (*Deus in adjutorium . . .*[247]) is proposed as a simple means {of} passing from the active to the contemplative life, and to the third renunciation and purity of heart.

b) Chapter 10:

1) In giving away possessions we are giving away what is really not our own, for we cannot own anything except what is in our hearts. For only what is in our hearts and part of our inmost self cannot possibly be taken away.

2) It is therefore only in the second renunciation that we give away what is really ours.

241. Col. 569A.

242. Blank space left for verse number in mimeograph.

243. Blank space left for verse numbers in mimeograph.

244. See Marsili, 66: "la perfetta carità è possible solo nella contemplazione" ("perfect love is possible only through contemplation"). On the following page Marsili says the converse is also true: "la perfetta carità si trova solo nella contemplazione e viceversa."

245. Purity of heart = perfect charity = contemplation.

246. Col. 826AB (which includes an additional clause between "*suae*" and "*unaquaeque*"): "According to the degree of its purity, each soul is built up and formed in its prayer."

247. Col. 832B ff.: "God [come to my] assistance."

3) Then in the third we renounce the *cosmos itself—cunctorum elementorum plenitudine* (573).[248]

4) After which a FOURTH STAGE IS ATTAINED: *"veni in terram quam tibi monstravero"*[249] (Gen. 12:{1}[250]). This is the *"perfectio summae beatitudinis"*[251] and is a pure gift of God alone, beyond any power of man to attain in any way whatever. *Id est, non quam tu ex temetipso nosse, vel industria tua poteris reperire, sed quam ego tibi non solum ignoranti, sed etiam non inquirenti monstravero* (574).[252]

Puritas Cordis: Finally, for a good understanding of the *"actualis scientia"* in Cassian, we must return to the classical passage: the first *Conference*. As we treat this in detail elsewhere[253] it will be sufficient to run through the main points briefly here.

(a) Note that in *Conference* 5, chapter 27,[254] it is pointed out that purity of heart is the result of victorious struggle against the eight capital sins. It is therefore the crown of the active life and is part and parcel of *"actualis scientia."*

(b) It is also identified with *love of virtue* (not mere restraint of passion), a positive inclination to the good for its own sake, hence related to "pure love," *caritas*. See *Conference* 11, chapter 6.[255] This sketches out a doctrine that is familiar to St. Bernard.[256]

248. The text reads *"plenitudinem"*: "the fullness of all the elements."

249. Col. 574A: "come into the land that I will show you."

250. Blank space left for verse number in mimeograph.

251. The text reads *"perfectionem"*: "the perfection of the highest blessedness."

252. "It is not something you can know from yourself, or find out by your own effort, but something I will show you who are not only ignorant of it but not even looking for it."

253. See *Cassian and the Fathers*, 204–18.

254. Col. 642B.

255. Cols. 852A-853A.

256. See Gilson's discussion of pure love in Bernard (141–47); see also *On the Song of Songs*, 83:5: "Pure love has no self-interest. Pure love does not gain strength through expectation, nor is it weakened by distrust. This is the love of the bride, for this is the bride—with all that means. Love is the being and the hope of a bride" (Bernard of Clairvaux, *On the Song of Songs* IV, trans. Irene Edmonds, CF 40 [Kalamazoo, MI, Cistercian Publications, 1980], 185), and the third

Conference 11 is on perfection. Abbas Chaeremon says (c. 5) there are three motives which prompt men to restrain their vices: fear (especially of hell)—this is the "servile state" of the Prodigal far from his father's house tending swine (c. 7); hope (of heavenly reward)—this is the state of {the} "hired servant" to which the Prodigal aspired when planning to return to his Father's house; love—this is the state beyond fear and hope, the *filiorum gradus*[257] which is that of perfect likeness to the Father (in love). The perfect love of the "son" is therefore identical with *puritas cordis*, the same thing seen from another aspect. {These are} characteristics of it: whereas *timor* and *spes* are "proper to men" (c. 5; col. 852) the pure love of the son *SPECIALITER DEI EST, ET EORUM QUI IN SESE IMAGINEM DEI AC SIMILITUDINEM RECEPERUNT*.[258] Such a one does good: *nullo metu, nulla remunerationis gratia provocante* *SED SOLO BONITATIS AFFECTU* (col. 852).[259] Such a love never sins, *Caritas numquam cadit* (c. 6).[260]

(c) Purity of Heart and *Caritas filiorum* are *essential for uninterrupted prayer*. That is to say that they are the summit of the active life and the key to the true contemplative life. That is to say that purity of heart and purity of love are the guarantee that the monk will pray *eo fervore ac puritate, qua debet* (*Conf.* {9}, c. 3; col. 773).[261] For this *immobilis tranquillitas mentis*[262] (same as *puritas cordis*) the monk must possess all the virtues, and they are all united in one in *caritas*. {See} *Conference* 9, chapter 2 on prayer:

---

degree of love in Bernard's *De Diligendo Deo*, to love God for God's own sake (Bernard of Clairvaux, *On Loving God*, trans. Robert Walton, OSB, in *Treatises* II, CF 13 [Washington, DC: Cistercian Publications, 1974], 118–19).

257. Col. 854A (which reads "*gradum*"): "the level of sons."

258. "belongs especially to God and to those who have received the image and likeness of God in themselves."

259. "motivated not by fear, not by hope of reward, but by love of goodness alone."

260. Col. 852A: "Charity never fails."

261. "with that fervor and purity which it ought to have" (mimeograph reads: *Conf.* 8).

262. Col. 771A (which reads "*immobilem tranquillitatem*"): "unchanging tranquillity of mind."

> Every monk (who looks for the perfect way) aims at uninterrupted prayerfulness. As far as is possible to a frail man, he struggles for imperturbable peace and purity of mind. This is the reason why we try so unwearyingly to practise the different disciplines of the body and the spirit. The discipline of the body and spirit on the one side, and unceasing prayerfulness on the other, cannot help having a mutual effect upon each other. The keystone in the arch of all virtues is perfect prayer, and without this keystone the archway becomes rickety and insecure. Conversely, without the virtues no one can attain the continual serenity of prayerfulness which I am discussing. Therefore, I cannot rightly and shortly treat of the effect and chief object of prayer (which is perfected in the truly virtuous life), unless first I treat systematically the way of avoiding sin and attaining goodness. As the Gospel parable teaches, the man who is going to build a tower first takes care to estimate and assemble his materials. But it is impossible to build a fine tower upon this prepared material unless the ground is cleared of rotten or dead rubbish and the foundations are built in firm (or 'lively' as they say) soil or on rock. So it is in the realm of the spirit. To build a tower of the spirit, you must clear the soul of its sins and passions, and build firm foundations of simplicity and humility upon the Gospel: this is the only way the tower can rise unshakable, as high as heaven. Then, though the tempests of passion be poured down upon it, though the floods of persecution beat upon it like battering-rams, though the storm of hostile spirits blows upon it, it shall still stand, and stand undamaged.[263]

{He emphasizes} the mutual interaction between virtue and prayer. Pure prayer is the keystone of the arch of the virtues. But it also depends on all the virtues, since a keystone cannot hang in the air by itself. {In} *Conference* 9, chapter 4, the soul {is} compared to a feather which when it is "dry" will naturally float easily in the air and be carried away by the lightest breeze. So the soul, if it retains its *natural* purity ("dryness") not weighed down by the "moisture"

263. *Western Asceticism*, 214–15 (cols. 771A-773A).

of passion, will easily be carried away by each breath of prayer. The things that most "weigh down the soul" {are} especially "*surfeiting* and *drunkenness* and the *cares of the world.*" *Videte ne graventur corda vestra crapula* etc. (Luke 21:34).[264]

> There is a good comparison between the soul and a delicate little feather. If a feather has not been touched by damp, it is so light that the slightest breath of wind can puff it high into the air. But if even a little damp has weighed it down, it cannot float, and falls straight to the ground. In the same way the mind, if not burdened by sin and the cares of daily life and evil passion, has a natural purity which lifts it from earth to heaven at the least breath of a meditation upon the invisible things of the spirit. The Lord's command is sufficient warning—'Take heed that your hearts be not *weighed down* by surfeiting and drunkenness and the cares of this world.' So if we want our prayers to reach the sky and beyond the sky, we must make sure that the mind is so unburdened by the weights of sin and passion as to be restored to its natural buoyancy. Then the prayer will rise to God (*Conf.* 9, c. 4).[265]

And the corollary {is that} care for temporal things, anxiety about our life, leads to *useless work*, i.e. for what is not necessary. This activism which springs from anxiety about our temporal needs produces overwork which is a *drunkenness of the spirit*. READ: *Western Asceticism*, p. 216 bottom and 217 top.[266] This is basic for monks. "If all you need to earn is one dollar (to pay for essentials) why earn three or four?" Correlative to this {is} *being satisfied with simple essentials of life*, restricting one's needs to {a} minimum, {finding}

264. Col. 774C (which reads ". . . *nequando . . . vestra in* . . ."): "Take care lest your hearts be weighed down by surfeiting . . ."

265. *Western Asceticism*, 215–16 (cols. 774B-775A).

266. "For example: suppose that a job with a wage of a shilling would satisfy our needs, and we try to work longer hours for two or three shillings: or suppose that two tunics are sufficient, one for the night and one for the day, yet we become owners of three or four; or suppose a hut of one or two rooms would be adequate, yet we build four or five rooms—then we are moved by secular pleasure and desire, and are letting worldly passion reign, so far as is possible for people in our situation" (cols. 776B-777A).

liberty from needs and consequently from anxiety, hence freedom to "pray at all times" without ceasing. The two go together.

(d) *Puritas Cordis* is therefore the "immediate goal" (*skopos*) of the ascetic life. The ultimate aim (*telos*) is the Kingdom of heaven (*Conference* 1). The monastic life is an "art" like any other. One must know how to live it, one must know its rules. {In} the art of farming, the farmer endures labor and difficulty to clear his land and plough it so that it is free of brambles, broken up and ready to receive seed. This is the "immediate aim" (*skopos*) of his labor. The ultimate end (*telos*) is the harvest. Applied to the monastic life: the immediate goal of ascetic labor {is} purity of heart, the ultimate aim, the Kingdom of heaven.

> 'In the same way, the ultimate goal of our life is the kingdom of heaven. But we have to ask what the immediate goal is: for if we do not find it we shall exhaust ourselves in futile efforts. Travellers who miss their way are still tiring themselves though they are walking no nearer to their destination.' At this remark we stood and gaped. The old man went on: 'The ultimate goal of our way of life is, as I said, the kingdom of God, or kingdom of heaven. The immediate aim is purity of heart. For without purity of heart none can enter into that kingdom. We should fix our gaze on this target, and walk towards it in as straight a line as possible. If our thoughts wander away from it even a little, we should bring back our gaze towards it, and use it as a kind of test, which at once brings all our efforts back onto the one path' (*Conf.* 1, c. 4).[267]

To be exact: the *principalis scopos* is *puritas cordis id est caritas* (*Conf.* 1, c. 7).[268] {The} New Testament basis is 1 Corinthians 13. Without charity all the virtues are lifeless and without value. This *caritas* IN SOLA CORDIS PURITATE CONSISTIT (c. 6; col. 488).[269] *NAM QUID EST ALIUS, NON*

267. *Western Asceticism*, 196–97 (cols. 485C-486B).

268. Col. 489B (which reads "*principalem scopon, id est, puritatem cordis, quod est charitas*"): "the principal end, that is purity of heart, which is charity."

269. The text reads "*quae*" for "*caritas*": "[love] which consists in purity of heart alone."

AEMULARI, NON INFLARI etc.[270] (list from 1 Cor. 13) . . . NISI COR PERFECTUM AC MUNDISSIMUM DEO SEMPER OFFERRE, ET {INTACTUM} A CUNCTIS PERTURBATIONIBUS CUSTODIRE (*id.*).[271] Note the last phrase is simply a roundabout way of describing what is signified by the unacceptable term "*apatheia.*"[272] Hence *puritas cordis* is at once pure love, *caritas filiorum*[273] and *apatheia*. All these converge in one reality. This is the pure doctrine of Evagrius. Hence everything in the ascetic life is done *for the sake of acquiring purity of heart or charity*.

> To this end everything is to be done. Solitude, watches in the night, manual labour, nakedness, reading and the other disciplines—we know that their purpose is to free the heart from injury by bodily passions and to keep it free; they are to be the rungs of a ladder up which it may climb to perfect charity. If by accident some right and needful occupation prevents us from keeping these acts of discipline, we should not be guilty of gloom or annoyance—for the aim of these acts is to drive away these faults. The loss you incur by being irritated outweighs the gain of fasting; dislike of your brother cannot be counterbalanced by reading the Bible. These practices of fasting, watching, withdrawal to the hermitage, meditation on the Scriptures, are all subordinate means to your chief aim which is purity of heart, or charity, and we ought never to allow them to take precedence over charity. Charity will not suffer hurt if some necessary reason prevents us fulfilling our disciplinary rule. None of these practices are of any profit at all if the purpose for which they are undertaken is lost (*Conf.* 1, c. 7).[274]

(e) Finally, what is meant by the *telos*, the Kingdom of Heaven? On the basis of *Conference* 1, chapter 13, Dom Salvatore

270. The text reads "*alium*": "For what else is it but not to be envious, not to be puffed up . . ."

271. The mimeograph reads "*intanctum*": "except to offer always a perfect and most pure heart to God, and to keep it safe from all disturbances."

272. "passionlessness," the term Evagrius uses for the goal of ascetic effort, for which Cassian regularly substitutes purity of heart.

273. "the love of sons."

274. *Western Asceticism*, 198–99 (col. 489AB).

Marsili says categorically: the *skopos* is *charity*, the *telos*, or *regnum Dei*, is *contemplation*.[275] The *regnum Dei* is realized in us when we are given to uninterrupted prayer, and contemplation. *Hic igitur nobis principalis debet esse conatus, haec immobilis destinatio cordis jugiter affectanda, ut divinis rebus ac Deo mens semper inhaereat* (c. 8; col. 490).[276] Anything other than this is either *secondary* or *noxious*. Contemplative life which will be the life of heaven begins on earth; but active life will be taken away in heaven—it is only for the earth. Hence *contemplatio* is *regnum Dei*. See chapters 10 and 13. It is true that in the flesh we cannot remain perfectly and continually united to God in contemplation all the time. But we can have the fixed intention to devote our minds to God, and constantly recall our thoughts to that target. *Totum namque in animae consistit recessu* (col. 497).[277] The sign of a soul thus pure in heart and united to God is therefore not *actual* and conscious contemplative union, but its disposition to regard as "spiritual fornication" every concern with anything other than God. This expression is not to be taken too literally: it means that the monk experiences the worthlessness and futility of all other endeavors, when contrasted with the *unum necessarium*[278] of union with God. Read chapter 8:

> It should be our main effort, the immovable and steadfast purpose of the heart, to cleave with our mind to the things of God and to God himself. Whatever is not this, however important, should be put second, or last, and judged to be hurtful. There is a lovely type of this mental attitude in the Gospel story of Martha and Mary. When Martha was per-

275. Marsili, 38–41; see also 107, n. 1; while Marsili cites *Coll*. 1, c. 13 for the identification of the Kingdom of God with contemplation, the identification of purity of heart with *caritas* is, as already indicated above, *Coll*. 1, c. 7 (see Marsili, 40, n. 1).

276. The text reads "*Hic ergo* . . .": "For this should be our principal effort, this unchangeable goal of our heart constantly to be sought, that the mind always cling to divine things and to God."

277. C. 13: "For the whole thing depends upon detachment of mind."

278. "one thing necessary."

forming her act of holy ministry in serving the Lord and his disciples, Mary was sitting at Jesus' feet, which in faith she had kissed and anointed, and was hanging upon his words as he taught the things of the spirit. The Lord praised Mary above Martha, because she had chosen the better part and that which should not be taken away from her. For when Martha was working away, in a truly religious spirit, and was busy about much serving, she saw that, unaided, she could not serve so many people, and asked the Lord that her sister might help her, saying: 'Carest thou not that my sister has left me to serve alone? bid her therefore that she help me.' She was calling Mary to no lowly task, but to an excellent work of ministry. Yet the Lord replied: 'Martha, Martha, thou art anxious and troubled about many things: we need few things, or even one thing. Mary has chosen the good part, which shall not be taken away from her.' The Lord, you see, placed the chief good in divine contemplation. All the other virtues, however necessary and useful and good we deem them, must be placed on a lower plane because they are sought for the sake of this one thing. When the Lord said: 'Thou art anxious and troubled about many things, but we need few things or even one thing,' he was putting the supreme good, not in the pursuit of virtue, however excellent and fruitful, but in the pure and simple and singleminded contemplation of himself. When he said that few things were needful, he means, that contemplation which begins with meditation upon a few holy subjects. From the contemplation of these few subjects, the soul in its progress mounts with God's help to one thing, the gazing upon God: the soul passes beyond saintly acts and ministries and attains the true knowledge of God and feeds upon his beauty. 'Mary therefore has chosen the good part, which shall not be taken away from her.' Mark the text. When he says: 'Mary has chosen the good part,' he is silent about Martha and seems in no way to blame her. Yet in praising Mary, he declares the work of Martha to be lower. Again, when he says: 'which shall not be taken away from her,' he shows that Martha's part could be taken away from her.

> To minister to the body is a transitory work: to listen to his word is the work of eternity (*Conf.* 1, c. 8).[279]

{(3)} Prayer and Contemplation in Cassian—The key to Cassian's whole doctrine on the spiritual life and prayer is his equation: *Puritas cordis = perfecta caritas = contemplatio*. It might also be added that *pure prayer* is also identical with the above. They are all aspects of the same thing. Another expression of it is: *solius Dei intuitus*[280]—seeing God alone. Hence for Cassian the contemplative life, which is the crown of the active life of ascetic purification, is not necessarily a vision of God (that will come in heaven) but a purity of heart, love and prayer which means constant attention (at least implicit) to God—if not constantly seeing God, at least constantly looking at God—but not at a form of God, for this presence of an objective form would be incompatible with *puritas cordis*. The desire for union with some objective form would also be incompatible with the third renunciation. A description of the contemplative state {is given in} *Collatio* 9.18 (see *Western Asceticism*, p. 222). This description is not psychological, and it involves nothing in the way of an "extraordinary state." It is the habitual condition of one living in purity of heart, therefore of perfect love, therefore of contemplation. *Sublimior status* [it is a state] *qui contemplatione solius Dei et caritatis ardore formatur*.[281]

Two elements make up this state: contemplation of God alone and ardor of love—ardor or intensity is equated with purity; the more our mind seeks and sees God alone, the greater the ardor of our love for Him alone, and (*e converso*)[282] *per* {*quam*} *mens in illius dilectionem resoluta atque rejecta*[283] (foreshadowing the language of later authors on abandonment, annihilation, etc.—{the} idea that the self is "lost" in God, cast away, carried

279. *Western Asceticism*, 199–200 (cols. 490B-493A).

280. The phrase, which Merton translates, is not found in Cassian.

281. Col. 788B (which reads "*charitatis*"): "a higher state which is formed by contemplation of God alone and by the ardor of love."

282. "conversely."

283. Col. 788BC (mimeograph reads "*quem*"): "through which the mind has been dissolved and thrown back into love for him."

away, totally forgetful of self, etc., etc.). FAMILIARISSIME DEO, VELUT PATRI PROPRIO, PECULIARI PIETATE COLLOQUITUR[284] (this gives {it} a clearly Christian character, firmly based in New Testament theology—Romans 8: this is the work of the Holy Spirit in us, the Spirit of Sonship, the perfect likeness to God as Sons in Christ, hence the completion of one's baptismal commitment to live as a son of God, etc.). The only thing about this description is that it is not precise enough as a description of *mystical* union; it is simply the ordinary life of prayer in a very pure state, under the guidance of the Holy Spirit, with definite implications of passivity (*resoluta et rejecta*) but without any attempt to satisfy the exigencies of later theologians in their efforts to distinguish what, precisely, is mystical prayer. *But for the monk this is an amply satisfactory description. The monk comes to the monastery to seek God and not to be a mystic.*

This description is to be completed by other passages in *Conference* 9—for instance chapter 14. The highest prayer is to be seen in the context of pure *gratitude* (cf. pure love) which is beyond three other degrees, *obsecratio, postulatio, oratio* (cc. 11-13).[285] Gratitude is marked by INEFFABILES EXCESSUS[286] and is beyond words, or thoughts, a kind of "ecstasy," but not in the sense of an unusual psychological phenomenon. Note: chapter 15 points out how *obsecratio* is perfected in *compunctio cordis; oratio* is fulfilled in *fiducia* and *completio votorum; postulatio* (for others) culminates in *ardore caritatis* (i.e. *fraternae*);[287] *gratiarum actio*[288] is expressed in the *oratio ignita, prayer of fire,* beyond words. MENTE PURISSIMA TRACTANTES, AD ILLAM IGNITAM, ET QUAE ORE HOMINUM NEC {COMPREHENDI} NEC EXPRIMI POTEST, ORATIONEM FERVENTISSIMO CORDE

284. Col. 788C: "it converses with God intimately, as with its own Father, with particular devotion."

285. Cols. 783A-785B: "supplication, intercession, prayer."

286. Col. 785B: "indescribable ecstasies."

287. Col. 785C: "compunction of heart . . . fidelity, fulfillment of vows . . . ardor of [fraternal] love" (n.b. these are not the precise terms used in the text).

288. Col. 785B: "act of thanksgiving."

RAPTANTUR (col. 786).[289] Note the word *raptantur*—an early suggestion of the idea of "*raptus*" in mystical prayer. The highest prayer *includes all these forms of prayer in one.*

> Yet sometimes the mind which is advancing to the true state of purity and has begun to be rooted in it, can conceive all these kinds of prayer in a single action; it cannot be understood, but may be compared to the leaping of a flame. It consists of a powerful and wordless pouring forth of prayer to God, which the spirit, with groanings that cannot be uttered, sends up though not conscious of its content. In that moment it conceives and puts forth what no one can describe, and which the mind apart from that moment cannot remember. So it happens that, whatever state of life a man has reached, he sometimes can offer pure and devout prayer. Even in the lowliest place where a man is repenting from fear of punishment and the judgement to come, his 'supplications' can enrich him with the same ardour of spirit as the man who has attained to purity of heart, gazes upon God's blessing, and is filled with an ineffable happiness. As the Lord said, he begins to love the more, who knows he has been forgiven the more (*Conf.* 9, c. 15).[290]

This is a very important and unusual text. Moments of special grace, touches of purity of heart, *suddenly occur at any level of the spiritual life.* Even one whose normal level of prayer is repentant *obsecratio* and *compunctio cordis*, may suddenly be struck by this grace, and at once *all the graces of all the levels* occur at once, as he is taken out of himself. This is due purely to the initiative of divine love, gratuitous grace of the Holy Spirit. *PRECES PURISSIMI VIGORIS EFFUNDERE QUAS IPSE SPIRITUS INTERPELLANS GEMITIBUS INENARRABILIBUS, NOBIS IGNORANTIBUS, EMITTIT AD DEUM* (col. 786).[291] Points to observe:

289. The mimeograph reads "*comprehendit*": "Drawn by a most pure mind they are swept up by a most fervent heart to that fiery prayer which cannot be understood nor expressed by the mouth of men."

290. *Western Asceticism*, 221 (col. 786BC).

291. The text reads "*ignorantibus nobis*": "to pour out prayers of the purest vigor, which the Spirit himself, interceding with unutterable groans, sends forth

a) This clearly distinguishes the *state of prayer* and the *momentary acts of pure prayer which transcend any and every state.*

b) Normally, the man whose habitual prayer is on the level of gratitude, is praying in a better way than the others. He is *closer* to the completely pure and ineffable gratuitous act of prayer, given by direct action of God alone.

c) But even in the lower state of prayer, one who is completely humble and in earnest can be lifted to the same heights, in this *act* of the Holy Spirit's love, and on this level *all meet, beyond every state.*

d) For all, too, the same condition obtains: the grace is transient. *AD HORAM COMPUNGITUR*.[292] This term recurs frequently in medieval mysticism.

e) In the brief moment when they are, to use St. Bernard's expression, "rapt above themselves,"[293] that is to say above their normal state, they are all equally pleasing to God, and in His eyes there remains no distinction between them.

f) This special act has more in it of the nature of gratitude than of the other "states." But it *consists in a greater love* than is implied by any of the states.

g) There is some slight confusion in the fact that the fourth state is said to be one of *purity of heart*. But perhaps this passage gives us light on the distinction between the *skopos*, purity of heart, as a *state* and the *telos* which is the kingdom of heaven, or "*raptus*." This gives special nuances to Cassian's ideas of mysticism. It is in the gratuitous act of God that we have genuine

---

to God, without our knowing." (This is a more literal translation than that included in the passage immediately above, and one which takes "*spiritus*" as referring to the Holy Spirit, as Merton suggests, not the human spirit.)

292. Col. 786C: "he is, at the time, pierced" (the translation above does not render "*ad horam*" into English).

293. See *PL* 183, col. 1194B (*SC* 85:13): "*rapitur . . . a seipsa, ut Verba fruatur*" ("[the soul] is rapt out of itself, that it might enjoy the Word"). For a general discussion of "*raptus*" in St. Bernard, see Gilson, 106–108; for consideration of specific texts, see Cuthbert Butler, *Western Mysticism: The Teaching of Augustine, Gregory and Bernard on Contemplation and the Contemplative Life*, 2nd ed. ([1926]; New York: Harper Torchbook, 1966), 115–17.

mysticism. The "states" even of purity of heart and the fourth kind of prayer, are as yet not on the level of mysticism, in our modern terminology. This shows that the "description" quoted above, from *Collatio* 9.18, is a description of a *state* but not of the exceptional *act* in which one is lifted above all states.

h) Chapter 16 shows that we must, as far as possible, aim for those *states* of prayer which are based on the contemplation of future goods (in heaven) or on *ardor caritatis* (ardent prayer for salvation of others), i.e. *postulatio* and *gratiarum actio*. This is also to be completed by *Collatio* 9, chapter 25 in which it is said that the Lord's Prayer (which he has just explained) leads beyond all states to the act of pure prayer, *oratio ignita*, *QUAE OMNEM TRANSCENDENS HUMANUM SENSUM, NULLO NON DICAM SONO VOCIS NEC LINGUAE MOTU NEC ULLA VERBORUM PRONUNTIATIONE DISTINGUITUR, SED QUAM MENS INFUSIONE CAELESTIS ILLIUS LUMINIS ILLUSTRATA, NON HUMANIS ATQUE ANGUSTIS DESIGNAT ELOQUIIS, SED CONGLOBATIS SENSIBUS VELUT DE FONTE QUODAM COPIOSISSIMO EFFUNDIT UBERTIM* (col. 801).[294]

And finally, chapter 3l gives the criterion of this purest act of prayer: "To teach you the feeling of true prayer, I will give you, not my opinion, but that of St Antony. I have known him sometimes so long at his prayers that the sun rose before he had finished. And I would hear him, still in a rapture of spirit, cry out to the sun: 'Why do you hinder me? The rising of your light draws my mind away from the true light.' And St Antony also uttered this heavenly, inspired, saying on the end of prayer: 'That prayer is not perfect in which the monk understands himself and the words which he is praying.'"[295]

294. "fiery prayer, which transcends every human sense, and is distinguished, I will not say, by any sound of the voice or movement of the tongue or any pronunciation of words, but which the mind, illuminated by the infusing of that heavenly light, does not describe by limited human words, after the senses have been put aside, but pours forth copiously as though from a most abundant fountain."

295. *Western Asceticism*, 229 (cols. 807A–808A).

Prayer without Forms—the Humanity of Christ? (cf. Gospel {for the} Fourth Sunday after Easter[296]): this then raises a problem which was much discussed later, but which did not exist for Cassian. If the most perfect prayer is prayer beyond all words, all forms, all "objects," then what happens to the Humanity of Christ the "One Mediator" between the Christian and the Father? No one can come to the Father but by Him.

The "Problem": the problem, which did not yet exist for Cassian, arose in later times when there was {a} question of *choosing between* a prayer without words, forms, etc., and a prayer that involved imagining the Sacred Humanity of Christ present, discursive acts, and so on. For Cassian this question of a choice was not relevant. He is not proposing *the prayer of fire as a method*. It must be clearly understood that the different modes and states of prayer proposed by Cassian are *not alternative methods*, which one may select according to taste, or under guidance of a director. They are rather appropriate ways of prayer for different stages of the spiritual life. They arise spontaneously according to need and to our condition, prompted by grace.

As for the *oratio ignita*, in the act of pure prayer which lifts one beyond the realm of forms and concepts, this is not an object of choice either. It is a work of God done in the soul without our own initiative. Hence for Cassian there is absolutely no question *of a conscious initiative* by which one might *reject the thought of the humanity of Christ* as though this were somehow an impediment to "pure prayer." In other words, though later writers may have done this, it would be a pure anachronism to imagine Cassian proposing "prayer without forms" as something one "chooses" as an appropriate method and which involves "turning away from all thought or image of the humanity of Christ."

296. John 16:5-14, in which Jesus tells the disciples he is going to the Father, but will send the Spirit to teach the disciples the truth—the pertinence of this passage is evidently that it is a reminder that it is to the Glorified Christ, human and divine, that prayer is directed.

It must be remembered that Cassian wrote against the Nestorians.[297] There is an implicit Nestorianism in this concept of the possible separation of the divine and human natures in Christ as *if they were two subsisting entities* (i.e. in effect two Persons). Nothing could be farther from the mentality of Cassian. He always fixes his attention on the *One Person of Christ, the Word Incarnate*. It never occurs to him to consider that Person as an obstacle, as a source of confusion, etc. On the contrary, the Person of the Lord is *ipse fons inviolabilis sanctitatis* (10.6; col. 827).[298]

1. The person of Christ in Pure Prayer (*Coll.* 10, c. 6):

(a) It is Christ Himself who leads us to pure prayer. *In seeking perfect purity of heart, without images and forms, we are following the example He has given us—Nos instruens suae secessionis exemplo, ut si interpellare nos quoque* [i.e., as He did] *voluerimus Deum* puro et integro cordis affectu, ab omni inquietudine et confusione turbarum similiter secedamus. . . .[299] Indeed, those who ascend to pure prayer are ascending *with Him* the mount of the transfiguration. *CUM ILLO SECEDUNT in excelso solitudinis monte.*[300] *Cf.* St. Ambrose—*Omnes regiae domus declinans tumultus,* [*Moyses*] *in secretum Aethiopiae se contulit: ibidem a caeteris negotiis remotus, totum divinae cognitioni animum intendit, ut gloriam Dei videret facie ad faciem* (St. Ambrose, *In Hexaem.* 1.2; *PL* 14, col. 125).[301]

(b) It is Christ Whom we see on the mountain: *QUI MERENTUR EUM MUNDIS OBTUTIBUS INTUERI* (col. 827).[302]

297. *De Incarnatione Christi, Contra Nestorium* (*PL* 50, cols. 9-272).

298. "himself the fountain of inviolable holiness."

299. Col. 827BC: "Instructing us by the example of his own withdrawal, so that if we also wish to address God with pure and complete commitment of the heart, we might likewise withdraw from all disturbance and confusion of crowds."

300. Col. 827A: "They withdraw with him to the high mount of solitude."

301. "Shunning all the commotions of the royal palace, [Moses] betook himself into the wilds of Ethiopia; removed once again from other concerns, he focused his whole soul on knowing God, so that he might see the glory of God face to face."

302. The text reads ". . . *mundis animae* . . .": "who merit to look upon him with the pure gaze [of their mind]."

(c) Christ Himself of course had this pure prayer without any need of purification. *Hence to pray without images and forms is to pray as He did*. It is, in fact, a most important aspect of our likeness to God in sonship, in union with Him (827). He did not need solitude to avoid distractions, but sought it as {an} example for us.

(d) It is He Himself *who purifies hearts* of images and forms, as well as of vices. *Qui universa polluta emundat atque sanctificat* (827).[303]

2. With this as our context, let us see what Cassian then says about the "humanity of Christ" in pure prayer.

(a) He begins the chapter with a purely Platonic principle: *Secundum mensuram puritatis suae* {. . .} *unaquaeque mens in oratione sua vel erigitur vel formatur* (826).[304] The more pure the contemplative soul, the more it recedes from the contemplation of earthly things.

(b) But the "*humilis vel carneus Jesus*"[305] is of this earth. Indeed, those living in the *bios praktikos*[306] contemplate Jesus. He does not in this passage declare that they contemplate only the humanity of Jesus, or that it is the *humilis Jesus* and the *carneus Jesus*. *He just says that they see Him, but less clearly than contemplatives*. The inference *may be* that they are looking at *Jesum secundum carnem*[307] (II Cor. 5:{16} which he quotes above[308]). But quite probably this is an anachronistic interpretation. It seems certain that for Cassian, *all Christians* must now no longer know *Jesum secundum carnem*, since this is the obvious meaning of St. Paul. Cassian

303. "Who cleanses and sanctifies all that is defiled."

304. The text reads ". . . *mensuram namque* . . ." and includes another clause between "*suae*" and "*unaquaeque*": "According to the degree of its purity, each soul is built up and formed in its prayer."

305. The text reads: "*Jesum vel humilem . . . vel carneum*": "the lowly and enfleshed Jesus."

306. "the active life."

307. "Jesus according to the flesh."

308. Actually Cassian is about to quote this text, and Merton will cite the passage just below (blank space left for verse number in the typescript).

says: *NON ENIM POTERUNT JESUM INTUERI VENIENTEM IN REGNO SUO, QUI ADHUC SUB ILLA QUODAMMODO JUDAICA INFIRMITATE DETENTI, NON QUEUNT DICERE CUM APOSTOLO ET SI COGNOVIMUS SECUNDUM CARNEM CHRISTUM, sed jam nunc non novimus* etc. (826).[309]

(c) But he does say that those who ascend above the works of this life contemplate the divinity of Christ. *ILLI SOLI PURISSIMIS OCULIS DIVINITATEM IPSIUS SPECULANTUR . . . qui cum illo secedunt in excelso solitudinis monte.*[310] However, what does this mean? It means actually the humanity of Christ in glory, or rather the Person of Christ, in His glorified humanity as a manifestation of the divinity; it is the *GLORIAM VULTUS EJUS AC CLARITATIS IMAGINEM*,[311] and this is revealed by Christ Himself to those of pure heart, who no longer contemplate any form or image: *revelat his qui eum merentur mundis animae obtutibus intueri* (827).[312] Hence this opens the way to the Greek and Russian idea of the "Light of Thabor" or the light of contemplation coming from the glorified Savior.

PACHOMIAN CENOBITISM[313]

In discussing this very important topic, we have to take account of recent discoveries. However at the same time we must remember our purpose in these conferences: to discover the influences on pre-Benedictine monachism, especially in France at the time of Cassian. Hence we will be concerned with St. Pachomius primarily in connection with the forces that contributed to the

309. The text reads ". . . *nunc jam* . . .": "For they are not able to see Jesus entering into his kingdom who are still held back by a sort of Jewish weakness and are unable to say with the Apostle, if we once knew Jesus according to the flesh, we know him thus no longer . . ."

310. The ellipsis properly comes after "*qui*": "Only those who withdraw with him to the high mount of solitude see his divinity with most pure eyes."

311. Col. 827A (which reads ". . . *claritatis ejus revelat imaginem*"): "[reveals] the glory of his face and the image of his brightness."

312. The text reads ". . . *revelat imaginem* . . . *merentur eum* . . .": "reveals [the image of his brightness] to those who merit to look upon him with the pure gaze of their mind."

313. Merton had previously discussed the Pachomian *Rule* in *Cassian and the Fathers*, 39–45.

formation of Benedictine monachism. But first, a summary of the modern work on Pachomian cenobitism.

Coptic Texts.

Primitive Western monachism knew Pachomian cenobitism only through the *Vita Pachomii* and the *Rule*, along with fragments about the Pachomian school. The *Vita* is however a late compilation full of legendary material. Modern scholarship has made important texts available, especially in Lefort, *Corpus Pakhomianum* (Louvain, in the *Corpus Scriptorum Christianorum Orientalium*).[314] Here we have the following in Coptic texts and French translations: *Pachomius*: *Catechesis concerning a Bitter Monk* (the only complete one); *Catechesis on the Six Days of Easter*; *Excerpts*; *Rules*; *Theodore*: Three *Catecheses* and some *Excerpts*—Theodore was Pachomius' favorite disciple; *Orsiesius*: *Letters*; *Catechesis*; *Homily on Friendship*; *Excerpts* and *Rules*—Orsiesius was head of the congregation for 50 years; *Sarour*: *Prophecy of the Decline of Monasticism at Pebow*. For *Schenouti*,[315] not included in this volume of Lefort, we must consult another authoritative source, which also gives material on Pachomius: Ladeuze, *Étude sur le cénobitisme Pachomien*[316]—photostatic reprint of an earlier dissertation (1898; photostat, 1961).

It is agreed that these texts are representative of a rich monastic literature, much of which has been lost. Unfortunately the

314. *Oeuvres de S. Pachôme et de ses disciples*, éditées par L.-Th. Lefort, *CSCO* 159–160; *Scriptores Coptici*, t. 23–24 (Louvain: L. Durbecq, 1956); vol. 159 [t. 23] has the original Coptic, vol. 160 [t. 24] the French translation. English translations of all this material (except for Sarour) are now available in *Pachomian Koinonia*, vol. 2: *Pachomian Chronicles and Rules*, CS 46 (Kalamazoo, MI: Cistercian Publications, 1981) and *Pachomian Koinonia*, vol. 3: *Instructions, Letters, and Other Writings of Saint Pachomius and His Disciples*, CS 47 (Kalamazoo, MI: Cistercian Publications, 1982), both volumes assembled and translated by Armand Veilleux, ocso.

315. Merton will later use the form Shenoute, the name in Sahidic, the Coptic dialect the abbot himself used; Schenouti (or Schenoudi) is the form in Bohairic, in which the *Life of Shenoute* survives; see David N. Bell, ed. and trans., Besa, *The Life of Shenoute*, CS 73 (Kalamazoo, MI: Cistercian Publications, 1983), 27, n. 35.

316. Paulin Ladeuze, *Étude sur le Cénobitisme Pakhomien pendant le IVe Siècle et la Première Moitié du Ve* (Louvain: J. Van Linthout; Paris: A. Fontemoing, 1898; rpt. Frankfurt am Main: Minerva, 1961).

texts are only fragments, a small part of what once existed. Yet this literature which we now have proves the great importance of St. Pachomius, his originality and his genius. The *Latin* Pachomian texts have been edited by Dom A. Boon, OSB.[317] His part in the history and formation of monasticism has hitherto been underestimated. He is the great *organizer* and *systematizer* of monasticism. He founded not only the cenobium of Tabenna, strictly organized and disciplined, but a group of eight large cenobia, analogous to a monastic order, with his own headquarters at Pebow, or Pbow. His sister ran a community of nuns. He was a great leader of men and teacher. This is seen especially in his *Catecheses*, which are among the greatest documents in the monastic tradition. There is at present a kind of vogue of Pachomian monachism, in some monastic circles, as a kind of reaction against the long predominance of Evagrian trends. There is a feeling that the rediscovery of Pachomius represents a recovery of something original, primitive and "pure" which had been "corrupted" by Greek influences, Platonism, etc. Furthermore, Pachomius is invoked by those who wish to emphasize the thesis of the absolute superiority of cenobitism. But this is an error of perspective, for Pachomius is not an absolute cenobite, is not *against* hermits. He envisages *both* eremitical and cenobitic life, according to each one's grace. The Evagrian-Cassian trend (Antonian) tends to emphasize the superiority of the hermit life, and this has prevailed in Oriental monachism, at least as an ideal. The reaction against this has led to a great admiration of Pachomius, and the Pachomian ideal is substituted for the Antonian. It is for us to know the facts about this, and to evaluate them soberly, without getting carried away in partisan disputes which inevitably warp the perspective. One of the most favorable studies on Pachomius is by a Jesuit, H. Bacht, in *Théologie de la Vie Monastique*[318] (p. 39

317. *Pachomiana Latina: Règle et Épitres de S. Pachôme, Épitre de S. Théodore et"Liber" de S. Orsiesius—Texte Latin de S. Jérôme*, ed. Amand Boon (Louvain: Bureaux de la Revue, 1932).

318. Heinrich Bacht, SJ, "Pakhome et ses Disciples," *Théologie de la Vie Monastique: Études sur la Tradition Patristique* (Paris: Aubier, 1961), 39–71.

ff.; see also *RAM* 1950, p. 308 ff.[319]). We will base our general estimate of Pachomius on this study, plus texts from Lefort.

Pachomius as a Spiritual Master.

1. The first thing that must be admitted is that in St. Pachomius we have a great spiritual master, the head of an important school and movement, whose true doctrine has hitherto not been fully known or appreciated. He was considered the great master of Upper Egypt, so that in Coptic texts when the word *Apa* (Abba) is used alone without a name, it always refers to Pachomius.[320] The real value of Pachomius and his doctrine is only just being discovered.

2. It is also very important to counterbalance the exclusively Evagrian view of the Desert Fathers, by evidence from Pachomian texts. The Pachomian school is more truly Coptic, less Greek, more Biblical also. The atmosphere is quite different.

3. It is a pre-Evagrian, anti-Origenist form of monasticism. It is the monasticism of the ordinary Egyptians, not of the Greek intellectuals.

4. Bacht says of it that its Biblical quality is very striking, and makes it *more actual*, more applicable to monks of our times.[321] (There is no question that many feel this to be true, but we by no means have to accept it as an article of faith. Pachomius must be taken with discreet reserve. The texts show that not all was ideal in the Thebaid, and, compared with the *Apothegmata*, one can question whether the actual doctrine and practice of Tabenna was superior to those which were supposed, according to these texts, to have prevailed at Nitria and Scete.) Note that in *RAM*, 1950, pp. 314 etc. Bacht speaks of the "striking actuality" of the *Rule* of Pachomius and then refers to some conventional and even *out-of-date* observances in modern rules, which have come from

319. Heinrich Bacht, sj, "L'Importance d'Idéal Monastique de S. Pacôme," *Revue d'Ascétique et de Mystique*, 26 (1950), 308–26.

320. Bacht, "L'Importance," 308.

321. Bacht, "Pakhome," 40, 42–47.

Pachomius[322]—along with the normal regulations on silence, poverty, communal relations. The fact that these are *familiar* does not make Pachomius an example of "frappante actualité." However, Bacht praises Pachomius as "free from the stifling influence of Evagrius" and from "one-sided hellenism" (p. 41). This is worth noting, but again, these value judgements are necessarily to some extent subjective. They do not have to be taken as the last word on Egyptian monachism. We must not exaggerate the opposition between Evagrian and Pachomian spirituality—Evagrian texts in primitive times actually transmitted excerpts from Pachomian catecheses to the West (see Lefort, Part II, p. 1).[323]

Biblical Spirituality: There was great emphasis on learning long passages of Scripture by heart, and on the meditative recitation of Scripture. This is not, however, peculiar to Pachomian monachism. We see it everywhere in Egypt. The monastic precepts are, as far as possible, drawn from Scripture and backed up by Scripture. It can be said that the Pachomian texts are generally more Biblical than the *Apothegmata* which are rather records of charismatic experience, in which the Fathers themselves are at least implicitly regarded as mouthpieces of the Holy Spirit. The monastic life goes back to Scripture as the basic Rule: {it} is built on the *regula scripturarum*. (Follow this theme in the *Rule* of St. Benedict,[324] and above all in St. Basil.[325]) Note the importance

322. For example, the exterior posture of the monk; modesty of the eyes, especially at table; silence during work; weekly service in the church, the refectory, the kitchen; no entry into another's cell without permission; weekly instruction; penance in the refectory; chapter of faults; keeping the head covered at table; rank determined not by age but by length of profession.

323. Lefort notes that an apophthegm from Pachomius' *Catechesis on a Bitter Monk* is found in almost identical form in Evagrius' *Mirror of the Monk* and that Evagrius refers to "Lives of the Tabennesiots" in the *De Oratione* (*PL* 79, col. 1192).

324. See the final chapter (73) of the *Rule*: "For what page or what utterance of the divinely-inspired books of the Old and the New Testament is not a most unerring rule [*rectissima norma*] of human life?" (McCann, 161).

325. See Jean Gribomont, OSB, "Saint Basile," *Théologie de la Vie Monastique*, 104: ". . . la pensée de Basile, pour qui seule l'Écriture faisait loi" (". . . the thought of Basil, for whom Scripture alone was law").

of {the} *Sapiential Books*, especially Proverbs, in the *Catecheses* of St. Pachomius—also a preference for *Daniel*.[326] Scripture and the examples of the Old Testament saints are regarded as the most effective weapons in the combat against the devil. This emphasis is not absent from the monachism of Nitria and Scete. However the Pachomian texts have a great depth, unction and power in them—truly Biblical. {Note this} example from {the} opening of Pachomius' first *Catechesis*:

> My son, listen, be wise, accept the true doctrine, *for there are two ways*; be capable of obeying God like Abraham who, having abandoned his native land, went into exile and with Isaac dwelt in tents in the promised land as though in a strange land. He obeyed and humbled himself and took possession of the heritage. He was also tried in regard to Isaac; he was courageous in his trial and offered Isaac in sacrifice to God; for this God called him His friend. Take also an example from Isaac's simplicity; when he heard his father he was submissive to the point of total sacrifice, like a meek lamb. Take also an example from the humility of Jacob, his submission and his constancy; for thus he became a light seeing the Father of the universe and was called Israel. Take also an example from the wisdom of Joseph and his submission. Battle in chastity and in servitude, until you reign. My son, imitate the virtues of the saints, practice their virtues; rouse thyself, be not negligent . . . "rise up, do not sleep among the dead, Christ will enlighten thee" (Ephesians 5:14), grace will open out within thee like a flower. All graces are discovered by patience; it is by patience that the saints obtained what was promised them; the glory of the saints is patience.[327]

There is a strong belief that the words of Scripture are addressed directly and personally to each monk, who is now *living in the time of the fulfillment of the word of God*.

326. Lefort provides a Scriptural Index: vol. 159, 105–11; vol. 160, 109–15.
327. Lefort, vol. 160, 1–2 (Merton's translation from the French).

Monastic Tradition: There is a very strong, coordinated, well-organized sense of monastic tradition. This is not only the free-wheeling and spontaneous commitment to the spirit and the "way" of various Fathers (such as we find in the *Apothegmata*, with a great deal of latitude allowed for choice). But it is much more formal and already quasi-juridical. The *monastic institution* is already the embodiment of tradition handed down from the Founder: all must observe his precepts. In order to make sure that the precepts of the Master are preserved and observed in their purity, there is an institutional framework and a very active organizational structure, including an *annual chapter at Easter*. The disciples of St. Pachomius, meeting in chapter, seek above all to "recall the aims of our Father Pachomius."[328] They declare: "Let us love the way of life of our Father Pachomius in order to share in the glory which God has revealed to him in the other world . . ." (Theodore).[329] "Let us consider the observances of our Father set up as a ladder to the Kingdom of Heaven . . ." (Orsiesius).[330] In St. Jerome's translation of the *Doctrina Orsiesii* (*PL* 103) we have (c. 12): "*State in arrepto semel proposito, et* implete opus Dei, *ut Pater, qui primus instituit coenobia gaudens pro nobis loquatur ad Dominum: sicut tradidi eis, sic vivunt*" (col. 457).[331] This is justified as apostolic by a quote—1 Cor. 11:1-2. See also chapter 21: "*Vigilemus attentius, et sciamus quod magnam nobis Deus praestiterit gratiam per Patrem nostrum Pachomium, ut renuntiaremus saeculo; et omnem sollicitudinem mundi, et curas rerum saecularium pro nihilo poneremus*" (col. 461);[332] and chapter 22: "*Nolite obsecro*

328. Theodore, *Letter* 1:5 (Boon, 106).

329. Theodore, *Instruction* 2, c. 3 (Lefort, vol. 160, 39).

330. *Doctrina Orsiesii*, c. 22 (*PL* 103, col. 461C).

331. "Stand firm once and for all in your commitment and fulfill the work of God, so that our Father who first began the community might joyfully say of us to the Lord: as I have handed on to them, so they live."

332. "Let us be more vigilant and attentive, and know that God has bestowed on us great grace through our Father Pachomius, that we might renounce the world and regard all worldly care and the concerns of secular matters as nothing."

vos oblivisci semel arrepti propositi et traditiones Patris nostri scalas putemus ad coelorum regna tendentes" (col. 461).[333]

Here there is a quite different concept of monasticism from what we have seen in Anthony, Evagrius, Cassian etc. There is the *basic idea of an authoritative institution* and the emphasis on the primacy of {the} *Rule*, and a common *opus Dei*—the fulfillment of the Founder's will and precepts. In the Antonian-Evagrian framework, the idea is that the monk follows the Holy Spirit, seeks the best way to purify his heart, according to the guidance of his own spiritual Father, and then arrives at contemplative union with God. In the Pachomian tradition, the founder and first fathers have been chosen instruments to point out the way to God. The followers, though not in direct contact with them, follow their will and their tradition in the *Rule and observances* left by them. The emphasis is not on contemplative purity of heart but on *spiritual combat*, eschatological warfare. The Pachomian idea is closer to Qumran than to the Evagrian texts. The central concept is *obedience*. Purity of heart in the Pachomian context means freedom from sin rather than the more absolute and contemplative purity of heart in the Evagrian tradition—which implies *apatheia*, freedom from passion and liberation from distracting thoughts. The outlook is *much more pessimistic*. The weakness and proneness to evil of each man and each monk is always in the center of attention. To preserve the monk from sin, absolute obedience is necessary, reinforced by many punishments. It is considered dangerous to allow the monk to delude himself with notions of lofty contemplation. What matters is for him to *submit* and take his place obediently in the organization without which he cannot manage his life properly. One of the deepest ideas of this spirituality is its *pessimism about the individual* and *relative optimism about the organization, the institution*. This is in contrast to the basic optimism of Antonian-Evagrian-Origenist

333. "Do not, I beseech you, forget the resolution you have made, and let us be mindful of the traditions of our Father, a ladder aimed at the kingdom of heaven" (cf. Merton's own translation of the latter part of this sentence immediately above).

spirituality and its belief in the perfectibility of the individual, its trust in the inherent value of the *personal life of the spirit*.

However, within the framework of the communal life there is room for great optimism because that life is a *life of love*. It is *love*, not just regularity and observance, that makes the cenobite. See *Doctrina Orsiesii*, chapter 23: "If we love one another we show we are *truly servants* of Our Lord Jesus Christ, and *sons* of Pachomius and *disciples* of the common life" (col. 462).

Basic Principles of Pachomian Spirituality:

A. God. The God whom they serve is the stern lawgiver of Sinai.

1. He does not invite to {a} union of love or to contemplation. He demands obedience and absolute submission to His representatives, and He punishes severely the slightest infractions of {the} Rule. However, this is not purely negative.

2. He is also the God who chose and blessed the Patriarchs, the God of Moses, Who *blesses and rewards* those who keep His law. When He sends trials, hardship, poverty and insult He is to be blessed for giving us a share in the sufferings of His Beloved Son. The Holy Spirit especially keeps the monk alert and vigilant to avoid neglect in his monastic life of asceticism. Hence the aim is a life *blessed by God* as was the life of the Patriarchs and of *Apa* Pachomius (see Orsiesius, in Lefort, II, pp. 97–98),[334] a life of *loving and happy service* in the fear of the Lord.

3. The fear of God is completed by zeal for His glory, love of His supreme Holiness: but a love never without awe. We must always humble ourselves before Him and strive with earnest zeal to keep His Law. However, there is always the sense that God is profoundly displeased with men, including monks. Pachomian texts are full of *preoccupation with decadence*. Already in the next

334. *Horsiesii Regulationes*, 54; see Armand Veilleux' argument that these are probably not by Horsiesios but by a later superior, in *Pachomian Koinonia*, 2:11-12.

generation after the founders, it is declared that everything is going to the dogs. All is bad, and all is going from bad to worse. Pachomius himself had already threatened {that} decadence was on the way. At the same time there are severe threats of punishments for those who relax the monastic life, diminish the austerity, and induce relaxation.

{B.} *The Monastic Life is essentially an eschatological combat.* The monk, living in the last days (a fact proved by general decadence everywhere) is charged with putting up a last stern fight for the glory of God against His adversary. This combat begins within the monk himself. For instance, {see} Pachomius, *Catechesis 1* (Lefort, Part II, p. {25-26}[335]):

> Now then, my brother, let us battle with our own selves. You know that darkness arises up on various sides. The Churches are full of men who bicker and who are stirred up; monastic communities have become ambitious; pride reigns as master; there is no longer any one left who shows any concern for his brother; on the contrary, "each one oppresses his neighbor" (Mich. 7:2). We are submerged in suffering. There is no longer any prophet or any gnostic; no one gives convincing arguments to his brother because hardness of heart abounds while those who really understand remain silent because of the evil times; each is his own master. They contemn what they should not contemn.
>
> As for you, watch yourself in every trial: do the work of a preacher, be constant in facing trial, *fight until the very end the combat of monasticism*: fight humbly, with meekness and trembling at the words which you shall hear; keep your virginity; avoid indiscretion and those abominable words uttered out of due season; remain within the writings of the saints and firm in your faith in Christ Jesus our Lord . . . etc.

335. Typescript reads: "p. 20".

These are the final words of the *Catechesis* n. 1 "against the bitter monk." (N.B., the idea of combat [*militia, militare*, etc.] in St. Benedict![336])

{C.} *Idea of Man, and of Salvation*: {There is} great emphasis on humility and obedience, the royal way, whereas *neglect* is the source of all evils, because *it implies acceptance of an intolerable state which is an insult to God, the state of sin*, in which the divine image is defiled and man is the prisoner of the devil. One cannot be careless in the presence of such a great evil. Eve, "deceived by the devil, attacked the divine dignity and lost her human dignity."[337] Adam, a rebel, was thrust out of paradise like an impure sinner thrust out of the Church. The monastic life of asceticism and penance is essentially a "new creation," a restoration of God's work which was marred by the sin of Adam and by the actual sins of all men since then. Hence {there is} zeal for restoration of God's image by {the} ascesis of common life. See the *Catechesis* 2 of St. Pachomius "on the six days of the pasch." This is a catechesis on the importance of fasting and penance during Holy Week:

> Let us struggle, my beloved, during these six days of the pasch, for they are granted to us each year in order that we may save our souls, and that in them we may do the work of God [not liturgy, ascetic restoration]. Indeed, it was in six days, beginning with the creation of heaven and earth, that God worked upon the cosmos until He finished it and on the seventh day He rested from His work.
>
> These days have been created by God for us in order that each of us may, according to his profession, work at the work of God. Silence, manual work, abundant prayers, custody of the tongue, purity of body and of heart, each according to his occupations. And then let us rest on the seventh day

336. See the Prologue: "*Christo vero Regi militaturus*" ("to fight for the true King, Christ"); "*sanctae praeceptorum obedientiae militanda*" ("to fight under the holy obedience of his commands"); c. 1: "*militans sub regula vel abbate*" ("serving under a rule and an abbot"); c. 2: "*sub uno Domino aequalem servitutis militiam*" ("to serve alike in the army of the same Lord"); c. 61: "*uni Regi militatur*" ("fight for the same King") (McCann, 6/7, 10/11, 14/15, 18/19, 138/139).

337. *Catechesis* 1, c. 24 (Lefort, vol. 160, 9).

> and celebrate the Sunday of the holy Resurrection, taking to heart the celebration of the holy *synaxes*, and sending up our homage to the Father of the Universe who has had pity on us. He has sent the Good Shepherd of the scattered sheep in order to bring us back into His flock. . . .
>
> Let each of us be watchful and constant in order that we may fulfill what was written in the Acts of the Apostles: "some on planks and others on pieces of the ship: and thus all got to the shore" (Acts 27:44).[338]

(See below {the} basic idea that the world is already judged.[339]) Note that this catechesis is addressed to everybody, including men in the world, the rich, emperors, etc. It is a common work of salvation—but each has to make his own efforts. *Basically the monk, and every Christian, is confronted with a radical choice between two ways.*

At the beginning of the *Catechesis* 1, he points out the right way, that of the Patriarchs who obeyed God, humbled themselves and devoted their hearts purely and entirely to the fulfillment of His will (see above[340]). He never explicitly contrasts the second way with the first in the beginning of the *Catechesis*, but the "way of sinners" is frequently described elsewhere. *There is a quite refined psychology of vice and passion* in the *Catecheses* of Pachomius. He does not, as Cassian does, or Evagrius, go into an extended and professional treatment of the "eight principal vices." However he does show how the chief vices are interconnected:

> My son, I beg you to watch and stand on your guard against the enemies that lie in wait to kill you. The spirit of *cowardice* and of *suspiciousness* walk together. The spirit of lying and of questionable dealings walk together. The spirit of avarice and of commercialism walk together with dishonesty, perjury and jealousy. The spirit of vanity and gluttony go together. The spirit of fornication and impurity go together. The spirit of hostility and of sadness go together. [Cassian

338. *Catechesis* 2, cc. 1–2 (Lefort, vol. 160, 26–27).

339. See page 89.

340. See page 77.

> observed this.[341]] Woe to the poor soul in whom these install themselves and gain control. They keep that soul far from God, for it is in their power. The soul struggles and strives this way and that, without results, until at last it falls into the abyss of hell (Lefort, II, p. 2{-3}).[342]

(References to Lefort can only be understood if we remember that in one bound volume we have the Coptic texts, followed by the French texts. The section of the French texts, where the pagination begins anew, is here referred to as Lefort II.[343])

Like many ascetic writers, Pachomius speaks of now one vice, now another as the "root of all the others." PRIDE is certainly a case in point—also NEGLIGENCE. In effect, we see how they are connected in his mind. The proud man is neglectful because he is satisfied with himself and seeks only the fulfillment of his own will. He is not zealous for restoration of the divine image by humility. He is content with the defaced image. "Guard against negligence, for it is the mother of all the vices. My son, fly from concupiscence, for it blinds the spirit [clouds the spirit] and prevents it from discovering the secret of God; it makes you a stranger to the language of the Spirit; it makes you unable to carry the Cross of Christ; it prevents you from giving your attention to the praises of God. . . . Guard against pride for it is the beginning of every evil; *the beginning of pride is turning aside from God and after that comes hardening of the heart . . .*" (all this is on the same page—Lefort, II, 7).[344] Another magnificent passage sounds like the Good Friday *improperia,* and shows the profoundly Christian depths of Pachomian asceticism. Christ addresses the monk as follows:

341. See *Instituta* 9, c. 4 (*PL* 49, col. 355AB).

342. *Catechesis* 1, c. 10.

343. This is not universally the case: vols. 159 and 160 (which Merton refers to as I and II respectively) are separate volumes, separately bound, in the edition consulted by the editor.

344. *Catechesis* 1, c. 18–20.

> "Have I ever left you lacking anything in my passage through the world? Did I not give you my Body and my Blood as food of your life? Have I not tasted death for your sake, in order to save you? Have I not made known to you the heavenly mystery in order that I might make you my brother and my friend? Have I not given you the power to tread under foot serpents and scorpions and all the power of the enemy? Have I not given you countless remedies of life with which you may be saved? My miracles, my prodigies, my marvels, in these I clad myself as if in armor, and I gave them all to you for your equipment that you might strike down Goliath, that is to say the devil. And now what do you lack, that you have become a stranger to me? Your negligence alone has cast you down into the abyss of hell" (Lefort, II, p. {18}[345]).

We must note the context of this. It is connected with an exhortation to *mutual pardon* which is the heart of Pachomius' cenobitic ascesis. The negligent monk is like Samson, blinded and bound by his enemies, forced to turn the mill wheel as their slave (Lefort, II, p. 11).[346]

To what extent can monks fall? For documentation on sinfulness in the cenobium, we might consider the *Homily of Orsiesius on Particular Friendship* (Lefort, II, p. 75).[347] It is a bitter lamentation, very graphic and moving, no doubt based on an actual problem. How widespread {was it}? To what extent was it a deep problem? The problem of chastity in the Egyptian cenobia has been a much debated question. Ladeuze[348] takes it up and censures the hostile generalizations made by a nineteenth-century scholar, Amélineau,[349] who discovered (and *highly exaggerated*) evidence of sodomy in the Pachomian monasteries and thereafter generalized and said that *all the monks* in Egypt were given to

345. *Catechesis* 1, c. 42 (typescript reads: "p. 17").

346. *Catechesis* 1, c. 26.

347. *Instruction* 7 (Lefort, vol. 160, 75–80).

348. Ladeuze, 336–41.

349. E. C. Amélineau, *Histoire de S. Pakhôme et de ses Communautés. Annales de Musée Guimet*, 17 (Paris: ADMG, 1889), 108 f.

this vice, whereas there is no serious evidence of widespread unchastity at Nitria or Scete. On the contrary everything points to the fact that the monks there were very strict and chaste.

The structure of Orsiesius' homily is this: against a background of lamentation and apocalyptic warning about the danger of sin, as a *possibility* at least, Orsiesius offers advice to "a brother," and the concrete advice given, the chief concern, is to avoid possible danger. The homily is not addressed to people in sin, but to people who may not realize a *danger* of sin. Conclusion: the *possibility* of homosexual offences is admitted, and this is based on the fact of "seduction" which has been known to occur. But in actual fact what is being attacked is the "unhealthy friendship," the attachment seen rather in its beginnings than in a fully developed perverse state. "O sick friendship, detested by God and by His angels! O perverse laughter that savors of gall. Cursed be thou, o sick friendship of which I speak, and which will be pursued by the divine wrath. O sick friendship whose smile has ruined superiors, dignitaries, priests, superiors both of men and of women . . ." (Lefort, II, 75{-76}).[350] It is to be noted that *temptations* to impurity are described, sometimes in much detail, in the documents. Actual sins are acknowledged to have occurred, but the indication is that sin itself is relatively rare. What is a problem is the *atmosphere* of "sick friendship." Most of the evidence concerns Pachomius discovering *evil thoughts* and unmasking *temptations*. Orsiesius describes the "sick friendship" which is marked especially by surreptitious exchanges of gifts and messages, by private "nests" in which food and other objects are surreptitiously accumulated and enjoyed by the clique. There are evidences of unhealthy emotional attachment. There is an unhealthy use of rings and other ornaments, etc. However, contrasted with sick friendship there is a healthy friendship which is admitted and praised. It is the friendship of the true monks, who are austere, fervent in the practice of monastic regularity, humble and wise, concerned with peace and purity. These also have the following character-

350. *Instruction* 7, c. 4.

istics: "They accuse no one, they rejoice at no man's fall, they do nothing to make a monk feel less friendly towards his companions, they do not try to avoid trials, but they persevere in the work that is pleasing to God" (Lefort, II, 78).[351] Note: the enemies of Pachomius attacked him before a local council and tried to destroy his work. *No mention was made* of unnatural vice. They certainly would have used this as a weapon if there had been a general scandal. In effect what we mostly retain from this situation is a group of rules that guarantee a certain austerity in fraternal relations and reduce sensual contacts to zero. *Nullus lavare poterit alium, aut ungere, nisi ei fuerit imperatum. Nemo alteri loquatur in tenebris. Nullus in psiathio cum altero dormiat. Manum alterius nemo teneat, sed sive steterit, sive ambulaverit, uno cubito distet ab altero. Spinam de pede alterius, excepto domus praeposito et secundo et alio cui jussum fuerit, nemo audebit evellere. Et omnino absque jussione maioris in alteram cellam nullus audebit introire*" (from Jerome's translation of the *Rule*, quoted in Ladeuze, p. 283).[352]

{D.} *The Monk and the World*: To protect himself against every form of sin is the first duty of the monk. Even in the monastery he has to struggle against sin. What would he be in the world? Hence monastic *conversatio* is a matter of:

1) Completely leaving the world and all that is characteristic of the world, all evidences of the worldly spirit.

2) Generously struggling against all the vices and passions, even sinful thoughts, in the monastery. The chief means of this struggle are prayer, tears, obedience and humility, fasting and

351. *Instruction* 7, c. 11.

352. *Regula*, cc. 93–95, 112 (*PL* 23, cols. 78AB, 79BC): "No one may wash another, or anoint another with oil, unless he has been ordered to do so. Let no one speak to another in the dark. Let no one sleep with another on his pallet. Let no one hold another's hand, but whether standing or walking one should keep a distance of one cubit from another. Let no one dare to remove a thorn from the foot of another, with the exception of the head of the house, his assistant, and anyone who has been ordered to do so." (The text reads "*alterum poterit*" for "*poterit alium*" [as in Ladeuze] and includes "*sive sederit*" ["or sit"] after "*ambulaverit*"; Ladeuze does not indicate the lacuna before the last sentence.)

vigils, faith. But first of all detachment from the world is necessary. *The world is in league with the devil*, against those who, like the monk, seek to liberate themselves from sin and give themselves to God. The world is full of occasions of sin, some of them under the guise of good. When the monk falls into sin, he falls under servitude to the devil, becomes a slave of the devil: hence the danger of the world to the monk. If the monk believes the seductions of the world he becomes an enemy of God, according to the Pachomian tradition. {It is} very frank on this point.

Leaving the World: One of the essential elements of Pachomian monachism is the clear, visible separation between the "holy *koinonia*" and the outside world. All is within an enclosure wall (not the more or less informal and spontaneous community groupings such as those of Anthony, and at Nitria). The enclosure wall has *one gate* and all passing in and out are under the observation and control of the gatekeeper, specially chosen for his task.

> *Ostiarii cura sit, ut omnes advenientes intra januas recipiat; dans eis responsum honestum cum humilitate et reverentia, ac statim nuntians vel abbati, vel senioribus, quis venerit, et quid petierit. Nec ullus extraneorum patiatur injuriam; neque habeat cum aliquo de fratribus necessitatem ac facultatem loquendi, absque scientia abbatis vel seniorum praesentia. Si quid vero cuicunque de fratribus missum mandatumque fuerit, nihil ad ipsum perveniat priusquam abbati vel senioribus indicetur. Ante omnia ostiarius monasterii haec observabit, ne quemquam de fratribus foris januam exire permittat* (Pachomian *Regula Orientalis*, c. 26; *PL* 103, col. 481).[353]

The monks it is true may go out, not only to work in nearby fields, but even to do business in the cities or to visit their relatives. But

353. "Let the charge of the gatekeeper be to receive within the gates all who arrive, giving them an honest reply with humility and reverence, and immediately announcing to either the abbot or senior monks who has come and what he wants. Let no outsider endure scorn; let him have no need or opportunity for speaking with any of the brothers without the knowledge of the abbot or the presence of senior monks. If anything is sent to any of the brothers, it may not be delivered to him before it is approved by the abbot or senior monks. Before all else the

the principle is that there are no contacts with the world, coming or going, except under strict control and strictly limited. *Note*: when relatives visit the monastery and bring fruits and sweets, the monk may eat some, but he must take what is left *for the sick brethren in the infirmary*—this is a nice indication of the cenobitic spirit.[354] It was strictly forbidden to relate news of the world in the monastery (cf. *Rule* {of} St. Benedict).[355]

Taking off the secular garb is then a highly significant action: it means casting off servitude to the demons and rejection {of} domination by the world and its spirit. Putting on the monastic habit is putting on Christ. To take off the worldly habit is to die mystically to the world, to vanish from the world, and live again, hidden from the world and from the demons, in Christ. It therefore becomes supremely important to keep the spirit of the world out of the monastery. This means extreme caution in all one's dealings with the world (for these are inevitable)—{a} recognition of the world as a deliberately hostile milieu, *in which men will actively try to frustrate the monk's vocation*. Sinners, when they cannot subtly lead the monks into worldly ways, will actively persecute the monks.

{E.} *Judgement*: The chief remedy against all this is a profoundly eschatological outlook. *The world is already judged*, and the monk is seeking to escape from that judgement. The last end is a matter for each individual to decide. The judgement of the world and its condemnation are already accomplished, and only

---

gatekeeper of the monastery will observe this, that he may not allow any of the brothers to go outside the gate." (This *Rule* is "a patchwork of literal borrowings from the *Rule* of Pachomius, free citations from 2RP [*Second Rule of the Fathers*] and original material from the anonymous redactor" and is "dated to the last decades of the fifth century"; it was said by its seventeenth-century editor, Holstenius [Lukas Holste] to have been put together by the otherwise unknown deacon Vigilius [*PL* 103, cols. 477-78], but this attribution "does not have any historical basis" [*Early Monastic Rules*, 12].)

354. *Regula*, c. 52 (*PL* 23, col. 74AB).

355. See c. 67, on monks who are sent on journeys: "Nor let anyone presume to tell another what he has seen or heard outside the monastery, because this causes very great harm" (McCann, 155).

need to be promulgated in the sight of all men. But individuals can save themselves from this shipwreck. They must make their choice, and in order to facilitate this, they must remember the *shame and disgrace of sinners* as individuals, in the judgement. Angels with swords "will force the obstinate sinner to acknowledge his infamy" before all.[356]

This then is the atmosphere of monastic asceticism. Let us consider some texts. *Pachomius*: *Catechesis for the Bitter Monk*: "Do not easily get into the habit of complaining and insulting, but on the contrary bear every trial gladly. For if you only knew *the honor that is the result of bearing trials* you would not pray to be delivered from it. It is far better for you to pray and weep until you are saved, than to relax your efforts and be taken away captive. O man, what are you doing in Babylon? *You have grown old in a strange land*, because you have not submitted to *docimasia* and because your relationship with God is not right. Therefore, O my brother, do not relax your efforts" (Lefort, II, p. 6).[357] *Dokimasía* = proving or testing (of metals), examination. The *Dókimos* is the *probatus*, the proven man, who is proved *real* by testing. (Compare the *Similitudes* of St. Anselm, c. 95; *PL* 159, col. 662.[358]) Note this idea that the monk is an exile in Babylon, struggling for his liberty,

356. *Catechesis* 1, c. 38 (Lefort, vol. 160, 16).

357. *Catechesis* 1, c. 16.

358. This chapter is entitled "*Similitudo inter monachatum et ignem*" ("A comparison between monasticism and fire"): "Frequently a false coin seems genuine, but if it is put in the fire its actual nature is disclosed. Likewise, many times an ill-natured man seems to have good habits while in the world, but if he becomes a monk, and has been rebuked according to the rule for the faults that have become evident subsequently, right away he is proved to be other than what he appears to be. One who apparently was humble and patient is soon found to be proud and impatient. If he blames the rule for this, it is like the coin saying to the fire, 'You made me false.' For the fire does not make the coin false, but shows what it was already. In the same way the rule doesn't make a person ill-natured but reveals the ill nature already there. So he should blame himself rather than the rule, and change bad habits into good ones. For unless he is seen to be of good character, the good works he does exteriorly are of little worth."

is prominent in the *Doctrina Orsiesii*, who quotes Baruch 3 at greater length.[359] (READ Baruch 3:9-14.)[360]

Pachomius continues: "You must not be reduced to shame and filled with lamentation in the *Valley of Joshaphat*, where all the creatures of God will see you and reproach you: 'Each day we thought you were a sheep, and behold you are a wolf: go now into the abyss of hell, cast yourself into the heart of the earth.' O what shame! In this world you walked as one praised among the elect, and when you arrive in the Valley of Joshaphat you are found to be naked. Everyone contemplates your sins and your vileness laid open before God and men. Woe to you at such a moment! . . . What will you do when you hear the words: 'I must wipe out from the city of the Lord all those who practice iniquity'?" (Lefort, II, pp. 13, 14).[361] (Here—discuss Eadmer—*De Beatitudine*, c. 8[362] in contrast—read context.) It is better then to walk in this world as a nobody, and to be regarded as worthless, so that at the Judgement one may be covered with glory (see p. 14).[363]

Pachomius recommends strongly a spirit of interior discretion, humility and spiritual solitude—a kind of reticence, not confiding in other men, being very careful with even seemingly

359. *Doctrina Orsiesii*, 1 (*PL* 103, col. 453A).

360. "Hear, O Israel, the commandments of life: give ear, that thou mayst learn wisdom. How happeneth it, O Israel, that thou art in thy enemies' land? Thou art grown old in a strange country, thou art defiled with the dead: thou art counted with them that go down into hell. Thou hast forsaken the fountain of wisdom: For if thou hadst walked in the way of God, thou hadst surely dwelt in peace for ever. Learn where is wisdom, where is strength, where is understanding: that thou mayst know also where is length of days and life, where is the light of the eyes, and peace" (Douay-Rheims translation); this quotation (along with verse 15: "Who hath found out her place? And who hath gone in to her treasures?") opens the *Doctrina Orsiesii*.

361. *Catechesis* 1, c. 33.

362. The chapter, entitled "*De sapientia*" ("On wisdom"), focuses on the redeemed at the last judgement, who will not be abashed or downcast by the revelation before all of their sins, but will rejoice in this evidence of the mercy and love of God as shown in the work of salvation by Jesus Christ, which justifies them even before the angels (*PL* 109, cols. 593C-596A).

363. *Catechesis* 1, c. 34.

good friendships, keeping to oneself, and *"sitting under the shadow of God"* ({he} quotes Ps. 90:1).[364] *"Think about the Lord and about the heavenly Jerusalem. When the heavenly city comes to your mind, you are under a blessing and the glory of God will carry you away"* (Lefort, II, 14).[365] While one must keep to himself and mind his own business, he must guard against uncharitableness. It is especially important to be at peace with all the brethren. At the Judgement, the Lord will say to uncharitable and argumentative monks: "If you have hated your brother, you are a stranger to my Kingdom; if you have fallen out with your brother and have not forgiven him, your hands and feet will be tied behind your back and you will be thrown into the exterior darkness where there is wailing and gnashing of teeth. If you have struck your brother you will be turned over to pitiless angels, and they will whip you in torments of eternal fire" (Lefort, II, 17, 18).[366] "You have insulted the poor man, then you have insulted me. You have struck the unfortunate, then you are one of those who struck me when I was humiliated upon the Cross" (*id.*).[367] Note the strictly evangelical character of this doctrine, but also note that it is not peculiar to the Pachomian cenobites. We find it just as much in the teachings of the hermit monks. Note the importance of *solitary compunction in the struggle to learn mercifulness* and charity. "If you have had the thought, 'My brother does not deserve the praises he receives,' if in your mind you agree with this suggestion of the devil, if hostility grows . . . then take refuge in solitude with the awareness of God, *weep alone with Christ, and the spirit of Jesus will penetrate your understanding*. It will convince you of the fullness of the precept: for what need is there for you to fight alone like a beast as if this poison were in you?" (Lefort, II, p. 24).[368]

In short the charity of Pachomius is very real, but also very interior. In view of the temptations of certain Coptic types, ex-

364. *Catechesis* 1, c. 35 (Lefort, vol. 160, 14).
365. *Catechesis* 1, c. 35.
366. *Catechesis* 1, c. 41.
367. *Catechesis* 1, c. 41.
368. *Catechesis* 1, c. 58.

pressiveness is not encouraged, fraternal love tends to be silent, and to some extent negative. But still it is deeply real, based on a profound and humble esteem of all one's brothers (affection not encouraged), a respect for their rights, minding one's own business, pardoning all, being the servant of all and at peace with all. A beautiful passage from Pachomius gives us once again the general atmosphere of Pachomian asceticism: "Now my Son, clothe yourself in humility, take the Christ and His Good Father for Counsellors. Be the friend of a man of God having the law of God in his heart. Be like a poor man, carrying the Cross and loving tears, with head veiled. May your dwelling be to you a tomb, where you await the time for God to raise you up and place a diadem of victory upon your head" (Lefort, II, 24).[369]

The Monk is a Perfect Christian then, according to the norms of the Gospel as Pachomius and his school understood them. The monastic community leads "an angelic life perfuming the whole *oikumene*" (Orsiesius).[370] He lives in the *koinonia*, the perfect Christian community, with others who seek God like himself, who give him good example and help him by fraternal correction and advice. The monks stimulate each other "*to love with all their heart the rule of the koinonia.*"[371] All work together to carry out the necessary tasks and to join in the common work of prayer and seeking holiness. All support the organizational framework, which is very strong and important. Yet at the same time there is no question that a *strong spirit of individualism* existed within the communities, and the very way in which Pachomius describes fraternal relations as well as the problems of the common life, suggests this. In point of fact there were constant rivalries, disputes and schisms in the Pachomian communities.

Non-Contemplative Character of Pachomian Monasticism. The Pachomian monastery may be "contemplative" in a broad, external sense such as we have today. That is to say, the monks live an enclosed life and do not engage in active pastoral works. But

369. *Catechesis* 1, c. 57.

370. *Instruction* 1, c. 2 (Lefort, vol. 160, 67).

371. Theodore, *Third Catechesis*, c. 30 (Lefort, vol. 160, 54).

the spirit of St. Pachomius is essentially ascetical (active) and non-contemplative (non-mystical). However, the contemplative ideal is understood and encouraged in the sense that *hermits are approved and the hermit life is permitted*. The Pachomian literature is not anti-contemplative or anti-eremitical. It is simply concentrated on the cenobitic life and does not give more than passing consideration to the other. However, Pachomius certainly has a preference for the cenobitic ascesis as more sure and more accessible to the majority. In his mind, cenobitic ascesis = obedience. Hermit ascesis tends toward extreme feats of corporal asceticism. (However remember discretion {is} recommended in the *Apothegmata* etc.[372])

{Note the} words attributed to St. Pachomius in a life of him: "The least of the brethren in the common life, who do not give themselves to the extraordinary practices of exaggerated asceticism, but who walk simply in obedience and docility in the purity of their body and following the established rules, may not seem to the anchorites to be living the perfect life. But they will be found perfect in the law of Christ by reason of their constancy." (See *RAM* 1950, p. 323.[373]) Pachomius seems to accept the ordinary Egyptian distinction: active life = cenobitic life, and contemplative life = hermit life. But he does not bother with the latter. The Patriarchs are models for the active life, the prophets for the solitary life (Lefort, II, p. 6).[374] He does not say much about one vocation being better than another; what matters is for *each one to live up to his own vocation* whatever it may be (Lefort, II, p. 17, 1. 24).[375]

Pachomian Ascesis. We have treated the Pachomian spirit in its general outline. Now it is important to concentrate on the

372. See *Cassian and the Fathers*, 76, 80, for discretion in the *Apothegmata*, and especially 222 for St. Anthony's teaching on discretion as the most important of the virtues (as related by Abba Moses in Cassian's second *Conference* [*PL* 49, cols. 525A-527B]).

373. Bacht, "L'Importance," quoting from the Boharic *Life of Pachomius*, ed. L.-Th. Lefort, *CSCO* 89 (Paris: Typographeo Reipublicae, 1925), 178 (c. 105).

374. *Catechesis* 1, c. 18.

375. *Catechesis* 1, c. 41.

cenobitic ideal of St. Pachomius, as well as his means of putting it into effect.

A. *The Theory of Cenobitism, and its Practice.* Cenobitism is an ideal with St. Pachomius: that is to say, he has a mystique of cenobitism, a spirituality of cenobitism, and he does not institute collective monastic life merely for pragmatic or economic reasons. There is more to it than organization. St. Jerome emphasizes this, when he says of Pachomius: *"fundavit conversationem cenobiorum a principio per mandatum Dei."*[376] That is to say the cenobitic *conversatio* (a much more accurate term than "ideal") is an expression of a divine mystery of salvation. (Comment on {the} word *conversatio.*[377]) And this phrase (*a principio*) gives to Pachomius the honor of being the true founder of cenobitism, so that the cenobitic *conversatio* is really his work, and his original contribution to the Church and to monasticism. To what extent he was influenced by Therapeuts,[378] etc. {is a question} still unsolved.

Pre-Pachomian "Community" Life. In Egyptian monasticism, St. Anthony had groups of disciples living with him. Nitria was a semi-eremitical community, in many respects (see above[379]). Differences:

a) "Community life" in Antonian monachism is always very loosely knit and informal. There is no organization, and the bond of union is the charismatic authority of the Abbas *only* (no Rule). The cells are close together, relatively to other hermit groups. There is common worship in the church, but not every day. There are common bakeries and shops. There is a Council of Elders.

376. Title to the *Regula Pachomii* (*PL* 23, col. 67C): "he founded the monastic way of life at the beginning by the command of God."

377. See Merton's essay "Conversion of Life," in Thomas Merton, *The Monastic Journey*, ed. Brother Patrick Hart (Kansas City: Sheed Andrews and McMeel, 1977), 107–20, for an extensive discussion of the meaning and usage of the term *conversatio morum* in the *Rule* of Benedict.

378. The Therapeuts were a Jewish community in Egypt similar to the Essenes, known through *De Vita Contemplativa* of Philo; see *Philo of Alexandria: The Contemplative Life, Giants and Selections*, trans. David Winston (New York: Paulist, 1986), 39–57.

379. See pages 38–39.

But this is not sufficient to constitute a "cenobium" in even a very loose sense.

b) There is no *uniformity*. There is no *obligation to remain* in the group. There is not poverty in the sense of {an} *inability to own anything*. The hermit still retains proprietorship, but exercises extreme austerity in the use of it, cutting down to the barest minimum, etc. Still, he is a proprietor.

c) In Antonian monasticism there is obedience, but it is not the keystone of the whole edifice. It is a personal matter, a function of personal asceticism, docility to the Abba in view to conquering passions and illusions. It is not permanent. The disciple eventually leaves the Abbas and lives on his own. It is not guided or limited by a Rule.

The Pachomian Conversatio.[380] The *koinonia*. The "Community" is in the deepest and most religious sense a community, a "common life" in the Spirit of Christ; its principle of cohesion is the love of Christ and the common search of salvation as a collective pursuit. The Antonian idea is certainly not that one's salvation is dependent upon belonging to a particular group as such, or that one finds Christ in the group. {There is a} sense of the community as "mystery." Bacht says of Pachomius: "*Il a donné à la vie commune un contenu qu'elle n'avait jamais connu jusque là.*"[381] He adds also, "*et il lui a imprimé une valeur canonique.*"[382] The *canonical character* of Pachomian common life is secondary but none the less important. *It confirms and clarifies the spiritual mystery of koinonia*. {It highlights the} relation of Law and Spirit in the Church.

The Enclosure: The fact and the obligation of the enclosure is the main "canonical" expression of the community as a mystery, an entity separated from the world, living a totally different life from the world. There is one wall with one gate ({cf. the} old idea

380. This entire section relies heavily on Ladeuze, 274–303: "Exposé des Règles Pakhômiennes."

381. "He gave to the common life a content it had never previously known" (Bacht, "L'Importance," 316).

382. "He impressed upon it a canonical value" (Bacht, "L'Importance," 316, which reads "et lui a comme imprimé . . .").

of {the} sacred precinct, *temenos*[383]). At this gate is the porter who controls all exits and entrances (see above[384]). Ideally speaking, the monk is at home only within the enclosure. He certainly cannot leave it without permission. This is "the foundation stone of cenobitism" (Bacht).[385] {It suggests} the mystical significance of the community, a heavenly city, defended against the attacks of the evil one (cf. *Vita Pachomii*, c. 41; *PL* 73:259).[386]

Common Life: Within the enclosure, worship is carried out in common. Offices were in common, in the church. Some common prayers were said in the "houses," v.g. the "six prayers" at night,[387] corresponding to our Compline ({there was} no Compline in early monasticism). Meals are taken in common (with exceptions, see below[388]). However there is some latitude. Each monk has an individual cell (?). Those who wish to eat alone may do so in their cells if they take just bread and water.

Work is common in the sense that *tasks are divided*, and various groups and individuals contribute part of a common effort. The work of the community {is} *seen as a strictly common effort in which everyone shares*. This too is of the essence of the cenobitic life. Superiors participate in the common work, and set the standard. Work is carried out in silence, accompanied by meditation (of Scripture); singing of psalms was permitted. When something

383. See Joseph E. Fontenrose, "Temenos," in *Oxford Classical Dictionary*, ed. N. G. L. Hammond and H. H. Sculland, 2nd ed. (Oxford: Clarendon Press, 1970), 1042: "in Homeric usage, signifies either a king's or a god's domain, a space marked off and assigned to his use. In later times it is nearly always used of a god's domain. . . . The rules governing the sanctity of precincts varied from cult to cult; entrance was sometimes forbidden except to certain persons at certain times. In most cults whoever entered the precinct had to be purified first."

384. See page 88.

385. Bacht, "L'Importance," 317.

386. In this chapter Pachomius and his monks are invited by a bishop to build a monastery on land he gives them, but local people, "blinded by the envy of the devil," tear down by night what the monks have built by day, until an angel of the Lord comes and surrounds the foundations with a ring of fire, which makes the completion of the building possible.

387. *Regula*, 155, 186 (*PL* 23, cols. 83CD, 89B).

388. See the section on "Uniformity" immediately below (pages 98–99).

is needed, *signs are made* in place of speech. *Specialized trades* are a later introduction—after Pachomius himself. Palladius saw in Akhmim—15 tailors, 7 blacksmiths, 4 carpenters, 12 cable makers and 15 fullers (dry cleaners).[389]

Farming: large scale development {came} *after* Pachomius. However, large numbers of monks went out on common expeditions to gather reeds, etc. Accounts of work done {were} kept each week and turned in to {the} Econome. Pachomius was not anxious to organize the work as a profitable industry, but only as an occupation forming part of the monk's spiritual life. Intensive organization came *after* Pachomius. Then came excess production and riches. This in turn led to divisions and {the} threat of schism in {the} "order."

Family? The Pachomian community cannot be called a family. The idea of *Familia* is basically Roman. Those who emphasize the "family" life in St. Benedict tend to do so by placing extraordinary stress on the supposed "Roman" elements in his *Rule* and spirit. But perhaps he is less purely Roman than these theorists make out.[390] The Pachomian community is too large, too fragmented, too organized to be a genuine family. See below[391]: the Structure of the Institution.

Uniformity: {This is} another characteristic of cenobitic life—uniformity in schedule, clothing, food, style of life—but not ab-

389. *Lausiac History*, 32.9; while Ladeuze translates καμηλαριους as "fabricants de câbles" (295), in Palladius, *Lausiac History*, trans. Robert T. Meyer, ACW 34 (Westminster, MD: Newman Press, 1965), 94, the translation speaks of camel drivers rather than cable makers, as does the Latin translation of the Greek text in Migne (*PG* 34, cols. 1100D, 1105A; *PL* 73, cols. 1138-39).

390. The "familial" character of Benedictine life is based on the use of the term *"paterfamilias"* in chapter 2 of the *Rule*, on the abbot (McCann, 16): see Herwegen, *St. Benedict, A Character Study*, 82, and 67–71 on the abbot as father generally. But as the note on this passage in *RB 1980: The Rule of St. Benedict*, ed. Timothy Fry, OSB (Collegeville, MN: Liturgical Press, 1981) points out, "While Abbot Herwegen saw comparisons between the Roman *paterfamilias* and the Abbot of the monastery, it seems better to understand the term according to biblical and ascetic tradition. It is Christ, not the abbot, who is the *paterfamilias*" (173, n. 2.7).

391. See page 106.

solute uniformity. Pachomian life was much less uniform than ours. Did monks eat at {the} same time? {This is} disputed—see Ladeuze, pp. 298–299. {The} aim of uniformity {was} THE SUPPRESSION OF SUBJECTIVISM. Hence the "objective" facts of the common life are taken to have value in themselves as willed by God for the monk and playing an important part in the mediation exercised by the *koinonia*: uniformity applies to superiors and subjects, {supporting the} concept that all alike are bound by the *Rule*, but allowing for wise exceptions and mitigations in special cases. The Pachomian life was not inflexible, though very minutely organized. Some see certain "democratic implications" in the Pachomian setup, but they are not to be taken without a grain of salt. In actual fact (see below[392]), the structure is quite totalitarian, and hierarchical.

Poverty plays a central role in the setup. It is for one thing a guarantee of uniformity. It is a function of the common life. Everyone has "the same," and under much the same conditions. *No one owns anything*. The community is Christ, and all belongs to Him. This was reached by gradual stages.

1) At first the Pachomian monks worked, as the hermits did, and turned in half their income to the common fund. In other words, they made their individual contributions to the community, while remaining proprietors and masters of their own work.

2) When this failed to work, Pachomius demanded *complete renunciation of all ownership*. Each monk was in total dependence on the Superior for everything. {He} worked in dependence, in total renunciation, without exercising his own choice and his own judgement. All independent acts of proprietorship {were} proscribed (lending, borrowing, giving, concealing, etc.). Care {was} to be taken that nothing is wasted or spoiled. This is the origin of {the} modern concept of religious poverty. {The} business of {the} monastery {was} conducted by {the} "Great Econome"

392. See page 122, where rigidity is attributed to Shenoute rather than to Pachomius.

(cellarer) who alone does all the buying and selling. {The} "Little Econome" (interior cellarer) takes care of food, etc.

Obedience: The whole Pachomian structure is built on obedience. This is not just the docility of the hermit to a director, but the lifelong obedience of the subject to the superior, as well as of the son to the Father. It implies a real concept of self-emptying and subjection, a real renunciation of one's own freedom, for keeps. It is "the distinctive factor of the new monasticism" (Bacht).[393] Elements {include}:

a) All are to obey the *Rule*, superiors and subjects. No one in the monastery is to follow his own will (cf. St. Benedict, *Reg.* c. 3).[394] The heads of houses and their assistants had to weave a certain number of baskets in a certain time, as a *norm* for the others to meet.

b) This strikes deep into the heart of the "mystery" of common life. If superiors do their own will and inferiors merely comply with that will, then there is not yet a religious mystery. This is constituted by the participation of all in the sacrifice and obedience of Christ, in His self-emptying. *All are in a kenotic state, as regards self-will.* All have renounced their will. The Holy Spirit then breathes in and through *all.*

c) However, the Superior must command, and he is to be obeyed as God. Furthermore the brethren are to obey one another, but above all the Superiors. In commanding, the Superior himself obeys God who wants him to command according to the *Rule*.

d) All must obey meekly and willingly, without murmuring. *Unwillingness and resistance show lack of faith* and seriously affect the spiritual vitality of the mystery of the common life. It is not just an individual defect. It affects the community.

e) Obedience is the highest value (with charity) in the common life. It is "greater than sacrifices."[395] That is to say that em-

393. Bacht, "L'Importance," 321.

394. "Let no one in the monastery follow the will of his own heart" (McCann, 25).

395. Ladeuze, 285.

phasis is systematically placed on what is enjoined by obedience, over what may be inspired by our own spontaneous religious desires, however good. This is another fundamental principle of cenobitism. What is enjoined *in the name of the community* (i.e. in the name of Christ by the Superior who, as head of the community, represents the common will which is also the will of God) leads to life much more surely and effectively than what is merely suggested by individual inspiration. However, this is not taken absolutely by Pachomius, who encouraged spontaneous sacrifices in matters of food. He did not make a fetish out of absolute uniformity. The sick could abstain from the relief offered them, etc.

Pachomius burned 500 mats that had been woven by the cook in the kitchen, while he was cooking. He had been ordered to cook, only—not ordered to weave mats. The work of supererogation was not acceptable, because outside obedience. Hence works of extra sacrifice are acceptable only when the approval of obedience brings them within the ambit of the common will and the common life. When a good work, of personal choice, is approved by the Superior, then it becomes part of the common spiritual striving and merit of the community; it becomes a work of Christ. But any work, however good, that is deliberately kept out of and apart from the common life-stream, ceases to be a work of Christ. Hence it is not blessed. Hence it is a potential danger, to the individual and to the community.

f) Obedience is *according to the Rule*: there is no longer any purely subjective and arbitrary command permitted. In commanding, the Superior must himself obey the *Apa*, the founder, and carry on the founder's will. He must run the institution according to the thought and mind of the founder, which is embodied in the *Rule*. The *Rule* represents the personal thought and desire of *Apa* Pachomius, and is not a mere legal document.

Discretion: Though extremely detailed in its ordinances of all kinds of minor points, and often very rigid and austere, there is still in the *Rule* of St. Pachomius a spirit of discretion. Everything is ordered so that *common duties* can be performed well, and monks can live at peace. The *sick* are treated with great kindness, well fed, get wine and meat. *Fires* {are} permitted for warmth. Monks could *oil* their hands, if injured. (However, see *Vita*, c. 52.)[396] The *common office of prayer* is not long, and is fairly simple. Pachomius says: "I have made these laws [for prayer] so that those who are not yet advanced in the ways of perfection may submit without too much difficulty. As for the perfect, they have no need of a law in this matter, for even when they are in their cells they consecrate their whole life to meditation" (quoted in Ladeuze, p. 290).[397]

Work is to be moderate. *Ne plus operis fratres compellantur facere,* sed moderatus labor omnes ad laborandum provocet (*Rule* [trans. Jerome];[398] cf. St. Benedict[399]). Two meals a day are permitted. Two tunics are allowed. Mitigations are allowed for the sick,

396. This chapter (*PL* 73, cols. 269D-271A) tells of the monk Zachaeus, who despite a disease that forced him to live away from the other monks was faithful to all the monastic exercises, including work making mats, which caused his hands to bleed profusely. Another monk convinced him to anoint his hands with oil, which only caused them to bleed more profusely when he worked. Pachomius visited him and admonished him not to trust in the oil but in the Lord, who had given him this disease that caused his hands to bleed for his spiritual growth. The monk acknowledged his fault and continued to bear his suffering until his death, and he was held up to the other monks by Pachomius as an example of fidelity and good works.

397. Actually these are words spoken by the angel to Pachomius, who had objected that there were too few prayers, in the revelation of the *Rule* in *Lausiac History*, 32.7 (Meyer, 94); see also *Vita*, 22 (*PL* 73, col. 243AB).

398. "Let the brothers not be forced to work excessively, but let moderate labor draw all to work" (*Regula*, 179 [*PL* 23, col. 87D]).

399. See c. 41: "If they have field work or the summer heat be extreme, this dinner at the sixth hour shall be the daily practice, according to the abbot's discretion. And let him so arrange and ordain all things that souls may be saved and that the brethren may do their work without justifiable murmuring"; and c. 48: "then are they truly monks when they live by the labour of their hands, like our fathers and the apostles. Yet let all things be done in moderation on account of the faint-hearted. . . . Sick or delicate brethren should be assigned a task or craft of such a kind that on the one hand they be not idle, and on the other be not overborne by excessive toil or driven away from the monastery. The abbot should have consideration for their weakness" (McCann, 99, 111, 113).

the old, the children, etc. Sometimes St. Pachomius is easier than St. Benedict in the matter of penances etc.[400]

Reading has an important part to play. All must learn to read and *lectio* is an essential element in the life, giving the monk food for thought in prayer and at work.

Fasting: There were *two* meals a day but monks could skip one if they wished. {They included} bread and vegetables and "sweets" (distributed after meals)—fruits, {but} no wine, fish soup or meat. Pachomius wanted the meals to be plentiful so that the monks could freely deny themselves a part (see *Vita*, c. 43).[401] *Fast days* {were} on Wednesday and Friday of each week, outside Paschal Time ({in accordance with} current custom). Private vows of fasting or special abstinence were encouraged.

Vigils: The monks slept in their cells with the doors open. {They} could take part of the night for prayer (outside of {the} regular office). {They followed the} Egyptian custom in vigils and prayer: usually half the night in prayer and half in sleep.[402] This was learned by Pachomius from Palamon. St. Anthony divided the night into three parts, the middle part for sleep, the others for prayer. For the day time, the *ideal* is "constant, uninterrupted prayer"[403] (with work). Work {is} frequently interrupted for prayer. Sometimes one brother chanted psalms while {the}

400. The wrongdoer is typically admonished a number of times for his fault (e.g. six times for anger [*Regula*, 161; col. 85C], ten times for disobedience [*Regula*, 165; col. 86CD], three times for leading children astray [*Regula*, 166; col. 86D-87A] before punishment is imposed); for Benedictine punishments, see *Rule*, cc. 23–30, 43–46 (McCann, 73–81, 103–109).

401. *PL* 73, cols. 260B-261B: this is the story of the cook who stopped preparing vegetables because the brothers were not eating them, and spent his time making mats instead; after burning the mats, Pachomius admonishes the cook for depriving the monks of an opportunity to freely deny themselves the food and so win merit for their virtue.

402. Ladeuze, 301.

403. See Ladeuze, 318: "D'ailleurs, les moines de Schenoudi devaient, eux aussi, avoir soin de prier et de méditer en silence pendant tout la journée, même durant leurs autres occupations" ("Moreover, the monks of Shenoute as well had to take care to pray and meditate silently throughout the day, even while engaged in other tasks").

others worked. {There were} two *synaxes*—Lauds and Vespers, {the} basis of {the} day office. {The} office consists of 6 psalms, each psalm followed by a prayer. After Vespers and supper all gathered for a conference of the Superior (*collatio*). Before retiring there was a *collecta domus*,[404] evening prayer in the separate houses. *Night vigils* in the Pachomian *typikon* began about 2 a.m. {and came to an} end before sunrise. It is thought that the Egyptian monks long *resisted* the introduction of fixed "day hours" in order to cling to the tradition of "constant prayer." *Later* the *collecta domus* is merged with Vespers = 12 psalms.

Penances: Punishments for faults. Detractors were {for} seven days excluded from {the} community, fasting on bread and water.[405] Angry monks had to take {the} last place for a while.[406] Murmurers were sent to {the} infirmary as a humiliation.[407] (Probably this was not systematic!!)

The *Vita Pachomii* (c. 22 ff.; *PL* 73:242) makes discretion stand out. In {the} revelation of the angel, the *first thing* given is the following precept (to Pachomius): "You shall grant to each one to eat and drink according to his strength, and you shall make them work according as they eat; nor shall you prohibit them from eating sparingly and from fasting. The stronger ones and those who eat more shall work harder; you shall impose easier work on the weak and on those who are abstaining."[408] In chapter 24 the program is again summarized: *Moderatum cibum, vilissimum vestitum, somnium etiam competentem* (col. 244).[409] Chapter 25 {discusses} his special care for the old, sick and children.[410] {In} chapter 38 his patience and kindness effects a deep change in a dissipated monk whom the brethren desired to be expelled from

404. See Ladeuze, 288–89.

405. *Regula*, 160 (col. 85BC).

406. *Regula*, 161 (col. 85CD).

407. *Regula*, 164 (col. 86C).

408. Col. 242B; the same message is given in *Lausiac History*, 32.2 (Meyer, 92), the evident source of this material, the so-called "Rule of the Angel," which is not found in the Coptic or Greek *Lives*.

409. "Moderate food, very poor clothing and sufficient sleep."

410. Col. 245D.

the monastery. He then gets such a strong gift of tears that they all beg him to stop weeping, at least during meals (it takes away the appetite of others) (256). {Note} Pachomius' praise of this brother (256–257) who overcame the devil by perfect humility. {The} death of Silvanus {is then recounted}—his soul {is} offered to God by angels "*velut electam hostiam*" (257C).[411]

Pachomian Discretion and the Benedictine Rule. What we have seen of the spirit of discretion in St. Pachomius and his deep sense of the cenobitic mystery compels us to disagree with the following statement of Dom Cuthbert Butler, which has hitherto been so commonly accepted in monastic doctrine as to be almost an axiom: "The twofold *break with the past*, in the elimination of austerity and in the sinking of the individual in the community, made St. Benedict's Rule *less a development than a revolution* in monasticism."[412] This is not the case.

Pachomian Foundations. Tabennisi or Tabenna {was} founded about 315 (?); Pbow, two miles down river from Tabenna, {at the site of a} deserted village, became {the} head of {the} "Order"; when Theodore was Abbot of Tabenna he used to go to Pbow in the evening for {the} conference of Pachomius; Sheneset {and} Tmoushons {are} the monasteries aggregated to the group; {also} Thbew; Pichnoum; Tse (under Abbot Pesso); Djodj; Tsmîne (under Abbot Petronius [?]); Psampester-Posen (where Pachomius had first lived alone).

411. "like a chosen sacrifice."

412. Cuthbert Butler, *Benedictine Monachism: Studies in Benedictine Life and Rule* (London: Longmans, Green, 1919), 45; there are no italics in the original, and the final word is "monachism" rather than "monasticism."

Structure of the Cenobitic Institute

The General Superior (at Pbow)

Monastic Superiors Monastic Superiors
The *Secundus*

Oikiakos *Oikiakos* *Oikiakos* etc.
(*Praepositus Domus*)

Secundus *Secundus* *Secundus*

Monks Monks Monks

"Tribe"

Under the Superior of the whole group of Pachomian monasteries, at Pbow, are the superiors of the individual monasteries. Under the superior is the "*secundus*," corresponding to our prior, the head of a "Tribe." The Tribe consists of "houses," perhaps many of them. Each house, presided over by a *praepositus domus*[413] (*oikiakos*[414]) aided by a *secundus*, consists of a small group of monks, about a dozen. They are selected by reason of traits they may have in common and put in groups with others, for instance exercising a similar trade, or coming from the same country. For instance there was a house of Greeks, with a superior and aide, with twenty monks. Jerome estimated 40 in a house.[415] *The House* (*domus*) consisted of a common room and individual cells (Ladeuze).[416]

Spiritual Instructions. The *oikiakos* gave two conferences a week to the members of his house. The superior of the monastery gave three catecheses a week to {the} whole community. Repetitions: the house group would review spiritual instructions in common, perhaps twice a day, v.g. after morning prayer and after supper. In addition to these regular talks and classes, additional talks might be given by the first superior at *any* time. See *Vita Pachomii*, c. 30 (col. 250): monks "meditating on {the} divine word

413. "superior of a house."

414. "housemaster."

415. See Jerome's Preface to his translation of the Pachomian *Rule* (col. 66A).

416. Ladeuze, 263, 275.

after Vespers." This could include "*disputatio*":[417] a monk relates {the} spiritual interpretation of Tabernacles, etc. he has heard from Pachomius; chapter 46 (col. 264) {describes} a conference of Pachomius after the Night Office "On Hastening by Good Works to the Heavenly Kingdom," basing one's fasts and labors on ever-present awareness of the coming Judgement.[418] All were required to learn to read. All had to learn some parts of the Bible by heart. Books could be kept from the library for a week.

Novices {were} carefully screened and tested, were admitted to guest quarters after about ten days of testing. There they underwent preliminary instruction, in prayers, reading, Scripture, Rules, etc. After examination, they were admitted into the community (without vows) and there was no more novitiate.

Vita Pachomii (translated from Greek by Dionysius Exiguus, *PL* 73).[419] Note: there are Greek, Arabic and Coptic lives of Pachomius.[420] In the Greek etc. we learn of trials and troubles of Pachomius who was accused before a Council at Latopolis shortly before his death (346).[421] {The} Prologue of Dionysius' translation is dedicated to a Roman Lady thought to be Galla, daughter of Symmachus, a noble widow, who lived a pious life (as {a} recluse?)

417. i.e. "public discussion or teaching"; in this chapter Theodore is motivated to seek out Pachomius by what he has heard of his teaching from this monk.

418. The chapter actually runs from col. 263D through 266A.

419. Cols. 227-72; this is closely related to, and may be a translation of, the so-called Second Greek Life of Pachomius; see Armand Veilleux, *Pachomian Koinonia*, vol. 1: *The Life of Saint Pachomius and His Disciples*, CS 45 (Kalamazoo, MI: Cistercian Publications, 1980), 12–14 for a discussion of the relationship.

420. Veilleux provides an overview of the entire biographical tradition and translations of *The Bohairic Life*, the *First Greek Life*, and the fragments of the *First*, *Second*, and *Tenth Sahidic Lives* in *Pachomian Koinonia*, vol. 1; the Greek lives were edited by F. Halkin in *Sancti Pachomii Vitae Graecae*, *Subsidia Hagiographica*, 19 (Brussels: Société des Bollandistes, 1932); the Coptic lives were edited by L.-Th. Lefort in *S. Pachomii Vita Bohairice Scripta*, *CSCO* 89 (Paris: Typographeo Reipublicae, 1925; Louvain: Secrétariat du Corpus SCO, 1964–1965) and *S. Pachomii Vitae Sahidice Scriptae*, *CSCO* 99, 100 (Paris: Typographeo Reipublicae, 1933, 1934; Louvain: L. Durbecq, 1952); the Arabic life was edited by Amélineau in *Histoire de Saint Pakhôme et de Ses Communautés*, 2:337-711.

421. See the *First Greek Life*, c. 112 (*Pachomian Koinonia*, 1:375-77).

at St. Peter's, Rome.[422] She had asked him for the translation. "*Avida voluntate beatorum Patrum cupitis instituta cognoscere, quatenus eorum studiis facta propria componentes, futuris saeculis documentum divini muneris singulare praestetis*" (col. 227).[423] {This} Prologue seems to reflect troubles and intrigues of the time of Symmachus and Boethius.

{The} Prologue of {the} *Vita* {focuses on the} origin of monasticism—the coming of Christ, growth of the faith, persecution of martyrs. Monks follow {the} example of martyrs. "*Quietem denique solitudinis appetentes, gaudia propriae salutis ac fidei divino munere sunt consecuti, caeterisque mox exempla sublimioris vitae sacratiorisque praebuerunt. Omnibus enim terrenis exuti negotiis, adhuc morantes in corpore, angelorum aemulati sunt sanctitatem*" (229).[424] They equaled the patriarch and battled with demons (229).

Chapter 6—{The} vocation of Pachomius {is} tested by Palamon (read).[425]

Chapter 7—Pachomius' novitiate.

Chapter 9—A proud monk {is} deceived by the devil (234–235).[426]

422. See Rosweyde's note, *PL* 73, cols. 271C-273B.

423. "You desire with eager will to learn about the way of life of the blessed Fathers, and by assembling as far as possible the proper facts about their devotion you will make available for future ages a unique record of divine generosity."

424. "Seeking at last the peace of solitude, they have pursued the joys of their own salvation and of faith through serving God, and have soon presented to others models of an elevated and consecrated life. Putting aside all worldly concerns, they rival the holiness of the angels while still remaining in the body."

425. Col. 233BD; in this chapter the newly converted Pachomius hears of an anchorite named Palamon and goes to him to ask him to teach him to be a monk; Palamon tries to discourage Pachomius, telling him of the many who have begun the eremitic life but did not persevere, and of his own strict discipline; he urges him to go to a monastery for a while to try out the life and then come back to him if he continues to be committed, but Pachomius persists in asking to stay and finally (at the beginning of chapter 7) the old man relents and lets him into the hermitage.

426. This chapter tells of a monk who challenges Palamon and Pachomius to walk on hot coals; Palamon rebukes him for his presumption, but the monk walks on the coals and is not burnt. The next day a demon in the form of a beautiful woman comes to him claiming to be fleeing from creditors; he lets her in, is

Chapter 10—Pachomius' progress; his purity of heart (235); his *lectio divina* (235D).

Chapter 12—The Rule of the angel (236).[427]

Chapter 13—Death of Palamon, fasting to the end (237).

Chapter 14–15—Pachomius begins life with his brother (237-238). His brother rebukes him for enlarging buildings and preparing for community. {The} brother wants {a} solitary life. Pachomius prays all night, moistening {the} ground with sweat and tears. His brother dies.[428]

{Chapter} 17—Devils try to delude him—one as a rooster attacks him (240). They try to make him laugh, dragging a leaf with a rope.

{Chapter} 18—Abbas Appollo tells him he is suffering beatings to win grace for other monks (241).

{Chapter} 19—As a result of his triumph over demons, he can ride crocodiles (241).

Chapter 21—The Rule of the Angel—note emphasis on discretion (c. 22; col. 242).

Chapter 23—His 3 first monks: Psenthessus, Suris and Obsis.

Chapter 24 (col. 245 top)—*why {there are} no priests in the cenobium*: "*Multo melius esse atque commodius monachis, non solum nullius prorsus honoris quaerere primatus et gloriae,* verum etiam

tormented by lust, and falls into a kind of fit. When he comes to, he returns to Palamon in shame, but is suddenly driven away by the evil spirit and eventually is hurled into the fire at a bathhouse.

427. This chapter tells of a heavenly voice coming to Pachomius when he is at Tabennisi and instructing him to remain there and build a monastery, and of an angel bringing him the *Rule* on a tablet; the story is told again in c. 21 (col. 242B) and the provisions are found in c. 22 (cols. 242B-243B). This "Rule of the Angel" is not found in any of the Coptic, Greek or Arabic *Lives* (though there is a brief angelic visitation in c. 22 of the Bohairic *Life* and c. 23 of the First Greek *Life* [see *Pachomian Koinonia*, 1:45, 311-12]), but is related by Palladius in chapter 32 of the *Lausiac History* (Meyer, 92–94); see the discussion of the Rule of the Angel in Veilleux' Introduction to *Pachomian Koinonia*, 2:5-6.

428. Not as a result of Pachomius' prayers (!), which were filled with repentance for his own anger at his brother, with whom he henceforth lived in humility and gentleness (col. 239B) until John died a short time later.

occasiones hujuscemodi de coenobiis amputare."[429] It was possible for cenobites to do without priests as nearby clergy could come to the monastery to offer Mass for the brethren. Ambition, like fire in the harvest, can destroy all the monks' good works. However, see {the} very interesting chapter 35: a neighboring superior has a monk who wants to be a cleric, though he is not worthy. The superior brings this monk to Pachomius hoping Pachomius will reprove him and convince him to give up his idea. On the contrary, Pachomius says, "*If he has this dignity, the responsibility may wake him up and reform him.*" So it turned out. The monk became humble and thanked Pachomius for saving his vocation by helping him to be promoted to the clerical state!! (col. 254).

Chapter 26—*Apostolate*: {Pachomius} has a church built for shepherds (246) and goes with {the} monks to *read* {the} *Bible* to them—as "*lectores*" (though not ordained??). Liturgy of the Word! {He} prayed with tears for conversion of idolators (247). (Later Shenoute would try to convert them by force.[430])

Chapter 27—His orthodoxy {is shown during a} visit of St. Athanasius (363 A.D.). "*Haereticos autem detestabatur plurimum, et maxime Origenem, velut blasphemum ac perfidum, vehementer horrebat*" (247).[431] He forbade the brethren to read Origen {and} threw

429. "It is much better and more suitable for monks not only not to seek positions of any honor and glory, but truly to remove from monasteries any opportunities for doing so."

430. Besa's *Life of Shenoute* features stories of Shenoute's forceful destruction of idols, though not of trying to convert idolators by force: see *Life*, cc. 83–84, 125–27 (CS 73, 66, 77–78); there is a story (c. 81 [65–66]) in which Shenoute chastises a pagan for oppressing the poor and is punched in the face, at which point a fearful figure emerges from the crowd, punches the pagan and drags him to the river, into which both disappear! E. C. Amélineau, *Les Moines Égyptiens: Vie de Schenouti* (Paris: Leroux, 1889), 317–19 tells of Shenoute's conflict with the authorities because of his opposition to paganism (based on the Arabic *Life*); see also Bell's discussion in his Introduction (18–19), where he says that Shenoute's opposition "seems to have accelerated the process" of the disappearance of paganism in Upper Egypt.

431. "He inveighed against heretics most of all, and he violently rejected Origen especially, as a blasphemer and perverter of the faith."

a volume of Origen into the river, saying that if the Name of God hadn't been in the book he would have burnt it.[432] {In} chapter 44—Some hermits come to visit and talk with him of "*rebus abditis atque arcanis*."[433] Pachomius detects a horrible odor {and} asks if they have read Origen. They deny it, but apparently not believing their denial, Pachomius declares that "every man who reads Origen and consents to what he reads there will end in the depths of hell" (261). Origen is mentioned again {in} chapter 53—Pachomius' dying admonition: "Stay away from Origen, Arius, etc."[434] Note he is more hostile to Origen than to Arius.

Chapter 28—His sister founds a convent of nuns. Monks help them with heavy or specialized work but return to their own monastery for meals (249). Nuns {are} buried in {the} monks' cemetery.

Chapter 29—Conversion of Theodore.[435]

Chapter 30—Meeting of Theodore and Pachomius. Theodore is "illuminated" by the sight of the Father and the *multitudo fratrum*[436] (mystery of {the} cenobium as an epiphany) (col. 251).

Chapter 31—Theodore refuses to see his mother who comes with letters of {the} Bishop commanding him to leave the monastery (col. 251).

Chapter 32—Departure of some tepid monks from {the} cenobium—even the earnest prayers of Pachomius could not save them from losing their vocation (252).

432. Col. 247CD.

433. Col. 261C: "hidden and secret matters."

434. Col. 271C: actually the order is reversed in the text: "*Nulla sit vobis conjunctio cum sectatoribus Meletii, vel Arii, vel Origenis*" ("You must have no contact with the followers of Meletius, or Arius, or Origen").

435. Since Theodore (unlike Pachomius himself) is described as "*Christianis ortus parentibus*" ("born of Christian parents") his "conversion" (a term used in the text ["*hoc modo conversus est*": "he was converted in this way"]) means taking up monastic life.

436. Col. 250D, which reads "*fratrum multitudinem*" ("the large number of the brothers").

Chapter 33—Why Pachomius admitted guests to {the} oratory but not to the refectory (253).[437]

Chapter 36—Cure of a consecrated virgin—Pachomius refuses to see her, {and} asks for a garment of hers to be brought—{he} declares, from seeing {the} garment, that she has been unfaithful to her vow (the garment, habit, is "not hers"[438]) (255).

Chapter 38—Silvanus, {a} converted actor, {is} given to dissipation in {the} monastery; the brethren want him expelled, but Pachomius by patience and love brings him to compunction (255-256).

Chapter 39—A monk of unworthy life is being buried with solemn obsequies. Pachomius forbids further psalmody and stops {the} solemnity—for the good of the monk's soul. {This is} interesting in relation to St. Benedict's concept of excommunication[439] (257–258). Pachomius says it is better for the monk to go to Purgatory in this case. "*Fons enim bonitatis Deus noster existens, occasiones quaerit, per quas opulenta super nos data pietatis suae effundat, remittatque nobis peccata, non solum in hoc saeculo, sed etiam in futuro.*"[440]

Chapter 41—Evil men try to destroy the enclosure wall of {a} new foundation—angels melt them like wax (259).

Chapter 42—Theodore confounds the vain speculations of a philosopher (260).

Chapter 43—The cook who was weaving mats. Pachomius comes on a visitation. One of the children in the monastery complains they are getting no vegetables. {The} cook says most of the

437. Pachomius explains to his friend Dionysius, who had questioned him about this, that because many of the visitors are young or new to the monastic life, he had decided that for the sake of his own monks' peace the visitors should eat in a separate place, where he cares for their needs himself.

438. Col. 254D.

439. Benedict discusses excommunications, which involve temporary exclusion from the common life of the community, in cc. 23–28 and 44 of the *Rule* (McCann, 73–79, 105–107); here too it is intended for the benefit of the monk's soul, though no mention is made of burial rites in Benedict.

440. "For our Living God, the fountain of goodness, seeks opportunities to pour out upon us the riches of His benevolence, and to forgive us our sins not only in this life but also in the life to come."

brethren fast on bread and water so why cook vegetables? He weaves mats instead. Pachomius then lays down this principle: he who abstains from what he can have is gaining more merit than he who abstains from what is beyond his power to have. *Cum plures escae appositae fuerint, si fratres parcius his utuntur propter Deum, tunc apud Deum sibi maximam spem reponunt. De cibis autem quos non vident, nec eis ad percipiendum facultas ulla tribuitur, quomodo pro parcimonia praemium conceditur? Ideoque propter exiguos sumptus tanta fratrum non debuit intermitti commoditas* (261{A}B).[441]

Chapter 45—Vision of the future decline of monasteries {due to the} negligence of superiors, divisions among the monks, ambition, neglect of exhortation. They will be in deep darkness. He complains to God and a voice says, "All things are under my mercy."[442] Then an angel promises him that the cenobitic life will persist until the end of time and even where it is not fervent, those monks will be saved who deny themselves and are serious about their salvation; cf. chapter 49—{a} long discussion with a devil who assures Pachomius that the monastic life will decline (268).

Chapter 46—On good works and avoiding {the} spirit of the world. A saeculi actibus . . . *Nimis anima illa probatur infelix, et omni lacrymarum fonte plangenda, quae saeculo renuntians, iterum saeculi actibus implicatur, et inutilibus dudum curis exuta, rursum redit ad durae servitutis obsequia* (264).[443] Note: here there is mention of contemplation as the fruit of asceticism: . . . *donec Spiritus Sancti calore succensa, supernae contemplationis mereatur auxilium, et a contagiis*

441. "When an abundance of food has been provided, if the brothers take less for God's sake, then they lay up a very great hope with God. But how is a reward for abstinence to be granted them for food they don't see and are given no opportunity to get? Such a great advantage for the brothers must not be taken away for the sake of small monetary savings" (N.B. the middle sentence is not in the original typescript but is included in the mimeograph).

442. Col. 263B.

443. "That soul is proved to be very unhappy, and must weep a veritable fountain of tears, which having once renounced the world, is once again drawn into worldly activities, and having once laid aside useless cares, returns again to a compliance with harsh enslavement." (The three opening words are a sort of title taken from the text: "From worldly activities," not a separate part of the text itself.)

exsoluta terrenis, divinis jugiter exsatietur alloquiis (265).[444] See {also the} following lines: *Philosophetur ergo . . .* etc.[445]

Chapter 47—Observance of silence—not a mere "human precept" {but one with} eschatological meaning (266). {Note the} humility of St. Pachomius who allows a child to correct him in his way of weaving mats (266).

Chapter 53—Death of St. Pachomius.

The *Doctrina Orsiesii* ("Doctrine" of Orsiesius)

This is an important Latin Pachomian document, also translated by St. Jerome. (It is found in *PL* 103, col. 453 ff.)[446] {It is} wrong to call this a Rule. Orsiesius knew no Rule but that of St. Pachomius. We do not need to go into details—it contains the same doctrine we have already examined. It begins, for instance, with a quotation from Baruch 3, a favorite text with the Pachomian cenobites: "How is it O Israel that thou art in the land of thine enemies?" God wills to save His children by penance. We must beware lest we are separated from "our city," Jerusalem, the monastic community, in the next life, and relegated to Babylon (hell) for having neglected the law of God (col. 453). Those who disobey, as soon as they enter the next world, "will quickly be separated from our Father [Pachomius] and the brethren who possess the place of victory" (454).[447] Hence the familiar exhortations against negligence. "Therefore let us examine our ways and judge our own steps; let us return to the Lord, and let us lift our

444. Col. 265A: "until enkindled by the heat of the Holy Spirit, it may win the assistance of heavenly contemplation, and released from earthly contaminations, be satisfied forever by words of divine encouragement."

445. Col. 265B: "*Philosophetur ergo, charissimi fratres, anima spiritalis quotidie adversus crassam carnis suae materiam; omnique circumspectione cum ea taliter agat, quatenus ad meliora sibi consentiat.*" ("Therefore, dearest brothers, may your spiritual self reason daily against the gross matter of its own flesh; may it so act towards the flesh with all prudence so that the flesh might conform to it for the better.")

446. An English translation is in *Pachomian Koinonia*, 3:171-224.

447. The text reads "*Patribus*" ("Fathers") rather than "*Patre*" ("Father").

hands and our hearts to heaven on high: that on the day of Judgement He may be our helper, that we may not be confounded when we speak with our enemies in the gate, but may rather be worthy to hear the words: Open the gates and the people that kept justice and truth shall enter in" (454; cf. Judith 15).

However we must again recognize the highly positive quality of this penitential doctrine. God is a God of mercy. He does not will the death of the sinner but that he may be converted and live. Chapter 33 of the *Doctrina Orsiesii* (col. {466}) quotes the Old and New Testaments, on the mercy of God calling us to return to Him by obedience. "And the most clement Lord, the source of all goodness, cries out to us in the Gospels saying: Come to me all you who labor and are burdened and I will refresh you. Take my yoke upon you etc. . . ." (Matt. 11). *Consideremus quod {bonitas} Dei ad penitentiam nos provocet, et sancti viri cohortantur ad salutem. Non induremus corda nostra . . .*[448] Compare this with the Prologue of St. Benedict: "*Ideo nobis propter emendationem malorum, hujus dies vitae ad inducias relaxantur, dicente Apostolo: An nescis quia patientia Dei ad poenitentiam te adducit? Nam pius Dominus dicit: Nolo mortem peccatoris*, etc." (Prol., lines 67–71, in Koenders, *Concordantiae*).[449] There is also the idea of waking from sleep to enter the spiritual combat: *Doctrina Orsiesii* 6 (col. 455) (cf. Prol.[450]) and other familiar themes.

{There is} an important passage {in} chapters 24 and 25 on not defending our brother when he is corrected (justly) by {the}

448. Col. 466D: "Let us consider that the goodness of God summons us to repentance, and holy men urge us to salvation. Let us not harden our hearts . . ." (typescript reads "406" and "*bonitatem*").

449. *Concordantiae Sanctae Regulae Beatissimi ac Deo Acceptissimi Patris Nostri Benedicti Abbatis: Textus Antiqui atque Recentiores*, ed. Henricus Koenders, OCR (Westmalle: Abbatia Cisterciensis, 1947), 3: "And the days of our life are lengthened and a respite allowed us for this very reason, that we may amend our evil ways. For the Apostle saith: *Knowest thou not that the patience of God inviteth thee to repentance*? For the merciful Lord saith: *I will not the death of a sinner . . .*" (McCann, 11).

450. "Up with us then at last, for the Scripture arouseth us, saying: *Now is the hour for us to rise from sleep*" (McCann, 7).

superior and not taking his part against the superior (cols. 462, 463). The superior who corrects is *erudiens in timore Dei.*[451] The brother who takes the part of the one corrected is *subvertens cor illius, . . . peccat in suam animam, subvertit eum qui corrigi poterat, consurgentem dejicit in terram, atque ad meliora {tendentem} mala persuasione decepit, errans ipse, et alios errare faciens.*[452] The following Scripture quotes are added: Hab. 2:15; Deut. 27:18; and Matt. 18:5.

There is an important chapter on the mystery of the cenobitic life (c. 28; col. 464-65): the traditions handed down by our Fathers (Pachomius, etc.) are commandments of God and lead to the Kingdom of heaven; we must therefore embrace them with all the desires of our hearts. If we merely follow the thoughts of our own hearts, we are in error, and if we fail to confess the error we are following a way that leads out of the "holy city," for we are likely to be asked: "Why have you defiled my holy place?" (cf. Ezech. 22). *SIQUIDEM CONCILIABULA MONACHORUM VERE DEI DOMUS EST, ET SANCTORUM VINEA*[453]—here {a} text of Canticles is applied: READ Cant. 8:11-12.[454] {See} also {chapter} 47 (col. 471): "We therefore are the imitators of the saints; let us not forget the observance which our Father, when he was still in this body, taught us to follow. Let us not put out the burning lamp which he has suspended over our heads. . . . God for love of this light has called us into His own family, giving us shelter as to wandering pilgrims, showing us a safe harbor while we were tossed on the stormy sea, giving us

451. Col. 462C (which reads "*erudiens eum . . .*"): "instructing him in the fear of God."

452. Col. 462C (which reads "*. . . quia subvertit . . . et consurgentem . . .*"; typescript reads "*tendens*"): "subverting his heart, . . . he sins against his own soul, because he undermines him who could have been corrected, throws to the ground one who was arising, deceives with evil argument one who was leaning toward better things—erring himself and causing others to err."

453. Col. 465A: "Indeed the communities of monks are truly the house of God and the vineyard of the saints."

454. "Solomon had a vineyard at Baal-Hamon; he gave over the vineyard to caretakers. For its fruit one would have to pay a thousand silver pieces. My vineyard is at my own disposal; the thousand pieces are for you, O Solomon, and two hundred for the caretakers of its fruit" (Confraternity translation).

bread in our hunger, shade in the heat, clothing in our nakedness . . . Let us not after his [i.e. Pachomius'] falling asleep forget such kindness and such undying benefits, etc. . . ."[455] The most interesting sections of this text deal with the relations of the various levels in the monastic hierarchy.

The *Doctrina* is especially directed to the various superiors, instructing them on their duties and the spirit with which they should exercise their responsibilities. {See} chapter 7: *Quapropter, o duces et praepositi monasteriorum ac domorum, quibus crediti sunt homines, et apud quos inveniuntur T, sive E, sive A, ut in {commune} dicam, quibus crediti sunt homines, singuli cum suis turmis exspectent Salvatoris adventum* (col. 455).[456] (The letters T, E, A seem to refer to a system of classification, monks being divided up according to their abilities and inclinations in the spiritual life.[457])

Some principles of direction:

—Not to become too concerned with temporal things (work) and neglect the spiritual development of the monks; not to overemphasize the spiritual and forget the care of the body. *SED ET SPIRITALES ET CARNALES CIBOS PARITER TRIBUITE ET NULLAM DETIS EIS OCCASIONEM NEGLIGENTIAE* (col. 455).[458] This is further background for the famous Benedictine discretion.[459]

455. The text reads ". . . *imitatores simus*, . . ." (". . . let us be imitators. . .").

456. Col. 455C (which reads ". . . *turmis suis* . . ."; typescript reads "*communi*"): "Therefore, superiors and masters of monasteries and houses, to whom men are entrusted and among whom are found T, or E, or A—as I say in ordinary speech, to whom men are entrusted—let each await with his group the coming of the Savior."

457. This explanation of the use of Greek letters is found in *Lausiac History*, 32:4-5 (see Meyer, 93), but there is evidence from the *Letters* of Pachomius that they were also (?) used in more esoteric ways, which may be intended here: see *Pachomian Koinonia*, 3:5, and 3:216: *Hors. Test.*, c. 7, n. 2.

458. Chapter 7: "But offer them both spiritual and bodily food equally, and may you give them no opportunity for negligence."

459. See the famous lines toward the close of the Prologue: "Therefore must we establish a school of the Lord's service; in founding which we hope to ordain nothing that is harsh or burdensome" (McCann, 13).

—*Unde et laborem et refrigeria cum ipsis habeamus communia, nec discipulos servos putemus* (455).[460] But if this had to be said, there was doubtless some danger that the brethren were being overworked (cf. c. 8).

—Avoiding favoritism (c. 9; 456) and anger (*id.*).

—Responsibility of superiors: they must give an account of their subjects at Judgement. This applies not only to the superiors, however, but to all the brethren. All are *responsible for all. Omnes invicem debent onera sua portare, ut adimpleant legem Christi* (col. 457).[461]

—Duties of *praepositi*: *Monete eos qui inordinati sunt, consolamini pusillanimes, sustinete infirmos, patienter agite ad omnes . . .* etc. (col. 458).[462]

—Duties of heads of monasteries: *Nec abutamini potestate in supplicia, sed exemplum praebete vos cunctis et subdito gregi . . .*[463]—to have St. Paul's zeal and compassion, to avoid negligence and scandal, to avoid hardness of heart, to contemn no one, and to realize that in saving the souls of his monks he is saving his own soul (458).

The Two Weeks. {This is} a special Pachomian "retreat" (cf. Kuhn: "The Observance of the Two Weeks in Shenoute's Writings," in *Patristic Studies* [Oxford, 1957; vol. 2, p. 427 f.]).[464]

460. "And so may we have both work and refreshment in common with them, and may we not consider disciples to be slaves."

461. Chapter 11 (which reads "*sua onera*"): "All should bear one another's burdens, and so fulfill the law of Christ."

462. These are instructions for superiors of individual houses: "Admonish those who are undisciplined; console the faint-hearted; strengthen the weak; act patiently toward all . . ."

463. Chapter 13 (col. 457D): "Do not abuse your authority in punishing, but set an example for all and for the flock under your care."

464. K. H. Kuhn, "The Observance of the 'Two Weeks' in Shenoute's Writings," *Studia Patristica 2: Papers Presented to the Second International Conference on Patristic Studies Held at Christ Church, Oxford, 1955*, Part II, ed. Kurt Aland and F. L. Cross (Berlin: Akademie-Verlag, 1957), 427–34.

What were the Two Weeks?

1. A special time of leisure for contemplation and prayer and for more perfect observance. "Our Father {. . .} endeavours to seize and draw us away from this lack of leisure which does not satisfy, that we may have leisure and rest in those two 'Sabbaton' more than we are at leisure daily." {It is} a time of intercession in view of the confusion of the world and its miseries. "Moreover, our Father did this because of the sufferings which take place in the world . . ."—famines or bad seasons, etc. (p. 428).

2. Only *necessary* work, and light work, {is} allowed during this period. "During the first 'sabbaton' of the Forty Days and the Great Holy Passover and also the two 'sabbaton,' they shall not constrain people by troubling them with difficult tasks nor shall they compel them to work except with regard to the very small things which are easy to do, or tasks which it is necessary to do, including those who are at the gate."[465] "Let not any man acquire work among us because of which he shall be detained from assembling, nor shall work be demanded of them, nor shall they be imposed upon, except what each one wishes to do of his own accord because of weakness for they are necessarily wearied in them . . ."[466]

3. Work done uselessly and outside obedience in this period especially (but perhaps also in other periods) *is to be burned* (p. 429{-30}).

4. The two weeks were *a time of fasting*. The negligent will be forcibly prevented from eating.

5. There are special assemblies.

6. The Weeks—*Sabbaton*—were not necessarily weeks of seven days. Kuhn thinks they were Holy Week and Easter week.[467] {The} problem {with this interpretation is}: would they fast in Easter week?[468]

465. Kuhn, 428–29.

466. Kuhn, 429.

467. Kuhn, 433.

468. Kuhn himself notes this: see 434.

Shenoute

Abbot of Atripé or the White Monastery (Adribah), {he was} the outstanding figure of *late* Pachomian monachism—{of the} fifth century (was Shenoute at {the} Council of Ephesus?)[469] {He is} interesting because there are no Greek and Latin sources. Shenoute is completely Coptic and has never entered into the Western tradition at all. And yet Coptic legends claim that the fame of Shenoute spread to Rome and that a sermon of his on death was read in Rome—not only that, but when a copy of this sermon was brought to the tomb of St. Peter, the Apostle put out his hand and touched it, speaking (to Shenoute present in the document): "Welcome today, on your arrival in this place, O friend, Master and pure Apostle. Surely as my lord Paul became the thirteenth Apostle, you shall be the fourteenth. . . ." etc.[470]

Other legends {state that} he walked about the monastery with Christ, Ezechiel, {and} many saints of {the} Old and New Testaments. On Saturdays he went into Paradise to hear the reading of the Apocalypse—if he was ill he sent one of the monks instead. Once when he wanted an apple, a monk brought him one from the garden of Eden. {He} travels about on a luminous cloud. His habit consisted of a belt that had belonged to St. John {the} Baptist, a tunic that had belonged to Elias, and underwear worn by the three youths in the fiery furnace. {He was the} son of a poor fellah {and} had been a shepherd. Then {he became} a monk under his uncle Bgoue, {and} became a great figure in {the} Coptic Church at {the} time of St. Cyril and {the} Council of Ephesus (431). {He is} said to have ruled 2,200 monks and 1,800 nuns.

469. According to Besa's *Life of Shenoute* (cc. 128–30 [78–79]) he did attend the Council of Ephesus; see also Bell's Introduction, 16–18, which confirms his presence at Ephesus and raises the question whether he was also present at Chalcedon twenty years later.

470. Ladeuze, 137–38.

Sources:

1) *Panegyrics on the anniversary of his death*—in Theban and Memphibic dialects[471] and in Arabic. These were studied at the end of the nineteenth century by Amélineau[472] and Ladeuze.[473] The panegyrics are idealizations of Shenoute, far from the reality, and Ladeuze comments: "In reading the work of Visa [author of {the} panegyrics] one would never imagine that the passionate and violent conduct of the Father [Shenoute] maintained in his monastery a state of permanent revolt" (*Étude sur le Cenobitisme Pachomien*, p. 137). We even see that civil authorities come to the monastery to restore order and Shenoute knocks down one of the magistrates and tramples on him. He appears to have killed a priest and a woman whom he suspected of sinning together (see Ladeuze, p. 139).[474]

2) *Letters and Sermons of Shenoute*—{These are} more authentic and reliable as historical sources. {They are} concerned with divisions and revolts in his monasteries and with reform of secular priests, attacks on idolatry, defense of the poor. {He was} "essentially impressionable . . . The greater part of his writings was written in moments of anger and fury; yet others bear the mark of delicate sensibility . . ." (Amélineau, in Ladeuze, *op. cit.*, p. 153).[475] We must recognize in Shenoute a great zeal for

471. These Coptic dialects are now called Sahidic and Bohairic, respectively: the former is the language of Upper Egypt, the latter of the delta (see Veilleux, *Pachomian Koinonia*, 1:2); Sahidic, the dialect of Shenoute, became "the standard literary idiom of Christian Egypt until it was itself supplanted by Bohairic in the later middle ages" (Bell, 1).

472. See Amélineau, *Les Moines Égyptiens: Vie de Schenoudi*, and Visa, *Panégyriques de Schenoudi*, Mémoires publiée par les Membres de la Mission Archéologique Française en Caire, vol. 4, ed. E. C. Amélineau (Paris: MMFC, 1895).

473. Ladeuze, 116–49.

474. According to the legend related here by Ladeuze, Shenoute struck the ground with his staff and the earth opened and swallowed them alive. In a different incident (see Ladeuze, 218) a monk died from a beating administered by Shenoute, even though "[t]he monk concerned was guilty of no more than a minor theft and a trivial lie" (Bell, 29, n. 59 [translating Ladeuze]).

475. Citation of *Vie de Schenoudi*, 233.

social justice and a love of the poor, also a very *active* idea of monasticism. His monks battled to exterminate paganism and to better the conditions of the poor.

3) *Rule of Shenoute*[476]—No "Rule" as such survives, but there are documents containing some of the innumerable regulations made by Shenoute, especially regarding *work*. Shenoute seems to be the originator of the *written schedule* of "profession," i.e. a kind of contract among the brethren to keep a similar observance of the common life (not yet vows). This pact was not binding for life. Shenoute insists on *uniformity* (against Pachomius); {he} reproves bakers for making extra bread for themselves. {He} attacks negligence at work, and keeping fruits of work for {one's} own use. Those who did not work hard enough were expelled. {He} conducted monastic schools for children. {The} *synaxis* consisted of {an} Invitatory (Ps. 94), {a} *Pater*, then immediately {a} reading from Scripture on which the monks then meditated—*a homily could be given*. {There was} solemn liturgy on Sundays—laypeople came in crowds and were fed by {the} monks after {the} sacrifice. Study was emphasized, especially study of the Scripture, and *memorizing* long parts of {the} Bible. There was a scriptorium and a fine tradition of manuscript copying and illumination. *Fasting* {was} more strict than Pachomian fasts; Shenoute allowed *one* meal a day, and greater austerity was demanded in the diet. Also he suppressed the liberty allowed by Pachomius and insisted that all should be exactly alike. {The} only exceptions {were} for the sick, in a special refectory, not to be seen by others. His penal code does not exist today, but documents record many beatings of monks, imprisonments, expulsions, etc.

Conclusion: The generalizations about Pachomian cenobitism in its "rigidity," "military organization" etc. seem to be based on Shenoute more than on Pachomius. We must clearly recognize the *genius*, *sanctity*, and *discretion* of Pachomius, especially his great warmth of humanity and his breadth of view. While recognizing the picturesque elements of violence in Shenoute, we

476. Merton relies here on Ladeuze, 305–26.

must not oversimplify. He too is evidently an important figure in monastic history, militant and active, and not without compassion for the poor—the oppressed class from which he himself came.

Saint Basil[477]

Cappadocian Monasticism and its Influence in the West. One of the most important monastic influences upon the West is, as we see from the Benedictine *Rule* (c. {73}),[478] the work of *St. Basil*. A more detailed study of St. Basil is being made in the Juniorate,[479] so such a study is not necessary here. We shall confine ourselves to a brief introduction to St. Basil and his background, and then look a little more closely at some of the *Basilian documents in Latin that were widely known in the West in the sixth century*. We are here concerned only with the "monastic" ideas of St. Basil, and not with his theology as such.

Life: {we give here} the bare outline of those facts which concern us. {In} 351 A.D., Basil's mother and his sister Macrina, with a younger brother, Peter, retire to live ascetic lives at Annesi, Cappadocia, while Basil goes to Athens to study. In Athens he meets Gregory Nazianzen; they discuss monastic life. Basil breaks with Classical culture, though not completely rejecting it (see Letter on Greek Literature[480]) and begins to investigate {the} monastic life. *Flight from the world* {is} one of his great themes. Before 358, having come under the influence of Eustathius of Sebaste in

477. Merton discusses St. Basil in *Cassian and the Fathers*, 45–51.

478. McCann, 161 (the chapter number is left blank in the typescript).

479. Fr. John Eudes Bamberger was teaching a course on Basil to the juniors (newly professed monks) at this time and in fact gave two lectures on Basil (Sept. 15 and 22, 1963) during Merton's regular conference period while Merton was in the hospital.

480. *Ad Adolescentes Quomodo Possint ex Gentium Libris Fructum Capere* ("To Youths, on How to Profit by Pagan Books") (*PG* 31, cols. 563-90); Werner Jaeger calls this oration the "charter for all Christian higher education for centuries to come" (*Early Christianity and Greek Paideia* [Cambridge, MA: Harvard University Press, 1961], 81).

Asia Minor, {he} visits Egypt, but returns disillusioned with the hermit monasticism of Lower Egypt. There is no evidence that he visited Pachomian monasteries of Upper Egypt, and it is entirely inaccurate to say that he adopted Pachomian ideas and took them to Asia Minor, giving "extreme" Egyptian cenobitism a "prudent" adaptation more fitted for the Greek mind, etc., etc. After 364 {comes the} composition of the *Rules* ({see the} comment on this name below). {In} 370 {he becomes} Bishop of Caesarea. He rewrites the *Rule* in a longer version, which Gribomont[481] calls the "Grand Asceticon" (not to be confused with the "Long Rules" or General Principles of ascetic life—QQ. 1-25 of {the} *Grand Asceticon*; {there is} much confusion in the use of these names). As Bishop of Caesarea, he orients his monks in a distinctively *active* direction by the erection of a hospital which they serve. {He} dies {in} 379 before finishing his fiftieth year.

"Rules" of St. Basil?? We now return to the question of the Basilian *Rules*. *The name Rule is inaccurate.*

1) Basil had no intention of *writing a Rule*. For him, there was but one Rule for the Christian, namely the Gospel.

2) The *Morals* or *Moral Rules* of St. Basil are nothing but a collection of New Testament texts, in which St. Basil seeks to outline systematically the basic teachings of the Gospel on Christian renunciation and the duties of the Christian life. It would be false to imagine that the *Morals* are unimportant, or accidental. They are the very substance of his teaching, though without any personal comment of his own. It would be false to imagine that they were a "Rule" written accidentally "for laymen" as distinct from a supposedly "more important Rule" written "for monks." The *Asceticon* is simply an elaboration of these Gospel principles in question and answer form. {It involves the} same principles, {the} same Christian life. However the *Morals* represent a reaction against the ascetic extremism of certain monastic groups, not those of Egypt so much as those of Asia Minor, particularly the Eustathians. Basil appeals to the simple Gospel and supports *sane*

481. "Saint Basile," 104.

asceticism of {the} Eustathians. The *Asceticon* (*Long Rules, Short Rules*) represents not a "more moderate form of monastic life" against an "extreme monastic life" of Eustathius, but a *more normal Christian life* as against the extremism preached as genuine Christianity by the more radical Eustathians. THE *ASCETICON* AND THE *MORALS* OF ST. BASIL ARE THEN PROGRAMS OF CHRISTIAN PERFECTION FOR ALL CHRISTIANS AND NOT SPECIALIZED RULES FOR MONASTIC COMMUNITIES LIVING TOTALLY APART from the ordinary faithful. But he does envisage ascetic community life. {For} *example,* {see} excerpts from the *Long Rules* (QQ. 37–41) on daily work and prayer. These instructions to "the brethren" are very interesting when seen as addressed to Christian ascetics "in the world" rather than monks entirely out of the world. See *Ascetic Works of St. Basil* (The *Fathers of the Church* Series, p. 309 ff.[482]):

p. 309: The canonical hours: N.B. some may not be able to be present at tierce. This is obviously a different system from the monastic ideal of uninterrupted prayer.

p. 311: What trades are suitable for the brethren? those which permit a minimum of disturbance and do not pander to false tastes of the "consumer."

p. 312: marketing the products of the brethren's work (Q. 39).

p. 313: not doing business at shrines (Eustathius' influence!).

Community life—see p. 295[483] (brethren {are} freed from care for relations).

p. 305: those who leave.[484]

p. 245: need of retirement.[485]

Cf. *Morals* (*Rule* 2, p. 74), and *Preface* to *Long Rules* (p. 223) (here it is stated {that} their aim is the "devout life").

N.B.: *Photius* (ninth century) on a codex of *Ascetic Works* of St. Basil containing the *De Judicio Dei, De Fide, Moralia* and the

482. St. Basil, *Ascetical Works,* trans. Sister M. Monica Wagner, csc, FC 9 (Washington: Catholic University of America Press, 1950), 307–17.

483. Question 32.

484. Question 36.

485. Question 6.

Rules {wrote}: "This is a most useful book *for all those who tend to perfection* and to the possession of eternal goods, and *especially for those who live in common* [ἐν κοινοβίῳ] *the ascetic life* [or rather the ascetic struggle—τὸν ἀσκητικὸν ἀγῶνα] . . . . He gives, arranged in chapters and without explanation, the characteristics of the Christian [the *Morals*] and he also gives corresponding characteristics for those who are to preach the word. Then he presents as it were certain ascetic rules, disposed as question and answer . . . [*The Rules*]" (from *PG* 103:633-637; cf. Dom Guétet in *Mélanges Bénédictins* [1947], p. 61-62).[486] It is therefore misleading to regard these texts as (monastic) "Rules." Such is the thesis of Dom Gribomont, OSB.[487] Yet the fact remains that they reached the West as "Rules" and were read and meditated on in the West as "Rules." They are in fact rules of perfection for all who seek to be perfect Christians, especially those living an ascetic life in common—not necessarily for *organized monasticism* as we know it.

Eustathius of Sebaste and his doctrine. Eustathius was Basil's friend and guide, who introduced him to the full ascetic ideal, {and} urged him to go to Egypt. Basil long remained under the influence of Eustathius but gradually came to differ with him, though it would be wrong to think that he turned against him. It is true that Basil later broke with Eustathius, because the latter was in dogmatic error regarding the divinity of the Holy Spirit (see cc.10–27 of *De Spiritu Sancto*[488]). Yet when Basil was bishop he continued to follow the Eustathian ideas and he founded his hospital on the pattern which Eustathius had used, and with advice from two disciples of Eustathius.

486. F.-M. Guétet, "Une Recension Stoudite des Règles Basiliennes?" *Mélanges Bénédictins: Publiés à l'Occasion du XIVe Centenaire de la Mort de Saint Benoit, par les Moines de l'Abbaye de Saint-Jérôme de Rome* (Paris: Éditions de Fontenelle, 1947), 61–68.

487. See especially Gribomont, "Basile," 104.

488. See St. Basil the Great, *On the Holy Spirit*, trans. David Anderson (Crestwood, NY: St. Vladimir's Seminary Press, 1980), 45–103; for a summary of the controversy, see J. N. D. Kelly, *Early Christian Doctrines*, revised ed. (San Francisco: Harper & Row, 1978), 258–63.

Who was Eustathius? Bishop of Sebaste (Armenia) who had travelled in Egypt, admired the monks, propagated asceticism in Asia Minor, had many followers and many opponents. The left wing of Eustathius' following tended toward heresy and exaggerated asceticism, preparing the way for Messalianism. The influence of Eustathius precipitated a crisis reflected in the Council (Synod) of Gangres in 341,[489] more than ten years before Basil came under his direct influence, though Basil's family embraced ascetic life under {the} influence of Eustathius about ten years after the council. At the Council of Gangres, opposition to Eustathius by conservative elements in {the} Church crystallized in a "condemnation" of Eustathius or rather of the extreme tendencies which some of his followers promoted. From this council it is clear that the left-wing Eustathians *tended* toward schism, asserting that only the perfect ascetics were worthy the name of true Christians. Married clergy were despised. {The} hierarchy {was} condemned for compromising with the world of Imperial power. Ascetes were accused of disrupting {the} social order, breaking up marriages, urging slaves to flee masters and officials to leave jobs to become monks. Monks refused to pay taxes, etc. Ascetes {were} accused of contempt for {the} ordinary liturgical life of the Church, feasts of martyrs ({which} tended to be social festivities), contempt for created things, etc. Extremists on the other hand found that Eustathius himself was not strict enough. Some of the ascetes protested against his foundation of a hospital at Sebaste as a source of distractions and worldliness. They departed into the mountains with a group of men and women bound to celibate and ascetic life. These extremists, as later the Messalians, exalted {the} life of prayer beyond all else; prayer supplied for everything, better than work. {They} also practiced sacred dances and preached "liberation of women."

St. Basil and Eustathius. Rather than saying that St. Basil reacted against Eustathian ascesis, it would be better to say that St. Basil took *what he considered best* and most evangelical in the

489. See Gribomont, 99–100.

doctrine and practice of his master, and affirmed it, as against the extremism of the left wing, which involved total separation from the ordinary faithful, condemning them as un-Christian. In other words, after the Council of Gangres, St. Basil emphasized what was genuine and truly traditional in the doctrine and practice of Eustathius, and worked out a way of life for all Christians to be perfect, according to the teaching of the Gospel. This way of life was not strictly speaking *monastic* life—though tradition regarded it as such. If by monastic life is meant withdrawal from the ordinary Christian community as well as from the world, then Basil was not "legislating for the monastic life." If by monastic life is meant ascetic communities within and in contact with the Christian community as a whole, then this is what Basil envisaged! He is talking of what we mean today by the *religious life*—especially that of active congregations, rather than of "contemplative monks." The love of money and rank were to be renounced, along with the love of pleasure, comfort, etc. Emphasis was placed on a life of prayer *and work*, as opposed to the one-sided emphasis on prayer preached by the extremists.

St. Basil's opposition to hermits is to be seen in this light entirely. In his mind, the hermit is associated with the extremist asceticism of the Eustathian left-wingers, and with their "exaggerated" flight from the world. In this sense, Basil's opposition to hermits can be interpreted as simply *anti-monastic. He was against all flight from the normal Christian community life*. The hermit fled from the mutual responsibilities, duties, work, and communal relations of the ordinary Christian community, and therefore, in St. Basil's mind, was seeking something better than the Gospel—than which there can be no better way. St. Basil was not therefore saying simply that cenobitic monasticism was preferable to eremitical monasticism. He was saying that the ordinary life of the Gospel in the Christian community was by far preferable *to any form of monastic separation*. Hence to quote his censure of hermits as a defence of some other form of monastic life is to misunderstand St. Basil's true meaning, though it may be a more or less valid application of his ideas to another situation not envisaged by him.

On the other hand, for St. Basil *the Christian life itself is somewhat marginal* in relation to ordinary worldly society. For him, the Christian is obliged to follow the narrow way of the Gospel in all its strictness, and therefore without compromise with the world, as well as without ascetical extremism. The ordinary Christian is *out of the world. The ordinary Christian life is essentially and obligatorily a life of penance.* The ordinary Christian life is by its very nature a life of *metanoia* and of renunciation of the world. The perfect Christian life is lived in a community, apart from the world, under the guidance of a superior who discerns God's will for the community as a whole, but not one who hands down arbitrary commands to each member of the community. The life of the Christian community is a life immersed in the will and the love of God, present in the community. Charity is the common will and life of the Christian community, living in the Spirit, in Christ. Each must fulfill his obligation as a living member of a body united in the love of Christ, hence {the focus on} work, obedience, humility, good works, helping others, self-renunciation. Each strives to progress in charity to the perfect love of God, but the emphasis is always on active Christian charity, NOT ON CONTEMPLATION. St. Basil then does not legislate for contemplative monks, but writes a directory, based on {the} Gospel, for ordinary active life of Christians seeking salvation in community, united in the love of Christ and in a common flight from the world.

SOME TYPICAL BASILIAN TEXTS: in these texts what is important is not their authorship but their influence, in the West, as ascribed to St. Basil.

A. *Letter* 2, to St. Gregory Nazianzen.[490] (Contrast the serenity of this letter with *Letter* 1 of St. Bernard.[491]) {This is} thought

490. *PG* 32, cols. 223-234.

491. This letter was written to Bernard's "nephew" (actually his first cousin) Robert, who had abandoned the Cistercians for the less rigorous life of a Cluniac monk, and whom Bernard very emotionally begs to return to Clairvaux; see *The Letters of St. Bernard of Clairvaux*, trans. Bruno Scott James (Chicago: Henry Regnery, 1953), 1--10.

by Dom D. Amand[492] to have been written at {the} beginning of Basil's "monastic" conversion, about 358, 359. {It} is regarded as a first sketch of the ascetic doctrine in the *Rules*. Basil certainly lived a life of chastity and poverty in retirement from the world, and in a framework of obedience that was however not quite strict monastic obedience as we know it, or as it was found in Pachomius. His was certainly a life of penance and austerity and good works, to purify his soul, a life of prayer and meditation. But it was not in Basil's eyes precisely the same kind of thing as the eremitism which he viewed with suspicion and identified as the "monastic life" in the sense of a life opposed to and removed from the ordinary Christian life, which in his mind was essentially a renunciation of the world. Henceforth, with these qualifications, we will speak of St. Basil's "monastic" ideas and preserve the term without further comment.

Letter 2, though to Gregory, is essentially an open letter to all his intellectual friends, justifying his departure from the world.

1) He explains that he has left the world (the "business of the city"), but that now his great struggle is to leave *himself*. He is like a seasick man who has left a large boat to get into a smaller one, but is still seasick. Seasickness refers to the passions.

2) The aim of his conversion {is} *to take up his cross and follow Christ*. {He} quotes Matt. 16:24.

3) In order to do this, he needs *tranquillity*. He seeks to escape the agitation and multiple distractions of the world, in order to focus quietly on the *truth*. Here we see something of the neo-Platonic and classical background (Plotinus, philosophy of the Cynics). The Cynics sought independence, *autarcheia* (self-rule) by flight from the cares and responsibilities of the world. This classical flavor is deliberate, {intended} for Basil's friends in Athens. The program:

492. David Amand, *L'Ascèse Monastique de Saint Basile: Essai Historique* (Maredsous: Éditions de Maredsous, 1948), 86; this work includes a French translation of *Letter* 2 (87–94).

—to forcefully detach the soul from its complicity with the body and its inclination to favor the flesh;

—to get free from the world, not so much by physical separation as by interior detachment, that is by liberating the soul from fleshly complacency with the world. He uses the word *anachoresis* for separation from the world, but makes clear it is not bodily (*somatikos*). Interior detachment makes one: ἄπολιν = without city; ἄοικον = without home; ἀνιδιον = without property; ἀφιλέταιρον = without friends; ἄκτημονα = without possessions; ἄβιον = without means of livelihood; ἀπράγμονα = without business; ἀσυναλλακτον = without contracts to sign and without knowledge of human teachings;

—to live in ignorance of profane studies (however compare his letter on Greek literature);[493]

—"Preparation of the heart"—to cleanse the wax tablet of the heart from all imprint and make it ready to receive the writing of God. Solitude tames the passions. Hence Basil and his companions have chosen a place where they will not be disturbed by other men. Their *ascesis* must be continuous. Their life is an uninterrupted *exercise of piety* (*ascesis eusebeias*). It is an angelic life of praise, imitating the hymns and chants of angelic choirs on earth. This is the happiest kind of life—going out to work at sunrise with prayers on one's lips. Freedom from care is the foundation of joy, tranquillity the necessary basis of purification. {It is necessary} to turn one's thoughts from desire to see beautiful bodies, to hear melodies composed for pleasure, to listen to jokes —all this slackens the energy of the soul. (Read p. 7, Fathers of the Church edition: *Letters of St. Basil*.[494]) When the soul is tranquil

493. See above, n. 480.

494. Saint Basil, *Letters*, vol. 1, trans. Sr. Agnes Clare Way, CDP, FC 13 (New York: Fathers of the Church, 1951), 7: "A life of piety nourishes the soul with divine thoughts. What, then, is more blessed than to imitate on earth the choirs of angels; hastening at break of day to pray, to glorify the Creator with hymns and songs, and, when the sun is brightly shining and we turn to our tasks, to accompany them everywhere with prayer, seasoning the daily work with hymns, as food with salt? For, the inspirations of the sacred songs give rise to a joyousness that is without grief. Silence, then, is the beginning of purification in the soul,

it enters spontaneously into itself and ascends to God. *It forgets itself and is illumined by His splendor*. This is effected in the reading of Scripture, which is the perfect medicine for the passions (cf. *medicamina scripturarum*, St. Benedict[495]), {and by} examples of the Old Testament saints. *Lectio divina* leads to prayer and constant thought of God, {and so to} living with God.

THE ASCETIC LIFE IS AN ANGELIC LIFE OF JOY WITH GOD, RISING EARLY TO PRAISE HIM AND WORKING THROUGHOUT THE DAY WITH HYMNS AND SPIRITUAL CANTICLES OF LOVE FOR HIM.

Prayer is especially effective when the mind has been rejuvenated by reading and is filled with thirst for God. "Beautiful is that prayer which imprints upon the soul a keen awareness of God [ἔννοια]. This is the indwelling of God: to have God established in our memory."[496] Thus we become temples and sanctuaries of God. But we must fly from vice and do what pleases God. *Silence* plays an essential part in this ascesis. It is not a matter of absolute monastic silence, but of restraint in speech which could be proper to any gathering of Christians: first avoiding all vain and self-satisfied speech; giving credit to others if one's ideas are borrowed from them; moderating the voice; thinking carefully beforehand in preparation to speak; treating others with humility and kindness, especially when correcting them (Basil is very interested in fraternal correction). (See *Fathers of {the} Church*, p. 9.[497])

---

since the tongue is not busied with the affairs of men, nor the eyes looking around at fair complexions and graceful forms, nor the ears lessening the harmony of the soul by listening to melodies made for fleeting pleasure or to the sayings of wits and jesters, a course of action which tends especially to weaken the spiritual timbre of the soul."

495. *Rule*, c. 28: "the medicine of the Scriptures" (McCann, 78/79).

496. This is evidently Merton's own translation from the French; it is not from FC 13.

497. "He must at all times avoid harshness, even when there is need of censure. For, if you yourself have evinced true humility, your ministrations will be pleasing to him who requires them" (9–10); Basil goes on to cite the example of Nathan and King David in 2 S 11:12.

External Conduct: (See *Fathers of {the} Church*, p. 10[498]). This letter emphasizes certain exterior details of conduct: keeping the eyes on the ground as a sign of mourning (cf. {the} twelfth degree of humility {in} St. Benedict[499]); unkempt hair and clothes not necessarily clean (mark of {the} pagan philosopher); special ways of walking, wearing the belt, etc.; diet: bread, water and vegetables, eaten quietly and slowly with {the} thought of God; vigils: not yielding to bestial sleep; praying at midnight. {For} further information from {the} *Letters* of St. Basil, see *Letter 14*[500] for {a} description of his solitude (*Fathers of {the} Church*, p. 46–48); *Letter* 22 is entitled "On the Perfection of the Monastic Life" but we note that all its precepts are concerned with "*the Christian*."[501]

B. *The Sermo Asceticus* (*De Renuntiatione Saeculi*). {This} is thought by Gribomont to be not the work of Basil.[502] It is translated in {the} Fathers of {the} Church series *Ascetical Works of St. Basil*, p. 15 ff.[503] Obviously {it} long exerted an influence as a "work of St. Basil." Note how it opens:

> "Come to me, all you that labor and are burdened and I will refresh you," says the Divine Voice, signifying either earthly or heavenly refreshment. In either case, He calls us to Himself, inviting us, on the one hand, to cast off the burden of riches by distributing to the poor, and, on the other, to make haste to embrace the cross-bearing life of the monks by ridding ourselves through confession and good works of the load of sins contracted by our use of worldly goods. How truly admirable and happy, then, is he who has chosen to

498. Merton lists the instructions from this page and the next in the following lines.

499. This final degree focuses on an outward demeanor of humility corresponding to inner humility of heart (c. 7; McCann, 47, 49).

500. Written to Gregory Nazianzen.

501. *Letters*, 1 (55–60).

502. "Saint Basile," 111, citing his own "L'Exhortation au Rénoncement Attribuée à Saint Basile," *Orientalia Christiana Periodica*, 21 (1955), 375–98.

503. "An Ascetical Discourse and Exhortation on the Renunciation of the World and Spiritual Perfection," 15–31.

> heed Christ and hastens to take up the life of lowliness and recollection! (p. 15, *Fathers of the Church* series).

{Note the} emphasis on monastic life as {a} response to a clear call. However he insists that rigorous preliminary training is required, to prevent a relapse and a return to the world. (READ p. 15.)[504]

Within the state of renunciation, there are *two possible states*: marriage {and} virginity. Marriage is for those who cannot bear the trials of virginity. But such must also be saints, and follow {the} example of saints of {the} Old Testament like Abraham, who, in his willingness to sacrifice his son, preferred God before all; {he} kept the door open to travelers, {showing} hospitality; "For he had not heard the counsel 'sell what thou hast and give to the poor'" (p. 16)—in other words, hospitality as {a} substitute for poverty.

> Does it not seem to you, then, that the Gospel applies to married persons also? Surely, it has been made clear that obedience to the Gospel is required of all of us, both married and celibate. The man who enters the married state may well be satisfied in obtaining pardon for his incontinency and desire of a wife and marital existence, but the rest of these precepts are obligatory for all alike and are fraught with peril for transgressors. Christ, when He preached the commands of His Father, was speaking to persons living in the world; He clearly testified this by His answer on one occasion when He was privately questioned by His disciples: "And what I say to you, I say to all." Do not relax your efforts, therefore, you who have chosen the companionship of a wife, as if you were at liberty to embrace worldliness. Indeed, you have need of greater labors and vigilance for the gaining of your salvation, inasmuch as you have elected

504. "But, I beseech you, let no man do this thoughtlessly nor promise himself an easy existence and salvation without a struggle. He should, rather, undergo rigorous preliminary discipline with a view to proving his fitness to endure tribulations both of body and soul, lest, exposing himself to unforeseen stratagems, he be unable to resist the assaults against him and find himself in full retreat to his starting point, a victim of disgrace and ridicule."

> to dwell in the midst of the toils and in the very stronghold of rebellious powers, and night and day all your senses are impelled toward desire of the allurements to sin which are before your eyes (p. 17).

Note the negative idea of marriage—close to Messalianism, Catharism, etc.

However, the better way is the way of monks. "But, you who aspire to become a lover of the celestial polity, an active participant in the angelical life, and a fellow soldier of Christ's holy disciples, brace yourself for the endurance of tribulations and *manfully betake yourself to the company of the monks*":[505] renouncing relatives above all; renouncing earthly goods (giving them to the poor); renouncing friends and relatives to be united with Christ crucified; submitting one's soul to {a} spiritual father.

> With much care and forethought set about finding a man skilled in guiding those who are making their way toward God who will be an unerring director of your life. He should be adorned with virtues, bearing witness by his own works to his love for God, conversant with the Holy Scripture, recollected, free from avarice, a good, quiet man, tranquil, pleasing to God, a lover of the poor, mild, forgiving, laboring hard for the spiritual advancement of his clients, without vainglory or arrogance, impervious to flattery, not given to vacillation, and preferring God to all things else. If you should find such a one, surrender yourself to him, completely renouncing and casting aside your own will, that you may be found a clean vessel, preserving unto your praise and glory the good qualities deposited in you. For, if you suffer any of your former vices to remain within you, those virtues that were placed in you will become contaminated and you will be cast out like a vessel unfit for use (p. 19).

The job of this Spiritual Father is to "place all our sins before our eyes and correct them" (p. {19-}20). Hence, do not seek one who will condescend to vices, and leave you to pamper the body. Having found a true teacher, one must *do nothing against his will*.

505. *Ascetical Works*, 18 (emphasis added).

The rest of this text is concerned with characteristic and familiar ideas on humility, retirement in the cell, energetic self-discipline and renunciation, including a condemnation of eating between meals, or "nibbling in secret."

> The vice of gluttony is wont to display its proper force not with regard to a great quantity of food, but in the appetite for a little taste. If, therefore, desire of some bit of food succeed in making you subject to the vice of gluttony, he will give you up to destruction without further ado. For, as the nature of water that is channeled along many furrows causes it to make verdant the whole area around the furrows, so also the vice of gluttony, if it issue from your heart, irrigates all your senses, raising a forest of evils within you and making your soul a lair of wild beasts. I have seen many who were slaves to vice restored to health, but I have not seen this happen in the case of even one person who was given to nibbling in secret or gluttonous. Either they abandon the life of continency and are destroyed by the world, or they attempt to remain undetected among the continent and fight in league with the Devil by leading a luxurious life. They are liars, profane, perjurors, quarrelsome, pugnacious, noisy, given to disavowing their gluttony, mean, effeminate, querulous, prying, lovers of darkness, and deliberately hostile to every virtuous mode of life; in their efforts to cover up the vice of gluttony they are caught in a swarm of evils. In appearance, indeed, they seem to be among the number of the saved, but by their conduct they are included with the reprobate (pp. 24–25).[506]

Whether or not this text is by St. Basil, it is rather characteristic of his thought, especially in its advocation of stern austerity and its condemnation of little self-indulgent acts of gluttony (for as the above text shows, he means by gluttony eating unnecessarily for pleasure, especially "snacks" here and there, rather than huge banquets and large quantities, which are naturally excluded from monastic life).

506. The typescript reads "abandoned . . . pugnacious, not given . . ."

He concludes with the exhortation to examine one's conscience. "Examine the actions of each day, and compare them with those of the previous day and press on towards improvement"[507] (one of the rare texts explicitly recommending *examen* in the monastic tradition).

C. *The Admonitio ad Filium Spiritualem*—(not by St. Basil).[508] This "Basilian" text evidently was very influential in the West. There are passages clearly echoed in the Benedictine *Rule*, and it is included in a collection of "*Exhortationes ad monachos et virgines*" which is printed in {an} appendix to Benedict of Aniane's *Codex Regularum* in *PL* 103,[509] and it is thought to have been first brought together by him. With two texts of St. Athanasius,[510] this collection also includes *Sententiae*[511] of Evagrius and sermons of Faustus[512] and Eucherius[513] which we hope to discuss. {There are} indications that this may have been a text well known at Lérins.

1. The Proemium and first chapters of the *Admonitio* definitely remind us of St. Benedict.

a) Proemium: It begins as follows: *Audi, fili, admonitionem Patris tui, et inclina aurem tuam ad verba mea, et {accommoda} mihi libenter auditum tuum, et corde credulo cuncta quae dicuntur ausculta*[514]—cf.

507. *Ascetical Works*, 31, which reads ". . . each day, compare . . . toward . . ."

508. But note that Johannes Quasten (*Patrology*, 3 vols. [Westminster, MD: Newman, 1951–60], 3.215-16) points out that the latest editor of this work, which exists only in Latin, believes the letter to be authentic, translated by Rufinus; while somewhat skeptical of Basilian authorship, Quasten does think it is a translation of an Eastern work: "Everything points to the Egyptian monasticism of the Scetis as the place of origin" (215).

509. Cols. 665-702; the "*Admonitio*" occupies cols. 683-700.

510. Cols. 665-84.

511. Printed in *PL* 20, cols. 1181-1186.

512. Printed in *PL* 58, cols. 869-890.

513. Printed in *PL* 50, cols. 865-868, 1207-1212.

514. Cols. 683D-685A: "Listen, son, to the instruction of your father, and incline your ear to my words, and freely focus your hearing on me, and with a believing heart attend to all that is said." (Typescript reads *"accomoda."*)

the *Incipit* of the Benedictine *Rule*.[515] Incidentally, in the light of this, we can question the idea of those who said, piously but without basis, that St. Benedict in his *incipit* must have referred to the Holy Spirit and not to himself. Here there is no doubt that the Abbot himself speaks, or in any case the writer of the *Admonitio* (*Abbas* in the ancient sense of spiritual Father, rather than canonical superior). Immediately this sentence follows: *Cupio enim te instruere quae sit spiritualis militia et quibus modis regi tuo militare debeas*.[516] This idea is continued in the first chapter, *De Militia spirituali* (col. 685). Ideas on the *militia* of the monk:

(1) *Si cupis, fili, militare Deo, illi soli militabis*[517] (cf. *soli Deo placere*[518]). This {is} followed by {an} analogy of obedience of {an} earthly soldier: how much more must one obey the heavenly King? *Multo magis miles Christi sine aliquo impedimento regis sui debet imperio obedire*.[519]

(2) The earthly soldier fights visible enemies: our enemies are invisible. There follows a trope on the "panoply" of the spiritual warfare, Christ our helmet, breastplate, etc. Our weapons: *divina eloquia jaculare*[520] (Scriptural prayer).

(3) Our enemy never sleeps, {but is} always active against us. He is much more clever than any earthly enemy.

(4) The arms of the earthly soldier are heavy to carry. Ours are light for those who love Christ.

515. "*Ausculta, o fili, praecepta magistri, et inclina aurem cordis tui et admonitionem pii patris libenter excipe et efficaciter comple*" ("Hearken, my son, to the precepts of the master and incline the ear of thy heart; freely accept and faithfully fulfil the instructions of a loving father") (McCann, 6/7).

516. Col. 685A: "For I wish to teach you what the spiritual army is, and by what means you must serve your King."

517. Col. 685AB (which reads "*Si ergo cupis . . .*"): "My son, if you wish to serve God, you will serve him alone."

518. St. Gregory the Great, *Dialogi*, Book II (*The Life of St. Benedict*), c. 1: "*soli Deo placere desiderans*" ("desiring to please God alone") (*PL* 66, col. 125).

519. Col. 685B: "Much more so the soldier of Christ should obey the command of his King with no hindrance."

520. Col. 685B: "to hurl the spear of divine eloquence."

(5) The earthly soldier, after the battle, returns to his wife and children. We enter into the Kingdom of heaven. *Coeleste enim donum exspectet monachus, qui terrenos actus a semetipso projicit,* ne implicet se negotiis saecularibus militans Deo. *Difficile namque est servire duobus Dominis; nec potest quisquam serviens mammonae spiritualia arma portare, sed jugum Christi suave ac leve a semetipso repellit ac projicit: et quidquid grave et onerosum est animae suae, hoc ei videtur suave ac leve. Istiusmodi vir a propriis armis vulneratur* etc. (col. 685).[521] The chapter concludes: you are about to build a high tower, out of virtues: consider the cost, and take care not to work in vain. It is easy to see here not only the general spirit of St. Benedict but the same language and train of thought. But Benedict condenses all this in the sentence: *quisquis abrenuntians propriis voluntatibus, DOMINO CHRISTO VERO REGI MILITATURUS obedientiae fortissima atque praeclara arma assumis;*[522] and also: "*a saeculi actibus se facere alienum*"[523] (from the Instruments of Good Works).

Chapter 2—*De Virtute Animae*.[524] This is reminiscent of chapter 4 of the *RB*, "Instruments of Good Works."[525] {It is} continuing the idea of serving one King: he who wishes to serve Christ will try to please Him in all things and displease Him in nothing. Our whole life must be centered in one thought: *ne occupes in diversis*

521. The text reads ". . . *dominis; . . . spiritalia* . . .": "For the monk may expect a heavenly reward, who banishes from himself earthly actions lest one enrolled in God's service become involved in worldly business. For it is difficult to serve two masters; and no one serving mammon can carry spiritual arms, but repels and drives away from himself the sweet and light yoke of Christ: and whatever is heavy and burdensome to his soul seems sweet and light to him. In this way a man is wounded by his own weapons."

522. "whosoever thou mayest be that renouncing thine own will to fight for the true King, Christ, dost take up the strong and glorious weapons of obedience" (Prologue; McCann, 6/7 [which reads "*sumis*" for "*assumis*"]).

523. *Rule*, c. 4: lit. "to make oneself a stranger to the actions of the world" (McCann, 26/27, where it is translated "To avoid worldly conduct").

524. "On the Virtue of the Soul" (col. 686AC).

525. McCann, 27–33.

animum tuum.[526] This thought is, by "*virtus animi*"[527] to cut off carnal love lest it destroy the fear of God in us (cf. {the} first degree of humility in St. Benedict[528]). {This is the} basis of monastic asceticism. Then {follows} a list of good works which constitute *virtus animae*: first love, then patience, chastity, etc. Each virtue is paired off with {its} opposite vice: v.g. *Virtus animae est avaritiam spernere, et voluntariam assumere paupertatem* (686).[529]

Conclusion: "all these virtues you can easily obtain if you set aside all worldly cares and prefer heavenly things to those that are passing. AND IF YOUR WILL BE OCCUPIED IN THE PRAISES OF GOD AND IF YOU ZEALOUSLY MEDITATE ON HIS JUDGEMENTS DAY AND NIGHT, you will be like a tree planted next to the rivers of water, all spiritual fruits will grow from you, and instead of a servant of God, you will be called His friend" (686). Note here themes which we find often in the Cistercian Fathers: the idea of the "friend" of God rather than the servant;[530] the idea (above[531]) that when we love God the spiritual warfare is light and easy, and when we do not love Him, worldly pleasures which are in reality a burden and sorrow for the soul, appear to us to be light and pleasant. This gives us the general tone of the *Admonitio*. The rest can be looked at more summarily.

Chapter 3. *The Love of God*, purity of intention, seeking to please Him alone. "*In simplicitate cordis*"[532] is the keynote—God

526. Col. 686B, which reads "*nec . . . diversis rebus . . .*": "Do not occupy your soul with various matters."

527. Col. 686B, which reads "*virtus animae*" (as below in Merton's text).

528. The first degree of humility focuses on keeping the fear of God present in the mind as a way of preventing evil actions and avoiding evil desires (McCann, 39, 41).

529. "The virtue of the soul is to scorn avarice and take up voluntary poverty."

530. See St. Bernard, *On the Song of Songs*, 59.1: "And those whom he loves he calls friends, not servants. The master has become the friend; for he would not have called the disciples friends if it were not true" (Bernard of Clairvaux, *On the Song of Songs* III, trans. Kilian Walsh, OCSO, and Irene Edmonds, CF 31 [Kalamazoo, MI: Cistercian Publications, 1979], 121).

531. In #5 (col. 685).

532. Col. 686D: "In simplicity of heart."

sees our intentions (cf. c. 7 of {the} *RB*, first degree of humility[533]). Here also {are the} reasons of loving God above all: obvious ones, but they are taken up again in St. Bernard's *De Diligendo Deo*, cc. 2, 3 etc.[534]

Chapter 4. *Love of Brethren*: he who loves his brother is truly a son of God. He who loves his brother has TRUE PEACE. (This {is} another important theme of the *Admonitio*.) The idea may be summed up {thus}: love of brother means conquering all one's self-love, forgiving injuries etc., rendering good for evil, truly evangelical perfection, which is at once a *proof of the reality of our love for God* and the true guarantee *of inner peace*. "He who loves his brother has his heart in tranquillity. But he who hates his brother is surrounded by a tremendous storm. The kindly man, even when he suffers injury, regards it as nothing. But the wicked man looks upon any action of his neighbor as bringing harm to himself. He who is full of love goes forth with a most placid countenance; but the man full of hate goes about in a rage" (688). Note the style, reminiscent of the Book of Proverbs.

Chapter 5 is entirely devoted to Peace: *DE STUDIO PACIS*[535] (688). (N.B.: *PAX*—{the} unofficial Benedictine motto.) Note {the} essential connection between *peace* and *truth*. Peace is based on perfect inner sincerity: love without simulation, {having} no inner desire to hurt anyone. This is the basis of peace because if we desire to hurt a brother we are in reality trying to hurt one who

533. "let him consider that God is always beholding him from heaven, that his actions are everywhere visible to the eye of the Godhead, and are constantly being reported to God by the angels. The prophet teaches us this when he represents God as always present in our thoughts: *God searcheth the heart and the reins*; and again: *The Lord knoweth the thoughts of men*; and again he saith: *Thou hast understood my thoughts from afar*" (McCann, 39).

534. Bernard points out that God gives the basic necessities, food, sight, air, for the body, and the higher gifts of dignity, knowledge and virtue for the soul (n. 2), and then goes on to point out the interdependence of these higher gifts, such that dignity without knowledge is unprofitable, since one is unaware of one's stature, and dignity without virtue becomes an obstacle, since one falsely takes credit to oneself rather than giving it to God (n. 3) (*Treatises* II, 95–96).

535. "On Dedication to Peace."

is a "part" of our own self, a "member" of the one Body, from which we draw all our life—hence the importance of reconciliation as {the} basis of peace, and true sense of community—not to let night fall without reconciliation. "He who embraces peace in the house of his mind prepares a dwelling for Christ in himself. For Christ is peace, and seeks to rest in peace. . . . The peaceful man has his mind always in security, etc." (688). Peace illuminates the secret recesses of the mind, but envy fills the inmost heart with obscurity (688). Note, throughout he contrasts the peaceful man with the envious man (*invidus*);[536] {it is} important to note this. He has referred above to envy of the virtues of others in the community life (c. 4). SECTARE FILI DESIDERABILE NOMEN PACIS, UT FRUCTUS PACIS POSSIS ACQUIRERE (689).[537]

Chapter 6. Patience.

Chapter 7. Chastity and continency. Here the emphasis is on avoiding the slightest contamination of lust, watching the smallest beginnings and thus preventing danger, especially by custody of the eyes, etc. {The} *motive* {is} the love of Christ, and the realization that we have dedicated our bodies to Him. Note that he speaks of clerics or monks (this is not exclusively for "monks") going to the house of a virgin. The mere entering {of} the house is undesirable. They should not seek opportunities of conversation, not prolong talk, etc. On not touching a woman even slightly {he writes}: "just as straw too close to the fire catches alight, so he who touches the flesh of a woman does not escape without harm to his soul" (689–690).

Chapter 8, on flight from the world, continues the above. The context is chastity. {There is} a long passage on the vanity of loving the flesh that must die and be corrupted—how quickly beauty fades (a literary trope). Age makes the loved one an object of repulsion. {Concerning} death, he suggests contemplation of the dead body of the beloved, falling into corruption. Read the passage where he repeatedly asks, "Where are the . . . smiles,

536. Col. 688D: "envious."

537. The text reads ". . . *fili, ergo*, . . .": "My son, follow the desirable name of peace, so that you might be able to gain the fruits of peace."

joking words, the vain joys etc." (col. 690). Hence, the *dangerous love of beauty* must be avoided at all costs. It leads to ruin; it darkens the eye so that it cannot see truth: a great passage (cf. St. John of the Cross, *Ascent* III, cc. 21, 22, 23[538]). {What is} the remedy? "Turn then thy soul from these obscene loves and direct all thy love to the resplendent beauty of Christ, that the rays of His glory may enlighten thy heart and all the mists of darkness may be driven out of thee" (690).

Chapter 9. Against avarice, for voluntary poverty and labor to help in almsgiving.

Chapter 10. Humility: {note the} contrast between the proud man and the humble man.

Chapter 11. Prayer: {he emphasizes} the humility necessary for prayer; never presuming on any merits of our own, we should base our petitions not on any confidence in ourselves, but on God's goodness alone. Hence we should confess our sins in prayer, and not be like the Pharisee. Our prayer must be silent, *non clamore vocis orabis*.[539] It must be simple, in few words. *QUIA NON IN MULTILOQUIO, SED EX MENTE PURISSIMA PLACABITUR DOMINUS*[540] (cf. *RB* c. 20[541]). {Note the} importance of forgiving our brother before we pray; and of thanking God after we pray.

This theme is continued in chapter 12, on Vigils. Prayer should be based on {the} hope of finding God: *Quaere Dominum*

538. Chapter 21 says that to rejoice in gifts of body and soul for themselves alone is vanity and deception, a focus on the gift rather than the Giver, and such gifts are transitory; chapter 22 discusses the particular evils that arise from finding one's joy in natural goods: vainglory, complacency, self-deception, clouding of mind and spirit, distraction, aversion to divine things; chapter 23 focuses on the benefits of detachment from material goods, including humility, charity toward others, self-denial, inner tranquillity, lack of desire for evil, generosity of soul (Peers, I:257-64).

539. Col. 695D: "you shall not pray with a loud voice."

540. Col. 696A: "because the Lord will be pleased not with many words but by a very pure mind."

541. "*Et non in multiloquio, sed in puritate cordis et compunctione lacrimarum nos exaudiri sciamus*" ("And let us be sure that we shall not be heard for our much speaking, but for purity of heart and tears of compunction") (McCann, 68/69).

et invenies eum, nec dimittas cum tenueris, ut copulatur mens tua in amorem ejus.[542] Pure prayer {is} to be offered to God: *Hic stude in vita tua, ut orationem puram offeres Deo.*[543] {A way of} fighting distractions {is to} realize the presence of God (cf. *RB* c. 19[544]). {He} speaks of two kinds of prayer (which go to make up vigils): *tempus orationis*—importance of *puritas; tempus psalmorum*—importance of *sapientia* and *vigilantia;*[545] in both these we must avoid sleep; *ne dissonans sit sensus et lingua*[546] (cf. *RB* c. 19[547]); *in tempore psalmodiae sapienter psalle*[548] (cf. *RB* c. 19[549]) ({Note the} full implications of *sapienter*); *per* orationes purissimas *omnia quae nobis sunt utilia tribuuntur a Domino, et cuncta quae noxia sunt procul dubio effugantur*[550] (col. 693) (examine all the implications of this). The *Virtus Psalmorum*[551] (693): they "soften the heart"; they are very sweet on the lips, but only to those who sing "with vigilance and wisdom." The mind must pay attention to the meaning of the words. The interior man is nourished by these sacred words, just as the exterior man is nourished by food. Vigilance must go over into all our acts so that in all of them we may please God (once

542. Col. 693B (which reads "*copuletur*"): "Seek the Lord and you will find him, and when you have possessed him do not send him away, so that your soul might be joined in his love."

543. Col. 693B (which reads "*Hoc . . . offeras . . .*"): "devote yourself to this in your life, in order to offer pure prayer to God."

544. "Let us then consider how we ought to behave ourselves in the presence of God and his angels" (McCann, 67, 69).

545. Col. 693B, which reads "*in tempore orationis vel psalmorum*" ("in the time of prayer and of psalmody"); the references to purity, wisdom and vigilance are found in the passage quoted below.

546. Col. 693B: "let there be no dissonance between sense and word."

547. "*sic stemus ad psallendum ut mens nostra concordat voci nostrae*" ("so sing the psalms that mind and voice may be in harmony") (McCann, 68/69).

548. Col. 693B: "at the time for psalms, pray psalms wisely."

549. "*Psallite sapienter*" ("*Sing ye wisely*") (McCann, 66/67, a quotation from Ps. 46 [47]:8).

550. The text reads ". . . *nobis quae* . . .": "through most pure prayers everything that is useful to us is bestowed by God, and let all that is harmful be fled from without hesitation."

551. "Power of the Psalms."

again {there is an} emphasis on purity of intention, serving one master) (col. 694)—hence {the importance of the} examination of conscience: *Quotidie actus tuos discute curiosius* etc. (694).[552]

SPIRITUALITY OF ST. BASIL'S "RULES" (*The Asceticon*). A brief outline will be sufficient. We are mainly concerned with the version of Rufinus in Latin (*PL* 103, col. 485 ff.)[553] (Gribomont[554] calls this "*Le Petit Asceticon*.") Rufinus, in his preface, tells Urseius about the *Rule* of St. Basil. His friend Urseius is a Western abbot having a monastery on a sandy island dotted with pine trees. He has asked Rufinus not a lot of curious questions about the places where the monks of the East live, but about their observance. Rufinus will translate the "*instituta monachorum*"[555] of St. Basil, which he gave in reply to "his monks" when they asked him questions. He does not call this a rule but "*velut sancti cujusdam juris responsa*,"[556] *definitiones, sententias*,[557] etc., *sancta et spiritualia instituta*,[558] containing a way of life and prayer which he hopes Western monks will follow, "as it is followed in the monasteries of Cappadocia."[559] (Note: Sozomenus says [see *PL* 103, col. 483][560] that this "*liber de institutis monachorum*"[561] had even been attributed to Eustathius, who "is said to have been the first to have instituted the monastic life and its regular observance.")

The Prologue {is} briefer in Rufinus than in *Fathers of* {*the*} *Church*,[562] which has the later redaction. (Note: the earlier, shorter redaction is often *clearer* and a better indication of {the} author's thought.) Rufinus simply states the situation in the Church: some

552. "Thoughtfully examine your acts daily."

553. Cols. 483-554.

554. Gribomont, 104.

555. Col. 485B: "the monastic way of life."

556. Col. 485B: "the answers, as it were, of holy law itself."

557. Col. 486A: "definitions, judgments."

558. Col. 486A: "holy and spiritual practices."

559. Col. 486A.

560. *Historia Ecclesiastica*, III.13.

561. "book of the way of life of the monks."

562. *Ascetical Works*, 223–31.

teach; others are taught. This is the *ministerium verbi.*[563] Those who have this ministry must be ready at all times to instruct souls in the way of perfection:

a) sometimes *in communi Ecclesiae auditorio*[564]—instruction given to *all*, together.

b) at other times *secretius,*[565] for the more perfect, to answer questions of concrete detail. This "secret" instruction is concerned with the greater perfection, and it is in regard to this that he gives the answers that make up his "Rules." These are then the fruits of spiritual conferences of the brethren, apparently after vigils. He spurs them to ask questions. All together will pray that God may give him relevant answers. *Tamquam ergo scientes* quia stabunt ante faciem vestram verba haec ante *tribunal Christi . . . ita et intendite animum vigilanter ad haec quae dicuntur* (487).[566]

Love, the basis of the Christian Life:

Q. 1. Is there an order in the commandments of God—are some things more important than others? Love is more important than all: first of God, then of neighbor.

Q. 2. Rufinus here develops the basic doctrine of love ({in} *Fathers of the Church*, this is spread over QQ. 2–6).[567] The power to love is implanted in us by nature. We do not "learn" love. Love is a natural "seed" which is cultivated by observance of the commandments of God. It is a spark which is enkindled to flame by the preaching of the Word. It contains within itself the seeds of all the other virtues. The task of the Spiritual Master is to awaken these latent seeds and sparks. We must remove obstacles: sins. Even beasts love their progenitors—how much more we should love God our Father (hence this seed of love is directed first of

563. Col. 487A: "the ministry of the word."

564. Col. 487A: "in the common hearing of the Church."

565. Col. 487A: "more privately."

566. The text reads "*Tanquam*": "Knowing, then, that these words will stand before the judgement seat of Christ as they do before your face, . . . incline your soul attentively to what is being said."

567. *Ascetical Works*, 232–47.

all to Him from whom it came). The greatest of miseries is to be alienated from the love of God, as all our being draws us to Him. The love of our brother is also natural to us. It is the same love which draws us to God. Right use of the inborn natural drives which lead us to love God and neighbor, is virtue. Wrong use of these drives is sin.

Disciplina Placendi Deo.[568] But right use of our natural powers has to be learned. It is an "art." This art is called the *disciplina placendi Deo*. Hence the spiritual education of the Christian and above all the monk is training in how to please God by loving Him in all things. But in order to please Him more perfectly we must break all ties with the world, and devote ourselves, in separation from the world, to total attention to His service. This gathers everything into one single intention, *unus prospectus*,[569] having only one aim in view—to give pleasure to God. The *Regula placendi Deo*[570] recurs throughout the *Rules*: {see} for instance Q. 14 (Rufinus), the *Affectus bonus*,[571] or the true interior dispositions of the servant of God. It is present when we have a *DESIDERIUM VEHEMENS ET INEXPLEBILE PLACENDI DEO* (col. 506).[572] This *affectus* has various aspects: *THEORIA*—that is to say "the knowledge [*gnosis*] by which we can apprehend and behold the magnificence of the glory of God";[573] *cogitationes pias et puras*;[574] *memoria bonorum, quae*

568. This particular phrase does not appear here; the text does say, "*unus terminus fixus est, quo Deo placere debeamus*" (col. 492D) ("one end has been established, by which we should please God"). The phrase "discipline for pleasing God" appears in the *Long Rules*, Q. 5 (*Ascetical Works*, 242) but there is no direct equivalent in the Latin here, and the Latin translation of the original Greek in *PG* 31, col. 919C reads "*exercitatio ad placendum Deo*"; Merton may have created the Latin phrase from the English translation, paralleling "*regula placendi Deo*," which does appear.

569. Col. 492D.

570. Col. 547D (title to Q. 65, which reads "*Regulam*"): "the Rule of pleasing God."

571. Col. 547D: "good inclination."

572. "a powerful and insatiable desire to please God."

573. Col. 506C.

574. Col. 506C: "reverent and pure reflections."

nobis a Deo collata sunt.[575] In remembering the mercies of God to us we are inflamed to love Him with our whole heart. *Sicut cervus . . .*[576] The result of this {is} that nothing can separate us from the love of Christ (col. 506).

We find it again in Q. 47—{which has a} very short answer: *Quis est mansuetus?*[577] Response: *Qui non transfertur a judiciis suis,* quibus statuit vel studet Deo placere.[578]

QQ. 56 to 65[579] are all concerned with the *Regula placendi Deo*:

1. To do everything for the sake of God or in obedience to His command, and not for the sake of pleasing men (Q. 56).

2. Detail: how to eat and drink in a way that pleases God (Q. 57): {by} remembering that it is God who feeds us; trying to thank Him with both body and soul; realizing that we are being sustained for His service that we may have strength to fulfill His commandments.

3. Pleasing God in everything (Q. 58): doing everything *cum intenta mente, et fixo desiderio placendi Deo;*[580] with all care lest we be deflected from the right path, with no thoughts except of God and "His work which we are doing."[581] *Tamquam si artifex faciens vas aliquod indesinenter et ejus meminit qui opus injunxit et vas quod versat in manibus, si recte et fabre veniat, intuetur* (col. 516).[582]

On the other hand (Q. 59), it is evident that we are not trying to please God but working for men if: when those who may

575. Col. 506C (which reads "*memoriam*"): "The memory of good things, which have been bestowed on us by God."

576. Col. 506D: "As the deer . . ." (beginning of Ps. 41 [42]).

577. Col. 514C: "Who is the gentle person?"

578. Col. 514C: "The one who is not altered in his commitments, by which he has decided and is eager to please God."

579. Cols. 516A-518A.

580. Col. 516B: "with an intent mind and a committed desire to please God."

581. Col. 516B.

582. The text reads "*tanquam*": "just as an artisan making some vessel, who constantly remembers both him who ordered the work and the vessel which he turns in his hands, considers if it may come out right and skillfully."

praise us are present we do a good work which we omit in the presence of those who would blame us, or when no one is around (or do more carelessly in such circumstances). If we would please God we are always equally zealous no matter who sees us or does not see us.

{What is the} cure of this? {See} Q. {60}:[583] practice of the *presence of God* and *fixa sollicitudo Deo placendi*,[584] and desire of beatitude with God. Pride (Q. 61) is noted when we seek the higher place, *eminentiora*.[585] Unlearning pride is like unlearning a language: one must get away from the people who speak that language. Consequently one must leave the world and live in an environment where one may preserve the uninterrupted *memory of God* (Q. 2). Read translation (*Fathers of {the} Church*, p. 241, Q. 5).[586] *Ut possimus orationi vacare oportet secretius habitare* (col. 493).[587] But this does not merely imply leisure and withdrawal: it means the Cross, because of the labor of overcoming one's old habits and acquiring new ones. {It is} useless to bring one's self into solitude (cf. *Letter* 1)[588] without changing anything.

583. Typescript reads "61".

584. Col. 516D (which reads "*fixam sollicitudinem*"): "a determined care to please God."

585. Col. 516D.

586. This question is entitled "On avoiding distraction." It warns that love of God and neighbor, the main end of the Christian life, cannot be achieved without focus and concentration, just as no skill can be learned without training and discipline. Basil calls for detachment and withdrawal from the distractions of life in the world (including marriage, citing St. Paul). One should always keep in mind the will of the One who called us and not be concerned about the opinions of others.

587. The text reads ". . . *oportet primo secretius* . . .": "In order that we might be free for prayer, it is necessary first of all to live more privately."

588. *Letter* 1 (1:3-4) is written to a philosopher, Eustathius, with whom Basil says he desired to study; it has no reference to solitude; Merton evidently intended to refer to *Letter* 2, to Gregory of Nazianzus, discussed above, which begins with Basil's lament that though he has abandoned the city and its distractions and entered into solitude, he has not yet managed to achieve inner peace: "Since we carry around with us our innate passions, we are everywhere subject to the same disturbances" (1:5).

ABNEGATIO: *Oportet nos* PRIMO OMNIUM ABNEGARE NOS IPSOS ET TOLLERE CRUCEM CHRISTI.[589] This abnegation has the following elements: *oblivio*,[590] forgetfulness of old customs and habits; renunciation of our own will, {which is} impossible without this forgetting of old ways; avoiding those who do not have the same kind of purpose, for they will revive constantly the old ways in our mind and we will not be able to deny ourselves. Even if one lives with worldly people and tries to live for God, there is constant distraction in trying to avoid imitating them and correcting our inevitable faults which will be much more numerous. There is also danger of pride if we compare ourselves with them and are content with being just a little better than they are. One cannot have the *memoria Dei*[591] living with worldly people, and without this *memoria* one cannot have the joy and strength that are necessary for the true life of virtue pleasing to God. Nor can one take delight in hearing His word, and one comes to forget His judgements and to act negligently, which leads to habitual contempt for His will. This is the worst of all states, and is characteristic of life "in the world." One must live in company with men desirous of holiness, not in solitude. The beginning of abnegation is then RENUNTIATIO, renouncing all we have in the world. But the perfection of *abnegatio* is to be free from all passion while one is still living in the body.

CONTINENTIA—In order to attain to this perfect self-denial we must practice "continency," or mortification. Q. 8 {includes} numerous examples from Scripture; lives of all the saints and of Christ Himself all urge us to lives of *continentia*.

1. {This is obtained} primarily {through} *fasting*, abstinence from unnecessary food, and from *all* the things that are desired by the bodily senses except in so far as strictly necessary, from *all pleasures of body and soul*, and from all vices.

589. Col. 493C (which reads "*Oportet ergo* . . ."): "It is necessary for us first of all to deny ourselves and take up the cross of Christ."

590. Col. 493C reads "*praeteritae consuetudinis obliti*" ("forgetful of former patterns of behavior").

591. Col. 494A: "the remembrance of God."

2. Hence {there is need for} abstinence from the desire for glory and reputation, from anger, from SADNESS (n.b., comment on this), from distractions *"ab omnibus quae occupatas tenere consueverunt ineruditas animas et incautas"* (col. 500);[592] from curiosity, "wandering eyes,"[593] ears avid for news . . . from inordinate laughter. He that shakes with laughter shows he is not continent, when it is necessary only to smile: *subridendo tantummodo laetitiam mentis oportet indicari*[594] ({he} quotes *"stultus in risu"* etc.—cf. St. Benedict[595]) (see *Fathers of {the} Church*, p. 271[596]). He says that Christ had all the "necessary passions" and He even wept: but He is not said to have laughed. Q. 9 {adds,} however, there is not one measure of continence for all. All must avoid sin, but in legitimate things each has different needs, and the measure of his mortification will therefore differ.

Other points on continency: {one must} especially {observe} silence—for beginners above all (see *Fathers of {the} Church*, Q. 13; p. 263[597]). In order to make sure one is not a heretic who despises matter as evil, one should "taste everything"—this is in the later redaction (see *Fathers of {the} Church*, p. 273; Q. 18[598])

ROMAN MONASTICISM IN PALESTINE, FOURTH CENTURY AND SAINT MELANIA

(cf. *Studia Anselmiana*, 46, p. 85 ff.—article by G. D. Gordini[599])

592. "from everything that customarily preoccupies untrained and unguarded minds."

593. Col. 500C.

594. Col. 500C (which reads *"oporteat"*): "one should show inner joyfulness by smiling only."

595. *"Decimus humilitatis gradus est, si non sit facilis ac promptus in risu, quia scriptum est: Stultus in risu exaltat vocem suam"* ("The tenth degree of humility is that he be not ready and prompt to laughter, for it is written: *The fool lifteth up his voice in laughter*") (McCann, 46/47; the quotation is from Sirach 21:23).

596. Q. 17: "That laughter also must be held in check" (271–73).

597. "That silence is a useful discipline for novices."

598. "That we should taste everything set before us" (273–74).

599. Gian Domenico Gordini, "Il Monachesmo Romano in Palestina nel IV Secolo," *Studia Anselmiana*, 46 (Rome: Herder, 1961), 85–107.

Origin—the pilgrimages to the Holy Places also encouraged interest in the monks of the East. Thus many were inspired to imitate the hermits and remain in the East. Western pilgrims preferred to remain as monks in the Holy Land because of the memory of Christ, and the Holy Places. {There were} *three main Latin Communities* in {the} Holy Land, {which} exercised a great influence ({for example, running} hospices for pilgrims).

1. *That of St. Jerome and St. Paula* at Bethlehem. Note: {this was} typical Latin monasticism from the start! Jerome had begun as a hermit in Syria {but} left because of controversies. In Rome {he exercised an} ascetic influence on noble matrons. A violent campaign against Jerome and monasticism prompts him to return with his feminine disciples to the East (385). He also had monks with him from the West: Paulinianus and Vincent. The monks had a monastery outside {the} town. Jerome and Paula visited Nitria, then settled permanently at Bethlehem. A monastery for virgins was erected at Paula's expense, near {the} Basilica of {the} Nativity, then a guest house for pilgrims (389). The nuns were divided into three groups according to social origin—each group had its own superior and the three groups came together only for prayer. {Note the} *active work* of Jerome's monks. They gave hospitality to pilgrims ("*De India, de Perside et Aethiopia monachorum cotidie turbas suscipimus*" [*Ep.* 107.2])[600] and catechetical instructions (to about forty catechumens in 396). {Jerome was} preaching homilies etc. to people on Sundays. Many important visitors came from all parts of the world—contacts were made and Jerome had a great deal of letter-writing to do, {with} replies to questions about Scripture, asceticism, etc. Monks {were} busy copying manuscripts which were eagerly demanded. Paula's nuns carried on active works of mercy. Even *education in humanities* {was} given to children of Bethlehem. {The} *Origenist controversy* caused strife with the other Latin groups in {the} Holy Land—it brought out what was probably an already existing ri-

600. *PL* 22, col. 870 (the text reads: "*India, Perside, Aethiopia . . . quotidie . . .*"): "Daily we receive crowds of monks from India, Persia, Ethiopia."

valry. The monks of Jerome were for a time excommunicated and it appeared that they would be expelled but peace was restored. Origenism was condemned and Jerome triumphed. But the monastery was now threatened by marauders from the north. Jerome built fortifications. {The} *Pelagian controversy* {began} around 415. Jerome {was} deeply involved. Pelagians attacked his monastery in 416 {and} burned some of the buildings. Monks and nuns took refuge in {the} tower. After the death of Jerome in 420, Barbarian invasions gradually wiped out Latin monasticism in Palestine.

2. *The Community of St. Melania the Elder*. This was the first Latin community of women to be founded in Palestine (373–374). St. Melania, {a} Roman noble of the *gens Antonia*, {a} relative of St. Paulinus,[601] lost her husband and two children at {the} age of 22 and decided to leave the world. (One son remains in Rome.) {She} left for Egypt in 372, visited Nitria, then went to Palestine to get away from Arianism. {She} founded {a} convent on {the} Mount of Olives with {a} guest house for pilgrims. {She} died at Jerusalem in 410. {A} friend of Rufinus, she was attacked, with him, by St. Jerome. Her nuns participated in the liturgical celebrations at the Holy Places.

Important material on St. Melania is found in the *Historia Lausiaca*, written in 419–420, for Palladius was a guest at Melania's convent in 405. (See *Paradise of the Fathers*, vol. 1, c. 40.)[602] {He exhibits} great praise for Melania and Rufinus: "among men one would not quickly find one who was more understanding, and gracious, and pleasant than he."[603] For twenty-seven years they gave hospitality to pilgrims without charge. They "healed the

601. See above, n. 20.

602. *The Paradise or Garden of the Holy Fathers: Being Histories of the Anchorites, Recluses, Monks, Coenobites, and Ascetic Fathers of the Deserts of Egypt between A.D. CCL and A.D. CCCC Circiter, compiled by Athanasius, Archbishop of Alexandria, Palladius, Bishop of Helenopolis, Saint Jerome, and Others*, ed. and trans. Ernest A. Wallis Budge, 2 vols. (London: Chatto & Windus, 1907), 1:156–60; this is a translation of Syriac versions of various early monastic documents.

603. Budge, *Paradise*, 1:157.

schism of the Paulinists [monks]."[604] "Now as concerning the possessions of which she stripped herself, and the money which she distributed, being hot as fire with divine zeal, and blazing like flame with the love of Christ, I alone am not able to recount it, for it belongeth also unto those who dwell in the country of the Persians to declare it; for there was no man who was deprived of her alms and gifts, whether he came from the east, or the west, or the north, or the south."[605] She returns to Rome to rescue her granddaughter Melania the Younger from the world and incidentally converts many others.

> She contended with all the women of Senatorial rank and with all the women of high degree, and strove with them as with savage wild beasts, for the men tried to restrain her from making the women do even as she had done . . . (forsaking) their worldly rank and position. And she spoke to them thus: "My children, four hundred years ago it was written that that time was the last time. Why do you hold fast thus strenuously to the vain love of the world? Take heed lest the day of Antichrist overtake you, and keep not fast hold upon your own riches and the possessions of your fathers." And having set free all these she brought them to the life of the ascetic and recluse.[606]

In Palestine she rebuked an ascetic for washing his hands and feet, and declared she had not washed any part of her body, even her face, since becoming an ascetic. Nor has she slept in a bed. However, she is fond of reading and reads Gregory (Nazianzen?), Pierius, Basil, "and of other writers, more than two hundred and fifty thousand sayings. And she did not read them in an ordinary fashion just as she came to them, and she did not hurry over them in an easy and pleasant manner, but with great labor and understanding she used to read each book seven or eight times. And

604. Budge, *Paradise*, 1:157; these were evidently monks who rejected the divinity of the Holy Spirit: see Meyer, 206, n. 419.

605. Budge, *Paradise*, 1:158 (slightly revised).

606. Budge, *Paradise*, 1:159 (slightly revised).

because of this she was enabled, by being set free from lying doctrine, to fly by means of the gift of learning to great opinions, and she made herself a spiritual bird, and in this wise was taken up to Christ her Lord."[607] Note in all this a spirit of aversion and estrangement from the world (cf. St. Benedict's *a saeculi actibus se facere alienum*[608]).

3. *The Community of St. Melania the Younger*. Melania the Younger, granddaughter of the above, was born in Rome {in} 383. Married at 14, {she} adopted a penitent life after the death of two sons,[609] {eventually accomplishing the} total liquidation of an immense fortune. {She} met with opposition from Roman society. {In} 406, {she} moves to Nola with St. Paulinus. (Her husband goes with her). {In} 408, {she goes} to Sicily with Rufinus, {and in} 410, to her properties in Africa ({where she begins a} friendship with Augustine). {In} 413, {she travels} to Jerusalem via Egypt {and} settles on {the} Mount of Olives, {where she} imitates Egyptian hermits. {She} founds {a} convent of virgins on {the} Mount of Olives, near {the} Basilica of {the} Ascension, {and lives an} intense life of prayer and penance. She died in 440.

Characteristics of Roman Monasticism in Palestine.

1) {It is} dominated by {the} influence of Nitria and Scete, i.e. by hermits.

2) {There is an} attraction to the Holy Places—monks and nuns furnish choirs for churches at {the} Holy Places in Bethlehem, Jerusalem (N.B. *Roman* Liturgy[610]).

3) {There is a} preponderance of *nuns*.

4) {There is a strong} influence of Jerome (positive or negative)—hence {the} importance of *study* and intellectual activity.

607. Budge, *Paradise*, 1:160 (slightly revised).

608. See above, n. 523.

609. According to Palladius, but Gerontius writes of a son and a daughter; see the second "Note Complémentaire" in Gorce (111–12), which suggests that two sons may have died at birth and a daughter as a young child.

610. But see Gorce, 107–109 for a nuanced discussion of the "Roman" character of the liturgy in Melania the Younger's monasteries.

5) These communities exercised an influence *by letters* on the West, and attracted visitors from there. Jerome received financial support from St. Exuperius, bishop of Toulouse (cfr. G. D. Gordini, "Il Monachesmo Romano in Palestina nel IV Secolo" in *Studia Anselmiana* 46.[611])

We can now consider a few characteristic texts.

From the Life of St. Melania the Younger by Gerontius (see *Sources Chrétiennes*, n. 90).

1. *Her Ascetic Life in North Africa:*

a) *Fasting* {was} extremely strict, a little liquid nourishment in the evening; at other times, {she} ate only on Saturdays and Sundays (dry bread and water)—"*Hebdomadary*."[612] But when she began fasting in the Easter Season her mother reproached her for ignoring the holy tradition (n.b. {the} Eustathians {were} condemned for this at Gangres). "It is not right for a Christian to fast on the day of our Lord's Resurrection but one must take bodily nourishment along with the spiritual."[613] (Easter {was} extended through Paschal Time and to all Sundays of the year.)

b) *Watching*: After sleeping two hours, she would wake the virgins living with her (mostly her former slaves), saying, "Just as the Blessed Abel and all the saints offered to God their first fruits, so let us also employ the first fruits of the night in glorifying God. For we must watch and pray at every hour, because we do not know when the thief will come."[614] She gave the virgins strict rules of silence and directed them, having them manifest their thoughts to her.

c) *Lectio*: She read the whole Bible two or three times a year, copying out what was especially useful for her (n. 26).[615] She chose Thagaste in order to study Scripture there under Alypius,

611. Gordini, 106–107.

612. See Gorce, 90, n. 1 for the use of this term for week-long fasters.

613. Chapter 25 (Gorce, 177).

614. Chapter 23 (Gorce, 175, 177).

615. Gorce, 180 ("three or four times a year" in the text).

{the} friend of Augustine. She was "*philologos*"—a lover of literature, reading—and the Bible "was never out of her holy hands" (n. 21).[616] She liked private recitation of {the} whole Psalter—{she} completed privately the psalms not said in Office that day (Daily Psalter) (n. 26).[617] {She was} perfect in both Greek and Latin; she read all the Patristic treatises she could get (n. 26).[618]

d) *Austerity*: When she was rich, the embroidery of a rich garment she wore had scratched her tender skin and caused inflammation. But now she wore the *maphorion* and cowl of coarse hair cloth (n. 31)[619] (*cilicium*—from Cilicia[620]). She had obtained strength from the Lord by prayer. "Ask and you shall receive."[621]

e) *Reclusion*: She wanted perpetual reclusion in North Africa but renounced it in order to maintain contact with people who needed her. But {she} spent a great part of her time in her cell, in solitude, lying in a box.[622]

2. *Her Monastic Life in the East:*

a) {She went} to {the} Holy Land as an integral part of *Sequela Christi*.[623] {She} meets St. Cyril at Alexandria.[624] Reaching Jerusalem, {she} gives money in secret through others, and is registered among poor pilgrims.[625] {She} lives at {the} Holy Sepulchre, praying there at night.[626]

b) In Egypt, {she} tries to give gold to hermits, {but is blocked by} their refusals (p. {199}).[627] {She} meets the Abbot of Tabenna,

616. Gorce, 170, 173.
617. Gorce, 179.
618. Gorce, 179, 181.
619. Gorce, 187.
620. See Gorce, 186, n. 4.
621. Chapter 31 (Gorce, 189).
622. Chapter 32 (Gorce, 189).
623. "the following of Christ."
624. Chapter 34 (Gorce, 191).
625. Chapter 35 (Gorce, 193, 195).
626. Chapter 36 (Gorce, 195, 197).
627. Chapter 39 (typescript reads "200").

Victor, {and} visits Nitria and {the} desert of Cells. "The hermits received her as a man."[628]

c) On {the} Mount of Olives {she} retires to her mother's cell, {and} encloses herself there in sackcloth and ashes, after Epiphany.[629] Then {she} builds a convent for about 90 nuns, {with a} special emphasis on rehabilitating fallen women.[630]

d) Ascetic Teaching. {Its} *basis* {is}:

(1) They have come to give their virginity to Christ, body and soul: *body*—total separation from {the} world of men; *soul*—vigilance in prayer, in fear and {in the} presence of angels, avoiding all evil thoughts[631] ({note the} Evagrian background).

(2) All ascesis is based on *purity of love* for God and one another. Without this their asceticism is false. The devil can imitate all the virtues but not love and humility.[632]

(3) *Faith* {is the} essential foundation of all true ascesis.[633]

Practice {entails the following}:

(1) She has them fast, but would guard against pride in fasting. Hence fasting is "the last of the virtues"[634] and for its merit depends on obedience. To neglect other virtues and depend on fasting alone is like a bride who appears in old clothes but only has a pair of very fine shoes. However, they must persevere in *fasting with joy* and be generous in it. They must enter by this narrow gate.

(2) *Obedience* "consists in this: doing what you do not like to do, for the satisfaction of the one who commands you, and doing violence to yourself for the sake of Christ."[635]

628. Chapter 39 (Gorce, 201, 203).
629. Chapter 40 (Gorce, 203).
630. Chapter 41 (Gorce, 205, 207).
631. Chapter 42 (Gorce, 209).
632. Chapter 43 (Gorce, 209, 211).
633. Chapter 43 (Gorce, 211).
634. Chapter 43 (Gorce, 211).
635. Chapter 44 (Gorce, 213).

e) Liturgy. They rose at night after a short sleep—"Not having satisfied one's desire for sleep"[636]—but then returned to bed afterwards. Night Office {consisted in} "Three responsories, three lessons and fifteen antiphons"; {there were also} "Morning Office" (Lauds); Tierce "because then the Paraclete came upon the Apostles"; Sext "because then Abraham received the Lord"; None "when Peter and John went to {the} Temple"; Vespers, {a time of} "special fervor—{the} hour when {the} disciples of Emmaus travelled with Christ, {the} Hour of *peace*."[637] {There was} Mass on Friday, Sunday and Feasts. {The church contained} relics of Zachary,[638] St. Stephen, and {the} forty martyrs of Sebaste.[639]

An Example of Jerome's Monastic Controversy: St. Jerome against Vigilantius (*PL* 23)[640] (406 A.D.). This text is important for us because Vigilantius was *in Gaul* and Jerome attacked him on request from two Gallic priests (see *Ep*. 109):[641]

1. *The opening tirade against the person of his opponent.* "Many monsters have been generated on the earth. Centaurs, sirens, '*ululas*' and '*onocrotalos*' (Isa. 13 & 35) are read of in Isaias. Job describes Leviathan and Behemoth. . . . Poets tell us of Cerberus, the Stymphalides, the Erimathean boar, the Nemean lion, the many-headed hydra etc., etc. Sola Gallia monstra non habuit, *sed viris semper fortibus et eloquentissimis abundavit. Exortus est subito Vigilantius, seu verius Dormitantius, qui immundo spiritu pugnet contra Christi spiritum, et martyrum neget sepulchra veneranda; damnandas esse dicat vigilias: numquam nisi in Pascha alleluia cantandum: continentiam, haeresim; pudicitiam, libidinis seminarium*"

636. Chapter 46 (Gorce, 215).

637. Chapter 47 (Gorce, 217).

638. i.e. the prophet Zechariah (see Gorce, 218, n. 3).

639. Chapter 48 (Gorce, 219).

640. Cols. 337-352 in the copy of *PL* 23 in the Gethsemani library, which Merton cites in his references; other editions have different pagination; page numbers of the Vallarsi text used by Migne, which are included in *PL*, will be provided to avoid confusion.

641. *PL* 22, cols. 906-909.

(339).[642] The spirit of Jovinian[643] lives in him again—who, condemned by the Church, vomited up his soul among pheasants and swine's flesh; and Vigilantius, a tavern keeper, continues to adulterate wine with water, only now it is the wine of faith adulterated with the poison of perfidy. In secular banquets he rants against the fasts of the saints—philosophizing among the bottles, he enjoys a psalm or two, but only at dinner. "I say this," Jerome ends, "not in mockery but with a grieving heart."[644]

2. *Points of Controversy*. Veneration of relics of martyrs is not superstition or paganism. The martyrs can intercede for us. Vigilantius complained of candles being burned in daylight. "*Quando legendum est Evangelium, accenduntur luminaria, jam sole rutilante: non utique ad fugandas tenebras: sed ad signum laetitiae demonstrandum*" (346).[645] Vigils are not to be reproved because of occasional abuses. Miracles {take place} at shrines of martyrs. {He relates} how Vigilantius ran out to church and prayed, waked in an earthquake. Jerome declares he himself trembles to enter basilicas of the martyrs when he has been angry or had a nocturnal pollution (349).[646] Jerome accuses Vigilantius of not wanting Christians to fast and be sober as this would hurt business in his tavern (349).[647] Vigilantius claims that it is better to keep property and give alms to the poor. Jerome defends total renunciation (351).[648]

642. Text reads "*nunquam*": "Gaul alone had no monsters, but has always abounded in brave and very eloquent men. Suddenly Vigilantius, or more accurately Dormitantius, has arisen, who with an unclean spirit fights against the Spirit of Christ, and declares that the tombs of the martyrs should not be venerated; he says that vigils should be condemned, that the Alleluia should never be sung except at Eastertime; that continency is heretical, modesty, the seedbed of lust" (Vallarsi, 387).

643. The *Two Books against Jovinian* are found in *PL* 23, cols. 205-338 (Gethsemani copy); Vallarsi, 231–384.

644. Chapter 1 (Vallarsi, 388).

645. Chapter 7 (Vallarsi, 394): "When the Gospel is to be read, candles are lit, even when the sun is already shining; not at all to chase away the shadows, but to exhibit a sign of joy."

646. Chapters 11–12 (Vallarsi, 397–98).

647. Chapter 13 (Vallarsi, 398).

648. Chapter 14 (Vallarsi, 399).

3. (#15) *Defense of Monastic Life as such*: Vigilantius "with viper's tongue"[649] has calumniated the whole monastic state: if all go into the desert who will take care of the churches? Who will save souls? Who will exhort sinners? If all are virgins the human race will perish. (Translate passage—351.[650]) Jerome replies: *Monachus autem non doctoris habet, sed plangentis officium: qui vel se, vel mundum lugeat, et Domini pavidus praestoletur adventum: qui sciens imbecillitatem suam . . .* etc.[651] (He avoids the sight of women). This is the foundation stone of De Rancé's ideas about monastic studies.[652] "Why do I go to the desert? Indeed, that I may not have to see and hear you, that I may not be plagued with your fury, and suffer your attacks: that the eye of a whore may not ensnare me, lest lovely forms lure me to unlawful embraces" (351-2).[653] Is this cowardice and evasion? "*Nulla securitas est vicino serpente dormire.*"[654] "*Idcirco urbium frequentias declinamus,*

649. Vallarsi, 400.

650. Merton has already paraphrased the content of Vigilantius' argument, omitting only Jerome's jibe, "if everyone were as ridiculous as yourself, who would be wise," and his sarcastic development of Vigilantius' argument against virginity, that if all were virgins there would be no children crying in their cradles, midwives would turn beggars, and "Dormitantius" would lie alone in his bed, cold and wide awake.

651. "The duty of the monk is not to teach but to weep; let him weep whether for himself or for the world; let him fearfully await the coming of the Lord; knowing his own weakness and the fragile vessel that he bears, he fears to offend, lest it be struck and fall and be broken" ("*. . . et vas fragile quod portat, timet offendere, ne impingat, et corruat atque frangatur*") (Vallarsi, 400).

652. See François Vandenbroucke, OSB, "L'Esprit des Études Monastiques d'après l'Abbé de Rancé," *Collectanea Ordinis Cisterciensium Reformatorum*, 25 (1963), 224–49, especially 226–27: "And so it is that Rancé comes to that form of work that is study. In this matter, he believes, one must return to the principle that he borrows nearly word for word from Saint Jerome, according to whom 'monks have not been intended for study but for repentance; it is their role to weep rather than to teach, and the purpose of God, in raising up solitaries in his Church, has been to form not teachers but penitents.'"

653. Chapter 16 (Vallarsi, 400).

654. Chapter 16: "There is no safety sleeping with a serpent nearby" (Vallarsi, 400).

ne facere compellamur, quae nos non tam natura cogit facere, quam voluntas" (352).[655]

Conclusion. "This is just a brief note dictated in one evening to Brother Sisinnius hastening to depart for Egypt. But if Dormitantius wakes up and starts detracting us, I will devote to him a whole night's vigil the next time—and to those who think one cannot be a priest unless he has a woman with child."[656] *Remarks*: Jerome argues like a Kentucky politician.

Some Monastic Ideas of St. Jerome.[657]

1. {Note the} importance of St. Jerome for the *Rule* of St. Benedict. He is quoted[658] as often as St. Basil—after Cassian, St. Augustine, St. Pachomius and the *Historia Monachorum*.

2. The SOLITARY: St. Jerome is the first to use *monachus* in Latin.[659] He takes it to mean "solitary." *Quid facis in turba qui solus es?* (*Ep*. 14).[660] Essentially {the monk is} a pilgrim to the promised Land, an exile, following Christ. His state does not normally allow of the priestly office (which would mean being in town). He belongs in paradise. *Tua regio paradisus . . . serva quod nata es . . . revertere.*[661]

655. Chapter 16: "For this reason we shun the crowds of cities, lest we be forced to do things that are not our nature but our will makes us do" (Vallarsi, 401).

656. Chapter 17 (Vallarsi, 401–402).

657. Merton discusses St. Jerome in *Cassian and the Fathers*, 63–69.

658. P. Antin, "La Monachisme selon S. Jérôme," *Mélanges Bénédictins*, 71, citing Cuthbert Butler's edition of the *Rule*, 3d ed. (1935), 131; most of the following material on Jerome is based on Antin's article.

659. *Ep*. 14:6 (*PL* 22, col. 350): "*Interpretare vocabulum monachi, hoc est nomen tuum*" ("Understand the meaning of the word *monachus*; this is your name."). This sentence directly precedes the one quoted immediately below.

660. Chapter 6 (*PL* 22, col. 350): "What are you doing in a crowd, you who are a solitary?"

661. *Ep*. 22:19 (*PL* 22, col. 406): "Your homeland is paradise. Retain your birthright. . . . 'Return [to your rest, my soul' (Ps. 124:7)]."

Monastic *Propositum*: "Profession" (*Propositum*) {is} a second baptism,[662] because a *martydom* (*Ep*. 108).[663] Monastic life {is} a *ludus* (athletic training) (*Ep*. {118}).[664] Here strength and generosity are much needed. It is also a *militia*, under Christ the *Imperator*[665] and *Archistrategos*[666] (*Christo vero Regi*: cf. St. Benedict[667]). To abandon one's monastic profession is to deny Christ, like departing from the army.

Praise: {Monastic life is an} *angelic life* of praise, in proportion as we sing to God with pure hearts and a record of good works. ("*Christus non audit vocem sed opera.*"[668]) *Psallite omnibus membris vestris. Psallat manus in eleemosyna, psallat pes vadens in opere bono.*[669] Compare what he says below on *chant*. The spiritual and intellectual life of the monk and nun {is} based on the Bible (*Ep*. 107-108).[670]

Silence. *Silence* {is central}. The monk helps the world by weeping in silence, not by preaching. "*Non loquendo, et discursando, sed tacendo, et sedendo*" (*Ep*. 50)[671] (cf. Dom Leclercq: "*Sedere*"[672]).

662. *Ep*. 39.3 (*PL* 22, col. 468).

663. Chapter 31 (col. 905): "*mater tua longo martyrio coronata est*" ("Your mother [Paula, mother of Eustochium] has been crowned after a long martyrdom"); see also *Ep*. 22.38 (col. 422), 44 (col. 480), 69.6 (col. 660).

664. *Ep*. 118.2 (col. 961) (typescript reads "108"); see also *Ep*. 154.13 (col. 557).

665. *Ep*. 14.2 (col. 548).

666. *In Abdiam* 1.1 (*PL* 25, col. 1155B).

667. *Rule*, Prologue: "[to fight for] the true King, Christ" (McCann, 6/7).

668. "Christ does not hear the voice but the works" (*Commentarioli . . . Tractatus sive homiliae in Psalmos . . .* , *Anecdota Maredsolana*, ed. Germain Morin [Maredsous, 1895–1903], 3.2, 148, 21, cited in Antin, 89, n. 100).

669. "Sing with all your members. Let the hand sing in almsgiving, the foot sing while going out on a good work" (*Anecdota Maredsolana*, 3.2, 147, 71, quoted in Antin, 90 [which reads ". . . *elemosyna* . . .]).

670. See Antin, 91.

671. Chapter 4 (col. 544): "not by speaking and discoursing but by sitting down and keeping quiet."

672. Jean Leclercq, osb, "*Sedere*: À Propos de l'Hésychasme en Occident," *Le Millénaire du Mont Athos: 963–1963: Études et Mélanges*, 2 vols. (Chevetogne: Éditions de Chevetogne, 1963–1964), 1:253-64.

Work. *Work* {is important}, at least the copying of manuscripts. Be slow to write books: "*Ne ad scribendum cito prosilias, et levi ducaris insania. . . . Multo tempore disce quod doceas*" (*Ep.* 125).[673] The monk *may* teach young children.

{See the} *satire* on *pseudomonachi* (*Ep.* 57; 22).[674] {He is} against the *bath* and light-colored clothing (cf. *Ep.* 79).[675] {It is} better to marry than to be a proud, disobedient monk. *Stability* {is} emphasized (at least the spirit) (cf. "*La Monachisme selon S. Jérôme*" by Dom P. Antin in *Mélanges Bénédictins*—Fontenelle, 1947).

St. Jerome—Letter 125 to Rusticus (*PL* 22:1072 ff.). {This is an} important letter on the monastic life written to a young monk in Gaul (at Marseilles). Jerome advises against ascetic life *at home* and urges joining a cenobitic community. The community is probably *inside* the town of Marseilles and close to the Church of St. Victor, and this later became Cassian's monastery (417). This fact accounts for Jerome's supposition that Rusticus may become a cleric. Note: Mabillon says of this letter, "This has always been considered a kind of monastic rule in which he claims to form a solitary and not a cleric" (*Reflexions sur la Réponse de M. l'Abbé de la Trappe*, p. 42).[676]

1. The glory and the risks of the monastic life. *Lubricum iter est per quod ingrederis . . .*[677] {He stresses} the hope of great glory and the risk of greater ruin. {Is this} an over-dramatic exaggeration? (1073).

2. Jerome will give Rusticus the fruits of his own experience. *Quasi doctus nauta, post multa naufragia, rudem conor instruere vec-*

673. Chapter 18 (col. 1082): "Do not rush forward quickly to write, and be drawn away from such trivial nonsense. Spend much time learning what you may teach."

674. See Antin, 94 (*Ep.* 57); 94–95 (*Ep.* 22).

675. Chapter 7, cols. 729–30.

676. Jean Mabillon, osb, *Reflexions sur la Réponse de M. l'Abbé de la Trappe au Traité des Études Monastiques* (Paris: Charles Robustel, 1693).

677. Chapter 1 (which reads "*esse*"): "It is a slippery path which you are entering upon."

torem . . .[678] He will tell him where the pirates are, the whirlpools, etc. (1073). He describes the way to India with its perils, which merchants risk in order to reach the fabulous mountains of gold. If they risk so much—*quid Christi negotiatori faciendum est, qui venditis omnibus quaerit, pretiosissimum margaritum?* (1074).[679]

3. Some personal details on Rusticus {are provided} (#6). He is a Gaul who has studied in Rome, to discipline the flow of Gallic speech (i.e. education in humanities). He is now living as {an} ascete at home (1075). This was the result of {the} foresight of a spiritual mother who had his interests at heart. Jerome takes {this} occasion to warn against friendships with pious ladies which easily turn into matrimonial adventures (1075).

4. *Monastic virtues* (#7). Rusticus must be a real monk and not just have the appearance of one. This means he must have care only for his own soul and not for exterior things:

a) Treatment of the body—*Sordidae vestes candidae mentis indicia sint: vilis tunica contemptum saeculi probet: ita dumtaxat, ne animus tumet, ne habitus sermoque dissentiant* (1075).[680] What concerns Jerome here is the *symbolism* of the monk's garb, not its "dirtiness." {He advises:} avoiding baths (sc. Roman public baths); fasting (but in moderation); watching out for contacts with women—careful of his mother's maids! Imitate the love of solitude that characterized St. John {the} Baptist and the "sons of the prophets" (1076). {Cultivate} solitude in the cell and love of reading—these protect chastity. *Habeto cellulam pro paradiso: varia Scripturarum poma decerpe: his utere deliciis: harum fruere complexu*[681] (i.e., the joys of Scripture are a sublimation of sensual desire)

678. Chapter 2: "Like a veteran sailor, after many shipwrecks, I am trying to instruct an inexperienced traveler."

679. Chapter 4: "What should Christ's merchant do, who, having sold all, seeks the finest of pearls?"

680. "Let soiled garments be signs of an unspotted soul: let a shabby tunic demonstrate scorn for the world: so that at least your mind will not be puffed up and your words and your clothes will not be at odds."

681. Chapter 11: "Take your cell for your paradise; pick the various fruits of the Scriptures; make use of these delights; enjoy their embrace."

(1076). Hence he must be constantly reading the Bible: *Numquam de manu et oculis tuis recedat liber* (1078).[682] *Corpus pariter et animus tendatur ad Dominum . . . Ama scientiam Scripturarum, et carnis vitia non amabis.*[683] Hence {one should} avoid even his own mother because of the dangers of leaving {the} cell and going where there are serving girls, etc.

(#8) The love of solitude: *Mihi oppidum carcer, et solitudo paradisus est* (1076).[684] *Quid desideremus urbium frequentiam, qui de singularitate censemur?*[685] {This is a} reference to the desire for clerical life. Jerome does not reprove it but considers priesthood and monastic life two different vocations, between which Rusticus has already chosen. However if he is later ordained, a worthy monastic life will have been a good preparation for priesthood (col. 1082).

(#9) Choice of cenobitic life: Jerome advises cenobitic life as preferable to complete solitude—for example and instruction: *ut habeas Sanctorum contubernium, nec ipse te doceas . . .* (1077).[686] *In solitudine cito subrepit superbia . . .*[687] The hermit may be tempted to overestimate his own virtues and despise others. He begins to follow his own fancies, thinking himself always right. He is more often in the city than in his cell. Hence the solitary life, which is very praiseworthy (*quippe quam saepe laudavimus*)[688] is only open to those who have had a long formation in the cenobium (1077). *Sed de ludo monasteriorum, hujuscemodi volumus egredi milites, quos eremi dura rudimenta non terreant* (1077).[689] The solitary life is for exemplary monks only.

682. "Never let the book disappear from your hand and your eyes."

683. Col. 1078: "Let body and soul be equally directed to the Lord. . . . Love knowledge of the Scriptures and you will not love the vices of the flesh."

684. "A town is a prison for me, and solitude is paradise."

685. Col. 1076: "Why should we who have resolved on solitude desire the bustle of cities?"

686. "that you may have the companionship of the saints, and not be your own teacher."

687. "In solitude pride quickly creeps up."

688. "which we have certainly praised often."

689. "We want only such soldiers whom the stern challenges of the desert do not terrify to go forth from the school of the monasteries."

(#11) Manual labor: besides reading, and study—there should also be *manual labor*. {The} Apostles {are cited} as examples of this. Jerome suggests basket-weaving and gardening, bee-keeping (*monasteriorum ordinem, ac regiam disciplinam, in parvis disce corporibus*),[690] making fishing nets, copying books (*Scribantur libri, ut et manus operetur cibum, et animus lectione saturetur*).[691] *Aegyptiorum Monasteria hunc morem tenent, ut nullum absque operis labore suscipiant*, non tam propter victus necessitatem, quam propter animae salutem (1079).[692]

(#12) Study: {he is told} how Jerome himself undertook the study of Hebrew as a young monk, to fight distractions (1079) {as well as} his labors and difficulties with this study. *Et gratias ago Domino, quod de amaro semine litterarum, dulces fructus carpo* (1079).[693]

(#13) Example of cenobitic training: a Greek youth in {an} Egyptian cenobium is tempted to impurity and cannot overcome temptation by fasting or labor. His Abbas has someone calumniate and persecute him, and all bear witness against him (the Abbas alone defends him *ne abundantiori tristitia absorberetur*[694]—cf. *Rule* of St. Benedict, c. 27[695]). This goes on for a year. The Abbas asked what happened to his former temptation. *"Papae, inquit, vivere mihi non licet, et fornicari libeat?"*[696]

690. "Learn the order of monastic life and the royal discipline from these small bodies."

691. "Books are copied both so that the hand might earn food and so that the mind might be filled with reading."

692. "The monasteries of the Egyptians keep this custom, to accept no one without ability to work, not just on account of the need for sustenance, but for the salvation of the soul."

693. "And I thank the Lord because from the bitter seed of literary study I pick sweet fruits."

694. Col. 1079: "lest he be swallowed up by too great sadness."

695. This chapter focuses on the abbot's solicitude for a brother who has been excluded (excommunicated) from community life (though Benedict does allow "old and prudent brethren" to provide comfort as well, in private) (McCann, 77).

696. Col. 1080: "'Father,' he said, 'I'm not able even to live—how could I fornicate?'"

(#14). {Here is} another reminiscence of St. Benedict[697]—{he} quotes Ps. {33}: *Declina a malo, et fac bonum. . . . Pax quaerenda ut bella fugiamus.*[698] *"Quaere pacem et sequere eam."*[699] {This is} the peace that surpasses all understanding and which is the *habitatio Dei* (1079).[700]

(#15) *Nulla ars absque magistro discitur. . .*[701] Hence he needs to live in a monastery *sub unius disciplina Patris* (1079)[702] and among examples of virtue. *Non facias quod vis, comedas quod juberis, vestiare quod acceperis, operis tui pensum persolvas, subjiciaris cui non vis, lassus ad stratum venias, . . .* etc. (1080-1081).[703] (*Choir*) *Dicas Psalmum in ordine tuo;* in quo non dulcedo vocis sed mentis affectus quaeritur . . .[704] ({he} quotes *Psallite sapienter*).[705] Obedience, hospitality, humble subjection, not judging the commands of superiors {are other values}.

(#16) *False monks*: {these} change only their habit but not their *pristina conversatio* (1081).[706] They are not poor or solitary. They are not humble. {They} become melacholy in their cells. *Hippocratis magis fomentis, quam nostris monitis indigent* (1082).[707] Others need worldly occupations and business to distract them (1082). They make more money in the monastery than in the world.

697. *Rule*, Prologue: "*Deverte a malo et fac bonum; inquire pacem et sequere eam*" ("*Turn away from evil and do good: seek after peace and pursue it*") (McCann, 8/9, a quotation from Ps. 33 [34]:15).

698. "Avoid evil and do good. . . . We must seek peace to escape wars" (typescript reads "36").

699. "Seek peace and pursue it" (text has "*persequere*").

700. "dwelling place of God" (col. 1080).

701. "No skill is learned without a teacher."

702. "under the direction of one Father."

703. "Do not do what you want, eat what you are ordered to eat, wear what you have been given, put in the effort of your work, be subject to another against your own wishes, come to bed exhausted . . ."

704. "Recite the psalm in your turn, seeking not sweetness of the voice but stirring of the soul."

705. "sing wisely" (Ps. 46 [47]:8).

706. "former pattern of behavior" (the text reads "*conversatione*").

707. "They need the prescriptions of Hippocrates more than our admonitions."

(#18) He must be slow to write and teach others (1082). {He must} not believe those who praise him. {Jerome provides a} caricature of a pedant and detractor (1083)—the type to avoid (#19).

(#20) {He} recommends he follow advice of Bishop *Proculus* of Marseilles and {the} example of Exuperius of Toulouse. *Nudum Christum, nudus sequere. Durum, grande, difficile; sed magna sunt praemia* (1085).[708]

The Pilgrimage of Aetheria and Eastern Monasticism in {the} Fourth Century

({A} Pilgrim—*peregrinus* [*per-agrum*]—{is} one who makes a long journey to a sacred place, as an act of faith and devotion.) *Aetheria* {is the} author of a narrative of a pilgrimage made to {the} Holy Land, Sinai, Mesopotamia and Egypt in the fourth or fifth century. Her name was at first not known when the ms. from Monte Cassino was discovered by Gamurrini in Arrezzo in 1884.[709]

First theory: "Sylvia"—he called it the *Peregrinatio Sylviae*, identifying {the} author as Sylvia or Galla Placida, {a} noblewoman from Aquitaine.

Second theory: "Aetheria"—{in} 190{3}, Dom Férotin,[710] basing himself on the discovery of the letter of the Spanish monk Valerius in praise of Aetheria, identifies the *Pilgrimage* with more or less certainty {as the} journey of a Spanish nun, whom Valerius praises as a saint. But there are still doubts as to her precise identity, as well as the correct version of her name. Férotin calls her Etheria (Aetheria).

708. Chapter 20: "Naked, follow the naked Christ. It is hard, imposing, difficult, but the rewards are great."

709. G. F. Gamurrini, "I misteri e gl'imni di S. Ilario Vescovo di Poitiers ed una Peregrinatione ai Luighi Santi nel Quarto Secolo," *Studii e Documenti de Storia e Diritto*, 5 (1884), 81 ff., and "Della Inedita Peregrinazione ad Luoghi Santi," *Studii e Documenti di Storia e Diritto*, 6 (1885), 145 ff.

710. M. Férotin, "Le Véritable Auteur de la 'Peregrinatio Sylviae': La Vierge Espagnole Étheria," *Revue des Questions Historiques*, 74 (1903), 367–97 (typescript reads "1906").

Third theory: "Eucheria"—Dom Morin,[711] and Dom Wilmart at first,[712] preferred *Eucheria* on {the} theory that she was related to Eucherius, the uncle of Theodosius, who himself came from Galicia. There seems to be evidence that Eucheria travelled with strong support from on high in the Empire. She used the official imperial relay system (*cursus publicus*).[713] In his article in *Revue Bénédictine*, 1913, p. 174 ff. (vol. 30) Dom Morin, analysing a cryptic passage in Jerome's *Letter to Furia* (*Ep*. 54, n. 13),[714] says it is directed at Eucheria, without naming her, and criticizes some unmentioned person for travelling in too great style and with too much freedom and luxury, in a "royal equipage recalling the weddings of Nero and Sardanapalus. Let us learn from this painful lesson . . ." etc. Yet it is not even clear that Jerome is referring to a woman. This letter is certainly no *proof* of anything. There is some *probability* in Morin's theory, who reconstructs Eucheria's journey as follows: {in} 393, she reaches Jerusalem and makes it her base of operations for three years of travelling about in Egypt, Sinai {and the} Near East. {In} 396, she goes to Edessa and then returns to Asia Minor and finally to Constantinople. In all this she neglected either to consult or even to visit Jerome, and Morin thinks this was enough to rouse his ire.[715] (But did she neglect to consult him? This is by no means certain. She need not have mentioned it, and parts of the book are missing.) This presupposes that Eucheria is a noble and well-to-do traveller, and indeed one with strong official support (quite likely). Morin surmises that the execution of a Comes at Antioch in 393, for refusing a "favor" that was asked somewhat illegally by Eucherius, might have been connected with offering military protection to Eucheria on the highway, for she had (according to Morin's

711. G. Morin, "Un Passage Énigmatique de S. Jérôme contre la Pèlerine Espagnole Eucheria?" *Revue Bénédictine*, 30 (1913), 174–86.

712. A. Wilmart, "L'Itinerarium Eucheriae," *Revue Bénédictine*, 25 (1908), 458–67.

713. See Éthérie, *Journal de Voyage*, ed. and trans. Hélène Pétré, SC 21 (Paris: Éditions du Cerf, 1948), 24, 25–26.

714. *PL* 22, col. 556.

715. Morin, 180–81.

theory) passed through Antioch some time before this (historical) execution took place (*RB*, p. 186).

Fourth theory: "Egeria"—Dom Lambert,[716] followed by Wilmart in his change of opinion,[717] calls her *Egeria* and links her up with another letter of Jerome (to Ctesiphon: *Ep.* {133}[718]) and this places her a little later, early in the fifth century. This links up Egeria with a background of *Priscillianism* in Spain, and Dom Lambert supports his claim by Egeria's frequent references to the "inspirations of the Holy Spirit" and other personal intimations of the divine will. Is this solid?

Other choices, as to the name: Echeria, Heteria, Aetheria, Eiheria. The more recent *Sources Chrétiennes* preserves Éthérie (Aetheria or Etheria).[719] Since this is the most common, we might as well stick to it, with some leaning toward Dom Morin's ingenious identification of her with Eucheria related to Eucherius. (Here—sample text—Epiphany in Jerusalem, p. 202.[720])

Character: Aetheria is impressive for her really unusual character. The very fact of undertaking such a journey and carrying

716. A. Lambert, "Egeria. Notes Critiques sur la Tradition de Son Nom et Celle de l'*Itinerarium*," *Revue Mabillon*, 26 (1936), 71–94, and "Egeria, Soeur de Galla," *Revue Mabillon*, 27 (1937), 1–42.

717. A. Wilmart, "Egeria," *Revue Bénédictine*, 28 (1911), 68–75, and "Encore Egeria," *Revue Bénédictine*, 29 (1912), 91–96; it will be noted that Wilmart's identification of the author as Egeria precedes that of Lambert by more than two decades.

718. *PL* 22, cols. 1147-1161 (the typescript reads "113").

719. It should be noted that scholarly consensus now favors the name Egeria: see *Egeria: Diary of a Pilgrimage*, trans. George E. Gingras, ACW 38 (New York: Newman Press, 1970), 2–7. The new volume in the Sources Chrétiennes series replacing the Pétré edition also uses Egeria [Égérie]: see *Journal de Voyage: Itinéraire Égérie*, ed. Pierre Maraval, SC 296 (Paris: Éditions du Cerf, 1997).

720. This section, which comes immediately after a missing page in the manuscript, begins by describing a procession from Bethlehem back to Jerusalem after a vigil service for the feast of the Epiphany at the Church of the Nativity. At dawn the community gathers at the Anastasis, the Church of the Resurrection, and then later at the Martyrium, the Church of the Cross on Golgotha. A description is included of the elaborate hangings and sacred vessels, and of the liturgical services celebrated during the octave of Epiphany (c. 25).

it out under such difficulties points to a person of unusual courage, independence, determination, and one who is completely set on fulfilling what she conceives to be a demand of grace. She is powerfully impelled to visit *all* the holy places that she has read about in the Bible. She has a holy and insatiable curiosity. (Sample text: nn. 13-14 [Sedima], p. 146[721]). She travels with two guidebooks in hand: not Baedeker, but the *Bible* and the *Onomasticon* of Eusebius in Jerome's Latin translation.[722]

The Biblical character of her spirituality must be emphasized:

1) Her aim is to visit and to pray on the very sites where great events narrated in the Bible have taken place. She wants to see exactly where the Hebrews crossed the Red Sea. She wants to reconstruct all the events at Sinai, and to make the sacred text absolutely clear in her own mind. She wants to see Horeb, the tomb of Job, etc. She is even curious about very small details—what happened to Abraham's brother at Haran?

2) She wants to see the *martyria* of the great saints and apostles.

3) She is also very interested in the great *monastic centers.* The ms. unfortunately is incomplete and her account of her (probable) visit to Scete and Nitria is lost. But generally she does not aim precisely to visit monks. She finds them all around the places she visits, because it is the natural thing for monks to settle near the sites of the great interventions of God in sacred history. Thus her interest in monasticism, though very keen, is subordinated to her interest in Biblical sites.

4) Above all, she wants to see the exact spots of the great mysteries of our redemption. Like all the other pilgrims she wants to adore the TRUE CROSS and join in the liturgy that takes place every day at the Anastasis, the Holy Sepulchre, at Jerusalem.

721. These chapters focus on the early stages of a journey to the tomb of Job; on the way she stops at the village of Sedima, which she is told was Salem, the city of Melchizedek, and visits a church which is supposed to have been built on the site where Melchizedek offered sacrifices of bread and wine.

722. See Pétré, Introduction, 27.

In a way we can say that Aetheria's pilgrimage was a charismatic return to sources in all the best ways available to her.

Other traits of character: she is an extremely *active* personage, very energetic, audacious, and unable to resist the challenge of difficulties. She *has to* climb mountains. This may have been due as much to her psychology as to grace. Was she perhaps "acting out" deep interior obsessions? Or was she really a saint? Who can say? Perhaps both. One drawback—her piety, though genuine, lacks interior depth. Though her pilgrimage is admirable, one feels at times a certain aimlessness and haste—and perhaps her continued assertions that all this is willed by God smack of self-justification. Another trait—she is credulous, almost naive. This adds to the simple charm of her style, which is completely genuine, and colloquial.

Her imagination and devotion. Aetheria had a very lively, concrete, deep, though somewhat primitive, prayer life, that worked itself out in her charismatic pilgrimages. The aim was to struggle on through all obstacles and difficulties to reach her goal (often the top of a mountain, or a remote place in the desert) and once arriving there to do the following:

1. Read the exact Scripture passages that narrate what took place there.
2. Sing a Psalm or Psalms that refer to the events that took place there.
3. To offer the Holy Sacrifice there if a priest is available and if there is a consecrated oratory (which there usually is). Often there is a priest there, one of the monks who has been ordained for this purpose.
4. In any case, to pray there fervently, by an *oratio* which was directed at penetrating the spiritual sense of the event as described in the Bible reading.

Valerius describes her as a charismatic pilgrim, who has responded to a very special grace given her by God. "[She] burned with the flame of desire of divine grace, helped by the power of the majesty of the Lord; with all her strength and with intrepid courage, she undertook an immense voyage throughout the entire world" (Appendix to *Sources Chrétiennes* edition of *Éthérie*, p. 268).[723] "The more she had acquired of the holy dogma, the more burned in her heart the unquenchable flame of holy desire" (*id.* 269).[724] "Bl. Etheria surpasses in courage all the men of the world, as her marvelous story relates" (p. 268).

To sum up the spirituality of Aetheria: Her concept of the world and of the Kingdom of God was something quite definite, clear and concrete. It is the concept that is proper to the fourth–fifth century, before the collapse of the Empire, but after the emergence of the Church from the catacombs. {It is} a triumphant, optimistic concept of the world as belonging to the Risen Christ and filled with visible, tangible, present and real signs of His victory.

a) Jerusalem {is} the place of the *True Cross*. The actual Cross of Christ is seen by the Pilgrims and adored by all on Good Friday. The True Cross is *standing* on the emplacement of Calvary (which she calls simply the *martyrium*). The Anastasis, the Holy Sepulchre, is the center of every liturgical celebration. The Bishop, surrounded by his clergy and the people, always goes to the Holy Sepulchre and many of the prayers are sung by him actually inside the Sepulchre. Jerusalem is then the place where everything speaks of the death and resurrection of Christ and the whole liturgical life of the Church is carried out at the very place where these great mysteries took place. (Monks are especially responsible for this worship in {its} entirety.) Hence the sense that Jerusalem is a center of the world, a sacred source of all Christian life. {The} power of this sense {is evident} in Aetheria.

b) The *martyria* of the apostles and other saints: {these are} places where the pilgrim venerates, in the relics of those who

723. Pétré, 268–74: Valerius, "Lettre à la louange de la bienheureuse Éthérie addressee par Valerius à ses frères, les moines du Vierzo" ("Letter in praise of the blessed Etheria sent by Valerius to his brothers, the monks of Vierzo"); Merton's translation of the editor's French version of the letter (the original Latin is not included in the text but is found in *PL* 87, cols. 421-26).

724. The French reads: ". . . de connaissance du saint dogme, . . ." (". . . of the knowledge of the holy dogma . . .").

have died for Christ, the *power of the resurrection* that acted in them.

c) The *monks* are living signs of the resurrection. They are holy, and work wonders and miracles in the power of the Spirit. They tend to gather at the sites of holy events, or else in the deserts of Egypt, etc. But they are always for her *sancti* and she seeks their blessing, their company, in prayer, their narration of the sacred events (they are custodians of the traditional narratives as well as of the Holy Places). Through the monks also she is in contact with the Risen Savior. Her visits to them, meals with them, etc. are also a kind of participation in the Resurrection life. Valerius says of her: "fortified by the blessing of the saints and comforted by the sweet food of charity" (she leaves Egypt, etc).[725]

d) Her special ambition is to go to *all the places* where the power of the Resurrection is to be encountered in this manner, and she makes a point of travelling toward the (dangerous) Persian frontier and into the parts of Mesopotamia that are still to a great extent pagan in order to see the *martyrium* of St. Thomas, which pilgrims usually do not visit (at least not the ones from the West). Note: Pilgrimages in the fourth century {are a} very important phenomenon, characteristic of the time, dominant in the spirit of the time, closely related to {the} origin of monasticism, especially Western monasticism. {By} 125, Jerusalem had been destroyed by Titus and then Hadrian,[726] {the} Holy places desecrated, {the} Holy Sepulchre buried, with Golgotha, and a Temple of Venus erected on the site. This remained for two hundred years. {In} 326, {the} *Pilgrimage of St. Helena* {led to the} excavation and restoration of the Holy Places. Great Basilicas replace the pagan temples, razed by Constantine. ({The} True Cross: {the} story of {the} invention {was} elaborated about 400, but it is already venerated by 359.) {In} 333, {a} Pilgrim of Bordeaux records still seeing {the} equestrian statue of Hadrian in {the} ruins of {the} old

725. Pétré, 269 (Merton's translation).

726. Actually the Second Jewish War, waged by Hadrian, took place in 132–135; Titus had captured Jerusalem and destroyed the Temple in 70.

Temple;[727] Jerome also mentions this.[728] {In} 335 {there takes place the} DEDICATION OF {THE} BASILICA OF {THE} HOLY SEPULCHRE with great solemnity. After this pilgrimages multiply. {In} 385 Jerome comes to {the} Holy Land to establish himself there with Paula. From 385 to 415 {is the} great age of pilgrimages.[729]

Monasticism in the Journey of Aetheria.

1) Sinai and Palestine. There had been hermits at Sinai since the third century. It was a very unsafe region. Monks were massacred by Bedouins quite frequently. Only in the sixth century (527–535) under Justinian, was the fortified monastery of St. Catherine constructed. The sixth and seventh centuries were the great days of this monastery, which still exists. Raithu, on the Red Sea, was a monastery dependent on St. Catherine. {St. Catherine had an} important library ({cf. the} discovery of *Codex Sinaiticus* by Tischendorf in 1844). Much of this MS material is now on microfilm. Her accurate description of Sinai and surroundings is important for the traditional Christian identification of the Mountain. She ascends Djebel Mousa, accompanied by monks. {There are} *monasteria* around Sinai. {Note the} early use of the word "monastery" in the sense of a hermitage. She also uses it in the sense of a military outpost in the desert of Egypt (see *SC* p. 122[730]). The

727. "*Sunt ibi et statuae duae Adriani*" ("There are two statues of Hadrian there"): *Itinerarium Burdigalense* in *Itinera Hierosolymitana Saeculi IIII–VIII*, ed. Paul Geyer, *CSEL* 38 (Prague: F. Tempsky, 1898; rpt. New York: Johnson Rpt, 1964), 22; according to Henri Leclercq, "Pèlerinages aux Lieux Saints," *Dictionnaire d'Archéologie Chrétienne et de Liturgie* [*DACL*], 30 vols. (Paris: Letouzey et Ané, 1924–1953), 14:77, one equestrian statue was of Hadrian, the other of Antoninus (Pius).

728. "*de Adriani equestri statuo, quae in ipso sancto sanctorum loco usque in praesentem diem stetit*" ("concerning the equestrian statue of Hadrian, which stood in the very Holy of Holies up to the present day"): *In Evangelium Matthaei* 4:24 (*PL* 26, col. 184B).

729. See Leclercq, "Pèlerinages," cols. 65-176, for a survey of these developments.

730. See Pétré, 123, n. 2: "Le mot employé ici *monasteria* est le même que celui qui désignait les habitations des moines." ("The word *monasteria* used here is the same as that which designated the dwellings of the monks.")

monks live in *monasteria*, small individual dwellings, whether huts or caves, surrounding a church. They grow fruit trees.

Humanitas. She constantly speaks of the cordiality and hospitality with which the monks receive her, using the word "*humanitas*" which appears in {the} *RB* in the chapter on guests (*RB*, c. {53}).[731] Old monks, too old to come out and meet her, greet her in hermitages *valde humane*.[732]

Eulogias—as an example and aspect of this *humanitas* is the offering of *eulogias* (cf. *RB*, c. 54).[733] When they ascend Sinai, after the Mass *eulogias* are distributed and eaten: they consist of fresh fruits from the trees grown by the monks.[734] Later she refers to this as a specifically monastic custom (SC p. 180) (when she is in Syria): *Nam et eulogias dignati sunt dare michi, et omnibus qui mecum erant, sicut est consuetudo monachis dare, his tamen, quos libenti animo suscipiunt in monasteriis suis*.[735] (Comment on connection with *RB*.[736])

Her ascent of Sinai: here the monks are her guides (at all the holy places she receives guidance and explanation from the monks who live nearby, and who tell her the traditional stories, pointing out details). They climb "straight up the side of the mountain"[737] instead of taking a spiral ascent. She comments on this. At the top they celebrate Mass in a small chapel "which has

731. "*omnis ei exhibeatur humanitas*" ("let all kindness be shown to him") (McCann, 120/121; the chapter number is left blank in the typescript).

732. Chapter 5 (116); see also chapter 11 (136).

733. This chapter forbids the monk from receiving letters, "devout tokens" ("*eulogias*") or anything else without the abbot's permission (McCann, 122/123); McCann notes of the word "*eulogias*" that "These 'devout tokens' regularly took the form of blessed bread, which one gave or sent to a friend as a sign of communion or charity" (192, n. 80).

734. Chapter 4 (106).

735. Chapter 21: "For they also deigned to give gifts to me and to all who were with me, as it is the custom for monks to give to those whom they receive with willing mind into their hermitages."

736. The reference is presumably to c. 53, "On the Reception of Guests" (McCann, 119–123), which discusses the hospitality to be shown to guests coming to the monastery, who are to be received as Christ and greeted with humility, to have their feet washed, and to be fed and lodged in the guest house.

737. Chapter 3 (102).

in it great grace" at the place "where the Law was given."[738] She then describes the view to her sisters. In all the discussion of Sinai she takes pains to situate and explain everything. She then sees the cave of Elias, and they read there the proper passage of Kings (III K. 19). This is on Horeb, a mountain adjacent to Sinai. ({Note the} importance of this for {the} Carmelite tradition.) She sees the Burning Bush *"qui usque in hodie vivit et mittit virgultas."*[739] Monks live all around. The Monastery of St. Catherine is not yet built ({it dates from the} time of Justinian). She is therefore before St. John Climacus and the other famous monks of Sinai. But she does speak of numerous hermitages (*monasteria plurima*)[740] with a church and a beautiful garden: *"hortus gratissimus habens aquam optimam abundantem, in quo horto ipse rubus est"* (*SC*, 110).[741] She arrives here and it is the tenth hour. They can no longer offer Mass ({an} interesting point for liturgical history), but wait to do so until the next morning (perhaps because they had broken their fast; in any case the implication is that a second Mass might have been offered here). When she leaves, many monks accompany her for a long stretch of her journey. Her conclusion: *Et illis omnibus sanctis nec sufficio gratias agere, qui meam parvitatem dignabantur in suis monasteriis libenti animo suscipere vel certe per omnia loca deducere, quae ego semper iuxta scripturas sanctas requirebam* (SC, p. 118).[742] Here as everywhere in the book we get insight into her character, her devotion, her "special grace" and also can guess at the wonder and excitement of the monks at receiving this most unusual visitor. She emphasizes their *humanitas*, but one also

738. Chapter 3 (104).

739. Chapter 4 (110), which reads *"qui rubus usque in hodie uiuet et mittet uirgultas"* ("the bush which lives and puts forth shoots right up to the present day").

740. Chapter 4 (110).

741. Chapter 4 (110–11): "a very pleasant garden with a very abundant water supply, in which the bush itself is found."

742. Chapter 5: "I cannot adequately give thanks to all those holy men who with willing mind deigned to receive my insignificant self in their cells, and to guide me surely through all the places that I was always seeking, in accordance with the holy scriptures."

supposes that there were some who may have thought that the attention given her was extreme.

Around Mt. Nebo. She finds monks there living around a small *martyrium* near a spring of water, reputed to be the spring struck from the rock by Moses (cf. Exodus 17:6; Numbers 20:8). Actually this is not the proper location for these events. {It is} probably {a} local tradition. {The} spring still exists and is called {the} spring of Moses. *Monachi autem plurimi commanent ibi vere sancti et quos {hic}* ascites *vocant* (*SC*, p. 136).[743] They are gathered around an *ecclesia {pisinna}*[744] (*pequena, piccina*) (cf. patois of Languedoc: "*pitchoun*"). Read {the} description of her visit to the monks at {the} foot of Nebo (n. 11; SC, pp. 136–138).[745]

The Tomb of Job. She meets "many holy monks"[746] coming from Hus to Jerusalem and they tell her the tomb of Job can be seen. She is inspired with the desire to undertake this "labor" and sets off with a party of monks. N. 16[747] describes how the tomb of Job was discovered by revelation: a monk told clerics to dig in a cave, and they find a tombstone with "Job" on it (!!). Note, on the way to this place she stops in an oasis where Melchisedec is supposed to have offered his "pure oblation."[748] In this same garden is a pool where John the Baptist is supposed to have baptised, where baptisms are performed at the Easter Vigil, and where monks come regularly to bathe.

743. Chapter 10: "Many very holy monks live there, whom they call ascetics here" (typescript reads "*his*" instead of "*hic*").

744. Chapter 10 (136): "little church"; Merton relates the non-classical word *pisinna* (which he mistranscribes as "*pissina*") to the word for "small" in Spanish and Italian, and in southern French dialect (which he may have remembered from his own childhood).

745. This chapter relates how the monks received the pilgrims into their cells, gave them gifts, showed them water flowing from a rock supposedly struck by Moses, and then those who were able ascended the mountain with them (by donkey most of the way and on foot for the last segment).

746. Chapter 13 (146).

747. Pétré, 156.

748. Chapter 13 (148).

2) *In Mesopotamia. "Deo jubente"*[749] (her usual expression) she starts off for Mesopotamia. *Volui jubente Deo etiam ad Mesopotamiam Syriae accedere ad visendos sanctos monachos, qui ibi plurimi et tam eximiae vitae esse dicebantur* . . . (*SC*, p. 158).[750] This is the first reason, apparently the most important. The second: *nec non et gratia orationis ad martyrium Sancti Thomae Apostoli* . . . (*id.*).[751] Here at Edessa reference is made to {the} legendary letter of Jesus to King Abgar, kept in the *martyrium* of the Saint. King Abgar V, Dukhama ("the Black") is supposed to have written a letter to Jesus asking Him to come and cure him. Jesus is supposed to have written back saying he was busy in Palestine, and would send a disciple. {He} sends Thaddeus, one of the seventy disciples, who cures the King ({the} story {is} in Eusebius[752]). {The} source {is the} Apocryphal "Doctrine of Addai the Apostle," traditions on {the} origin of {the} Church of Edessa. (Abgar IX, King of Edessa {at the} beginning of {the} third century, was converted to Christianity and the story probably arose at that time.) They stand in the gate where the letter is supposed to have arrived and the Bishop reads the letter there, aloud, to all, with prayers. She then copies the letter of Jesus to Abgar and that of Abgar to Jesus. {She encounters} *the monks* whom she would not otherwise have seen (very austere, {they} live in the mountains and come down to the feast of St. Elpidius whose basilica is on the site of Abraham's house in Haran—Elpidius {is a} monk and martyr {whose feast day is} April 23, in whatever rite that was). All the monks come for the feast, *etiam illos maiores, qui in solitudine sedebant quos ascites vocant*.[753] Note: she considers it a confirmation of the fact that she is traveling *jubente Deo*, that she arrived just on the day when the monks hap-

749. Chapter 17 (158, 160): "according to the will of God."

750. Chapter 17 (which reads ". . . *etiam et ad* . . ."): "I also wished, God willing, to go to Syrian Mesopotamia to visit the holy monks who were said to be numerous there and living very outstanding lives."

751. Pétré, 158 (which reads ". . . *nec non etiam et* . . ."): "and also in order to pray at the shrine of Saint Thomas the Apostle."

752. Eusebius, *Ecclesiastical History*, I:13 (*PG* 20, cols. 119B-130A).

753. Chapter 20 (174) (which reads "*etiam et illos* . . ."): "even those greater ones who used to remain in solitude and are called ascetes."

pened to be in the city, otherwise she would not have seen them. Other "signs" that God really willed her to go this far: *In nomine Dei transito flumine Euphrate . . .*[754] It is the power of God that gets her across this great and rapid river (p. 160). On p. 164 the Bishop of Edessa is quoted in support of her belief: *quoniam video te, filia, gratia religionis tam magnum laborem tibi imposuisse, ut de extremis terrae venires ad haec loca . . .*[755] After Edessa she says simply that it was necessary for her to go on to Haran. *Necesse me fuit adhuc in ante accedere in Charis* (Haran) (p. 172).[756]

About the monks of the mountains behind Haran, then, she says:

> I never had the slightest thought I would be able to see them, not because it was impossible to God to grant me even this, who had already granted me everything else, but because I had heard that they never came down from their places [in the mountains] except at Easter and on this feast, because they were such men that they worked many miracles, and I did not even know in what month this martyr's feast was. Therefore God commanded that on the very day which I had not even hoped for, I arrived. We spent two days there because of the martyr's feast and in order to see those saints, and they deigned to welcome me and speak to me graciously, which I certainly did not deserve. For they themselves, right after the martyr's day disappeared from that place and at once, by night, they sought the desert and each one made for his hermitage in which he lived (p. 174).[757]

To understand the lives of these monks one must read the hymns of St. Ephrem, who himself was a monk[758] in the mountains

754. Chapter 18 (162) (which reads "*Eufraten*"): "In the name of God the River Euphrates was crossed."

755. Chapter 19 (which reads ". . . *extremis porro terrae* . . .): "Because I see, daughter, that you have imposed upon yourself for the sake of religion so great a task that you come to these places from the very ends of the earth."

756. Chapter 20 (which reads: ". . . *usque ad Charris*"): "It was necessary for me to go on farther, all the way to Charris."

757. Chapter 20 (Merton's translation).

758. See below, pages 242–43, 244 for a different conclusion on this matter.

behind Edessa. He describes their solitary death in a special homily. "No one is there to close their eyes, no one to bury their bodies but the hymns of the heavenly spirits surround them. . . . No one knows their tombs, Paradise is their dwelling place. . . . As soon as the hermit's soul is separated from his body it is taken up into the radiance of eternal life and until the resurrection their bones are preserved in the desert. The angels perform the funeral rites, sent in legions to the tombs where the hermits were crowned after their heroic victories" (quoted by Beck, in *L'Orient Syrien*, 1958, p. 279[759]). Ephrem praises {the} absolute solitude of hermits who do not even participate visibly in {the} sacramental life of the Church. Some take {a} vow never to *see* another man. They remain in communion with the Church in the Spirit, by pure hearts: "*Corpora eorum sunt templa Spiritus, et* mentes eorum sunt ecclesia, *et oratio eorum est thuribulum purum.*"[760] "*Quocumque venerit unus eorum* erigit crucem suam et fit ecclesia."[761] "*Loco altarium, mentes eorum et orationes eorum pro sacrificiis Deo offeruntur.*"[762] "Though they live in the cliffs they are by their faith in the midst of the Church; where the oblation is offered they are present though in the desert. . . . The fact that they are absent in body does not make them cease to be sons of the Church" etc.[763] Their prayers support the whole Church (Beck, *l.c.*, 295, 296).

She adds that in the town of Haran, apart from a few clerics and some holy monks who live in the town, the inhabitants are all pagans. She asks the bishop to take her six miles out of town

759. Edmund Beck, OSB, "Ascetisme et Monachisme chez Saint Ephrem," *L'Orient Syrien*, 3 (1958), 273–98; this and the following quotations are taken from the homily "d-'al îhîdâyé w-abîlé," which Beck considers authentic (297).

760. Beck, "Ascetisme et Monachisme," 295: "Their bodies are temples of the Spirit, and their minds are a church, and their prayer is pure incense."

761. Beck, "Ascetisme et Monachisme," 295: "Wherever one of them has come he erects his cross and a church is made."

762. Beck, "Ascetisme et Monachisme," 295–96: "In place of altars, their minds and their prayers are offered as sacrifices to God."

763. Beck, "Ascetisme et Monachisme," 296, quoted from the "*Epistola ad Montanos*" (attributed to Ephrem, but not by him).

to see the well where Jacob gave water to the flocks of Rebecca (Genesis 29:{2-10}).[764] There she finds *multi monachi valde sancti et ascites et sancta ecclesia* (p. 178).[765] She would like to go on to Nisibis, but it is no longer in Roman territory, having fallen to the Persians (this happened {in} 363, hence {this detail} helps {in} dating the document[766]). She reports that the bishop, like the monks everywhere, told her much about the Scriptures and about the miracles of the saintly monks, whether those who have gone to heaven or those still *in corpore*.[767] And she adds: *Nam nolo aestimet affectio vestra, monachorum aliquando alias fabulas esse nisi aut de scripturis Dei aut gesta monachorum maiorum* (p. 178).[768] The monks at Jacob's well, who live a wonderful life according to the Bishop, receive her and give her *eulogias sicut est consuetudo monachis dare* (p. 180).[769]

Seleucia. Then she returns west, to Antioch, after which she goes into the mountains to Seleucia, to the shrine of St. Thecla, a center of monastic life for Asia Minor. First {she makes a visit} to the Bishop, *episcopum vere sanctum ex monacho*.[770] The shrine of St. Thecla is on a plateau outside the town, surrounded by monasteries without number of men *and women*. {Here is the} first mention of religious women. Also here evidently there is the first contact with monastic *community* life. Here she finds an old friend, the deaconess Marthana, whom she had known in Jerusalem as {a} pilgrim; she is superioress of a community: *monasteria*

764. Chapter 20 (178); chapter 21 (180) (space left for verse numbers; Merton means Rachel rather than Rebecca here).

765. Chapter 20 (which reads: ". . . *monachi ibi sunt ualde* . . ."): "many very holy monks and ascetes are there, and a holy church."

766. See Pétré, 178, n. 1.

767. Chapter 20 (178): "in the body."

768. Chapter 20: "For I do not want Your Charity [title given to her correspondent] to think that the stories of the monks had any other subject at all than the scriptures of God or the deeds of greater monks."

769. Chapter 21 (a number of words separate "*eulogias*" and "*sicut est* . . ." in the text): "gifts as it is the custom for monks to give."

770. Chapter 23 (182): "the bishop, a truly holy man and former monk."

{*aputactitum*} *seu virginum regebat* (p. 184).[771] She spends two days there seeing the "holy monks or {*apotactites*}, both men and women who were there, and having prayed and made my communion"[772] she returns to Tharsus, {and journeys} thence to Constantinople.

The term {*Apotactites*} {is} important here—from "*apotage*" or *abrenuntiatio*, "saying goodbye."[773] {It} is the word used in Luke 14:33: "Whoever does not say goodbye to . . . cannot be my disciple."[774] {Note the} distinction between *apotage* and *egkrateia*. *Egkrateia* (see *DS*)[775] {is} a Greek notion: "continency," *self*-control; restraint—temperance arrived at by discipline—in conformity with reason. This is a Greek, especially *Stoic*, approach. {It} is not Biblical—{there is} only a reminiscence of it in I Cor. 7:9 (the training of the athlete). The Greek approach = mastery over the senses by reason. {The} Biblical approach = renunciation of {the} world and submission to God. Discuss the differences! *Egkrateia* aims at a state of "perfection," "incorruptibility." Clement of Alexandria adopts the Greek idea, modifying it and stressing that Christian continency is a "gift of God" (*Stromateis* III).[776] St. Basil develops this idea (*Long Rules*, 16-17),[777] also Chrysostom, commenting on St. Paul, etc.[778] Compare by way of illustration: Ammonas, *Apothegmata* (Greek) #2 (Nau); (Syrian) #3 (Nau, p. 410).[779] {Here the focus is on} solitude and {the} conquest of pas-

771. Chapter 23 (184) (Merton mistranscribes "*apuctatitum*" for "*aputactitum*"—a mistake he makes throughout this section): "she governed monasteries of *apotactites*, or virgins."

772. Chapter 23 (184).

773. See A. Lambert, "Apotactites et Apotaxamenes," *DACL*, 1:2605.

774. Lambert, col. 2605.

775. Pierre-Thomas Camelot, "Εγκρατεια (continentia) Egkrateia," *Dictionnaire de Spiritualité Ascétique et Mystique* [*DS*], ed. F. Cavallera et al., 17 vols. (Paris: Beauchesne, 1932–95), 4:357-70.

776. Camelot, col. 361 (*Strom*. III.7, 57–59).

777. Camelot, col. 362 (*PG* 31, cols. 957-65).

778. Camelot, col. 362 (*In Ep. I ad Cor., Hom*. 19.2 [*PG* 61, cols. 153-54]; *In Ep. Ad Gal., Comm*. 2.2 [*PG* 61, col. 635]).

779. *Ammonas, Successeur de Saint Antoine: Textes Grecs et Syriaques*, ed. and trans. F. Nau, *Patrologia Orientalis* [*PO*], vol. 11 (Paris: Firmin-Didot, 1915), 391–

sion. {See} Ammonas, *Letter* I (Nau, p. 432 ff., esp. n. 6).[780] In the language of Syrian monachism chastity is a first degree of solitude, or *ihidaya*—"living alone in one's body"—*singularis* or single. {For} *Apotage* {see the} example of St. Marcianus in Theodoret, *HR* III: "Having *bid farewell* [to his palace, etc.] he went into the midst of the desert and built a little hut which was hardly enough for his body. This he surrounded with a fence, and remaining enclosed perpetually within, remote from all human contacts, but speaking with the Lord of the cosmos, he heard the Lord's sweet voice."[781] Baptism {is a form of} *apotage* or *renunciatio* of Satan. Monastic *apotage* {is} the factual renunciation of all possessions, and not just interior detachment. *Apotassesthai* {is the} same as *monachari* [782]—and in Cassian's *Institutes*,[783] monks are called *renuntiantes* (*De Institutis Renuntiantium*).[784] The monks are opposed to those who live a common life while retaining

504; actually the apothegm in both the Greek and the Syriac versions is #3: in the Greek (404) Ammonas simply says, "I have passed forty years at Scete praying God night and day to grant me to overcome anger"; the Syriac (410–11) begins with this identical saying, but adds a dialogue in which the brothers ask why Ammonas was in the desert for forty years without overcoming anger, and an elder responds that the tendency to anger was part of his constitution, but that the passions and demons fought against him as if he were a giant and a hero, for this is the way the demons attacked the Fathers, who nevertheless shone forth with patience and endurance during their prolonged struggles.

780. In section 6, the conclusion of this letter (432–34) (the twelfth in the Syriac ordering), Ammonas writes that since the time of Elijah God has shown what should be done by solitaries, and urges his correspondents to strengthen themselves in what they are doing, because those who abandon their solitude cannot overcome their own wills nor triumph in the battle they have undertaken against them, since God's power no longer dwells in those who submit to their passions. He concludes by urging them to overcome their passions and promising that God's power will then come to them.

781. *PG* 82, cols. 1323D-1326A (n.b. the term "*apotage*" does not appear in this passage; the Greek word for "having bid farewell" here is "ἐρρῶσθαι").

782. Lambert, col. 2606.

783. Lambert, col. 2606.

784. This is the title ("On the Institutes of Those Professing Renunciation") of Book 4 of the *Instituta* (*PL* 49, cols. 151–52), and also an alternative title for the whole work: see the note of Gazaeus at the beginning of Book 1 (col. 59B).

proprietorship and administration of their goods (v.g. Gregory Nazianzen[785]). In the *Rule* of St. Pachomius a monk is said to be one who wills to *genesthai* {*apotaktikos*}.[786] But in Asia Minor the term was especially used of those who, in imitation of the Apostles, wandered from city to city. {These included monastics of} both sexes (third and fourth centuries).

Jerome on the "Remoboth." This is the type of monk which Jerome does not like,[787] and criticizes severely (*Ep.* 22, n. 34;[788] see *PL* 49:1102-1108[789]). (He calls them *Remoboth*,[790] or Sarabaites.) He says they are a *genus teterrimum atque neglectum*.[791] *Bini vel terni . . . suo arbitrio ac ditione viventes*[792] (note {the} absence of poverty and obedience). *De eo quod laboraverint in medium partes conferunt ut habeant alimenta communia*.[793] (Note {the} reminiscence of Apostolic life however: cf. Acts 2:42 to end.) *Habitant quam plurimum in urbibus et castellis*[794] ({there is a} lack of solitude, but this seems to imply a stable form of life). *Et quasi ars sit sancta non vita quidquid vendiderint majoris est pretii*[795] (this attitude toward work is subject to a more favorable interpretation). *Inter hos saepe sunt jurgia quia suo viventes cibo non patiuntur se alicui*

785. *PG* 37, cols. 1349-1353, cited in Lambert, col. 2607.

786. "become a renunciant" (*PG* 11, col. 949, cited in Lambert, col. 2607).

787. Pétré makes this connection in her Introduction (88).

788. *PL* 22, col. 419.

789. This reference is to Cassian's discussion of the Sarabaites in chapter 7 of *Conference* 18.

790. The more recent critical edition of Jerome's letters (*Sancti Eusebii Hieronymi Epistulae*, vol. 1, ed. I. Hilberg, *CSEL* 54 [Vienna: Tempsky, 1910]) calls them "*remnuoth*": see the *Letters of St. Jerome*, vol. 1, trans. Charles C. Mierow, ed. Thomas Comerford Lawlor, ACW 33 (Westminster, MD: Newman Press, 1963), 170.

791. "a very low and careless type."

792. The text reads "*arbitratu*": "Two or three . . . living according to their own will and authority."

793. "They contribute part of what they have produced to a common fund so that they might have shared provisions."

794. "They live as much as possible in cities and villages."

795. "And as their work, not their life, is holy whatever they sell is of a higher price."

esse subjectos[796] ({cf. the} connection between obedience and poverty: sc. subjection). *Solent certari jejuniis*[797] (another familiar accusation of Eastern monks). *Affectata sunt omnia, laxae manicae, . . . crebra suspiria*[798] (cf. Cistercian accusations of Cluny and vice versa[799]). *Et si quando dies festus venerit, saturantur ad vomitum. . . .*[800] This is one reason why the Latin monks in Palestine prefer to live in the Egyptian style. Nevertheless we can see from Aetheria that in reality the {*apotactites*} were the most common type of monk in the Near East in the fourth century. They have a tendency to live in towns, around the churches where they fulfill the common prayer. But they frequently travel. They are strict in fasting. {They} form an intermediary class between clergy and faithful; {they} may be directly under the Bishop. In the *DACL*, see details about heretical tendencies that developed from this type of life and outlook (col. 2615 ff.).[801]

Conclusion: Aetheria is an essential witness giving us a living picture of Palestinian monasticism as she saw it. She tells only the best. All the monks are "saints" etc. Nevertheless we see from her that the institutions were somewhat different from those of the familiar Egyptian pattern and from what we meet in Jerome.

796. "Among them there are often quarrels because living by their own food they do not put up with being subject to another."

797. "They customarily compete in fasting."

798. "Everything is pretentious, wide sleeves, . . . frequent sighs."

799. For an overview, see David Knowles, "Cistercians and Cluniacs: The Controversy between St. Bernard and Peter the Venerable," in *The Historian and Character and Other Essays* (Cambridge: Cambridge University Press, 1963), 50–75.

800. "And when a feast day comes, they are glutted to the point of vomiting."

801. Lambert, cols. 2615-25.

Appendix I—Chant and the Monastic Life[802]

St. Jerome is one of the Fathers who is *opposed to chant* for monks. It would be well, at this point, to take account of the divergence of opinion among the Fathers on this subject. *St. Jerome* is of course against recreation in worldly music (*Epistola* 107:8).[803] But he is also against liturgical music. *Audient haec adolescentuli: audient hi quibus psallendi in ecclesia officium est,* Deo non voce, sed corde cantandum*; nec in voce tragoedorum modum guttur et fauces dulci medicamine colliniendas,* ut in ecclesia theatrales moduli *audientur et cantica,* sed in timore, in opere, in scientia scripturarum (*In Epist. ad Ephesios*).[804] Here he is speaking of *boy-cantors* in parish and cathedral churches, and a *theatrical* rendering of the chant with a special view to pleasing the ear. His opinion is that this sensible pleasure in the chant is unimportant and a bad singer can still be very pleasing to God in his prayer, if he is virtuous. *Quamvis sit aliquis ut solent illi appellare* cacophonos, si bona opera habuerit, dulcis apud Deum cantor est. Sic cantet servus Christi ut non vox canentis sed verba placeant (*In Epist. ad Ephes.*).[805] This rigorist view completely discounts the aethestic value of Church music.

St. John Chrysostom—The following text is not "against chant," and Chrysostom does not neglect the value of chant but

802. Merton's discussion in this appendix relies on P. Thomas, osb, "Le Chant et Les Chantres dans les Monastères Bénédictines Antérieurs au XVe Siècle," *Mélanges Bénédictins*, 405–47, which includes all the passages quoted.

803. *PL* 22, col. 874: "*Surda sit ad organa. Tibia, lyra, cithara, cur facta sint, nesciat.*" ("Let her be deaf to the organ. Leave her ignorant of the pipe, the lyre, the cithara and why they have been made.")

804. *PL* 26, col. 562A, which reads: "*Audiant . . . in tragoedorum . . . audiantur . . .*" (Merton follows the text as cited in Thomas, 410, n. 9): "Let youngsters hear this: let these whose duty it is to sing in church hear it: one should sing to God with the heart, not the voice; the throat should not be used in the manner of tragedians, nor the jaws besmeared with sweet potions, so that tunes and songs of the theater are heard in church, but one should sing in fear, in work, in knowledge of the Scriptures."

805. *PL* 26, col. 562A: "Although it is someone that is usually called cacophonous, if he has good works, he is a sweet singer before God. Thus let the servant of Christ sing so that not the voice of the singer but the words are pleasing."

he asserts that a virtuous man who is not a good singer can still be very pleasing to God. "If you are worn out with old age, or still young, if your voice is harsh or crude, if you are completely ignorant of rhythm, none of this is to be regarded as a fault. What is asked of you is a modest soul, a vigilant spirit, a contrite heart, a balanced reason, and a free conscience: if you possess this you can enter into the holy choir of God and take your place next to David" (*In Ps. 41*).[806]

Desert Fathers—A quotation attributed to Abbot Pambo by Paul Evergétinos[807] (see *Mélanges Bénédictins*, p. 410, note {9}) {says}: "The times are near when monks will abandon the solid nourishment, the Word of the Holy Spirit, to devote themselves to hymns and tones. What compunction or what tears can come from *troparia* when a man in church or in his cell is bellowing like a bull? . . . Monks do not come to this desert to stand before God . . . to sing hymns and melodies." Another Desert Father replied to a disciple who said he needed to *sing* in order keep awake in his prayer: "My son, to sing psalms with melodies is first of all pride. For this makes you think of yourself singing, while your brother is not singing. Secondly it hardens your heart and does not allow it to enter into compunction. *If therefore you want compunction, give up chant*; when you stand to pray let your mind think of the meaning of the verse, . . . [If you sing] that is the precise reason why compunction flies far from you. . . . Chant has led many into the depths of the earth, not only worldlings but priests who have become effeminate and have fallen into shameful passions" (cf. *Mélanges Bénédictins*, p. 411, n. {9}).

Diadochos, without reproving chant, says that in proportion as one's prayer becomes more spiritual, one sings more softly and the prayer is more interior:

806. *PG* 55, col. 158.

807. Evergétinos was an eleventh-century Byzantine scholar who assembled a vast collection of materials from the desert fathers, some of it not published elsewhere.

> When the soul is still in the abundance of its natural fruits, it gives itself to psalmody with a stronger voice and prefers vocal prayer. *But when it is moved by the Holy Spirit* it sings very quietly and softly [or perhaps, it sings *in silence*] and *prays with the heart alone*. From the first way of prayer springs joy in the imagination; from the second come spiritual tears and then a certain well-being that loves silence. Thanks to moderation of the voice the memory [of the meaning?] remains warm and prepares the soul to conceive peaceful thoughts that are propitious for tears. . . . However when we are weighed down by great desolation we should sing psalms in a stronger voice, raising by joy and hope the accents of the soul until the dark clouds are scattered by the breath of melody.[808]

This is a saner and more moderate view, which holds that *chant is sometimes very useful and good* but does not simply equate spiritual prayer with good singing. Naturally, he does not equate it with *bad* singing!

St. Ambrose is famous for his *hymns* which were very popular and effective in helping the people to participate in the offices.

St. Augustine {says}, "*cantare amantis est*."[809] He emphasizes that the *unity* of the choir in song is representative of the unity of Christ and therefore no voice must dominate (*In Ps*. 149:3).[810] Also if one is to sing in church he should try to sing as well as he can, in order to honor God (*In Ps*. 32:3).[811] In both these cases he is speaking to the laity, but monks are not excluded from this teaching.

808. Quoted in Thomas, 412, n. 10.

809. The full statement is: "*cantare et psallere negotium est amantium*" ("to sing and psalmodize is the business of lovers") (see Thomas, 411, n. 10).

810. *PL* 37, col. 1953.

811. *PL* 36, col. 283.

{Appendix II}—The Spiritual Doctrine of St. Ammonas

Ammonas—2nd Abbot of Pispir.

1. It is worth while to study some important texts editied by F. Nau and M. Kmosko[812] in *Patrologia Orientalis* 11. Ammonas is a disciple of St. Anthony {who is} commemorated in {the} Greek Church on Jan. 26 and on the Saturday before Quinquagesima (dedicated to "the ascetics"[813]) {and} in a Syrian Menology on June 10. {There are a number of} different persons of the same name:

a. *St. Ammon*—founder of Nitria—{he} married but lived {an} ascetic life with his wife from the beginning, {and} settled at Nitria about 330. His wife had a community of virgins in their home. He visited her twice a year. He died before St. Anthony, about 350 (see *PL* 73:1099-1100).[814]

b. *St. Ammonas*—Abbot of Tabennisi[815] (*Hist. Laus.* c. 48) died about 400. {Note the} rigorous asceticism of his community, especially in the matter of silence. {He is} confused with our Ammonas; {he is commemorated} in {the} liturgy {for} Jan. 26 (*PL* 73, col. 1153).

c. *Ammonas Parotes*—{was} one of the "Long Brothers" of Scete exiled by Theophilus in the Origenist controversy. {He is} called Parotes because he cut off his left ear to escape the episcopal dignity and when this was apparently not enough threatened to cut out his tongue. He was condemned as {a} heretic by Theophilus in 401, fled with the other three {"Long Brothers"} (and also Cassian) to Chrysostom at Constantinople, {and} died {in} 403.

812. *Ammonii Eremitae Epistolae*, Syriac text ed. Michael Kmosko, *PO* 10 (Paris: Firmin-Didot, 1913), 553–640; for Nau, see n. 779.

813. Nau, 395.

814. *Historia Lausiaca*, c. 8.

815. This reference is to the text as published in Migne; the critical Greek text as established by Butler does not include any notice of this Ammonas; the material is taken from the *Historia Monachorum*, where Ammonas is properly understood to be abbot of a Tabennisiot monastery, but not of Tabennisi itself: see n. 143 above.

Our Ammonas—began as a monk of Scete, befriended St. Anthony, {and} became Abbot of Pispir after Anthony's death. St. Athanasius took refuge there, and consecrated him Bishop. {He}was {a} friend of a monk of Syria exiled in Egypt (*PL* 73, col. 983).[816] He is dead before {the} redaction of {the} *Historia Monachorum*[817] (before 396?).

Teaching of Ammonas:

A—Greek Texts[818]

{There is an emphasis on the} importance of *metanoia*—repentance. First concern: is my repentance *genuine*?

1. The "Four Matters" (*Tessara pragmata*) (*PO* XI: 455 f.)—four things which make repentance impossible and render prayer unacceptable to God:

a. *Pride*—"When a man thinks he lives well {. . .} and others are being edified by him . . . that he has been liberated from many sins by retiring into the desert etc. *If he thinks this God does not dwell with him*." Rather he must remember Isa. 64:6. "If the soul does not bear witness in truth that he is more sinful than unreasonable beings, birds and dogs, God will not accept his prayer" (455). (Animals are not proud—they love those who care for them, but man does not love God who cares for him [456].)

b. *Rancor*—If a man bears a grudge and feels resentment toward another "even if that man has put out your eye"—prayer will not rise to God (456).

c. *Judging others*—He who condemns a sinner will be condemned himself "even if he works wonders and prodigies" (456).

816. Actually Nau says it was Poemen who was the friend of this monk, but that Ammonas knew Poemen (394–95); the *PL* 73 reference is to the *Verba Seniorum* (V, 18:16), which doesn't mention Ammonas, but does give the story of Abba John who came to Abba Pastor (i.e. Poemen) from Syria and received counsel from him in Greek (which Pastor didn't know).

817. Cf. *PL* 21, col. 517.

818. The page references in this section are to Nau, ed., *Patrologia Orientalis*, vol. 11.

"The Christian must judge no one for even the Father judges no one; He leaves all judgment in the hands of his Son, so that *he who judges before Christ is an Anti-Christ.*" "Many who are today thieves and lechers will be tomorrow holy and just, {. . .} for we do not see their hidden virtues . . ." (456).

d. *Lack of charity*—{he} quotes 1 Cor. 13:1-3. Even with miracles, lack of charity empties all of meaning. Charity hates no one, harms no one, suffers for others, has compassion for sinners in perfect imitation of Christ who ate and drank with sinners and loved everybody. Charity is for *all.* {It is} useless to do good to some and hate others (457).

2) *Christ the Master and Model of the Monk* (nineteen exhortations—each beginning "take care . . ."):

a. In His humiliation, taking the form of a servant (Phil. 2—Read);[819] in His redemptive suffering and death (Isa. 53: {the} Servant of Yahweh—model of {the} monk). The monk imitates Christ above all by meekness and non-violent acceptance of injuries (459). {He} accepts them in silence and if possible in a spirit of prayer, as due to him for his sins, in explicit *imitation* of and *participation* in the Passion. {He shows meekness by} praying for persecutors and benefactors who have done him a great good. The monk should fly from all honors and seek the lowliest tasks, in which he will conduct himself "with compunction and humility, without regret,

819. "Take care, my dear friend, because you have confidence and conviction that Our Lord Jesus Christ, who is God and possesses an ineffable glory and grandeur, became our model so that we might walk in his footsteps; 'he humbled himself' for our sake deeply, beyond all description, 'by taking the form of a slave,' without hesitation in the face of deep poverty or disgrace; he likewise endured numerous insults and injuries, and as it is written, 'He was led like a sheep to the slaughter, and as a lamb is silent before his shearer, so he did not open his mouth. It is in humiliation that his judgement was completed'; he even endured death with many insults for us; so that we too, according to his command, should willingly bear, for our own sins, whoever rightly or wrongly insults us, despises us, does evil to us, beats us even to death; so like a sheep led to the slaughter and like an animal without speech, make no objection, but rather, if you can, give yourself over to prayer, or at least, if you cannot, keep total silence with deep humility."

as if you were going to die and as if you were already dead to the world, indeed as if you were the last and greatest of sinners" (460; Read n. 4; p. 461).[820] In these tasks the monk will seek always what is most humiliating and tiring to body and soul, in so far as he can under obedience, keeping his body "without interruption in manual labor, in fasting, and other numerous humiliations according to God" (462{-63}), also in meditation of the Scripture and in tears.

b. *He should always "be in the same disposition of spirit as if he assisted at the Holy Sacrifice"* (463), and live in the awareness that he *belongs totally to Christ his Redeemer and not to himself*, "in confidence and in the persuasion that you are always before His eyes, *dying in thought and going out of this world* as if you remained before him and were there at all times" (463). As a servant with his master, the monk is "always before God in fear of body and soul"—in fear and dread—purifying his thoughts of all evil. To remain in this, persevere with *tapeinophrosune*—{lowly} mindedness; *praotetos*—meekness; *aidous*—respect; *epistemes*—circumspection (Nau translates "tact") and all humiliation, not daring to look up because of one's sins (464).

820. "Take care to ask sincerely for pardon of your sins, to seek in every way the salvation of your soul and the kingdom of heaven, and to work with all your power, in thought, word and deed, in dress and appearance, to humble yourself and abase yourself like dung, dirt and ashes, as the least of all, the servant of all, to consider yourself always in the depth of your heart, with all sincerity, as the least and the worst sinner among Christians, far removed from all virtue, and say to yourself, 'In comparison with a Christian, I am but earth and ashes, and "like the rag of a woman in her courses" [Is. 54:6], and it is only by great kindness and grace that I can find mercy before God, since I am more worthy of eternal punishment than of life. For, if he comes to enter into judgement with me, I can have no favorable verdict, as I am full of vileness.' While you keep your soul in mourning and humiliation and await death each day, cry out without ceasing to God, that with great mercy he would heal your soul and take pity on you, so that you feel overwhelmed by grief and groanings, to the point of never rejoicing or laughing; rather may your laughter always be changed to sorrow and your joy to sadness; walk always with a somber look while saying to yourself, 'my soul has been covered with scorn' [Ps. 37:8]."

c. As a result of this {there is} *total obedience to God, even to laying down of one's life* (meditation—{realizing the} presence of God). "{Be} ready to obey His will whether in life or in death, or in any affliction, with great good will and faith, as if you were expecting great and frightful temptations to descend upon you, even the worst afflictions and tortures and a dreadful end. And take care that in everything that befalls you, in word or act or thought, you do not seek your own rest or your own will, but seek with concern the will of God and desire to carry it out totally even though it seems to lead to affliction and death, for His command is eternal life" (464–465). This means *consulting Him* about every action, every smallest thing, and even doing all in His truth and confessing Him in all words and works, so as to love Him very much (n. 10; 465), and considering ourselves "useless servants," not asserting our right to a reward, nor taking for granted that our service is especially acceptable (n. 11; 465). {It means} belonging wholly to the Lord who has redeemed us (n. 13; 467) and hence not acting as one's own master. {It means} to *hope for nothing from anyone but Him* (n.16; 469), to accept nothing that does not come by God's will, i.e. not to accept fruits of injustice (n. 17; 469–470), {to value} silence (n. 18; 470).

3. *Letter to Solitaries (Peri ton thelonton hesuchazai):*

a. {He tells them} *to keep their lives simple and deep, by compunction and avoiding controversy.* "A love for inquisitive study of Scripture engenders discord and argument, whereas weeping for one's sins brings peace" (472). What he says of scripture applies equally well to liturgy, to monastic reform, spirituality etc. In detail: the monk who sits alone in his cell *sins* if he "curiously investigates" (*periergazesthai*) Scripture while neglecting his own sins. To be "*periergos*" is to be overcareful, officious, a busybody, prying into every little detail, with excessive and inopportune work. It is a way of *evading* the reality of our sins. {The} result of this {is that} "the monk falls into a *great captivity.*" He who wishes to avoid captivity prostrates himself before God. One way to captivity {is} "seeking resemblances of God." This is blasphemy. Avoid this by purity and fear of the Lord and imploring Him to deliver us from sin. Seek and *keep* His word rather than {trying} to penetrate it with full understanding. If the heart is pure and empty, the Lord will fill it with His gifts (472).

b. Read n. 2 (472-473): "He who is attached to his own ideas {. . .} comes into conflict [enmity—*echthras*] and is a captive of the spirit of sadness" (472). "He who sees the words of Scripture and observes them according to his own knowledge, relying on this knowledge and declaring 'This is so!'—he does not know his own glory and his true riches. But he who looks and says, 'I know not—I am only a man'—he gives glory to God. The riches of God dwell in such a one according to his strength" (473).

c. "Do not expose your ideas before all but only before the Fathers, or you will have sadness in your heart" (n. 3; 473). Sadness and aggression {are} two sides of the same coin.

d. The love of human glory begets lying (n. 4; p. 473). {One should show} respect for others—not speaking evil of them—not associating with those who speak evil of {the} brethren. Loyalty and plain dealing {are essential} (n. 6). "If anyone says one thing and has another in his heart, for evil, his whole liturgical office is in vain. Have nothing to do with such a man lest he infect you with his poison" (473). "Have no malevolence toward any man lest you make all your [monastic and ascetic] labors worthless" ({474}).[821]

4. *Instructions to Novices* ("Those who are beginning to serve God"): {cf.}[822] instruments of good works[823]—"to be read every day" (483-4). *Strength is found in tears before God*. The whole instruction is concerned with *fortitude and zeal* in asceticism, as against negligence and discouragement. "*The instruments of virtues are bodily fatigues suffered with understanding*" (n. 5; 475). {He} emphasizes peace, compassion, humility, modesty, fear of the Lord, solitude. "Decline of the spirit comes from love for distrac-

821. Mimeograph reads "473".

822. Mimeograph reads "of".

823. I.e. chapter 4 of the *Rule* of Benedict (McCann, 27–33).

tions [*agapan ton perispasmon*—love of wandering about?] but growth in knowledge [*hesychia en gnosei*] is restoration of the spirit" (n. 12; 475). "To maintain your will against your neighbor is a sign of [spiritual] ignorance" (476). {This is} apparently obvious, but in fact {is} a very deep truth {which} must be understood in depth. "Like a house without door or window, with which the snakes can enter as they please, such is the man who does his work without full attention" (477). "*Charity* is the end of virtues, to esteem oneself just is the fullness of passion" (477). "He who does not blame himself cannot withstand anger" (477). "Have no confidence in yourself, or the support of God will leave you" (478). "Seek always the advice of the Fathers and you will be at peace all the days of your life" (479). "With all your strength ask God to send you His fear so that with your desire directed towards God you may extirpate all the passions that attack your unfortunate soul, seeking to separate it from God and gain possession of it. . . . Therefore, brother, seek no rest while you are in the body in this world . . ." (481).

Fragments. "Let us keep away from useless meetings of men and be lovers of solitude [*monosis*] for getting together with other people is destructive of inner peace" (485). {See also his} meditation on the last things (p. 486).

B—Syriac Texts[824]

Letter I. "The Spiritual Life"—"True Health." The Latin version of this letter is among the letters attributed to St. Anthony in *PG* 40, col. 1030, *Letter* 15[825] (from a corrupt Arabic text). One would never get the real idea of Ammonas from this version which gives us commonplace moral maxims. It speaks of "bearing living fruits"[826] but this is never clear—it is simply reduced to the maxim "do good—avoid evil."

824. The page references in this section are to Kmosko, ed., *Patrologia Orientalis*, vol. 10.

825. Cols. 1030D-1032A.

826. Col. 1030D.

a) {The} *theme of the letter is "health"*—of *body, soul and spirit* (the whole man) (n. 3; p. 569); this is a gift of God, it is the "divine inheritance" (p. 567); {it} is the result of truth. The spiritual life, spiritual health, is *the whole man living fully in truth, standing upright in truth* (not of course simple care of the body!). "*I see your body is now standing upright and is entirely alive*" (p. 567). (Spiritual life {is the} whole man awake, restored to truth and attention to God, from torpor and spiritual death of error and sin). God desires this life and health in us—"For He has a care to preserve the living form [of man] in order that [man] may be numbered in the inheritance of God" (p. 567). "Therefore," says Ammonas, "I now rejoice for you and for your living body."

b) *Sickness and death*—A Scripture quote illustrates his idea of "illness." It refers to false asceticism, to fasting, etc., without justice and charity (p. 568; Read Isaias 58:1-5[827]). The source of this is *error*, from which man must be liberated by God (569). This error has its root in the world (*in saeculo maligno*) (569), especially in *vain glory* and the *desire of pleasure* (570). (This is taken up again in Letter III, p. 575.)

c) *The fruits of health*—If their health is preserved by God they will grow in truth and bear the fruits of life—fruits of holiness (569). These fruits are joy, *philanthropia*, love of the poor, and all good conduct. They will then lead a paradise life without evil thoughts and without corruptible fruits, but will be received into the "camp of the angels and the Church of the firstborn." (Read:

827. "Cry out full-throated and unsparingly, lift up your voice like a trumpet blast; tell my people their wickedness, and the house of Jacob their sins. They seek me day after day, and desire to know my ways, like a nation that has done what is just and not abandoned the law of their God; they ask me to declare what is due them, pleased to gain access to God. 'Why do we fast, and you do not see it? afflict ourselves, and you take no note of it?' Lo, on your fast day you carry out your own pursuits, and drive all your laborers. Yes, your fast ends in quarreling and fighting, striking with wicked fist. Would that today you might fast so as to make your voice heard on high! Is this the manner of fasting I wish, of keeping a day of penance: that a man bow his head like a reed, and lie in sackcloth and ashes? Do you call this a fast, a day acceptable to the Lord?"

Hebrews 12:18-29.[828]) (cf. *Epistola Dubia* I, nn. 7-8; p. 626,[829] on spiritual *maturity*, {with its} Biblical approach to the three degrees of spiritual life: childhood, youth, fatherhood [cf. 1 John 5:12]: "*Finem autem crescendi mensuram paternam dicit*" [626]).[830]

Letter II. "*Virtus*" (*Dunamis*).[831] This letter is one of the finest pieces of ascetic writing (indeed {it} is mystical) of {the} fourth century. {It speaks of} an angelic strength—the angel given by God to surround the monk and drive away devils from him (570). This angelic protection is fully effective only where the monk has passed through the following steps of conversion: total love for God begets fear, tears, then joy. The "*suavitas Dei*"[832] then produces "*virtus*" (571). But this true virtue is given to few—though

828. "For you have not approached a mountain that may be touched, and a burning fire, and whirlwind and darkness and storm, and sound of trumpet, and sound of words; which sound was such that those who heard entreated that the word should not be spoken to them; for they could not bear what was being said: 'And if even a beast touches the mount, it shall be stoned.' And so terrible was the spectacle that Moses said, 'I am greatly terrified and trembling.' But you have come to Mount Sion, and to the city of the living God, the heavenly Jerusalem, and to the company of many thousands of angels, and to the Church of the firstborn who are enrolled in the heavens, and to God, the judge of all, and to the spirits of the just made perfect, and to Jesus, mediator of a new covenant, and to a sprinkling of blood which speaks better than Abel. See that you do not refuse him who speaks. For if they did not escape who rejected him who spoke upon earth, much more shall we not escape who turn away from him who speaks to us from heaven. His voice then shook the earth, but now he promises thus, 'Yet once, and I will shake not the earth only but heaven also.' Now by this expression, 'yet once,' he announces the removal of things which can be shaken—created things—in order that the things which cannot be shaken may remain. Therefore, since we receive a kingdom that cannot be shaken, we have grace, through which we may offer pleasing service to God with fear and reverence. For our God is a consuming fire."

829. Chapter 7 focuses on King Hezekiah's request (in Isaiah 38) to live longer to perfect his soul; c. 8 is a reflection on 1 John 5:12-13, as noted immediately below.

830. "He says the process of growing ends with a father's stature."

831. "*Virtus*" here is not only virtue but power, strength, the Latin equivalent of the Greek "*dunamis*."

832. "sweetness of God."

all who dispose themselves can receive it. {The} Latin version (from Arabic) (*PG* 40, col. 1022)[833] emphasizes that most monks, *thinking they have already received* the *virtus*, do not seek it any more and do not receive it. One's whole effort should be directed to receiving this great gift. Complete sincerity in the service of God merits this gift.

Fruits of this gift:

1) The monk is not held back by the "powers of the air" that stand between him and God (572);

2) He is purified of all trust in the world and its wisdom;

3) He constantly prays in fasting and tears;

4) He finds rest and great liberty in which all his needs are taken care of.

Epistola Dubia II (Kmosko, p. 637) says the following: "Pray day and night that the divine '*virtus*' may be given you, and it will take away from the eye of your interior man all bitter thoughts and evil cares and will purify the eye of your heart so that it may chastely see God. It will purify your soul of all the cares of this world. And now, Beloved, implore God to send you the Paraclete from on high, for the Lord Himself promised He would give the Holy Spirit to all who asked Him . . . and His promises do not fail." (The *Virtus* is here identified with the Holy Spirit—cf. {the} distinction between created and uncreated grace, in Christ.) However, those who do their works to be seen by men do not obtain this gift (*Letter* III; p. 573). They are in bad faith. "Therefore the divine *virtus* does not dwell in them, but in all the works they do, they are weak. They ignore the divine *virtus* . . . their soul is heavy in all their works because it is double" (serving two masters) (574). The remedy is *wholeness*—"That your *whole body* may be acceptable and solid, living with its Maker, so that you may receive the divine *virtus*" (575). Those who allow themselves to be praised as saints are "taken apart" by the devil. "He disperses their body and extinguishes its light" (575) by mixing into their lives the desire to please men. They are left without *virtus* because

833. Anthony, *Epistola* 9 (cols. 1021D-1023A).

their "*bodies* are not disposed." To return to wholeness—"Summon your soul before you and question it," and pray to God ({he} quotes Psalm 142:4 ff.; 576–577). David {is presented as} an example. ({The} Latin [Arabic] version [*PG* {40}, col. 1024; *Epistola Antonii* X],[834] says to "weep over your love"[835] and restore it to life and to blow on the soul as on a fire to make the flames rise up.) Then God reveals the "greatest mysteries" (577). The custodian of *virtus* is *discretion*—an "illumination of the interior eye" (*Letter* IV; 578). {He} quotes Ephesians 3:14, 18. With the "joy of God," {there is} a "sweetness" in God, a revelation of mysteries (579). This is attained by prayer, both of the monk and of his spiritual father—and by *not associating with lax brethren*. Hermits without fervor are to be sent away for they seek only their own will, and are constantly speaking of worldly things so that they dampen the fervor of others (580). Such associations extinguish the Spirit (580) (I Thess. 5:19) by "empty words." But the *virtus divina* will grow in fervent monks and will reveal the *maxima divinitatis mysteria*[836] (*Letter* VI; p. 582), revealed to those who take up their cross. Note the unity between active and contemplative lives in the one *virtus*!! Also {note} the idea of apostolic fruitfulness: these "*accipiunt charismata et prosunt hominibus*" (583).[837]

Letter V deals with the relation of the monk to the Spiritual Father. It is brief (580-581)—{it speaks of the} prayer of the Spiritual Father for sons, and of brethren for one another; they are taught by the Spirit and confirmed in this doctrine by the Spiritual Father (581).

Letter VI. "When the Fathers receive their Sons, God is there in both of them" (583). {Here is an} example of {the} difference between {the} Syrian *Letters* of Ammonas (Kmosko) and {the} Latin (*PG* 40)—cf. *Letter* VI in Kmosko {and} *Letter* XIII of "St.

834. Cols. 1023A-1024D.

835. Col. 1024B.

836. "the deepest mysteries of divinity."

837. "receive spiritual gifts and are profitable to others."

Anthony":[838] {the} *Latin* is longer, contains irrelevancies, {and} does not bring out characteristic ideas of Ammonas (for instance the "*virtus Dei*"). {The} *Syrian* {reads}: "My prayer is that you reach [your full] measure and know the incomprehensible riches of Christ." And he adds that few reach this, even among monks. {The} *Latin* gives the impression that it *is reached* by monks rather than others, and adds: "by monks and virgins living in communities."[839] These "have reached perfection and thrones are prepared for them, on which they will sit and judge."[840] There are men like these in every generation ({the} implication {is} that there are plenty), and they judge their own generation. {The} *Syrian* says rather: "Those who have received the great promises of the Son *have charisms and do great good to men*. All generations *need* these men as *examples* . . ."

"The Charism of the Fathers" (cf. Romans 15:8): {this involves the} transmission of the *virtus Dei* to others. *Letters* VII, VIII and XIV speak of the monk as sharing in "that charism which your Fathers received" (VIII; p. 586). "By imitating your Fathers in the faith may you receive the promises, for you are numbered among their sons" (VII; p. 584). "As carnal parents leave to their sons an inheritance of gold and silver, the just leave to their descendants this inheritance: justice" (*Letter* XIV; p. 615). He makes clear that our inheritance as monks comes to us from the Patriarchs and prophets. {He} especially likes Jacob, Joseph, Moses, Elias, John {the} Baptist. By justice here, he means *eternal life* (616). As Jacob imitated his Fathers in everything, he obtained the blessing of the Fathers (*id.*, 584). Other examples: Elias and St. John {the} Baptist lived in the desert, not among men. "First they were in great silence and for this they received the power of God" (*Letter* XII; p. 604). In this case it was the *power to heal souls*. They are only sent to heal others when all their own infirmities are healed. Note: the Latin Version ("Anthony" *Letter* XIV; *PG* 40, col. 1029)[841]

838. Cols. 1027D-1028D.

839. Col. 1028B.

840. Col. 1028BC.

841. Cols. 1029A-1030D.

does not bring out the idea of the charism of the Fathers. The monks have simply prayed to follow their Father Ammonas to heaven. Jacob etc. {are} brought in as examples of filial devotion *to their* Fathers. The Latin is far short of the Syrian. In the Latin, emphasis is on the blessing of the Spiritual Father, which was grace for the monk. In the Syriac, emphasis is on hoping for the gift of the Holy Spirit who was given to the Fathers (i.e. {the} Saints of {the} OT) and will be given to us. {In the} Latin, {the} emphasis is on the obedience and subjection; {in the} Syriac, {the} emphasis is on *generosity, confidence, {the} gift of the Spirit, prayer of the Spiritual Father who bears witness to the generosity of his sons and testifies that they are "seeking God rightly in self-denial and the Cross."* {The} Latin has {a} reference to Evagrian "*apatheia*"[842] as {the} way to contemplation, and quotes Paul (Romans 8, end)—{this is} not in the Syriac. {It} also emphasizes Jacob's gifts to placate Esau, of which there is nothing in {the} Syriac. He does this "to obtain the blessing of his parents."[843] {The} *Syriac* {speaks} about the power of prayer "for others" given to the perfect monk. This is very important. None of it {is found} in the Latin. As a result of having received this blessing Jacob saw the ladder with the angels ascending and descending. The "Blessing of the Fathers" is then the guarantee of obtaining the promise and charism of the angelic life. This is obtained by prayer and by imitation of the Fathers, and by obedience to Christ. {Its} fruit {is} *security and joy in the Lord*. Also the prayer of the Spiritual Father himself is especially efficacious in obtaining for his sons the share in the promises of the Fathers (VIII; p. 586). *The "labor of body and of heart"* by which they enter into the promises of the Fathers {is discussed}: it consists above all in "praying to receive

842 .The Latin reads "*imperturbabiles sunt affecti*" ("they became imperturbable") (col. 1029D).

843. The Latin reads "*ad consequendam parentum suorum benedictionem*" (col. 1030C), but "*consequendam*" here seems to mean "imitate" rather than "obtain," as the blessing had already been given, and the quotation from Ecclesiasticus [Sirach] 3:11 following suggests the blessing is being transmitted to Esau: "*Benedictio patrum descendet in filios*" ("The blessing of the parents will descend upon the children").

the Holy Spirit" (VIII; 587); in keeping one's thoughts in heaven (*id.*); in firm faith that one can receive the Spirit who dwelt in the prophets. "*Do not give place in your hearts to thoughts of doubt,* but ask with a right intention and [the Spirit] will be given to you" (*id.*). The Spiritual Father adds his own prayer that the sons may receive the Spirit. They must empty their hearts and they will receive Him. When they have received the Spirit He will reveal to them the secrets of heaven, and things which cannot be expressed in words. He will also drive all fear out of their hearts and they will live as though they were already in heaven (*id.*). "And then there will be no further need for you to pray for yourselves but only for your neighbors" as Moses, after he had received the Spirit, prayed for the People of God (*id.*).

Yet this blessing does not exclude temptation and tribulation (*Letter* IX). "Wherever a man has received the blessing of God, immediately there comes upon him temptation from the enemies who seek to rob him of his blessing" (p. 589). For example when Jacob had received the blessing, Esau plotted against him (590). "So you, therefore, my Beloved, having received the blessing of God, *accept also these temptations until you overcome them* . . . then great joy will be given to you from heaven, more than you can understand" (*id.*). "*If God did not love you He would not bring temptations upon you.* . . . For the faithful, temptation is necessary, for all those who are free of temptation are not among the elect."[844] He quotes St. Anthony: "Without temptation no one can enter the Kingdom of heaven" (p. 591). {He} quotes also 1 Peter 1:6 ff.

In *Letter* XIII he says: "Temptation comes to no one unless he has received the Spirit. When he has received the Spirit he is delivered up to Satan to be tempted. Who delivered him if not the Spirit of God? It is not possible for Satan to tempt the *faithful* man unless God delivers him up" (610). Note: this applies to the temptations of the good—and of monks. This is based on Mat-

844. This passage is quoted in an identical translation in Thomas Merton, *The Climate of Monastic Prayer*, CS 1 (Washington, DC: Cistercian Publications, 1969), 136 (also published as *Contemplative Prayer* [New York: Herder & Herder, 1969], 126).

thew 4: the temptations of Christ in the desert. The Holy Spirit once given, nevertheless withdraws from man to see if man will seek Him. "There are some men who after the Spirit has left them and withdrawn, overcome with sadness, sit and remain immobile in sadness. They do not pray God to take the sadness away from them, or that the joy and sweetness which they had known might return to them, but because of their neglect and their self-will they remain strangers to the sweetness of God."[845] Thus in *acedia* monks become blind; they have the habit of monks but none of the *virtus* (593). They do not know the work of God. But if with prayer, fasting and tears they beseech God, a greater joy than before will be given them.

Letter X again takes up the subject of temptation and its place in the spiritual life. *Temptation is the sign of progress*, and stands between the joys of beginners and the much higher joy of the perfect. The beginner has fear of God {and} fervor, and loves all the observances of the life. In this sweetness, he learns to serve God (595, 596). But once he has learned, then the sweetness is taken away; "all that was before sweet to him becomes loathsome" (596). Those who remain in this state of disgust become carnal. The importance of Ammonas' doctrine here is the clarity with which he shows that the time of temptation is the time of choice and is decisive for further progress. Those who give up the spiritual life at this moment, fall back into the carnal way. "But if one resists Satan in the first temptation and conquers him, then God gives pacifying fervor, which is reasonable and patient" (596). {There is an} important distinction between the fervor of beginners, which is "agitated and irrational," and that of those who have passed through the initial temptations, which is much greater. It is marked by "imperturbable patience" (*apatheia*?) (596). It is in any case totally pacifying, *omnimode sedator*.[846] The reason

845. For a longer version of this passage, with a somewhat different translation, see *Climate of Monastic Prayer*, 137 (*Contemplative Prayer*, 127).

846. *Letter* X, #2 (596): "*pari ratione fervor secundus omnimode sedator est*" ("The second fervor, balanced with reason, is calming in every way").

why this "second fervor" is so stable and secure is that it comes from God: it purges out the old man and makes one a temple of God; it is obtained by those who become fully aware of their neglect, who pray earnestly to God and think constantly of the last things. He suggests that there are different levels of temptation. Besides the *first temptation* that precedes this state of rational peace, there is the "last temptation" which precedes final happiness. This last temptation is very severe and is compared to imprisonment in hell (*Letter* XIII; p. 611–612). The Latin version in *PG* 40 (*Antonii Epistola* XIX, col. 1052, 1053)[847] emphasizes this as the final purification of the writer himself by a descent into the prison of Hell.[848] The Syriac version {reads}: "And I think this is my last temptation" (611).

Letter XI {focuses} especially on *Perseverance* in the Monastic Vocation: The hermits to whom he writes are thinking of leaving their place, perhaps only going to another location. He says that if they do this by their own will God will not help them and will not go with them. He will not give them the "*virtus*" necessary to continue as monks (599). He quotes Prov. 14:12: (*Sunt viae quae videntur hominibus rectae*[849]. . . quoted in {the} Prologue of St. Benedict[850]). "This he [Solomon] said of those who do not understand the will of God but who cling to their own good pleasure. . . They receive from Satan fervor at first in the beginning which is like true joy but is not joy but after that he gives them sadness and ignominy. Those who cling to God's will get great labor in the beginning but in the end peace and joy" (600). There are three sources of "thoughts": the devil, our own hearts, and God. It is for the perfect to distinguish between these three. "Inquire within your own souls which of these three is soliciting

847. Cols. 1051B-1055B.

848. Col. 1053BC.

849. "There are paths that seem right to men, [but which in the end lead to death]."

850. This verse is actually quoted not in the Prologue but as part of the discussion of the first degree of humility in chapter 7 of the *Rule* (see McCann, 41).

you to leave your place." Ammonas says that he knows what is God's will for them, and that it is difficult to know the will of God. It requires self-abnegation and obedience (601). "I am your Father. But if I had not obeyed my spiritual Fathers from the beginning God would not have revealed His will to me." He therefore urges them to stay where they are!

Letter XII carries on the same topic. In this case, it is a question of going forth to "heal souls." The hermit should leave his solitude for others only if sent by God. Those who go by reason of their own will, are not pleasing to God, {and} cannot save their own souls, still less those of others. "They who are sent by God do not willingly leave their silence. For they know that in silence they have acquired the divine *virtus*." They only go forth in obedience to God and in imitation of the Word coming into this world, to take upon Himself the sufferings of men (605). "Behold, my beloved, I have shown to you the power of silence, how it thoroughly heals and how fully pleasing it is to God. Wherefore I have written to you to show yourselves strong in this work you have undertaken, so that you may know that it is by silence that the saints grew, that it was because of silence that the power of God dwelt in them, because of silence that the mysteries of God were known to them . . ." (606).[851] Hermits who have not been able to persevere in silence have not been able to overcome their own will (606). "Therefore they go to live among men because they are not able to contemn themselves and fly from the ways of men and fight in the battle" (606). Therefore they are not worthy of the divine sweetness and the "*virtus*" does not dwell in them (607). "When the *virtus* appears to them it finds them consoling themselves in the tabernacle of this world and in their passions of body and soul, and hence it cannot descend upon them" (607).

851. This passage is quoted, in a virtually identical translation, in *Climate of Monastic Prayer*, 60 (*Contemplative Prayer*, 50).

Letter XIII—The *Spiritus Paenitentiae* and the *Spiritus Sanctus*:[852] The Lord first gives the Spirit of penance, which is not Himself, but which purifies the soul to receive the Holy Spirit. The Holy Spirit fills the perfect monk with "a ravishing perfume and sweetness" (608). He also calls this the "Spirit of Truth" and says He descends upon very few from generation to generation (609). This Spirit of Truth is the precious Gospel pearl (609). {The} spiritual life {is symbolized} in the vision of Ezechiel (ch. 1). The face of the Cherub {represents} when the Spirit of God rests in the soul, disposing it to praise. The face of the man {represents} when the "spirit ascends and wishes to seek man."[853] The face of the ox {represents} when the soul is in suffering and temptation (i.e. as a victim). The face of the eagle {represents} when "the soul flies in the heights and remains near to God" (612).

852. Spirit of Penitence; Holy Spirit.

853. The Latin here actually reads "*ascendere vult et hominem quaerere*" ("wishes to ascend and to seek man").

PRE-BENEDICTINE MONACHISM

Series II

Syria, Persia, Palestine

ABBEY OF GETHSEMANI
NOVITIATE
1964

Monastic Chronology

About	*Egypt*	*Palestine, Sinai*
300	St. Anthony	Monks of Sinai
315	St. Pachomius Nitria	St. Hilarion
330	Macarius the Elder (Scete)	St. Chariton, *Laura of Pharan*
350	+St. Anthony (356)	
375		St. Melania the Elder
380	Evagrius Shenoute	
385	Cassian in Egypt	St. Jerome
390	Palladius in Egypt +Macarius the Great	
400		St. Euthymius (Pharan)
410		
420	Isaac of Scete	
450		

Syria, Persia	*Asia Minor*	*Constantinople*
Monks of Edessa	Monks in Armenia	
Lauras Julian Saba James of Edessa		
Aphraat		
	Eustathius of Sebaste	Heretic Monastery
	Basil	at Constantinople
St. Ephrem	+St. Basil (379)	
Monastery of Teleda (Syria)	Gregory {of} Nyssa Gregory Nazianzen	First Orthodox Monastery at Constantinople
Monastery of Johanan		
Nestorius		Chrysostom
St. Simeon Stylites Theodoret		
		Acemetes
	Council {of} Ephesus (431)	
		Council of {Chalcedon}* (451) Daniel {the} Stylite Stoudion (461)

* Typescript reads Constantinople.

PRE-BENEDICTINE MONACHISM SERIES II

Syrian and Persian Monasticism—a brief introduction:

The importance of Syrian monasticism has recently come into focus with studies like those of Vööbus and Festugière (see Vööbus: *History of Asceticism in the Syrian Orient—CSCO*—Louvain, 1960;[1] Festugière: *Antioche Paiënne et Chrétienne*[2]). Hence we must go back a little to include what ought to have been treated in the earlier series of conferences (see *Pre-Benedictine Monasticism*—Part I). Syrian Monasticism is especially important in {the} cultural history and indeed religious history of the Near East. Its influence reaches into other religions and cultures. "One cannot understand the sudden rise of the Islamic culture without the factor of all the accomplishments of {the} Syrian culture in the {formation} of which Syrian monasticism played the most {important} role" (Vööbus, *History*, intro. p. viii).[3]

> The influence of Syrian monasticism also embraced Abyssinia. Here too it effected a vitalization of religion. The start of christianization had been established earlier, but this,

1. Arthur Vööbus, *History of Asceticism in the Syrian Orient: A Contribution to the History of Culture in the Near East*, *CSCO* 184, 197 (Louvain: Secrétariat du Corpus SCO), 1958, 1960; a third volume (*CSCO* 500) was published in 1988.

2. A. J. Festugière, OP, *Antioche Païenne et Chrétienne: Libanius, Chrysostome et les Moines de Syrie* (Paris: E. de Boccard, 1959); see also A. J. Festugière, OP, *Les Moines d'Orient*, 4 vols. (Paris: Éditions du Cerf, 1961–65).

3. This and succeeding references are to the first volume; the typescript reads: ". . . of Syrian . . . information . . . most decisive role."

> according to all indications had remained dormant and the work of Frumentius had ended in stagnation. The Ethiopic tradition admits that the country owes the new impulses that helped bolster the strength of the Christian religion to Syrian monasticism. The arrival of a group of Syrian monks occurred in the second part of the fifth century, possibly towards the end of the century. In the Ethiopic sources, these men are celebrated as those who reshaped the spiritual face of the country. They introduced Christian discipline, reformed customs, and fostered religious, monastic and ecclesiastical institutions. They also gave the church its liturgy, and introduced a version of the biblical text. As the evidence laid down in the Ethiopic {biblical text shows, it clearly bears the mark of the Syrian biblical} traditions and the signature of the Syriac idiom. Thus, as the information stands, the impact made by Syrian monasticism upon Christendom in the land of the Negus, covered the entire field of spiritual life.[4]

Since Syrian monasticism shaped Nestorian Christianity, and this Christianity spread into China in the T'ang dynasty, the influence of the Syrian monks can be said to have reached China.[5]

{Note also the} influence of Syrian Christianity in India (Vööbus, *History*, Intro. pp. viii-ix): "The influence of Syrian monasticism can be traced in the Christianity of India. This seems to be mainly the merit of monasticism's missionary zeal that Christianity in India was brought into closer contact with the Syrian church in Persia and received fruitful stimuli from it for its growth. The route from Persia to India was covered with monasteries that created new communication lines and enlivened the interchange in the spiritual life between these areas." Of course influences were reciprocal (see later[6]). Influence from Iran and India affected Syrian monasticism through gnosticism, encratism

4. Vööbus, *History*, 1:viii (a line is dropped from the text in the mimeograph).

5. See Vööbus, *History*, 1:ix.

6. See Vööbus's theory that Indian and Persian ascetic traits entered into the formation of Syrian monasticism through Manichaean influence and intermediaries (*History*, 1:158-69).

etc. Syrian monasticism shaped the Christianity of Mesopotamia and Persia to the east, Armenia and Georgia to the north, reached south into Arabia and Ethiopia. Vööbus stresses the independence of Syrian monasticism from Egyptian and Greek influences. "As against Coptic and Greek monasticism in Egypt and Greek monasticism in Palestine and Asia Minor, Syrian monasticism is conspicuous as *a definitely independent phenomenon, engendered by its own spiritual genius* . . ." (Vööbus, p. iv).[7] Not only is it independent of these other forms, but it *antedates* them, says Vööbus.[8]

Origins of Syrian Monasticism

The area was Christianized by Jews and not by Greeks. Hence one will expect to find a Judaizing Christianity. Yet the extreme asceticism of Syria is not explained by ordinary Jewish sources. The ordinary Jewish belief and culture is ritualistic and strict in this sense but is nevertheless centered on a this-worldly existence. But Vööbus says that Syrian Christianity owed much to Jewish-Christian missionaries who were imbued with the spirit and doctrine of *Qumran* and the Essenes.[9] These Jews were in turn strongly influenced by Iranian mysticism (Zoroaster).[10]

Character{istic}s of this Primitive Syrian Christianity {include}:

1) *Covenant consciousness*: Christians {are} sons and daughters of {the} new covenant, committed to asceticism.

2) *Military terminology* and symbolism: life {is} an ascetic battle for the world. The Christian is a soldier engaged in this battle.

Vööbus traces this trend to John {the} Baptist, converts from Qumran and the disciples of the Apostle James (very ascetic).[11] "There is only one document which claims to know anything

7. Emphasis added in typescript.
8. Vööbus, *History*, 1:iv.
9. Vööbus, *History*, 1:17-30.
10. Vööbus, *History*, 1:21.
11. Vööbus, *History*, 1:15-16.

about the character of the most primitive Christianity in Edessa, namely the *Doctrina Addaei*. . . . Particularly interesting is the remark about virginity which was introduced into the new congregation. This practice is described in the following words: 'but all the *qeiama* of men and women was abstinent and glorious, and they were holy and pure and dwelt singly and abstinently without defilement, in watchfulness of the service gloriously'" (Vööbus, vol. 1, p. 10{–11}).[12] Conclusion: an ascetically oriented faction of Palestinian Aramaic Christianity moved east. {There is an} emphasis on baptism, ascesis, covenant, struggle, {along with} militant asceticism.

Tatian and Encratism

Tatian {was} an Assyrian convert in Rome. At first interested in Greek Philosophy, {he} turned against it and remained aggressively opposed to Greek influence in Christianity. In a rigorous opposition against Western Christianity, he emphasized extreme asceticism for all and even opposed marriage and procreation. He was condemned as {a} heretic in the West. He had a decisive influence in Syrian Christianity. Note his *Gospel Harmony*.[13] Vööbus gives examples of the way Tatian changed Gospel texts to suit his own rigorous views (pp. 40–41). {He} excluded wine from the Kingdom, omitted references to Joseph as Mary's "husband," etc. Note: Jerome, commenting on Galatians 6:8 ("He who sows in the flesh . . .") attributes to a most zealous heresiarch of the Encratists, Cassianus, the view that this is a text against marriage. This Cassianus may be "Tatianus" ({an} error of {the} scribe) or else Julian Cassianus, a Valentinian gnostic.[14] Defending fasting against Jovinian (*Adv. Jovin.* {2}.16; *PL* 23:309), Jerome mentions Tatian and Marcion as heretics who forbade certain foods out of

12. For the meaning of *qeiama* as covenant, see Vööbus, *History*, 1:97-103.

13. The *Diatesseron*, which combined the four Gospel accounts into a single narrative, was the official liturgical text for Syrian Christianity until the fifth century: see Quasten, *Patrology*, 1:224-25.

14. *PL* 26, col. 460A; see n. 2 (cols. 459D-460D) for a discussion of the proper identification.

"hatred for the works of the creator"—*ad destruenda et contemnenda et {abominanda} opera Creatoris*[15] (see below—Marcionites). The true Christian view: *Nos autem creaturam omnem laudamus Dei*[16]—but Christians fast nevertheless. Fasting is commanded by Christ, but not because any creature is evil. Tatian places great emphasis on *suffering* in the spiritual life.

Marcionites:[17] as a result of dualism, {Marcion separated} the "good God" of the New Testament and the evil principle of {the} Old Testament. Creation comes from the evil one. Hence to despise creation is to insult and contemn the evil principle. Marriage {was} treated with nausea. Only celibates could be full members of the Church (cf. Albigenses). {Marcion taught a} hatred of the body, {a} Docetist view of {the} Incarnation and {made the} claim that Christ hated {the} flesh. {He taught} hatred of food: eating is regarded as a bestial and evil action. {Marcionites showed} aggressive opposition to the world, courting persecution.

The Acts of Thomas (apocryphal):[18] {this work shows} a modified encratism, {with an} emphasis on virginity. Only the virgins are espoused to Christ, and they alone can enter with Him into the Kingdom. It is also necessary to leave all possessions, for Christ comes only to those who are stripped of all things. Vagrancy is praised.

In these sources and others (cf. {the} Apocryphal *Odes of Solomon*)[19] we see ascesis regarded as an *essential* part of the Christian message. The Gospel is only for those who practice extreme asceticism. We have seen this already in the background of St. Basil.[20] The idea was eschatological: the refusal of procreation had a cosmic significance. It was supposed to hasten the day of the end. The celibate took a real and concrete part in the "reduction

15. "for destroying and despising and detesting the works of the Creator" (Vallarsi, 351) (typescript reads "1.16" and "*abomnanda*").

16. "We give praise for every creature of God."

17. See Vööbus, *History*, 1:45-54.

18. See Vööbus, *History*, 1:66-67, 70-73, 85-86.

19. See Vööbus, *History*, 1:62-64.

20. See above, pages 127–28..

of the dominion and duration of {the} present world" (Vööbus, p. 90).[21] "Only a church with such qualities could be an instrument working towards the consummation of {the} cosmic upheaval and the expansion of God's dominion in the world" (p. 91).[22] Hence the sacraments were rewards for the continent (v.g. Baptism {as} a crown for the perfect, not an initiation).

Encratism:

1) {It is} dualistic, rejects {the} Old Testament {and} ascribes {the} division of {the} sexes to the demon.

2) Therefore {it} prescribed total abstention from marriage and meat.

3) A "metaphysical hatred of wine"[23] {was} carried to the point that water only was used at Mass.

Tatian taught that Adam was not saved because he married.[24]

Thesis of {the} Egyptian origin of Syrian monasticism. Vööbus disputes {the} theory that monasticism was brought to Syria by Mar Augen, a "disciple of Pachomius" (this is an eleventh-century story, he says).[25] The fact that St. Hilarion in Palestine was entirely influenced by Antonian monasticism proves nothing, says Vööbus.[26] In any case Jerome did not really know Syrian monasticism. (Why not? Did he not complain of the *Remoboth*?[27]) Theodoret, in his *Historia Religiosa*,[28] makes no reference to an

21. Typescript reads ". . . this present . . ."

22. Vööbus, *History*, 1:90; typescript reads ". . . of cosmic . . ."

23. See Georges Blond, "Encratisme," *DS* 4, col. 633: "Les hérétiques encratites ont pour le vin la meme repulsion de caractère dogmatique que ceux qui manifestant la tendence encratite" ("Encratite heretics have the same dogmatic repulsion toward wine as those who show a tendency toward encratism"); see also Vööbus, *History*, 1:84.

24. See Vööbus, *History*, 1:36.

25. Vööbus, *History*, 1:139, 217-20.

26. Vööbus, *History*, 1:140.

27. See above, page 186–87.

28. *The Religious History, or Ascetic Way of Life*, *PG* 82, cols. 1283-1522; Merton quotes from and translates the Latin version accompanying the original Greek text.

Egyptian origin for Syrian monasticism.[29] {In} Theodoret's account {the} origins {are} traced to *James of Nisibis*, who died in 338. Bishop in {the} early fourth century, he had been a monk before that,[30] probably about 280 to 300. This is certainly very early. But there were monks even before him in the mountains around Nisibis. *Julian Saba* died about 367 after 50 years as {a} monk (hermit). "The fact shines through all the early sources that the earliest monasticism in Mesopotamia shows no connection with Egypt" (Vööbus, p. 145). *Wandering monks* of Syria are, says Vööbus, entirely different from those known in Egypt.[31]

Theodoret—*Historia Religiosa: Seu Ascetica Vivendi Ratio*

{This is} the *basic document* for {the} study of Syrian monasticism (Canivet),[32] written about 444. He presents a full *variety* of ways to sanctity—from which one may choose—setting them in a general view of the ensemble of Syrian monasticism. {It is} not so much history as *panegyric*, without reference to deviations, {giving} "an impression of paradisiacal anarchy" (Canivet).[33] The book must be read in the light of his *Therapeutic*[34] which is already a preparatory monastic apologia, and note his discourse on charity at the end.[35] The martyrs were proclaimed by the Church as Victors in Christ, and he proclaims the victory of the confessors. Hence {the} emphasis on military and athletic terminology.[36]

29. Vööbus, *History*, 1:141.

30. In "Ascetisme et Monachisme chez Saint Ephrem," *L'Orient Syrien*, 3 (1958), 284–87, Edmund Beck, OSB disagrees, pointing out that according to St. Ephrem, James was an ascete but not a monk.

31. See Vööbus, *History*, 1:153-54.

32. Pierre Canivet, SJ, "Théodoret et le Monachisme Syrien avant le Concile de Chalcédoine," *Théologie de la Vie Monastique*, 241.

33. Canivet, "Théodoret," 243.

34. The *Cure of Hellenic Maladies*, an apologetic work (*PG* 83, cols. 783-1152; see Théodoret de Cyr, *Thérapeutique des Maladies Helléniques*, ed. and trans. Pierre Canivet, SJ, SC 57 [Paris: Éditions du Cerf, 1958]).

35. I.e., of the *Historia Religiosa*, not the *Therapeutic*.

36. See Canivet, "Théodoret," 244–47.

1. *Preface*: He intends to record the admirable exploits of Athletes of Christ, the great lovers of God. This will be medicine for Christians—to make them not oblivious of the great battles of the saints (as pagan writers narrate the victories of heroes). Statues and pictures are made of Olympic winners—so also of our saints. This book {is a} "proclamation of winners"[37]—cf. {the} proclamation of victorious martyrs in their cult. *Nos autem* vitam scribimus philosophiae magistram, *et quae illam vitae* institutionem imitata *est* quae agitur in caelis[38]—the invisible battle of Ephesians 6:12-17. Their victory was not of nature, but of grace. It came from love of God. Grace closed their senses to the attacks of the demons—for the demons can only reach us through sense. (Comment—see background notes above.[39]) They learned that "Death comes in by the windows" (Jerem. 9:21).[40] Hence they closed the windows of sense "with the locks and keys of divine laws."[41] {They} refused to see, touch, taste, etc. what was not for God's service. (Comment: mere closing of {the} senses does not make our life spiritual—{this is a} false anthropology.) {With} thoughts in harmony, {and} senses under control, the whole person is in order like a well-tuned musical instrument. The soul {is imaged} as {a} charioteer (Plato[42]) and harpist.[43] *All the senses like well-tuned strings respond in harmony to the hand of the player* (cf. Gregory Nazianzen[44]). The saints ignored laughter and "consumed

37. See Canivet, "Théodoret," 245; cf. also col. 1287B: "*Tam praeclaram retulere victoriam, ut fugerint adversarii, et his fugatis nemine obstante tropoeum erexerint*" ("they have gained such an outstanding victory that their adversaries fled, and after these had been put to flight they erected a memorial with no one blocking the way").

38. Col. 1286D: "For we write about a life directed by philosophy, and which copies that form of life that is lived in heaven."

39. Evidently a reference to the comments on encratism and Marcionism, pages 216–18 above.

40. Col. 1287D.

41. Col. 1287D.

42. *Phaedrus* 246b.

43. Col. 1290BC.

44. In his second *Oration* (c. 39; *PG* 35, col. 448A), Gregory says that the orator plays on his audience of various ages and conditions as though on a

their entire lives in grief and tears."[45] (Contrast Aphraat.[46]) {They} took "immense delight"[47] in psalms and canticles. *Veram philosophiam perfecte adamarunt.*[48]

2. He will describe the particular virtues of certain hermits of Syria *"qui {luminum} instar in Oriente fulserunt."*[49]

I. *James of Nisibis*—the New Moses: {he} is compared to several OT saints. (Was he a monk?[50]). *Solitariam et quietam vitam est amplexus.*[51] {He} lived in the high mountains, in summer under the trees of the forest, and in winter in a cave. {He} lived only on wild berries and herbs and totally refused the use of fire for cooking or heating (*Boskoi*).[52] {He} rejected wool as superfluous and dressed in goatskins. His mind purified, he became a "mirror of the divine Spirit."[53] {He showed} perfect confidence in God—{and had} gifts of prophecy, etc. He goes to visit Christian communities in Persia. On the way some girls are washing clothes in a fountain. Because they stare at him impudently he dries up the fountain and turns their hair grey. He could, like Eliseus, who delivered little girls (*sic*)[54] to the bears, have been more drastic. His merely turning their hair grey was due to Christian meekness. James is chosen as Bishop of Nisibis—{he} continues his

stringed instrument; in *Oration* 12 he speaks of himself as a divine instrument tuned and played by the Holy Spirit (c. 1; *PG* 35, col. 843A).

45. Col. 1290C.

46. See page 233 below.

47. Col. 1290C.

48. Col. 1290D: "They loved true philosophy perfectly."

49. Col. 1291B: "who shone in the East like heavenly lights" (typescript reads ". . . *lumine* . . .").

50. See above, page 219, n. 30.

51. Col. 1294C: "he embraced the solitary and quiet life."

52. "Shepherds," a term used by Sozomen in his *Historia Ecclesiastica* (6:33; *PG* 67, col. 1393) for itinerant Syrian anchorites; see Vööbus, *History*, 2:14, 24, 263.

53. Col. 1294D.

54. The text (col. 1295D) does not actually imply that Theodoret thought Elisha had cursed girls: "*impudentes illas puellas*" refers not to the children in the biblical story but to those whom James encountered.

austerities. {He} took part in {the} Council of Nicaea. After a severe day's fast of James, Arius who was "about to be pardoned"[55] died in the toilet (!)—"paying the penalty for his stinking blasphemy in a stinking place."[56] Thus James was a new Phineas (Ps. 105:30). When the army of SAPOR King of Persia besieges Nisibis with elephants and engines, James routs them by prayer which calls down a cloud of mosquitoes and fleas upon them—these drove the elephants mad, scattered them through the camp (this makes James a new Ezechias[57]). James showed great moderation and discretion, says Theodoret, in not calling down thunderbolts upon the Persians but only mosquitoes.[58] James of Nisibis is described by Ephrem in *Carmina NISIBENA* nn. 13, 14:[59] he was the educator of the Church of Nisibis in her childhood. His teaching was simple and severe, extirpating vice and frivolity. As bishop he lived the ascetic life in poverty. But Ephrem does not mention James living as a hermit in the mountains, and so some scholars[60] consider it doubtful that James was a monk in the strict sense. {Note the} military imagery—{its} background {is} the Essenian combat between {the} sons of light and sons of darkness. {There are} no explicit Essenian references in Theodoret; he is more purely Pauline.

II. *Julian Saba* (*sabas = senex*[61]) (in Syrian martyrologies {his feast is} Feb. 8th or 6th; or Aug. 26th, Dec. 5th—"The glorious elder Mar Julian, chief of monks, full of compunction."): {he} lived in a cave in the wilderness east of the Euphrates in the

55. Col. 1302B.

56. Col. 1302C; this legend has no basis in fact, since Arius died not at the Council of Nicaea but in Constantinople eleven years later: see Theodoret of Cyrrhus, *A History of the Monks of Syria*, trans. R. M. Price, CS 88 (Kalamazoo, MI: Cistercian Publications, 1985), 21–22, n. 6.

57. I.e. King Hezekiah: see 2 K 18–19; Is. 36–37.

58. Col. 1306A; this is also legendary, since James died during the siege: see Price, 21, n. 7.

59. See Beck, "Ascetisme et Monachisme," 284–85.

60. See Beck, "Ascetisme et Monachisme," 285–86.

61. I.e. "elder" or "old man," a term of respect for those mature in the ascetical life.

Parthian region. {He} ate once a week, drank very little water. His real banquets were "the hymns of David and fervent colloquies with God."[62] Of these he never had enough—savoring the words that expressed divine love, "*Atque illius* [sc. David] *qui haec dixit amorem in se transtulit*" (*Psalmody*).[63] Mysticism: "*Hic enim tanto amoris igne fuit incensus, ut desiderio inebriaretur, et terrenarum rerum nihil videret,* solum dilectum et noctu somnians et meditans interdiu."[64] See {the} comment below on "the love charm."[65] Here comment on *eros* and *agape*.

1) Usually desert father stories are confined to ascetic feats and miracles. Here is the language of mysticism. Later when Julian goes into solitude as a retreat from his disciples, "*solitus erat . . . se ab omni consuetudine humana separans, atque in seipsum rediens, privatim versari cum Deo, ac divinam illam et ineffabilem pulchritudinem speculari.*"[66]

2) Naturally the mysticism is that of Theodoret. However it is interesting to see it attributed to this very early hermit.

3) This is described as his *summa philosophia*.[67] It attracts many disciples to him. Soon he had a hundred disciples—all in the cave with him. Cenobitic life!!

4) The disciples begin to add herbs, etc. to the meal of bread. The cave is damp and bad for the herbs. They ask to build a cell. After hesitating he gives permission. While he is away in soli-

62. Col. 1307A.

63. Col. 1307B: "He transferred into himself the love of the one who spoke these words."

64. Col. 1307B: "For he was inflamed with such a fire of love that he was made drunk with desire, and saw nothing of earthly realities, dreaming only of his beloved at night and meditating on him during the day."

65. From the Greek of this passage: col. 1308B (φίλτρου); see below, page 231.

66. Col. 1310A (which reads "*Solitus enim erat . . . humana consuetudine* "): "he was in the habit of removing himself from all human intercourse and turning within himself, to commune privately with God and gaze upon that divine and unutterable beauty."

67. Col. 1307A (which reads "*summam . . . philosophiam*"): "most elevated philosophy".

tude, they build a larger one than he had permitted. He rebukes them but permits the new cell to continue. His concessions to the disciples are justified by texts of St. Paul (v.g. Rom. 12:16; 1 Cor. 10:33). {Note the} implications for cenobitic life, which necessarily implies certain compromises and adjustments "so that all may be saved."[68] (A hymn, *not* of Ephrem,[69] sums up Julian's doctrine: "you taught us daily *to keep truth in our bodies* that our community might be preserved by it."[70]) One of his disciples wants to go with him on his seven-day journey into the desert, in spite of warnings. The disciple collapses, and the tears of Julian make a spring of water come forth from the sand—again the theme of pity and assistance to the weak. This youth later becomes a great monk, Asterius, and founds a "*palaestra monastica*"[71] near Antioch. {He} taught Acacius the monastic life. However before that, Asterius used to carry things into the desert for his Master. Julian is characterized by sweetness and moderation; {he} accepts services given him in his old age, {and} accepts praise for the sake of those who praise him.

5) How he trains his disciples:

a) ascetic: "*curam corporis negligere*"[72] (contrast {the} Gospel);

b) prayer—{he} taught them "*intus communem hymnodiam*"[73]—interior prayer in common. How? {He} sent them out two at a time into solitude after dawn. One would prostrate in adoration of God while the other, standing, would sing fifteen psalms. Then they would change around. This went on for the whole day. At evening they would go apart to rest a little and then return to the cave all to sing Vespers.

68. Col. 1310B (quoting 1 Cor. 10:33, which reads "*multis*" ["the many"]).

69. Beck, "Ascétisme et Monachisme," 291–92, disagreeing with Vööbus (see *History*, 2:42-44, where he defends Ephrem's authorship of these hymns).

70. *Hymn* 18.10, quoted in Beck, "Ascétisme et Monachisme," 293.

71. Col. 1314B (which reads "*palaestram . . . monasticam*"): "a monastic training center."

72. Col. 1307C: "to neglect the care of the body."

73. Col. 1310B (which reads "*intus . . . communem . . . hymnodiam*"): "within, hymnody in common."

6) Thus begins the *philosophiae gymnasia seu monasteria*.[74]

7) Voyage to Sinai: {it is taken} with a few of his more intimate disciples, travelling only in {the} desert and avoiding all towns and villages, carrying bread, a wooden cup and a sponge on a rope (to get water from "deep wells"[75]). They adore God on Sinai and build an altar there (i.e. Julian is credited with building the chapel on Sinai).

III. *Eusebius*: {he is an} example of cenobitic Syrian monasticism (chapter 4). {He} lived a *common life as {a} recluse* at first ({there was a} group of recluses near Antioch). He lived in a cell with another recluse. Then {he} was advised to go out and bring others to the love of God. "*Quoniam tu Deum qui te fecit et salvavit, ardenter amas, fac alios tecum reddas amatores.*"[76] He consented to be superior to a group of cenobites. {He} encouraged private solitary prayer in addition to common prayer. "Each one in private, in the shade of some tree or by some cliff, or wherever he might find a quiet place, should pray the Lord and ask for his salvation, either standing or prostrate upon the earth."[77] Disciples of Julian Saba came to him after Julian died. {His was} an extremely ascetic community. Individual choice of extreme ascetic practices was the norm.

IV. *Publius* (c. 5):

a) Head of a community of hermits, {he} expressly forbids more than one living in a cell. {He} *visits the cells with a scale* and if he finds more than a pound of bread, calls them gluttons. {He} used to go around the cells at night to see if they were watching and if not would awaken them. Finally, the brethren, "seeing his labor,"[78] suggested that they could all live under one roof and a cenobium was formed. (Comment.)

74. Col. 1310D (which reads "*gymnasiis seu monasteriis*"): "monasteries or training centers of philosophy."

75. Col. 1315C.

76. Col. 1342D (which reads "*Quoniam ergo tu quoque . . .*"): "Because you also intensely love God who made you and saved you, make others lovers along with yourself."

77. Col. 1343B.

78. Col. 1354B.

b) The advantage of a community {is found in} the "exchange of virtues"[79]—just as in a market one sells bread and buys shoes, so in {a} monastery the virtues can be acquired from mutual edification.

c) *The community had two language groups, Greek and Syrian, and two liturgies.*

V. Theotechnus (c. 5): {he} succeeds Publius. {He} has {a} great gift of compunction. "So greatly was he endowed with spiritual grace that when he prayed all those present were silent and remained intent upon his sacred words alone, believing that just to hear him was a form of zealous prayer."[80]

VI. *Aphraat* (c. 8): that Aphraat, a Persian and {thus} a member of a despicable race, should have been a "philosopher" is an indication that "*hominum una sit natura, et philosophari facile sit volentibus.*"[81] {He} *left his country and lived as a recluse outside Edessa*. Then {he goes} to Antioch where he conducts a "*gymnasium philosophiae.*"[82] In time of conflict and persecution he leaves his solitude to defend the Church. Reproved for this, he replies that when the house is on fire it is not right for a virgin to remain lying in her marriage bed. Hence he leaves his "*quies*"[83] lest he be consumed in the general disaster. Various miracles {are attributed to him}.

VII. *Peter the Galatian* (c. 9): {he} left the world at the age of seven {and} died aged 99. After living {the} monastic life in Galatia, {he} went to Palestine, to {the} Holy Places. "*Veluti sponsi umbram aliquam videre desiderans, loca inquirebat, ex quibus salutares omnibus hominibus fontes profluxerant.*"[84] (See {the} context: pilgrim-

79. Col. 1354C.

80. Col. 1355B.

81. Col. 1367A: "the nature of men is one, and philosophizing is easy for those who desire to do it."

82. Col. 1367B (which reads "*gymnasio . . . philosophiae*"): "a training center of philosophy."

83. Col. 1374B, which reads "*quietem*".

84. Col. 1379B: "As if desiring to see some shadow of the bridegroom, he sought the places from which the streams salvific for all people had poured forth."

age {functions} in place of later "composition of place" in meditation on {the} sacred humanity.[85]) Outside Antioch {he} lives in a tomb (*inclusus*).[86] {He} delivered a possessed man who then lived with him as his "minister"—Daniel. This man was known to Theodoret—both in fact (as a child). Various miracles {are attributed to him}.

VIII. *Theodosius* (c. 10): near Rhosus, Cilicia, on a wooded mountain, he embraces {the} eremitical life, *"Parva sibi exstructa domuncula, vitam solus amplexus est evangelicam."*[87] His hair grew down to his feet. {He had a} zeal for manual labor. His disciples took baskets and other products to town by boat. He declared that it was ridiculous for monks to sit with their hands folded and live on the work of others while men in the world had to work to support families, pay taxes and give alms to the poor. In time of war {he} was persuaded to move to Antioch.

IX. *Zeno* (c. 12): {he} had been a messenger in {the} army of Valens. {He} left service and went *to live in a tomb* outside Antioch. "Solus ibi degebat, animam purificans, ejusque aciem expurgans, et divinae vacans contemplationi, *Deique ascensiones in corde suo disponens,* et alas optans instar columbae, et in divinam requiem evolare cupiens."[88] {He} had no bed, used no fire or light, had no books etc., but borrowed books one at a time from brethren. {There is an} interesting account of a visit made by Theodoret to him. *Zeno lived 80 years in this solitude, and went to Mass with the laypeople on Sundays.* {When} his death {arrived,} "tamquam Olympicus victor quispiam *ex studio discessit, non ab hominibus tantummodo, sed ab angelis quoque laudes referens."*[89]

85. See Canivet, "Théodoret," 266–67 for this connection.

86. Col. 1379C: "enclosed."

87. Col. 1387D, 1390A: "After building for himself a small cell, he embraced the evangelical life in solitude."

88. Col. 1365C: "There he lived alone, purifying his soul and cleansing its vision and freeing it for divine contemplation, placing the ways of God in his heart, longing for wings like a dove, desiring to fly to divine rest."

89. Col. 1399B: "He left like some Olympic victor from his struggle, bearing the praise not only of men but of angels."

X. *Macedonius* (c. 13): {he was} a wandering monk. {He} ate barley, and was called *Critophagos*.[90] "Pro palaestra et studio montium vertices habuit, non uno loco affixus, sed nunc *in hoc degens, nunc migrans in alium . . .*"[91] to avoid {the} attention of crowds. In his old age, {he} consented to build a hut, or would accept hospitality of others. Bishop Flavian of Antioch ordained him and he did not know what was going on. When he found out he went for Flavian with his cane. He meets a hunter {and} asks, "*ad quid venisti?*"[92] Then {he} says of himself, "*Ego vero Deum meum venor, et capere cupio; videre illum desidero, neque unquam ab hac pulchra venatione abstinebo.*"[93] A rich woman was an obsessive eater. One day she ate thirty chickens and was still looking for more. Friends called in Macedonius, who blessed water and gave {it to} her to drink, after which she was satisfied with a few small pieces of chicken at her meals.

XI. *Acepsimas* (c. 15): {he was a} *recluse*.

a) "*Is cum in domuncula seipsum inclusisset, annos transegit sexaginta, nec ulli visus, nec ullum alloquens: sed in seipsum intuens, Deumque contemplans, omnem inde capiebat consolationem.*"[94]

b) He received his food through an aperture that was not direct but oblique so that he could not be seen. He went out only at night to get water. Once {he was} seen by {a} shepherd who thought he was a wolf and was going to let go at him with {a} slingshot but was held back and later realized {his} error. Next

90. Col. 1399B: "barley-eater."

91. Col. 1399D: "For his training ground and place of effort he had the mountain-tops, not fixed in a single place but now living in this spot, and now journeying to another."

92. Col. 1403B (which reads "*quem in finem huc venisti?*"): "for what reason have you come here?"

93. Col. 1403B: "I am hunting my God, and long to catch him; I desire to see him, and I shall never give up this lovely hunt."

94. Col. 1414D: "When he had enclosed himself in a small hut, he endured for sixty years, neither visible to anyone nor speaking to anyone: but turning within himself and contemplating God, he received every consolation in this way."

day he goes to the *"virtutis gymnasium"*[95] (i.e. the hermitage) to ask pardon—{he} receives it *"non aliqua loquentis voce audita, sed ex manus motionibus benevolentiam intelligens."*[96]

c) A man climbs a tree to look into {the} enclosure of Acepsimas. Acepsimas has the tree cut down.

d) At {the} end of his life, knowing he would live only fifteen days more, he allowed himself to be seen by all. The Bishop came and ordained him purely as an honor. He accepted *because* he knew he was about to die.

Theodoret: Summary of his doctrine (see Canivet, *TVM*):

1) Demonology.[97] {There is the} usual emphasis, but not exaggerated. He seeks to avoid Messalianism, hence stresses *freedom* of the will. Demons act indirectly on {the} will through {the} passions. He is not very complete or subtle in his analysis of spiritual combat. {He} recommends severe asceticism ({cf. the} Syrian background {of} *hatred* of {the} flesh), but does not approve of the extreme, and endangering life. {He} tells superiors to moderate penances of subjects.

2) Note: the exterior of the monk—{this is} influenced by philosophers. {He is marked by} dirty ragged clothes, {a} beard with fleas, emaciation, downcast eyes. These are all signs that one has turned against the world (cf. Beatniks). This is called ἀγροικία (a*groikia*)[98]—*rusticity*. Carried to {an} extreme {it entails a} total rejection of civilization. For extreme examples see Festugière, *Antioche*, pp. 293–307.[99] Monks {are} simple people anyway; {they} do not need to know anything, says Chrysostom.[100]

95. Col. 1415A: "the training ground of virtue."

96. Col. 1415B: "not by hearing any voice speaking, but understanding his good will by the motions of his hand."

97. See Canivet, "Théodoret," 247–50.

98. See Canivet, "Théodoret," 250.

99. These examples comprise the bulk of chapter 9, "Traits Charactéristiques de l'Anachorétisme Syrien" (291–310).

100. *Hom. 21 in Ep. ad Ephes.* (*PG* 62, cols. 152-53; Festugière, *Antioche*, 291).

As {for a} need for culture, {they} will only speak to the wall and the roof, the desert, the tree, the bird. {See also} Chrysostom on Julian Saba (see Festugière, *Antioche*, p. 291);[101] {Theodoret on} Symeon—the chain and the lice (Festugière, p. 292)[102] (others condemned chains as "ostentatious": cf. St. Benedict[103]); {on} Eusebius—in a dry well with 120 lbs., plus 50 lbs. plus 80 lbs. = 250 lbs. of chains;[104] {on} Polychromius—and his oak root (Festugière, p. 294).[105] Read Baradates—{a} recluse etc. (295–296)[106]—*symmetry*. Read Salamanes—twice kidnapped (298).[107] {These are} the "fresh air" monks: *hypacthrioi*.[108]

101. Julian is called (in the same homily [col. 153]) a man of the fields, of humble origin, completely foreign to culture, yet filled with truthful wisdom.

102. Festugière quotes from Theodoret (c. 26; col. 1472BC) on Symeon Stylites before he mounted his pillar, when he wore a chain attaching him to a rock, and twenty large bugs were found beneath the leather covering where the chain was attached.

103. See Gregory the Great, *Dialogues*, trans. Odo Zimmerman, OSB, FC 39 (New York: Fathers of the Church, 1959), Book 3, c. 16 (144).

104. Festugière (*Antioche*, 293), quoting from Theodoret, c. 3 (col. 1337B); this is Eusebius of Chalcis, a disciple of Marcianus, not Eusebius of Teleda, the subject of chapter 4, mentioned earlier.

105. Festugière quotes from Theodoret, c. 24 (cols. 1460D-1461A) on Polychromius, who refused to wear a chain out of fear of pride, but placed a heavy oak root on his shoulders at night when praying; Theodoret himself was almost unable to lift it because of its weight.

106. Festugière quotes from Theodoret, c. 27 (cols. 1484D-1485B), which begins by noting that as the enemy of humanity has devised multiple ways of drawing people to destruction, so devotees of piety have discovered multiple ways of ascending into heaven, some communal, some solitary, some sheltered, some in the open air; Baradates spent time in a small box in which he could not stretch out full-length, until the bishop persuaded him to leave it, living from that time in the open air.

107. Festugière quotes from Theodoret, c. 19 (cols. 1428D-1429A), who tells of the hermit Salamanes, who was taken from his cell on the east bank of the Euphrates by villagers from Capersana, his home town, on the west bank, and then later taken back by villagers from the east bank, Salamanes all the while making no protest, having totally died to the world with Christ.

108. Theodoret, c. 27; col. 1485C (Festugière, *Antioche*, 295, n. 4; 299).

3) The monastic life is angelic and heavenly.[109] A place is prepared for them in the choir of angels and *on dying they go at once to occupy it* (cf. martyrdom)—*Bios Angelikos*[110] = λειτουργία—service:

a) service of God in constant praise;
b) *service of the elect*, like angels (Hebrews {1:6}[111]), doing good, *helping others on their way to salvation*.

Emphasis {is} on virginity but {he} admits married people can be saved. Even {the} second marriage of widows is legitimate. The word ἀπάθεια (*apatheia*) is in {the} *Historia Religiosa* only twice[112]—once in connection with Julian Saba—more as an ideal aimed at than as a reality attained on earth.

4) Monastic life is *philosophical*[113]—more a question of attaining *equilibrium* between body and soul, than simply dominating the body. Hence {the} emphasis on "thinking" ({a} monastery {is} a *phrontisterion*),[114] and on "reason." {One should be} seeking *symmetry* rather than *ammetry*.[115] {A} model of *symmetry* must be presented by {the} Spiritual Father. But above all Christ is the model—*especially in gentleness, refusal of violence, universal love, and {the} capacity to pardon*. ("Be ye perfect!")

5) *Contemplation*—with psalmody {and} *lectio*, {this is} *essential* to {a} monastic life. {It is} directed to {the} *beauty* of God—love of the divine beauty {is} awakened by {a} φίλτρον[116] which burns the heart with desire, inebriates the mind, {and} places the monk outside himself {so that he} forgets himself. This "charm" is God's gift of His own love. Seek His beauty in darkness. Ceaseless tears may be an effect of this "charm." {It leads to a} *flight* of the soul.

109. See Canivet, "Théodoret," 253–54.

110. Col. 1341B (c. 4).

111. Space left in typescript for chapter and verse.

112. Cols. 1285AB, 1324C (see Canivet, "Théodoret," 258, which erroneously reads "1385").

113. See Canivet, "Théodoret," 261–64.

114. "thinking place": Theodoret, c. 2, col. 1309D; c. 8, col. 1368B (Festugière, *Antioche*, 296, n. 1).

115. See Canivet, "Théodoret," 262.

116. Col. 1308B (see Canivet, "Théodoret," 271, 273).

Aphraat (Afrahat) "the wise" *(cf.* Hausherr, *DS I).*[117]

{He has a} special importance as an early writer whose authenticated works are available ({from the} middle {of the} fourth century): {his is} a Biblical spirituality unaffected by philosophy; {he} has not yet been studied as he deserves. {He} came to Antioch but knew only a few words of Greek; {he} lived as {a} recluse near Edessa. His writings {consist in} *Demonstrations*, written for ascetes, "Sons of the Covenant" (*Benai Quejama*),[118] who have dedicated themselves to *a special state of life* (*"pact"*). It is a life of *virginity* above all. Is it a *monastic* life? *Dem.* 6 {is entitled} *Ad Monachos*—is this {the} right translation?[119] They are "solitaries" in {the} sense of ascetic withdrawal, in the sense that they are not married. He called them *"blessed"*—not "mourners"[120] ({the} characteristic Syrian term). {Note} his exegesis of Genesis 2:24, Matthew 19:5: "Man will leave Father and Mother and cleave to his wife . . .": the Father = God the Father; {the} Mother = {the} Holy Spirit (feminine) (cf. exegesis of Origen[121]). (Comment.) To *leave* them is to marry and lead an earthly life of

117. Irénée Hausherr, "Aphraate (Afrahat)," *DS*, 1, cols. 746-52.

118. Hausherr, "Aphraate," col. 747.

119. Hausherr says not (col. 747).

120. Hausherr, "Aphraate," col. 747.

121. Origen's most extensive comment on Genesis 2:24 (which is not discussed either in his *Homilies on Genesis* or in the *De Principiis*) is found in his *Commentary on Matthew* (cc. 16–17), concerning Jesus' response to the Pharisees' question on divorce (Mt. 19:3): while he distinguishes between the verse "male and female He made them" (Gen. 1:27), which he refers to the initial creation of souls, and "For this cause a man shall leave his own father and mother" etc. (Gen. 2:24), referring to earthly creation, he goes on both to legitimate human marriage and to apply the passage to Christ's relation to the Church (and to the Synagogue): see John Patrick, trans., *Origen's Commentary on the Gospel of Matthew*, in Allan Menzies, ed., *The Ante-Nicene Fathers*, vol. 10 (New York: Christian Literature Co., 1896), 505–507. A briefer comment in his *Commentary on the Song of Songs* highlights the typological interpretation: "And among the prophets Adam too is reckoned, who prophesied *the great mystery in Christ and in the Church*, when he said: *For this cause a man shall leave his father and his mother, and shall cleave to his wife, and they shall be two in one flesh.* It is clearly with reference to these words of his that the Apostle says that *this is a great mystery, but I speak in Christ and in the*

forgetfulness, cleaving to the world through the wife. Ergo, perfection = {the} *indwelling* of "Mother" Spirit and this requires renunciation of marriage (748): cf. *Dem.* 18: {the} superiority of virginity over marriage—against {the} Jews.[122]

Faith {is the} basis of all life of Perfection (*Dem.* 1); without it no virtue is valid.

Charity {is} the height of perfection—{love} for {the} *Blessed Trinity*; for Christ; for other men, especially Christians. {The} *slightest defect in charity spoils all virtues, fasting, etc.*[123]

Dem. 9. *On Humility—"Makikoutha"*[124]—meekness, mildness {is the} basis of intimacy with God; {the} basis of peace with men; {the} basis of radiant joy, and even laughter (as opposed to Ephrem: "*perpetually sad*, bald and beardless"[125]).

Dem. 3. The most scandalous defect is lack of humility, especially among ecclesiastics. {Note the} connection of humility with fasting (all-embracing mortification).[126]

Constant Prayer (*Dem.* 4)—Any way in which God rests in us is prayer. To pray = *to give God rest*: to give Him rest is to give rest to the weary; good works for others = constant prayer; but one must make explicit effort to pray also. Types of prayer: *in tribulation*—petition for pardon; *in prosperity*—"confession"—acknowledgment of gifts, thanksgiving; *in joy*—praise of God for His works[127] (note {the} role of angels in prayer, especially Gabriel.[128]); pure prayer: without any defect of love. {There is a} preference for solitary prayer. {Does it include} mysticism? {It is} not formulated, but see *Dem.* 14:35, 17:7, 9:12.

Church" (Origen, *The Song of Songs: Commentary and Homilies*, trans. R. P. Lawson, ACW 26 [Westminster, MD: Newman, 1957], 149).

122. Hausherr, "Aphraate," cols. 748-49.

123. *Dem.* 2:17 (Hausherr, "Aphraate," cols. 748-49).

124. Hausherr, "Aphraate," cols. 749-50.

125. See n. 174 below.

126. Hausherr, "Aphraate," col. 750 (the first sentence actually refers to *Dem.* 14).

127. *Dem.* 6 (Hausherr, "Aphraate," col. 750).

128. *Dem.* 3:14, 4:8, 19:10 (Hausherr, "Aphraate," col. 751).

Summary: Discretion, Optimism, Solidity {are central} ({along with} faith, humility, love—Evangelical). *The Christian is "the child of peace."*[129]

Aphraat—Some readings from his works:

Demonstratio 6: *De Monachis* (*Patrologia Syriaca*, vol. 1. col. 239 f.):[130]

1. {The} theme of monastic vigilance and good works: "Let us now at last rise from sleep"[131] (cf. *RB*, Prol.[132]). Let us lift up our hearts to God in heaven so that when he comes he may find us watching. "Let us watch for the hour of the glorious Spouse so that with him we may enter the bridal chamber."[133] (See this in {the} context of his ideas on marriage!) Then follows a biblical program of ascetic purification. "Instruments of Good Works"[134]—{there is a} use of Biblical symbols appropriate to spiritual *experience*—also repetition and balance of statements: *arsis—thesis*:[135] prepare food for the journey on the narrow way; rejecting all impurity so as to merit {the} wedding garment; investing the talent we have received, to merit {the} name of good servants; to be faithful in prayer, to escape from the place of fear. "Let us purify our hearts from iniquity so as to see the Most High in His glory"[136]

129. *Dem.* 14:30 (Hausherr, "Aphraate," col. 751).

130. *Patrologia Syriaca, Pars Prima: Ab Initiis usque ad Annum 350*, ed. R. Graffin, 3 vols. (Paris: Firmin-Didot, 1894–1926), 1:239-311; Merton translates from the accompanying Latin.

131. Chapter 1 (col. 239).

132. "Up with us then at last, for the Scripture arouseth us, saying: *Now is the hour for us to rise from sleep*. Let us open our eyes to the divine light, and let us hear with attentive ears the warning that the divine voice crieth daily to us: *Today if ye will hear his voice, harden not your hearts*" (McCann, 7).

133. Chapter 1 (col. 239).

134. Benedict, *Rule*, c. 4 (McCann, 27–33).

135. These terms are used in Gregorian Chant, as well as other forms of music and prosody, to refer to alternating upbeat and downbeat, or stressed and unstressed syllables, though here Merton seems to be referring to the balance of the two halves of a line.

136. Chapter 1 (col. 239).

(note {the} difference from Evagrian purity of heart).[137] Let us be merciful so that God may be merciful to us. Let there be peace among us so that we may be called the brothers of Christ. He continues in this way, multiplying scriptural references. We must hunger and thirst for justice, we must become the salt of truth, we must weed out the thorns from among the good seed, build our house on stone and not on sand, sell all for the precious pearl, etc. (242). Good works are emphasized: "Let us visit the Lord in His sick, so that He may call us to stand at His right side" (242). "Let us be poor in this world that we may enrich many with the teaching of the Lord."[138] "He who prepares to enter into rest must get ready food for that sabbath."[139] The panoply of spiritual weapons is invoked (243). "Let us become strangers to the world as Christ was not of the world" (242). "Let us utter his own prayer in purity of heart so that it may ascend to the Lord of majesty. Let us be partakers of his sufferings so that in turn we may live by his resurrection"[140] (themes common to *RB*[141]). "Let us call no one on earth father, so that we may be the sons of the Father Who is in heaven."[142]

Prayer life {is} suggested as follows: "Let us be concerned with heavenly things and meditate on them, those realms where Christ has been taken up and glorified. Let us leave this world which is not ours, in order that we may reach that place to which we have

137. Merton is apparently referring to the completely scriptural use of the term in Aphraat, with its association of purity of heart and seeing God (cf. Mt. 5:8), as distinguished from the Greek philosophical associations of Evagrian *apatheia*, which Cassian regularly renders as purity of heart.

138. Chapter 1 (col. 246).

139. Chapter 1 (col. 251).

140. Chapter 1 (col. 242).

141. For becoming strangers to the world, see *Rule*, c. 4: "To avoid worldly conduct" (McCann, 17); for sharing in Christ's sufferings so as to share in his resurrection, see the conclusion of the Prologue: "Never abandoning his rule but persevering in his teaching in the monastery until death, we shall share by patience in the sufferings of Christ, that we may deserve to be partakers also of his kingdom" (McCann, 13).

142. Chapter 1 (col. 246).

been invited. *Let us lift our eyes to the things above that we may contemplate the splendor which is to appear. Let us raise up our wings like the eagles so that we may see where the body is*. Let us prepare a sacrifice for the King, desirable fruits, fasting and prayer" etc. (246, 247) (contrast "dove"). *The necessity of choice* is then stressed: "He who does not put on the wedding garment will be cast out into exterior darkness."[143] "He who wants to be a fisherman, let him cast his net assiduously."[144] "He who carries in himself the Body of Christ, let him cleanse his body from all defilement. He who is called a temple of God, let him cleanse his body from all impurity" etc. (251). Trust in God is emphasized. Finally, returning to {the} subject of virginity, {he emphasizes} vigilance, and silent trusting patience. "He who loves virginity, let him become like to Elias [meaning? cf. 263[145]]. He who bears the yoke of the saints, let him sit still and be silent. He who loves peace, let him wait expectantly for his Lord in hope of life" (254). So ends this chapter which is in effect a collection of "instruments of good works."

2. *The wiles of the enemy*. He is very clever, and seeks to weaken the monk, and the weak are under his sway, so that he does not have to work against them. But the strong he attacks, and they must resist strongly: by *flight*, and by avoiding his *spider web*; by *fearless trust* in God, for the enemy can do nothing against the sons of light who do not fear evil, since God has given them

143. Chapter 1 (col. 247).

144. Chapter 1 (col. 247).

145. "*De Elia scriptus est cum modo in monte Carmelo consedisse, modo in torrente Carith, et famulum suum ei ministrasse. Eo quod in caelo cor eius manebat, aves caeli afferebant ei cibum; quia angelorum caeli gerebat similitudinem, ipsi angeli panem et aquam ei praebuerunt, cum a Iezabelis conspectu fugeret; et qui totam cogitationem suam in caelo posuerat, ad caelum in igneo curru raptus est, ibique facta est habitatio eius in sempiternum*" ("Of Elias it is written that when he had settled sometimes on Mount Carmel, sometimes in the Brook Carith, his own servant had ministered to him. Because there his heart remained in heaven, the birds of the air used to bring him food; because he acted like the angels of heaven, angels themselves brought him bread and water when he was fleeing from the sight of Jezebel; and as one who had put all his thoughts on heaven, he was raised up to heaven in a fiery chariot, and that became his dwelling place for all eternity") (c. 5).

power to trod it down. They have become salt, and the serpent cannot eat salt (this occurs several times—see also n. 1[146]). {Note the idea of} being, not doing. *The spirit of childhood* gives them power to play unharmed where the asp is found (255). They resist his incitements to gluttony by fasting (this probably covers all forms of restraint). They resist the evil thoughts he suggests, by looking up to heaven (cf. the difference between {an} "antirrhetic" and {an} "anagogical" approach to temptation[147]). If he tempts them in their possessions, then they renounce possessions and bestow them on the poor. "And if he inflames them with the lust of Eve, they dwell alone and not with the daughters of Eve"[148] (reference to possible *subintroductae*?[149]).

3. Temptation arising from women. Eve tempted Adam, Joseph {was} tempted by a woman, etc.; also Samson, etc., etc. This whole number is given to biblical examples.

4. Conclusion: no co-habitation with women however holy (*subintroductae*). "Therefore my brethren if anyone is bound by vow [probably {a} wrong translation] or has professed [probably wrong][150] continency, and has embraced the solitary life, and wants to have a woman also bound by vow living with him, it would be better for him to marry openly lest he be enticed by lust. In the same way it would be better for the woman publicly to marry, or else to get away from that hermit."[151] Let women live

146. "*Sal efficiamur veritatis, ne in escam serpentis cedamus*" ("Let us become the salt of justice, lest we turn into food for the serpent") (col. 242).

147. An antirrhetic approach to temptation attacks and struggles against a particular sin (as in the *Antirrhetikos* of Evagrius, which provides scriptural resources for combating the eight principal vices), while an anagogical approach operates by focusing on the attraction of the life of virtue and of the final end of union with God.

148. Col. 255.

149. See Vööbus, *History*, 1:200; "*subintroductae*" (lit. "those who have been brought in secretly") were female ascetics who lived in celibate cohabitation with male ascetics.

150. See Hausherr, "Aphraate," col. 747, who says that these ascetics took no formal vows.

151. Col. 259.

with women, men with men. When married people embrace continency they ought to separate. It is in a word better to "remain solitary."[152] In this context he obviously means "solitary" in the sense of virginal and unmarried, but not necessarily completely alone as the "solitary" may be dwelling with another "solitary" of the same sex.

6. After more biblical examples of men living without women, he concludes that woman is a spider web to be assiduously avoided. The curse of the law is due to woman, so is death etc. in {the} Old Testament context. "Now however, due to the Son of Mary the thorns are rooted up, sweat is dried away, the barren fig tree is cursed, dust is turned into salt, the curse is nailed to the Cross, the flaming sword is taken away from the tree of life and it is given as food to the believers; to the blessed, the virgins and the chaste, paradise is promised, the door is opened, the fatted calf is killed."[153] He then goes on to speak of all the *joys of the virginal life* in eschatological terms without Greek resonances, purely biblical:

> Prepare yourselves, chosen ones! A pleasant and brilliant light has arisen, and garments not made with hands have been set out. The shouts of joy come closer, the tombs are thrown open, all that was in them is revealed. The dead rise. Full of life they run to meet the King. The banquet is set out, the trumpet is blown, the bugles rouse everyone. The angels of heaven hasten to the scene, and the throne of the Judge is set in place. He who has worked, let him rejoice. He who has fallen, let him tremble. He who has done evil, let him not approach the Judge . . . . Grace has passed, justice reigns: there is no penance there. The winter has come, the summer has passed [meaning?]. The sabbath of rest has arrived, labor is over. Night has fled, the dawn reigns . . . . The angels of heaven will minister to those who had no wives, and those who preserved their chastity

152. Col. 262.

153. Chapter 6 (cols. 266-67); the text reads ". . . due to the coming [*adventum*] of the Son of Mary . . ."; the final part of the quotation is compressed.

> will rest in the sanctuary of the Most High. All the Solitaries will receive joy from the Only Begotten in the Bosom of His Father . . . . Instead of the groans of the daughters of Eve, they will sing the canticles of the Spouse . . .[154]

7. Virgins are then exhorted to remember this, and not accept any invitation to live with a holy man. How to answer him: *"I am espoused to Christ."*[155] {Note the} importance of this in {the} history of mystical terminology.

8. {He provides} further moral and ascetic advice for "solitaries" (in the world): love of Christ, humility, constancy, mortification: avoiding the use of ointments and perfumes, or fine clothes, not going to parties, control of {the} tongue, etc.; not mocking others; not getting involved in business. "Let him not make fun of a penitent for his sins, not cavil at a fasting brother. Let him not, however, confound the brother who is not able to fast" (274). *Let him open the depths of his heart to some man who fears God*. But let him avoid the company of the perverse, etc. In conclusion to all this advice {he says}: "These things are fitting to monks who have taken upon themselves the yoke of heaven and are disciples of Christ. Thus it is right that disciples of Christ should become like to Christ their Lord" (275).

9. The example of the Lord: New Testament texts {are} multiplied, to show how Christ in His humility gave Himself to give us life.

10. Theology of {the} Spiritual Life (*"O admirabile commercium"!*[156]): God "left His nature to walk in our nature."[157] *We remain in our nature* in order to receive (participation in) His nature. "That which He assumed from us is preserved in honor . . . . *and we must have in honor the pledge He has left to us*" (279). We must honor the humanity of Christ in heaven. We must honor His

154. Cols. 267, 270.

155. Col. 271, which reads *"Viro Regi sum desponsata"* ("I am espoused to the Man who is King").

156. "O wondrous exchange!" (antiphon for the vigil of the octave of Christmas, Vespers, and for Matins: *PL* 78, cols. 741A, B).

157. Col. 278.

presence in our bodies by purity. *We must honor His Spirit which He has left as a pledge. "Christ sitting at the right hand of the Father at the same time dwells in men;* above and below He is Lord by the wisdom of the Father, and though one, dwells in many . . . . He is in us and we in Him" (282).

11. How *Christ being one dwells in many without there being many Christs.* As the Sun shines in many doors and windows and every patch of light is called "sun" there is still only one sun (283-286).

12. Christ dwells in all by His Spirit. Among {the} Scripture quotes—note that he renders 1 Cor. 15:28 as ". . . *and the whole God is in all, and in every man*"[158] (cf. n. 18: "Those who have received the Spirit of Christ shall bear the likeness of the heavenly Adam *who is the life-giving Lord Jesus Christ;* in them *that which is animal is absorbed by the spiritual*"[159]).

14. "Therefore, Beloved, we too [like the prophets, and St. John {the} Baptist (n. 13[160])] have received of the Spirit of Christ and Christ dwells in us . . . . Let us therefore prepare our temple for the Spirit of Christ and not sadden Him lest He depart from us."[161] *If we receive the Spirit of Christ in baptism and remain faithful, then when we die though our animal spirit dies with the body, the Spirit of Christ in us returns to Christ.* (Contrast this with {the} Greek idea of immortality.) "When one has kept the Spirit of Christ in purity, when this Spirit of Christ returns to Him it speaks thus: The body to which I came and which in the waters of baptism I put on, kept me in holiness. And the Holy Spirit will urge Christ to raise up that body by which it was kept in purity" (295).[162] Read {the} passage on resurrection (295–298).[163]

158. ". . . *et est Deus totus in omnibus et in omni homine.*"

159. Col. 307.

160. Cols. 287, 290-91.

161. Col. 291.

162. Cols. 294-95.

163. "*Cumque tempus advenerit consummationis finalis, appropinquante resurrectionis hora, Spiritus Sanctus qui in puritate fuerit servatus, virtutem magnam ex natura sua accipiens, Christum adibit, stabitque ad ostium sepulcrorum, ubi conditi fuerint homines qui eum in puritate servaverint, clamorem exspectans. Et statim ad*

15. The important thing then is to *keep the Holy Spirit* at all costs, lest one fall into the power of Satan. Prayer {makes this possible}—hence {the} importance of prayer: "In that hour when one is aware in his heart that he is not aflame with the Spirit, but that his heart has descended to thoughts of this world, let him realize that he does not have the Spirit. Let him therefore arise, pray, and watch so that the Spirit of God may return to him, lest he be overcome by the enemy."[164]

17. The enemy like a thief listens at the wall of the house. If he hears the Master within, he departs. So the devil observes our words and thoughts, and if they are of the Spirit, he stays away.

19-20. Conclusion: Since preserving the Spirit depends on purity of body and since to be pure one must live alone, hence {the} prime importance of solitary, ascetic and virginal life.

---

caelorum portas angeli coram Rege aperuerint, cornu sonabit, mittentque tubae vocem; Spiritus exspectatum clangorem audiens sepulcra festinanter pandet, corpora et quod in eis sepultum est suscitabit, induetque ea quam secum adduxerit gloria; ipse [*Spiritus*] *intra manet, ut corpus suscitetur, extra vero* [*manet*] *gloria, qua corpus ornetur. Spiritus animalis a Spiritu caelesti absorbebitur, eoque corpus possidente, totus homo spiritalis fiet. Mors absorbebitur a gloria, et corpus a Spiritu; et ille homo a Spiritu raptus, in occursum Regis evolabit, eumque cum gaudio excipiet. Christus autem corpori qui Spiritum suum in puritate servaverit benignum se ostendet.*" ("When the time of the final consummation arrives and the hour of resurrection draws near, a holy spirit that had been preserved in purity, receiving great virtue from its own nature, will approach Christ and will stand awaiting the signal at the mouth of the tombs where the men who had preserved their spirits in purity had been kept. And suddenly angels will appear before the King at the gates of heaven, the trumpet will sound, the horns will send forth their voice; the spirit, hearing the awaited sound, will quickly open the tombs, will raise up the bodies and what is buried in them, and will clothe them in that glory which it will have brought with itself; the spirit itself remains within, to raise the body, while the glory remains without, to adorn the body. The animal spirit will be absorbed into the heavenly spirit, which will take possession of the body, so that the whole person will become spiritual. Death will be taken up into glory, and the body into the spirit; and the one lifted up by the spirit will fly up to meet the King, and follow Him with joy. Christ will show Himself generous to the body which has kept its spirit in purity".)

164. Chapter 17 (col. 302).

St. Ephrem (d. 373)

I. *Life*: {There is} special difficulty in obtaining truth about Ephrem. {A} great diversity of opinions {exists} on him and his works. Born in Nisibis about 306, he came under the influence of St. James of Nisibis. Ephrem wrote hymns in praise of the austerity of life of James of Nisibis. Though in these he does not mention James's eremitical life, it is now taken for certain that James was a hermit (see *DS*, col. 788[165]). In writing of James, Ephrem says: "In the lively childhood years he was to me an educator to be feared, and his stick deterred me from play, the terror of him deterred me from vice, reverence for him deterred me from seeking my own pleasure."[166] Ephrem was also influenced and formed by Bishop Vologesius. He writes an ideal portrait of Vologesius, praising both his asceticism and his culture, his "graciousness" (τὸ χαρίεν).[167] *Carmina Nisibena* {is written} in praise of his models, James, Babu, and Vologesius.[168]

{In 363} Ephrem leaves Nisibis and goes to Edessa to escape the Persians. {He} taught at Edessa. Did he *found schools* at Nisibis and Edessa? Yes.[169] Voyages to Cappadocia and Egypt are legends.[170] It is certain that Ephrem was a deacon. It is said he evaded episcopacy by simulating madness, {but} this is not certain.[171] It is also doubtful whether he lived as a hermit.[172] Rather {he lived}

165. Edmund Beck, "Éphrem," *DS* 4:788-800, but Beck actually cites but does not endorse the sources that call James a hermit, and in "Ascétisme et Monachisme," Beck likewise describes James as an ascete but not a hermit (284–87).

166. *Carmina Nisibena* 19.16 (quoted in Beck, "Éphrem," col. 788).

167. Louis Leloir, OSB, "Saint Éphrem, Moine et Pasteur," *Théologie de la Vie Monastique,* 87.

168. Beck, "Ascétisme et Monachisme," 284.

169. See L. Leloir, OSB, "Éphrem le Syrien," *Dictionnaire d'Histoire et de Géographie Ecclésiastiques* [*DHGE*], ed. Alfred Baudrillart, 26 vols. (Paris: Letouzey & Ané, 1912–1995), 15:590-97; Vööbus (*History,* 2:108, 410) is more hesitant.

170. Leloir, "Éphrem," col. 591; Vööbus, *History,* 2:88-90.

171. Sozomen, *Historia Ecclesiastica* (*PG* 67, cols. 1085–93), quoted in Beck, "Éphrem," col. 789.

172. Beck, "Éphrem," col. 789.

as {a} solitary in Aphraat's sense. However he highly praises the hermit life. {See the} *Sermo de eremitis et de lugentibus*. This is admitted as genuine by E. Beck in *DS*.[173] The Syrian biographies' description of Ephrem as "bald, perpetually sad and refusing to laugh"[174] is perhaps *not* historical, but an "ikon"-like representation of Ephrem as {a} legendary hermit.

Ephrem records a "saying of Jesus": *"Ubi unus erit, ibi sum ego,"*[175] and adds, "Jesus said this to take away all motive of sorrow from hermits, *for He is our joy and He is with us*" (from {an} Armenian version of {his} Gospel commentary, quoted {in} *DHGE* 15:591). The angel announced the Nativity to Shepherds "in order to show that no one of those who live in the desert will be deprived of grace, but, saved, they will find peace, thanks to the joyous message of the Good Shepherd" (*id*. {591-}592).

Ephrem died June 9, 373. {He was} declared {a} Doctor of {the} Church {in} 1920. {His} feast {day is} 18 June (in {the} Syrian Liturgy, January 28).[176] See {the} Encyclical of Benedict XV: *Principi Apostolorum*.[177]

Biographical writings:

Vööbus—His *Testament* or *Confessions*: {there is} one genuine {version} in Syriac and one in Greek: {the theme is} self-castigation for sins.[178] Vööbus thinks Ephrem lived in retirement a semi-eremitical life near Edessa. "He lived in his cell in the mountains of Edessa, but {. . .} his seclusion was not absolute. He kept contact with the needs of the Christian community {in} Edessa" (vol. 2, p. 90).[179] Vööbus tends to admit as genuine any works of

173. Col. 789.

174. See Vööbus, *History*, 2:101 (citing *Historia Ephraemi*, 23, in *Ephraem Syri Hymni et Sermones*, ed. T. J. Lamy [Malines: H. Dessain, 1886–1902] 2, col. 41f.): "his stature was small, his countenance was always mournful, and never did he yield to laughter, and he was bald and beardless."

175. "Where there is one, I am there."

176. See Leloir, "Éphrem," col. 593.

177. See Beck, "Éphrem," col. 790.

178. Vööbus, *History*, 2:70-73.

179. Typescript reads ". . . but his . . . kept in contact . . . of Edessa."

Ephrem that support his thesis.[180] Hence Vööbus exaggerates Ephrem's eremitical doctrine to an extreme rejection of all humanism and all civilization. Monks live only among wild animals, without houses, never touching cooked food, eating only leaves and roots, etc. "Do not build houses lest you descend into the abyss. Do not have inner chambers lest you inherit outer darkness. Love the inner parts of the desert that Paradise may be your dwelling" (*Orient Syrien*, 1959, p. 305).[181] Contrast the *Mimré* of Ephrem for the Blessing of the Table (*Orient Syrien*, 1959).[182] Legends of Ephrem: "{There is the} historical Ephrem quite different from the Ephrem of hagiography" (Vööbus).[183]

II. Doctrine:

1. Church: In his youth he probably lived as an *ascete* rather than as a monk. But he was aware of monasticism along the Persian border (Beck).[184] {He} knew of hermits and small groups of monks, not big cenobia (Vööbus).[185] *He knew of the higher ideal of monasticism which not only embraced continency but also sought separation from all men*. Thus *the distinction of ascetes and monks is clear* in Ephrem. His idea of the Christian *covenant community*: these are divided into virgins, fasters, watchers[186] (some are all three). It is argued specifically that such people *overcome fate*. In other words their lives are an assertion of Christian freedom against predetermination by the stars or by nature.

2. *Nature*: {is} a fund, capital or "talent" given us by God to be used. He who "orders" nature, increases his capital, his talent.

180. So Leloir, "Éphrem," col. 593.

181. A. Vööbus, "Le Reflet du Monachisme Primitif dans les Écrits d' Éphrem le Syrien," *L'Orient Syrien*, 4 (1959), 299–306, quoting Lamy, 4:151, 153.

182. "Mimré de Saint Éphrem sur la Bénédiction de la Table," ed. François Graffin, SJ, *L'Orient Syrien*, 4 (1959), 73–109, 163–92, 285–98 (eleven poems in the original Syriac with Latin and French translations, by Louis Mariès, SJ and Léon Froman and by François Graffin, SJ, respectively).

183. Vööbus, *History*, 2:84.

184. Beck, "Ascetisme et Monachisme," 289.

185. Vööbus, "Reflet," 301–302.

186. See *De Paradiso*, 3 (Beck, "Ascetisme et Monachisme," 277).

He who disturbs the order of nature in his life by vice, must take the consequences (cf. {the} Hindu idea of karma). Conclusion: {there are} two ways of ordering nature: (1) Married life, which avoids sin and disorder (Ephrem admits marriage as good); (2) Virginal life which lives *above nature itself* (*jejunare a natura*).[187]

Mimre on the Blessing of the Table: The hymns of St. Ephrem on the blessing of the table, published in Latin and French in *L'Orient Syrien* for 1959, show us his attitude toward God's creation. {These are} hymns of praise and thanksgiving, without any indication of a pessimistic and rigorist attitude toward the use of creatures. Note however that these hymns are not specifically for *monks*.

Song 1.[188] This is expressly composed for a *feast*. {A} spirit of rejoicing and praise is evident. The rejoicing is directly referred to God's bounty. {The} refrain {is} repeated after each of sixty-six verses: BLESSED IS THE GOOD ONE WHO HAS STRETCHED FORTH HIS HAND AND FILLED OUR TABLE WITH PRAISE.[189] {The} theme {is} announced: "Give glory to God and thank Him in feasting."[190] "Whosoever is filled by His gift, let him give praise to His essence. And whosoever eats of His good things, let him praise His goodness."[191] Note {the} contrast between His *gifts* and His *being*, the former ordered to praise of the latter.

In *Memra 2*—"It is easy for God to give abundant gifts—and it is *easy for us to give thanks, so let us do this*."[192] He has done more difficult things. Let us thank Him for these also. *Vitis et triticum*

187. "to fast from nature" (*Contra Haereses*, 6.19, quoted in Beck, "Ascetisme et Monachisme," 281).

188. "Mimré sur la Bénédiction," 76–84.

189. "Mimré sur la Bénédiction," 76 (both the Latin and the French read "hands").

190. This is the editor's headnote for section A (76).

191. "Mimré sur la Bénédiction," 76 (1-A): the Latin reads "*gratias agat ei pro bonitate ejus*" ("let him give thanks to Him because of His goodness"), though the French reads "à sa bonté rendent gloire" ("let them give glory for His goodness")—the same phrasing as in the previous verse.

192. "Mimré sur la Bénédiction," 84 (II-A^{1}).

ex parte Ejus, oratio et amor ex parte nostri.[193] *Deliciae a voluntate Ejus et jubilationes a libertate nostra!*[194] (Cf. *Commentary on the Gospels*, c. 12.1: "*Propterea immiscuit, posuit dulcedinem in vino quod fecit, ut indicaret quanti thesauri laterent in vivifico sanguine suo.*"[195]) "He does not contemn our gifts even when they are contemptible. Let us thank Him for His gifts which are above all else!"[196] In *Memra 6*[197]—he adds: "God does not need our praise, but He wills that in praising Him our souls should be benefited along with our bodies."[198] {This is a} true theology of Christian joy. {See} *Commentary on {the} Gospels* c. 1, n. 14: Because Zachary did not come forth from {the} sanctuary praising and giving thanks, the people realized that his silence indicated an element of punishment in the angelic vision.[199]

"Whosoever drinks of His fountain, let him pour forth to Him from His words [i.e. scriptural praise]. Whosoever is filled at His table, let him sing to Him with His hymns."[200] He who is filled from His table, let him give alms from that table. (Receiving and giving are correlated. God gives abundance, and we share that abundance, pouring forth abundance of praise and giving alms to

193. "Mimré sur la Bénédiction," 85 (II-B): "The vine and the wheat come from Him, the prayer and the love from us."

194. "Mimré sur la Bénédiction," 86 (II-B): "The enjoyment comes from His will and the rejoicing from our freedom."

195. "Therefore he has mixed together, he has placed sweetness in the wine that he made so as to suggest how much treasure lies hidden in his life-giving blood" (Ephrem le Syrien, *Commentaire de l'Évangile Concordant*, Version Armenienne, trans. Louis Leloir, *CSCO* 145 [Louvain: L. Durbecq, 1954], 115).

196. "Mimré sur la Bénédiction," 86 (II-B[1]).

197. Mimeograph reads "IV" for "VI".

198. "Mimré sur la Bénédiction," 170–71: this is not an exact quotation but a conflation of the opening words of section 6-B: "*Non quod indigeret* [*Deus*] *benedictionibus, nos voluit docere id quod convenit.*" ("It is not that God has need of our blessings, but that he wants to teach us what is suitable") with section 6-B[1], on the double benefit to souls and bodies: see the editor's headnote: "La louange est à l'âme ce que le pain est au corps; en mangeant, ne séparons pas l'une de l'autre" ("Praise is to the soul what bread is to the body; in eating let us not separate one from the other").

199. Ephrem, *Commentaire de l'Évangile Concordant*, 7–8.

200. "Mimré sur la Bénédiction," 77 (1-A).

those who are less fortunate. {This is a} theology of openness, of generosity, of love.) *Qui amat filium vitis, amet voces gratiarum actionis. Et qui bibit abundanter, amet laudem magnam.*[201] (Certainly {this is} not manichaean.) To eat and be silent is to eat like a beast.[202] (Cf. *Memra 2*: "What good does he who eats gain, if he eats and does not give thanks!"[203]) Feasting requires praise and thanksgiving, which is the sign of man, the son of God. For to eat and then praise is to nourish the soul with doctrine. *The joy of food and drink is analogous to the joy of spiritual understanding and the two go together*: *Sicut suavis fuit potus ori, sicut suavis auri interpretatio.*[204] (This idea is developed in *Memra 3*: "Behold, Brethren: Body and Soul, Table and Doctrine. For the visible body, the banquet; for the hidden heart, doctrine."[205] *Requieverat corpus in manifestis, et requievit anima in occultis.*[206]) *God is the Master of the Feast.*[207] Hence let there be peace and harmony among those who are present and *let love reign in their midst*. This is essential to the spirit of praise. ({In} *Memra 5*, on the contrary, the Devil, who hates blessing and praise, incites us to condemn and detract while we are eating.[208])

{On} speaking and silence: at the feast some should speak, others should listen—the young, the sad, the chatterers, should not spoil the feast by saying stupid or depressing things. But those who know the Scriptures, those who are experienced, and those of sound mind should do the talking[209] (cf. monastic

201. "Mimré sur la Bénédiction," 77 (1-A): "Whoever loves the offspring of the vine, let him love the voices of the act of thanksgiving. And whoever drinks freely, let him love to give great praise."

202. "Mimré sur la Bénédiction," 77–78 (1-A[1]).

203. "Mimré sur la Bénédiction," 87 (2-B[2]).

204. "Mimré sur la Bénédiction," 78 (1-A[1]): "As drink was sweet to the mouth, so understanding is sweet to the ear."

205. "Mimré sur la Bénédiction," 88 (3-A).

206. "Mimré sur la Bénédiction," 89 (3-A): "The body had found rest in things seen, and the soul found rest in things hidden."

207. "Mimré sur la Bénédiction," 78 (editor's subtitle for section B of Hymn 1).

208. "Mimré sur la Bénédiction," 165 (5-A[1]).

209. "Mimré sur la Bénédiction," 79–80 (1-B[1]).

silence?). {He discusses} proper questions and answers: {there should} not {be} long questions, but *brevis et manifesta* {. . .} *dulcis et sana*.[210] The fountain of conversation should inebriate the ear and "*disputatio*"[211] should send forth its rays and illuminate the eyes. Note—we are in the sapiential tradition of the Jews. See Sirach on feasts (for instance, read Ecclus. 32:1-13).[212] {The} subject of conversation {should be} the virtues, purity of heart, sobriety, and the joys of heaven: *Habeatur sermo super mensa nostra de illa mensa Regni*.[213] To preserve temperance they should remember Jonadab and the Rechabites and drink sparingly[214] (but not abstain completely). Wine is not impure or evil, as the Apostle bears witness; however excess is to be avoided. These things should be discussed at the banquet.[215]

Conclusion to {the} first Hymn: Let the whole feast be replete with spiritual and bodily joy together, {with} praise to God, to Christ and the angels, merit to the host, hope for men, and a remembrance of the poet in their future banquets.[216]

THIRD HYMN—Whereas in the first and second hymn God is regarded chiefly as Creator whom we thank for His Gifts, here in the third the eye of the poet is fixed on Christ the Savior and His Apostles. The miraculous meals given to the multitudes are recalled. The wedding of Cana was a manifest miracle, but each day the hidden miracle takes place in which water becomes wine in the vine and grape. *Vini {paulum} in hydriis et laus magna in*

210. "Mimré sur la Bénédiction," 80 (1-B²): "brief and clear, sweet and sensible."

211. "Mimré sur la Bénédiction," 80 (1-B²): "discussion."

212. These verses provide instruction on hosting a dinner party, advise young men to speak briefly and modestly only after being asked, and recommend going straight home after the party is over.

213. "Mimré sur la Bénédiction," 81 (1-C): "May the speech at your table be about the table of the Kingdom."

214. "Mimré sur la Bénédiction," 81–82 (1-C¹); for Jonadab and the Rechabites, see Jeremiah 35.

215. "Mimré sur la Bénédiction," 82 (1-C²).

216. "Mimré sur la Bénédiction," 83 (1-B³).

bibentibus.[217] *Admiration* is therefore an essential element in the feast, admiration for the miracles of Christ and for the creative power of God, and His immense goodness. To admire is then to *discern* with human intelligence the reason and beauty of God's order, not to eat in a stupor like a beast.[218] (Cf. *Memra* 9, only a fragment: *In discernenti autem qui laudat tota creatio cithara est*.[219]) When Adam ate the forbidden fruit he ate as a beast, without praise. That is to say he ate ungratefully, as a rebel. But Christ repaired this sin. He broke bread, gave thanks and ate, and paid Adam's debt. And we, as we give thanks over our table in memory of Him, become worthy of sitting at His banquet.[220]

OTHER HYMNS—Note that the eighth Memra[221] in particular is devoted to blaming the Jews who did not thank Yahweh for manna in the desert, murmured at the quails, etc. etc., and had to be punished. But Lazarus in the parable is said to have offered God praise even though his belly was empty, while Dives murmured.[222]

3. *The World*: The world is good not only because created by God but above all because *blessed* by Him (Gen. 1:18). Without the blessing of God sin would have supervened and the world would have fallen into nothingness (cf. St. Ammonas—the "Blessing of the Fathers"[223]). *Paradise was the thalamus castitatis*:[224] the dwelling of God and angels; sexuality {was} absent from it. The earth, to which man falls, is the domain of sex and of sorrow.

217. "Mimré sur la Bénédiction," 90 (3-A²): "Let there be a little bit of wine in the cups and a great deal of praise in the drinking" (typescript reads "*paululum*").

218. "Mimré sur la Bénédiction," 90–92 (3-B-B¹).

219. "Mimré sur la Bénédiction," 184: "For the discerning one who gives praise, the entire creation is a lyre."

220. "Mimré sur la Bénédiction," 93–94 (3-C-C¹).

221. "Mimré sur la Bénédiction," 178–83; the seventh hymn (172–78) has a similar theme, focused on the bunch of grapes brought from the Promised Land (Num. 13).

222. "Mimré sur la Bénédiction," 180–81 (8-B).

223. See above, pages 202–204.

224. *De Paradiso*, 13.3, quoted in Beck, "Éphrem," col. 791: "the marriage bed of chastity."

Man {is} in {the} image of God by the power of {the} word, speech ({note the} implications for monastic silence!)—by intelligence—above all by free will. After the fall, man has become childish and irresponsible in his actions: death says to man "you are like a baby who laughs and cries at the same time . . . you are insipid in your sorrow and idiotic in your merriment, you cannot be perfect men because you do not laugh or weep as ones who know what is going on."[225] Why is this? The basis of realism is a healthy sorrow at knowing our real state. "Remorse of soul has crushed me because I have lost my crown and my stole and the bridal chamber of light."[226] He laments his sins but also recognizes his gifts. (Beck remarks[227] that one of the indications of spurious works attributed to Ephrem and false confessions are the inordinate expressions of sorrow. If people knew his sins they would spit in his face. The stink of his sins would drive everyone to seek shelter, etc., etc.) *"I was made a learned lamb . . . Blessed is He who made me His harp."*[228] Beautiful!

4. *Faith*:

1) {A} dialectic between *profession of faith and interior silence* {is} necessary for prayer. Both are essential. Faith comes from silence and leads to silence.

2) Man is *created with a "sense of God."*[229] {Is this} natural or supernatural? {They are} not distinguished. But it is a "gift of God" in any case.

3) God reveals Himself in *human images but these cancel one another out* lest man should imagine that he really knows the divine essence.

4) *Inter hominem et Deum stat fides et oratio, ut veritati Dei credes et divinitatem adores.*[230]

225. *Carmina Nisibena*, 62.6,9, quoted in Beck, "Éphrem," col. 791.

226. *De Paradiso*, 7.24, quoted in Beck, "Éphrem," col. 792.

227. Beck, "Éphrem," col. 792.

228. *Carmina Nisibena*, 17.12, quoted in Beck, "Éphrem," col. 792.

229. Beck, "Éphrem," col. 792.

230. *De Fide*, 2.488 (which reads *"divinitatem ejus"*), quoted in Beck, "Éphrem," col. 793: "Between man and God stand faith and prayer, that you

5) Faith {is} a true source of spiritual life. Look upon the "*Deum symbolorum*"[231] and He heals your heart (cf. {the} brazen serpent[232]). Faith both finds the truth and *is found by* the truth. (God seeks us in faith.) *Ex Patre fluit per Filium veritas quae donat vitam omnibus per Spiritum.*[233]

6) Even in the dead their faith is the destruction of death and a principle of resurrection.

7) Faith demands works that are in harmony with faith.

8) Faith and love are two wings, both of which are necessary.[234]

9) Love of God and neighbor is the supreme commandment: love of God in {the} form of desire for God, and filled with *ever-increasing confidence*, boldness.[235]

5. *Prayer*: One cannot reach God by intellectual speculation, but He can be reached by *faith, love and prayer* says the Hymn *De Fide*, 4.[236] "By the offering of prayers, a way is laid open by the Creator for His creatures to approach His door."[237] The birth of Christ made prayer efficacious: "*On this day* [*Christmas*] *the door of heaven has been opened to our prayers*."[238] This is as much as to say that all valid prayer is prayer *in Christ*; it reaches the Father through the mediation of the prayer of Christ. "*Beatus qui obtulit oblationem suam per Te*" (*De Virginitate*).[239] But in order to pray in Christ we must *strip ourselves of self-love and of all that separates us*

might believe in the truth of God and adore his divinity."

231. *De Fide*, 9.11 (which reads "*Dominum symbolorum*"), quoted in Beck, "Éphrem," col. 793: "the God [Lord] of the creeds."

232. *De Fide*, 9.11 (citing Numbers 21:4-9; John 3:14-15), quoted in Beck, "Éphrem," col. 793.

233. *De Fide*, 80, quoted in Beck, "Éphrem," col. 793: "From the Father through the Son flows the truth which gives life to all through the Spirit."

234. *De Fide*, 20.12, cited in Beck, "Éphrem," col. 794.

235. *De Ecclesia*, 9.10, cited in Beck, "Éphrem," col. 794.

236. *De Fide*, 4, quoted in Beck, "Éphrem," col. 794.

237. *De Fide*, 11.11, quoted in Beck, "Éphrem," col. 794.

238. *De Nativitate Domini*, 1.96, quoted in Beck, "Éphrem," col. 794.

239. *De Virginitate*, 31.2 (which reads "*suam oblationem*"), quoted in Beck, "Éphrem," col. 794: "Blessed is he who has presented his offering through You."

from our brother. Otherwise our prayer is not Christ's but only "ours." If we pray in Christ, a prayer for our brother is a prayer for ourselves, so there need be no fear that our own good will be forgotten if we ourselves forget it. *Oravisti pro proximo tuo, oravisti pro temetipso*.[240] "Our prayers stand before His door [Ephrem likes this image] and love opens the door before them. Offer your sacrifice with salt, as it is written: let the salt be love of your Lord."[241] Thus the idea of *unity* in prayer is much emphasized: unity with God, unity in Christ, unity with one's brother, and finally *unity of body and soul*. Prayer is not a "purely spiritual" activity from which our material part is excluded. Hence {the} stress on vocal prayer in which the body participates.[242] The relative contempt for vocal prayer as opposed to mental and contemplative prayer is something more modern. The prayer of soul and body through the mouth is an open *witness to faith*. However there is also *silent and interior prayer* "conceived in the mind and born there without a voice" (*De Fide* 20).[243] It (virginity of spirit) takes place in deep tranquillity. The words must not cross the threshold of the lips, and *the virgin mind must remain in her cell, which is truth*. Truth is the bridal chamber of the virgin spirit and the Lord. *Love is the crown of the virgin soul. Silence and tranquillity are the guardians at the door*, protecting her silent prayer. In contemplative prayer, Christ alone is perfectly mirrored in the soul.

> Let prayer be a mirror before thy face. O Lord, let thy beauty be outlined in the brightness of the mirror. Let nothing of the ugly and evil one be seen in that mirror, Lord, lest his filthiness infect the glass. A mirror reflects all that passes before it. Let not all our thoughts be impressed upon our prayer [reflected in it]. But let the movements of Thy face be revealed in [the mirror of our prayer] so that, as a mirror,

240. *De Ecclesia*, 4.8, quoted in Beck, "Éphrem," col. 794: "You have prayed for your neighbor, you have prayed for yourself."

241. *De Ecclesia*, 4.9-11, quoted in Beck, "Éphrem," col. 794.

242. *Carmina Nisibena*, 47.4, cited in Beck, "Éphrem," col. 794.

243. Quoted in Beck, "Éphrem," col. 795.

it may be filled with Thy beauties [*pulchritudinibus*, plural, suggesting the infinite depth of the divine beauty].[244]

({See} St. John of the Cross, *Spiritual Canticle*, XXXV).[245] He adds that this beautiful interior prayer is "born"[246] in the soul without the labor of the soul itself, though we must nevertheless dispose ourselves by generous effort to receive this holy gift.

6. *Fasting and Watching*: The special reward for abstinence from meat and wine {is noted}.[247] Fasting gives beauty to the soul and to the body together. This beauty is the sign of a supernatural transformation of nature, and prepares for the life of the risen body. To hunger and thirst and to deny oneself food and drink that are licit and available, and {to} do this with rejoicing—this is a sign of victory over earthly desires. One who has won this victory is disposed for contemplation. {There can be} no contemplation without penance and asceticism. (Compare Eastern and Western theology on this point.) (Note {the} danger of resting in this spiritual beauty for its own sake.) However, fasting from food and drink is by itself insufficient. One must fast from all vices. Those who watch are said to "shine in the night."[248] The

244. *De Ecclesia*, 29, quoted in Beck, "Éphrem," col. 795.

245. See the second verse of stanza XXXV (stanza XXXVI in the second recension): "And let us go to see ourselves in thy beauty," and John's commentary on the verse: "Let us so act that, by means of this exercise of love aforementioned, we may come to see ourselves in Thy beauty: that is, that we may be alike in beauty, and that Thy beauty may be such that, when one of us looks at the other, each may be like to Thee in Thy beauty, and may see himself in Thy beauty, which will be the transforming of me in Thy beauty; and thus I shall see Thee in thy beauty and Thou wilt see me in Thy beauty; and Thou wilt see Thyself in me in Thy beauty, and I shall see myself in Thee in Thy beauty; so that thus I may be like to Thee in Thy beauty and Thou mayest be like to me in Thy beauty, and my beauty may be Thy beauty, and Thy beauty my beauty; and I shall be Thou in Thy beauty and Thou wilt be I in Thy beauty, because Thy beauty itself will be my beauty" (Peers, II:156-57).

246. *Epistola ad Monachos* (not by Ephrem), quoted in Beck, "Éphrem," col. 795.

247. *De Paradiso*, 7.16, quoted in Beck, "Éphrem," col. 795.

248. *Contra Haereses*, 18.4, quoted in Beck, "Éphrem," col. 796.

hermits and ascetics are close to the angels because they watch in the night. Both monks and angels are called *"the vigilant ones."*[249]

7. *Virginity and Monasticism*: Even more than fasting and watching, virginity is an anticipation of the paradise life. It is a return to our "true country," the "land of the angels,"[250] not that of the beasts. Virginity makes the monk in a sense superior to the angels for he has to gain by bitter struggle what the angels possess without effort. The question of *spiritual virginity* {is raised}—undefiled by {the} "image" of the self. Attachment equals defilement—"marriage." "Actions" {are} born of this union.

See *Collectio Monastica* (Ethiopian—Louvain, 1963) n. 63—"Material and Spiritual Virginity": "A monk who thinks about the cares of this world will be unhappy in both worlds, both this one and the world to come. For he will not enjoy this present world, since he has abstained from marriage and its goods and in the world to come he will be tormented since he has made a promise to God and not fulfilled it. That which he left is matrimony *in order that he might be empty and withdraw from the cares of this world and take care to purify his heart day and night in prayer and fasting without interruption*. But if he once again thinks of the cares of this world, he will have made void the pact for which he abandoned matrimony."[251] {See also} *idem* n. 67:[252] since it is impossible not to have some semi-voluntary cares about food, clothing, etc., the monk will be purified of these by confession and by faith, trusting in God for everything. The implication: care for worldly things is tolerated to some extent if it is a *common care* embracing {the} needs of others. To renounce life with a mate in marriage is to renounce *all* claim to be justified in worldly cares.

The virgin is the bride of Christ. Christ came to earth to espouse virgin souls to Himself, for in them He meets no obstacle

249. *Carmina Nisibena*, 18.1, quoted in Beck, "Éphrem," col. 796.

250. Beck, "Éphrem," col. 796.

251. *Collectio Monastica*, trans. Victor Arras, *CSCO* 239 (Louvain: Secrétariat du Corpus SCO, 1963), 179.

252. *Collectio Monastica*, 180–81.

of any other love or attachment. This must be understood in the light of what has been said about prayer. {Note} the espousals: i.e. in the virgin and pure heart Christ is perfectly reflected. *Imago Domini tui formetur in corde tuo.*[253] *"Blessed, O Lord, is he in whose heart and mind Thou art present*. He becomes a palace by virtue of Thee, Son of the King. He is a holy of holies for Thee, O High Priest."[254] John the Apostle honored the Holy Temple in which Christ dwelt (i.e. Mary) "in order to teach us that today Thou dwellest in pure virgins."[255] He specifies: Christ dwells in the *bodies* of virgins—not physically of course. Ephrem is stressing the unity of the person, body and soul. John the Beloved Disciple is the model of virgins: he has recovered the purity of Adam and Adam's intimacy with God. "Thus was Adam loved when he was pure and holy, like John: thus are the virgins loved who are holy like John."[256]

{What about} solitaries? As in Aphraat, the term *ihidaya* refers to those who are single, unmarried. The *abile, lugentes,* mourners {is a} term more proper to monks, hermits—it is used only once in Ephrem.[257] The peculiarity of the *abile* is that they abandon the community to mourn in the desert. *Abiluta*, sorrowing,[258] was a lifelong activity of Julian Saba, says Ephrem.[259] Penance is then *a constant expression of love for God*, since it purifies the heart of all that is not God; it is manifested by prayer, fasting, vigils, tears. (Note, "prayer and penance" are sometimes separated and contrasted; prayer *is* penance, and so is fasting, etc.) Penance must be *constant*, a long therapy, healing wounds by its constancy. Penance is not just a temporary "city of refuge";[260] it must become

253. *De Virginitate*, 2.15, quoted in Beck, "Éphrem," col. 796: "Let the image of your Lord be formed in your heart."

254. *De Nativitate Domini*, 17.5, quoted in Beck, "Éphrem," col. 796.

255. *De Virginitate*, 25.10, quoted in Beck, "Éphrem," col. 796.

256. *De Azymis*, 14.4, quoted in Beck, "Éphrem," col. 797.

257. *De Virginitate*, 21.2, cited in Beck, "Éphrem," col. 797.

258. See Vööbus, *History*, 2:34, n. 88; 283 for the terms *abile* and *abiluta*.

259. Actually found in the apocryphal *Hymns to Julian Saba*, cited in Beck, "Éphrem," col. 797.

260. *De Ecclesia*, 34.5, quoted in Beck, "Éphrem," cols. 797-98.

a permanent refuge. Hence, he rebukes the soft, the lazy, the sleepers, who do not embrace life-long penance. Meditation on death and judgement nourishes the spirit of penance. Julian Saba always thought of his death standing at the front door: thus he kept doing penance.[261]

Note: in the *Diadema Monachorum* of Smaragdus[262] (ninth century) we find a trace of the rather notable influence of Ephrem in the West in the High Middle Ages. Chapters 87–88 (*PL* 102:680-681) deal with the last things from a Latin text ascribed to Ephrem (*De Beatitudine*) (see Dekkers 1143).[263] The *Diadema* is really an anthology of monastic and ascetic texts {which are} important because {they are} *before* Benedict of Aniane.

8. *Devotion to Mary*: The Hymns to Mary are contested, not by Ephrem perhaps (Beck),[264] but Ephrem's Marian devotion is found in the Nativity Hymns.[265] Mary, the Mother of the Savior, is blessed among all women. She delights to be in paradise with her Son and rejoices that the saved will share this joy with her. She saw God in the flesh with her very eyes: the faithful see Him in the Eucharist also with their very eyes. {Note the devotion to} *Jesus*: "Jesus, Name worthy of all praise, invisible bridge, leading from death to life . . . May Thy love become a bridge for Thy servant. Through Thee may I cross over to Thy Father. *May I pass over and say: Blessed is He who has tempered his strength in His Son.*"[266] "Floods of joy flow forth to the gathering of the seers from the Splendor of the Father, through His firstborn Son" (*De Paradiso*, 9).[267]

More points of doctrine and conduct—for ordinary Christians: Ephrem said that too much care for fine clothes was a sign of

261. *Hymns to Julian Saba*, cited in Beck, "Éphrem," col. 798.

262. *PL* 102, cols. 593-690.

263. Eligius Dekkers, OSB, *Clavis Patrum Latinorum* (Bruges: Beyaert; the Hague: M. Nijhoff, 1961), #1143: "Ephraem Latinus" (253–54).

264. Beck, "Éphrem," col. 798.

265. Beck, "Éphrem," col. 798; see for example the "Hymne de Saint Éphrem sur la Nativité," trans. Frère Alphonse, *L'Orient Syrien*, 2 (1957), 38–40.

266. *De Fide*, 6.17, quoted in Beck, "Éphrem," col. 799-800.

267. *De Paradiso*, 9.24, quoted in Beck, "Éphrem," col. 799.

worldliness and he who loved to dress well on earth would not be clothed in heavenly glory—also that too much refinement in washing and care of {the} body was a sign of slavery to vice. *On Compunction* (*Liber Scintillarum*, 6:28-30): "Compunction is the health of the soul. / Compunction is the illumination of the soul. / Compunction is the remission of sins. / Compunction draws the Holy Spirit to us. / Compunction makes the only-begotten Son dwell in us. / *Tears before God give us confidence always.*"[268] (Contrast a "worldly" idea of confidence which is security in having *nothing to regret*!)

St. Ephrem III—Texts in the *Collectio Monastica* (*Aethiopica*), ed. by Arras, *CSCO*, Vol. 239, p. 112–113.[269] *The Monastic Paradise* {is} cenobitic life (this shows Ephrem's interest in {the} common life). Paradise, full of delightful fruits and flowers, is the "*multitudo monachorum insimul ornatorum caritate Domini*" (p. 112).[270] The first part of the texts is simply a litany of symbolic comparisons: the fountain of water in the midst of paradise = *the fount of tears* with which the monk waters the psalms (cf. later Hymns on Paradise). Like a strong fortified city is the monastic community "*insimul sese portantes invicem in caritate Domini.*"[271] The good works of the community together form *one Image* of the heavenly King (p. 112). The *recollection* of the monastic community makes it like an army of angels. *Mutual Consolation and Charity* {is} like a spring for one dying of thirst in the desert: monastic life = solitude, {the} desert; charity = {a} divine oasis. Five of these comparisons appear in the *Liber Scintillarum* of *Defensor of Ligugé*,[272] and are accepted as genuine by scholars (see *Liber Scintillarum, Sources Chrétiennes*, Vol. II, p. 58).

268. Defensor de Ligugé, *Livre d'Étincelles*, vol. 1, ed. and trans. Henri Rochais, SC 77 (Paris: Éditions du Cerf, 1961), 126; the quoted passage is from # 29, and literally reads ". . . to itself" and ". . . in itself" rather than ". . . to us . . . in us".

269. *Collectio Monastica*, c. 22.

270. "multitude of monks adorned together with the love of the Lord."

271. "together bearing up one another in the love of the Lord."

272. Chapter 40, nn. 36–40.

Negative Images—the faults of the individual monk: he who sleeps in psalmody is like a sick man weighed down with a sack of salt (p. 112); impure thoughts fill the mind like thorns and brambles; hatred {is} like worm-eaten wood; pride makes of the monk a tall tree without fruit; {he writes of} instability: "*Sicut quando quis evellit arborum plenum fructibus et plantat eum in alio loco et fructus eius marcescunt et rami eius exsiccantur, ita monachus qui relinquit locum suum et per aliena loca vagatur*" (p. 113).[273] This comparison becomes a commonplace in monastic literature on stability. See for instance two interesting letters of Peter of Celles (*Ep.* 175, 176),[274] to some monks of Grandmont who had transferred to the Order of Cîteaux. He urges them to remain with the Cistercians. {He} uses the image of the tree, which he ascribes to Gregory (*PL* 202, col. 633).[275] {He} uses it again in col. 634: "*Teste philosopho primum argumentum bene compositae mentis existimo posse consistere et secum morari. Discurrere enim et locorum mutationibus inquietari, aegri animi jactatio est non enim coalescit vel convalescit planta quae saepe transfertur*" (*Ep.* 176).[276] {Concerning} impatience, {the text declares}: a monk without patience is a building without foundation.

Gloriatio Monachi ({cf.} meaning of *glory*)—another "litany" follows, on this theme (p. 113): *Gloriatio monachi patientia cum caritate . . . Gloriatio monachi laus coram angelis caeli et hominibus et humilitas in puritate et mansuetudine cordis . . . Gloriatio gloriationum quando Dominum diligit ex toto corde suo et proximum sicut*

273. "As when someone uproots a tree full of fruit and plants it in another place and its fruits wither and its branches dry up, such is a monk who leaves his own place and wanders through foreign lands."

274. *PL* 202, cols. 633B-636A.

275. "*Dicit Gregorius, quod plantae, quae saepe transponuntur, radices non mittunt*" ("Gregory says that plants that are frequently transplanted do not put down roots").

276. "I think, and the philosopher bears me witness, that the first proof of a well-settled mind is to be able to stay put and abide with oneself. For to run about and be unsettled by changes of place is the instability of a weak mind, for a plant that is frequently transplanted does not flourish or grow strong."

seipsum (p. 113).[277] ({This is} not very interesting from a literary viewpoint.)

IV. Some themes from Ephrem's hymns on Paradise (texts: see Beck, *Studia Anselmiana* 26;[278] *Hymn* 5: Daniélou, *Dieu Vivant* 22;[279] *Orient Syrien* 1960, vol. 5[280]).

Hymn 1: {This focuses on the} difficulty of the Paradise theme: the Torah tells the beauties of the garden, describes *what is seen* and praises *what is hidden*. Thus the poet remains caught between fear and love: "I will respect what is hidden and contemplate what is seen. In seeking I will gain, in silence I will find support."[281] {There are} two elements of contemplation, the seen and the unseen, {with} a dialectic between these two. In this double movement his spirit takes flight, but errs. "Discerning the splendor of paradise, but not what paradise really is, / Only what is given to man to see of it."[282] Hence what is said will be symbolic—it will be only in human images.

1. The height of Paradise: the deluge reached only to the edge of it.[283]

2. There the sons of light dwell in tents of light. The prophets and apostles are distinguished by their flights and their dancing on the surface of the sea, together with those whom they have instructed.[284]

277. "The glory of a monk is patience with charity . . . The glory of a monk is praise among the angels of heaven and men and humility in purity and gentleness of heart. . . . The glory of glories is when one loves the Lord with one's whole heart and one's neighbor as oneself."

278. Edmund Beck, OSB, ed., *Ephraems Hymnen über das Paradies, Studia Anselmiana*, 26 (Rome: Herder, 1951).

279. Éphrem le Syrien, "Hymne sur le Paradis," trans. Jean Daniélou, *Dieu Vivant*, 22 (1953), 77–86.

280. "Trois Hymnes de Saint Éphrem sur le Paradis," trans. René Lavenant, SJ, *L'Orient Syrien*, 5 (1960), 33–46; the three hymns are nn. 1, 2 and 7, the three that Merton discusses here.

281. "Trois Hymnes," 34 (1.2).

282. "Trois Hymnes," 34 (1.3).

283. "Trois Hymnes," 34–35 (1.4).

284. "Trois Hymnes," 35 (1.6).

3. Paradise is invisible, but it can be seen with the eyes of the spirit in its relation to the lower creation: it surrounds all the material creation with a ring of spiritual glory, like a halo around the moon.[285] This is compared with the crown around the altar of Moses (Exodus). "He crowned the altar with great magnificence, and thus also with magnificence is woven / The crown of paradise around all that is created."[286]

4. The fall from Paradise. ADAM fell only into the "lower part of paradise."[287] But the sons of Adam, continuing to sin, fell even from there. However, some of the creatures of God (called the "sons of God"[288]) remained in this lower paradise, and went down to wed the daughters of men (Genesis). The lower part of paradise is the place to which those go who on earth sinned out of foolishness and weakness rather than malice, when their sin is expiated. The higher paradise is reserved for the truly perfect.[289] (This division is common in Syrian theology—cf. Philoxenos.[290])

5. The just in Paradise look down and see the punishment of the wicked. There is an abyss between paradise and hell. The

285. "Trois Hymnes," 35 (1.8).

286. "Trois Hymnes," 35–36 (1.9).

287. "Trois Hymnes," 36 (1.10).

288. "Trois Hymnes," 36 (1.11).

289. "Trois Hymnes," 37 (1.16).

290. The division in question is apparently that between the just and the perfect, which Philoxenos explores in his *Homelies* 8 and 9 (see below, pages 283, 299–300), rather than that between two sections of paradise, which Philoxenos does not consider: see Jean Gribomont, OSB, "Les Homélies Ascétiques de Philoxène de Mabboug et l'Echo du Messalienisme," *L'Orient Syrien*, 2 (1957), 427: "Because all are not capable of following the Lord, salvation is granted to the just; but for the *Liber Graduum*, this salvation is only a beatitude of the second order: communion in the Holy Spirit, complete knowledge of the truth, entrance into the heavenly Jerusalem where one sees God face to face, are reserved for the perfect. On these various points, Philoxenos is not explicit—possibly he did not have completely clear ideas on the eschatology reserved for the just; it is not this ultimate consequence of perfection that interests him: his discussion continuously returns to emphasize the interior freedom which accompanies 'spiritual service,' and Christ's preference for this renunciation."

wicked also see the joys of paradise but cannot attain to them.[291] The cosmos remains *an integrated spiritual unity* for Ephrem. Nothing in it is lost or forgotten. All has a definitive "place." (Thus far, *Hymn 1*.)

Hymn 2:

6. Paradise is entered through the "gate of examination which is in love with men"[292] (which desires to admit them). {Note the} refrain of this hymn: "Blessed is He who was pierced and took away the sword from Paradise."[293] *We spend our lives making our own key* to the door of paradise. Each one has to have his own key. In our lives, the door "seeks us,"[294] smiles on us. "Door of discernment, it measures those who enter / Wisely making itself small or great according to its judgement / Fitting the stature of each . . ."[295] (Implied by Ephrem's treatment here is Christ's own statement "I am the door."[296])

7. Entering the gate, men suddenly see the true value or worthlessness of all they have loved in life. Riches are nothing. If their life was a lie then they enter into torment. But the sufferings of the just now vanish like a dream and give place to eternal joy. Their life was *truth*.[297]

8. The sweet odors of paradise and some of its radiance reach down to us on earth but they come to us impoverished and changed, since for us to appreciate them they have to take on something of the taste and quality of earth.[298] Thus also the waters of the rivers of Eden come to us through "canals"[299] which the Lord has disposed so that they reach us (in contemplation).

291. "Trois Hymnes," 36–37 (1.12-17).
292. "Trois Hymnes," 38 (2.1).
293. "Trois Hymnes," 38.
294. "Trois Hymnes," 38 (2.2).
295. "Trois Hymnes," 38 (2.2).
296. Jn. 10:7, 9.
297. "Trois Hymnes," 38 (2.3-5).
298. "Trois Hymnes," 39 (2.8).
299. "Trois Hymnes," 39 (2.9).

9. The ark and Mount Sinai are symbols of the order established by God among the souls in paradise—the ark: in the lowest part, animals; in the middle part, birds; in the highest part, Noe himself, in the place of God; the mount: at the bottom, the people; on the lower levels, the priests; half way up, Aaron; near the top, Moses; at the very top, the glory of the Lord, and the Lord of glory himself. Both the ark and the mount symbolize the paradise of the Church.[300]

Hymn 7:

10. "Courage, *Abiluta*":[301] this term refers to the mourning and compunction of asceticism.[302] *Hymn* 7 reminds each level of life in the Church that there is a special reward for its works. Time is like a night of sleep from which we presently awaken. The morning is near, let us not then lament that the night is too long,[303] and {the} "refrain" {reads}: "Blessed is he who by his keys has opened the garden of life."[304] Those who fasted and thirsted will be fed and refreshed with wisdom.[305] Those who lived on vegetables will be welcomed into special groves where the trees will honor them and provide them with unique fruits. So too the flowers will kiss the feet of those who washed the feet of the poor. Those who abstain from wine will be met by the grapes of paradise coming to refresh them.[306] {Here is the} *theme of reconciliation with* {*the*} *created world* (Biblical, not Greek!). In Paradise there is no nakedness; the saints are clothed in garments of light. The virgins dance in paradise, under the fig tree which says that they need no longer remember the day of shame when nature fled naked to it to hide in its leaves.[307] {There is a} reward also for the married: as a reward for the sorrow of childbearing, they will see

300. "Trois Hymnes," 39–40 (2.12).
301. "Trois Hymnes," 40 (7.3).
302. See "Trois Hymnes," 40–41, n. 1.
303. "Trois Hymnes," 40 (7.2).
304. "Trois Hymnes," 40.
305. "Trois Hymnes," 41 (7.3).
306. "Trois Hymnes," 43 (7.16-18).
307. "Trois Hymnes," 41 (7.5-6).

the little ones who died, playing like lambs in paradise, in familiar converse with the angels.[308] {There are} special rewards for the merciful.[309] The old should think more of paradise: "Old age, fix thy thoughts on paradise / Whose sweet fragrance will make you young again / Whose breath will bring you joy / All stain will be taken away by the glorious vesture that will clothe you!"[310] The beauty of glorified bodies is described, or rather suggested.[311] The glory of the martyrs is mentioned,[312] but note that there is much more emphasis on virginity and the ascetic life than on martyrdom.[313]

11. "At sight of this place, O brothers, I sit down and weep / Over myself and over those like me: O my days have come to their end / One by one they have melted away, they have vanished without my knowing they are snatched away / Remorse has descended upon me: I have lost my crown . . . / May all the sons of light pray for me . . . / That the Lord, in his mercy, may give me the treasure of his mercies."[314] Ephrem himself will also dwell (in the spirit, during the present life) in the antechamber of paradise, seeing the rewards of the just on one hand and the punishment of the wicked on the other, learning from the example of Dives and Lazarus.[315]

12. In closing, Ephrem prays the Lord to give him fear of HIM, the true God, instead of making his neighbor his god, fearing to offend his neighbor, seeking to please his neighbor and to be praised by him. Thus man is the slave of slaves: "God had given us the gift of liberty, but we have sold it into slavery"[316] by submitting to other men and being guided by their opinions etc. This is idolatry: "Let us then give up the lord that we have forged

308. "Trois Hymnes," 42 (7.8).
309. "Trois Hymnes," 42 (7.9).
310. "Trois Hymnes," 42 (7.10).
311. "Trois Hymnes," 42 (7.12).
312. "Trois Hymnes," 44 (7.19).
313. "Trois Hymnes," 43 (7.15-16, 18).
314. "Trois Hymnes," 44–45 (7.24-25).
315. "Trois Hymnes," 45 (7.26-27).
316. "Trois Hymnes," 46 (7.31).

and exchange it for Thy Lordship!"[317] This is what the Kingship of Christ meant to the early Syrians. Monastic vocation {is} to be seen in this light as a call to freedom to serve Christ the true King (*Rule* of St. Benedict[318]).

Ephrem—*Hymns on Paradise*: compare and contrast *the doctrine of Origen on Creation*:[319]

1. The primitive or original state of man: for Origen *"the spiritual man" is created in and with the "first heaven" on the "first day"* of creation—i.e. *outside of time*. This is man *in the Word*. He has no being other than the contemplation of God in the Word—in *perfect unity*. His being is entirely in God, and he has no being outside of God. The whole "heaven" created the first day is "in God" and not "in existence" outside of God.[320]

2. The firmament, created on the second day, is the world in existence outside of God. *Multiplicity replaces unity*. *Time* is now measuring *duration*. This already implies a *fall of being* into temporal existence. Spiritual beings then abandon perfect contemplation and engage themselves in *the concerns of temporal existence*. *Nous* becomes *psyche* and enters into history as a "cool" entity. But its rationality and intelligence shall make it in {the} image of the Word. The destiny of the rational being is then to *return to likeness and unity* in *theologia* or contemplation of God in the Word. {This is} the "spiritual man," the true theologian, {the} true man of prayer. God will then be once again all in all as He was in the beginning. Hence man becomes once again *nous* in the Word, and is deified by the vision of God. "It is not *through* or *by* the Word that the blessed see the Father as through an intermediary but *in* the Word and *with* Him by direct knowledge [His own knowledge]" (Lossky).[321]

317. "Trois Hymnes," 46 (7.31).

318. Cf. the Prologue: "*Christo vero Regi militaturus*" ("to fight for the true King, Christ") (McCann, 6/7).

319. Merton draws on Vladimir Lossky, *Vision de Dieu* (Neuchâtel, Switzerland: Delachaux & Niestlé, 1962), 49–59.

320. Lossky, *Vision de Dieu*, 50.

321. Lossky, *Vision de Dieu*, 54.

3. *Paradise*—for Origen is a place where those who have sought to study and contemplate God on earth devote themselves, so to speak, to "graduate work" in a *locus eruditionis* or *auditorium vel schola animarum*.[322] One then goes on through the various heavens, ascending to God, ever increasing in purity of heart so as to see God. Like Plotinus, his fellow student under Ammonius Saccas, Origen sees the material creation as a *degradation* of being and seeks salvation in a flight from matter.[323]

Hymn 5 on Paradise (from *Dieu Vivant*, 22, with introduction and commentary by J. Daniélou) *repeats some of the familiar themes*: the sweet odors and joys of paradise; the two divisions—the inner paradise of the perfect where they sit at the banquet table, rewarded for their works; the outer vestibule for sinners saved by pure mercy, who feast on the crumbs from the banquet table; Paradise is the true life; we are born into it by death, yet as the baby cries on emerging from the womb, we weep and lament when we must go forth from this world to which we are attached.

Full development of other themes {is also made}: (1) *Lectio Divina* as a way to paradise; (2) the idea of "place" and "space" in paradise; (3) how God is present in paradise.

1) *Lectio Divina*:

a) The creative Word is like the rock in the desert. There was no water in the rock but water came forth. The creative Word brings forth all from nothing.

b) "Moses in his book described creation in nature so that *nature and the book* might bear witness to the Creator—*nature by its use, the book by its reading are witnesses which reach out to every place* and are present in every time, and at all hours. They accuse him who does not believe, *because he has not rendered to the Creator the praise due to Him*."[324] Thus the creative word is present in na-

322. Lossky, *Vision de Dieu*, 56: "place of learning"; "lecture hall or classroom of souls."

323. See Lossky, *Vision de Dieu*, 57–59.

324. "Hymne sur le Paradis," 83.

ture and the book: we must hear and respond by praise—note {the} implications for Christian activity in the world. Use of nature is not profane.

c) Reading Genesis: "*I read the beginning of this book and I shuddered with joy / For the lines and verses stretched out their arms to me* / And the first one that came to meet me / Embraced me and led me to her companion / And when I reached the line where is written the description of Paradise, / That line lifted me up and transported me from that place / Into the bosom of paradise. // My eyes and my spirit crossed over on these lines as on a bridge / They entered together into the story of Paradise. // My eyes, in reading, led my spirit across the bridge / And my spirit let my eyes rest from their reading / And when the passage in the book was read there was rest for my eyes / And act for my spirit . . . // My eyes remained outside, my spirit entered within / And *I began to move about in that which Moses had not described* / The luminous abyss of Paradise is pure, splendid and lovely. / The book calls it Eden because it is the abyss of all good."[325]

2) *Explanation of "place" in paradise*. The spiritual bodies of the just will be as free and spaceless as the Spirit. When the spirit is recollected it is "somewhere."[326] But it can extend itself and be everywhere. A house is filled with the rays of many lamps, a flower with many good odors. Yet they move freely "in their festival."[327] "Thoughts without number inhabit a little heart / And yet they are out in the open / They are not cramped and do not cramp others."[328]

3) God in paradise. He does not "see" God, but a great cry of *Sanctus* goes up "like the tumult of a great camp filled with the crash of trumpets. / Hence the Godhead was in the midst of it / I believed that God was there, for the place was void / And I knew He was there because of the outburst of praising voices."[329]

325. "Hymne sur le Paradis," 83–84.

326. "Hymne sur le Paradis," 85.

327. "Hymne sur le Paradis," 85.

328. "Hymne sur le Paradis," 85.

329. "Hymne sur le Paradis," 85.

4) Conclusion: "*Hence Paradise has restored me with its peace and its beauty.* / There lives beauty without stain, there peace without fear. / Blessed is he who is judged worthy to be received into paradise / If not by justice, then at least by mercy. // {. . . .} Our region is a prison, and yet the captives weep when they must leave it . . . / Death is a birth. Those who are born weep in leaving the vast universe, the Mother of Sorrows, to enter the paradise of delights."[330]

FINALE: "May thy soul take pity on me, O Lord of Paradise / And if it be not possible for me to enter, hold me worthy / At least of the pasture which spreads out before the entrance. / The heart of paradise is the table of the rich / And its fruits at the gate fall out like crumbs for the sinners / Who live on thy bounty."[331]

EPHREM: more texts attributed to Ephrem in the Ethiopian Collection (from *Collectio Monastica*, ed. by Victor Arras, *CSCO* 239 [Louvain, 1963]). Number 23 is attributed to Ephrem but in reality is by Abbot *Isaias*.[332] A Latin version of the same is found in *PG* 40, col. 1108 ff.[333] It is worth reading here, for its own intrinsic interest (historical). It refers obviously to life in hermit lauras. It is a tract on *monastic formation*. "The things spoken by Abbot Ephrem concerning the young, *quoad juvenes*."[334]—especially in relation to others, above all *strangers*—hence these maxims relate to guests and to monks on a journey.

1. *Humilitas spiritus*[335] is necessary above all because only by humility of spirit does one "make empty the work of the false messias"[336] (cf. Gospel {for} 24th Sunday post Pentecost[337]). It is also a source of peace. What does it consist in?

330. "Hymne sur le Paradis," 86.

331. "Hymne sur le Paradis," 86.

332. See *Collectio Monastica*, 114, n. 1.

333. Cols. 1108-1112.

334. *Collectio Monastica*, 114.

335. *Collectio Monastica*, 114: "humility of spirit."

336. *Collectio Monastica*, 114.

337. Matthew 24:15-35, part of the eschatological discourse, warning against false messiahs and false prophets.

a) Not undue assertion of self. In all one's ideas, to take a submissive and unassertive attitude.

b) Not having a proud opinion of oneself, *"ut sis sine agitatione in omni cogitatione tua."*[338] Important: self-esteem is {the} source of restlessness, agitation, lack of peace.

c) Modesty and silence {is to be shown} in dealing with others, whether they are pilgrim monks who come to visit, or whether one is himself on pilgrimage with other monks. {One should observe} silence while traveling, and {be vigilant in} curbing curiosity, keeping hidden, and not being too demonstrative in public (n.b. *our own rules*[339] when going to town, etc.)

338. *Collectio Monastica*, 114: "so that one might be without agitation in all one's thoughts."

339. *Regulations of the Order of Cistercians of the Strict Observance Published by the General Chapter of 1926* (Dublin: M. H. Gill and Son, 1926), Book 8, chapter 13: "Of Religious who go on a Journey" (##403–405): "(403) When a religious is obliged to be absent on a journey (which should never occur except in a case of grave necessity), the Superior gives him an 'obedience' indicating the place to which he is going and the itinerary which he is to follow. Before his departure, he goes to receive the blessing of the Reverend Father Abbot. If a religious is sent out on a commission, and foresees that he will not be able to return in time for the repast, he asks permission to eat out of the monastery; otherwise he should not do so. If he is not to return the same day, he asks the prayers of the community (this is not to be taken literally as regards the Superior and the cellarer). Accordingly, at the end of the Canonical Office which immediately precedes his departure, he goes to the middle of the presbytery step, bows, salutes the two choirs by a moderate bow to the right and to the left, without turning his back on the altar, and then prostrates on the knuckles, if it is a ferial day; on other days, he bows toward the altar. If there are several, the seniors place themselves in the middle; but if one of the travelers is the Abbot, all the others go behind him. After the verse **Fidelium**, or after the **Divinum Auxilium**, if the Office of the Dead is to follow, the Hebdomadery says the versicles and prayer in the Breviary, the choir standing turned to the altar; on ferial days out of Paschal time, the Hebdomadery and the choir remain prostrate on the desks. The religious will do well to say, if he can, the prayers of the Itinerary at the moment of his departure. (404) The religious thus sent out shall only make such visits as the Superior shall determine. In his conversation he shall be careful to say nothing but what may edify. He may eat eggs and fish, but not meat, unless he is ill, or unless he obtains each time the permission of his Superior. Meat may, however, be eaten on a sea voyage. (405) On his return, the religious should first of all go and pray in the church, but

2. *Modesty and chastity* are strongly recommended, here especially in the context of the journey. The conditions of travel should not make one relax modesty and be too free with others, for instance sleeping under the same blanket with another. Modesty {is to be observed} when anointing oneself with oil, even though only the feet. Sitting with feet covered and knees together {is enjoined}.

3. *Conduct with guests at table*. Give them all that is necessary for a good meal. After they stop eating tell them to eat some more, and go on telling them up to three times. "And when you eat do not lift up your face to your brother and do not look about this way and that and do not speak any vain word [i.e. empty word, useless word]. And if you want something do not take it until you have said '*Benedic*.' And if you drink, don't make gulping noises in your throat. And when you sit with your brothers and you get phlegm in your throat do not spit in their presence but go and spit outside. And do not scratch yourself while others are looking. And if you start to yawn, close your mouth and it will go away."[340] {Observe} good manners {and} self-control.

4. *Humility with others*. Great stress {is laid} on asking pardon, *not defending oneself*, not fighting and bickering, quelling anger as soon as possible.

a) If one is not ashamed to ask pardon, anger will go away;

b) Appease the anger of others by admitting one's fault;

c) "If someone asks you 'why did you do this?' do not get upset, but prostrate yourself and say, 'I did wrong, and I will not do it again . . .' All this is a victory for the young."[341]

---

out of the choir. He then goes to the Reverend Father Abbot to ask his blessing and give him an account of his journey. On this subject, he maintains the most absolute silence with all his brethren. At the end of the first Office at which he can assist, he asks the prayers of the community, but this time, he prostrates at the presbytery step, whatever day it may be, and does not salute the choir. The Hebdomadery and the choir act as laid down in no. 403."

340. *Collectio Monastica*, 114: "*Benedic*": "Bless (the Lord)."

341. *Collectio Monastica*, 115.

5. *Work.* One must be diligent and also eager to learn. {One should} not {be} ashamed to ask questions and seek correction when needed. "When you do the work of your hands do not be negligent, but occupy yourself with it in the fear of the Lord so that you may not make a mistake without understanding."[342] One must also be willing to leave his work and go to do something else when commanded or requested by a brother.

6. *Silence, obedience.*

> When you have finished your meal, get up and go into your cell and say your evening prayer and do not stay outside indulging in useless talk. But if they are elders and are speaking of the things of God, say to him who sits with you, "Do you want me to stay and listen or should I go and get inside my cell?" And do what he tells you. And if he sends you somewhere else for an errand say to him: "Where do you want me to spend the night and what do you want me to do and what do you want me to buy?" And whatever he tells you, do just that, without adding or subtracting anything.[343]

(N.B. the "obedience" in our usages.[344])

7. Relations with other brothers. When the monk stays with another monk in a different place, for several days, he will work for the other monk if asked, will not relate what he has seen here and there, will not put on airs and try to seem important to the other and will not stick his nose in the other monk's business. In all conflicts of will, give in to {a} brother *ne sit ira et tristitia*.[345] "When others say, 'It is your turn to cook,' just go ahead and cook, after asking, 'What do you want me to prepare?' And if they say cook whatever you like, go ahead and do it in the fear of the Lord."[346]

342. *Collectio Monastica*, 115.

343. *Collectio Monastica*, 115.

344. I.e. the particular instructions for a journey: see the quotation above, n. 339.

345. *Collectio Monastica* 115: "lest there be anger and sadness."

346. *Collectio Monastica*, 115.

8. *Receiving a guest.*

> If a pilgrim brother [a monk from other regions] comes to you, show him a joyful countenance when you salute him and if he is carrying a package take it from him with joy and set it down . . . *Be careful that you do not ask him questions about anything useless* but invite him to pray and ask him how he is. That is enough. And let him sit [to meditate] and give him a book to read. If you know he is tired, refresh him and wash his feet. . . . If his clothes are dirty, wash them. If they are torn, repair them. If he comes begging, do not introduce him to your brethren but take care of him yourself in the fear of God. . . . If he is truly a poor brother do not send him away with empty hands but give him from the blessings which God has given you; for you must know that they are not yours but the Lord's.[347]

9. *Staying with another*. If the host leaves the guest alone in the cell, the guest should not go around looking at the books or prying into things and examining his pots, jugs, etc., but should ask for some work to do until the host comes back.

10. *Prayer*. "When you stand to pray in your cell do not be negligent. But when you wish to praise Him do not act like one who would provoke Him to anger, but stand in the fear of the Lord. Do not lean against the wall, and do not lift up one foot and rest on the other. And hold your heart firm lest it wander away with its desires, that you may offer the Lord your sacrifice. . . . And if you stand for the liturgical service keep your heart in the fear of the Lord that it may not be distracted and you may be worthy of Him and He will heal you."[348]

St. Ephrem: *Seven Hymns on Virginity* (from the Armenian: *Orient Syrien*, 1961).[349] {These are} original and varied. {They} *give {a} proper place to marriage*, {seeing} marriage and virginity {as}

347. *Collectio Monastica*, 116.

348. *Collectio Monastica*, 116–17.

349. "Hymnes Inédites de Saint Éphrem sur la Virginité," trans. François Graffin, sj, *L'Orient Syrien*, 6 (1961), 213–42.

complementary. Virginity is superior to marriage but is *a gift of God which no one can arrogate* to himself—without marriage there would be no one to be saved.[350] The prophets {are} models of virginity and solitude: ELIAS—"He remained alone on Carmel to guard his virginity" (2, p. 217). The prophets chose the rank of angels, and, as they could not attain to it, they chose the desert, which in some fashion resembles the heavenly dwelling. *For in the desert is no carnal desire; there the spirit can recollect itself. The desert is propitious to prayer because all thoughts vanish away.* It is good for the body to dwell alone, so as to be neither led nor dragged by the desires. . . .[351] {Note the} example of Christ: you have learned that the Son of God retired alone, apart from his disciples, and remained in prayer—to teach us both prayer and solitude together. "O Lord, give strength to the men of the mountains, give patience to the hermits. / And may those who remain in the village be protected / By the prayer of those who are far off" (*Hymn* 2, p. 220). The virgin will be carried to heaven in triumph on the chariot of Elias (*Hymn* 3, p. 221). {He contrasts} the reward of virgins who have kept virginity for love of Christ and the punishment of those whose virginity was kept for human praise (221). (Read *On the Reward*, p. 223.[352])

Debate between virginity and holy matrimony (see *Hymn* 4 {and} 5).[353] {Note} the comparison of examples from the Old Testament: examples of virginity (Josue, Elias) are compared with examples of holiness in marriage (Noe, Moses). It is admitted that the works of married saints were greater (Moses, Peter, etc.) but they were pure gifts of God.[354] The sacrifice of virginity is a greater and more pure offering to God. Note: the "debate" between vir-

350. See Graffin's introduction (214).

351. "Hymnes Inédites," 220 (2.135-44).

352. "Hymnes Inédites," 223–24 (2.119-28): "She is declared blessed who by struggling for a time . . . has won an eternal reward. At the hour when the sun goes dark, the eyes of the virgins are lit up; at the hour when the moon goes dark, their senses are alight with glory; and like the sun and the moon, they shine in the Kingdom."

353. "Hymnes Inédites," 224–32.

354. "Hymnes Inédites," 232 (5.137-46).

ginal solitude in the desert and holiness in the world recurs in Philoxenos, *Letter on Monastic Life* (*Orient Syrien*, 1961, p. 332–333).[355] Here the devil reminds the novice that many have been saints in the world: Abraham, Isaac, Jacob, etc. The devil also adds that the *labors* of virginity are indeed greater, and practically impossible. The young novice who undertakes them will be guilty of folly, will fail and be laughed at by all.

Hymn 6 on Virginity:[356] "I have vowed my person to God, rather than to be the mother of others, / *Instead of having sons, I have chosen to be the daughter of God / . . . Instead of espousing a mortal husband I am the spouse of the Son and Creator of Life* / Instead of the joy of one day, I have desired the joy that is everlasting. / . . . I have not regarded my face in the mirror for I do not make up my face for a husband. / But in the mirror of the commandments I shall behold my interior face / In order to cleanse the stains of my soul and to wash away whatever soils my spirit."[357] Contrasted with the sufferings of childbirth, the sorrows of marriage, *is the freedom of the virgin life*, subjected directly to Christ. "In her life, Christ protects her from everything for God has counted the hairs of her head / At her death He does not forget her: He makes her rise from the tomb. / . . . To her soul He gives wings; He smashes the barrier of the sword / He opens to her the gate of paradise and glorifies her amid the trees. / Because she weakened her body with fasting, she is fed in the pastures of Eden. / . . . After the rank of angels, in order, comes the rank of virgins. / After the virgins the saints [those holy in marriage], then finally the people of the world. / Let us hasten, also, to seek the highest rank while there is yet time."[358]

355. "La Lettre de Philoxène de Mabboug à un Supérieur de Monastère sur la Vie Monastique," ed. and trans. François Graffin, SJ, *L'Orient Syrien*, 6 (1961), 317–52, 455–86; 7 (1962), 77–102; for the question of authorship, see below, n. 401.

356. "Hymnes Inédites," 233–36.

357. "Hymnes Inédites," 233–34 (6.27-30, 33-36, 41-46).

358. "Hymnes Inédites," 235–36 (6.107-10, 113-18, 125-30).

Hymn 7—Jeremias, ordered by God to be a virgin, is the model of monks. "*He observed virginity after having received the order, not after having promised it.*"[359] Conditions of virginity according to Jeremias {include}: (1) taking upon oneself the yoke of the Lord and dwelling: in silence; (2) "with his mouth in the dust"[360] and accepting injustice and blows; (3) fasting; (4) solitude. "After having been hateful to all because of the chalice of wrath he gave them to drink / His virginity overflowed. He kept it and was crowned."[361] Jesus sowed the seeds of virginity in His Church. Virginity in the Church fulfills the figures of the Old Testament.[362]

Prayer—attributed to St. Ephrem by Alcuin in *PL* {101}:607:

> Pone, Domine, lacrymas meas in conspectu tuo *sicut in promissione tua, ut* avertatur inimicus meus retrorsum *et expavescens conturbet, cum viderit me* in loco quem {praeparavit} *misericordia tua.* Exspectans autem inimicus videre in loco quem mihi propter delicta mea praeparavit, *videat me in loco lucis et vitae aeternae et conversus in tenebris conturbetur,* quia nequaquam voluntas eius effecta est. *Ita benignissime, ita amator hominum, ita qui solus sine peccato es, effunde super me inaestimabilem et immensam misericordiam tuam et praesta mihi ut {et} ego et hi qui te diligunt regni tui efficiamur haeredes,* et videntes gloriam tuam, adoremus bonitatem tuam: *et dicamus pariter, qui digni fuerimus videre* insatiabilem pulchritudinem majestatis tuae:
>
> *Gloria Patri qui fecit nos*
> *Gloria Filio qui sanavit nos*
> *Gloria Spiritui Sancto qui renovavit nos*
> *Trinitas Sancta, une Deus,*
> *Sub umbra alarum tuarum nos protege*
> *Qui es benedictus in saecula. Amen.*[363]

359. "Hymnes Inédites," 238 (7.47-48).

360. "Hymnes Inédites," 238 (7.59, 77).

361. "Hymnes Inédites," 239 (7.83-86).

362. "Hymnes Inédites," 239 (7.95-100).

363. "O Lord, place my tears in your sight as in your promise, so that my enemy may be turned away and thrown into terror and confusion in seeing me in

Syrian Monastic Rules (see Vööbus, Syriac and Arabic Documents [Stockholm, 1960]):[364]

Admonitions of Mar Ephrem[365] (probably not by Ephrem). {It contains} no general principles of monasticism. {It is a} collection of rules and precepts patterned on Wisdom Literature. Perhaps some of Ephrem's works were used as a basis. Sometimes collected precepts were drawn from Ephrem's works in this manner, for instance a cycle of rules drawn from his homilies on virginity and translated into Armenian.[366] Also as these rules are for cenobites, they are not by Ephrem (Vööbus argues[367]) but after his time. Ephrem was not interested in cenobitism, says Vööbus.

General tone: {the emphasis is on} obedience, discipline, good example, learning wisdom. These are typical cenobitic concerns. Also {there is a} stress on learning maturity. Virtue, discretion and control are characteristic of maturity—impulsiveness, sensuality, etc. of immaturity.

Obedience: Abraham {is} the model. {The} monk should be in a state of "continuous listening" (1)[368] in order to learn. Obedience {is} the way to learn (5).[369]

---

the place which your mercy has prepared. Expecting to see me in a place which was made ready for me because of my offences, let him see me in a place of light and eternal life and find himself in darkness and confusion because his desire has in no way been fulfilled. And so, most kind lover of men, who are alone without sin, pour out upon me your unimaginable and immeasurable mercy and grant that both I and those who love you might become heirs of your kingdom, and seeing your glory, might adore your goodness, and may we who have been made worthy to see the unending beauty of your majesty say together: Glory to the Father who made us, Glory to the Son who healed us, Glory to the Holy Spirit who has renewed us, Holy Trinity, One God, beneath the shadow of your wings protect us, you who are blessed forever. Amen" (the typescript reads "102", ". . . quem praeparaverit . . . *ut ego* . . ."; "*Amen*" is added by Merton to the text).

364. Arthur Vööbus, *Syriac and Arabic Documents Regarding Legislation Relative to Syrian Asceticism* (Stockholm: Estonian Theological Society in Exile, 1960).

365. Vööbus, *Documents*, 17–23.

366. See Vööbus, *Documents*, 18, n. 6.

367. Vööbus, *Documents*, 18.

368. Vööbus, *Documents*, 19.

369. Vööbus, *Documents*, 20.

Honor one's Masters and be grateful for their care, especially by carrying out their teachings and exemplifying the truth of what they say (3).[370]

Maturity: {There is a} stress on definitely putting away "childish ways" in order to be able to learn by obedience (7, 11, 12).[371] Fear of the Masters begets discipline, maturity. (Read [copy] n. 9—p. 20).[372] Vainglory in particular is a sign of immaturity. One must take refuge in the Creator (by what we have elsewhere described[373] as anagogic acts). Read (copy) n. 13, p. 21.[374] Immaturity according to this text means: a) lack of discipline—passive surrender to emotions and sense appetites; b) vainglory especially, trusting in one's "image" of oneself. Question—in what way does a mature man place himself in dependence on another man? Discuss this modern problem.

Hope in God, taking refuge in Him by prayer and meditation on His word, is the chief way to escape sin, overcome passion, and mature. READ (copy) nn. 15, 16, 17, 18, 19.[375] This makes one steadfast. But irresponsible conduct, foolish laughter and talk deprive one of grace (20).

Summary: "Praise God who made you worthy of his (monastic) institution; and pray for your masters who have been

370. Vööbus, *Documents*, 19.

371. Vööbus, *Documents*, 20, 21.

372. "It is good for you that you are being educated in the fear of your masters; and become humble and chaste and disciplined, and do not become undisciplined."

373. See above, page 237.

374. "When the (thoughts of) vainglory increase in you like in a child, take refuge (lit. run) at the throne (lit. door) of the Creator and inter them there."

375. Vööbus, *Documents*, 21–22: "15. Hope in the deliverance by Him to whose throne (lit. door) you take the refuge (lit. you run); and say as the Son of Jesse: 'teach me, Lord, the way of Thy commandments and I shall keep them'; and again say: 'how love I Thy law! It is my meditation all the day.' 16. Exercise yourself in the holy psalms, and behold you save yourself like a bird from the snare of a hunter. 17. Slip your feet out from the nooses of guile by meditating on the law of the Lord day and night. 18. Your hunter is unceasing and shrewd—(but) there is the Artificer, God, and He is able to free you from his guile. 19. Call on God for your help, and He will make you a disciple of steadfastness."

wearied (by labor) because of you; and for your fathers who have brought you to the (monastic) instruction" (21).[376] {The} importance of living tradition in the monastic life must always be remembered.

Rules of Rabbula[377]—{In the} fifth century, Rabbula, a rich pagan, was converted to Christianity and to monastic life by a recluse {named} Abraham. After sending his wife and children to monasteries, he enters {the} monastery of Abraham. {He was} elected Bishop of Edessa {in} 411. His monastic life was cenobitic, but primitive and poor. These cenobites were of a special school who, *relying on God's grace, as a special program, avoided expansion, growing to complicated life, with much business and many exterior relations*. The *Rules* of Rabbula represent this conservative and primitive view, and resist the growth and expansion of large-scale and business-like cenobitic development.

The Rules are concerned above all with regulating contacts with the outside. {They emphasize the} danger of contacts with women: these must be kept out of the monasteries (1).[378] Contacts with {the} outside are to be restricted to one officer, the *sa'ura*. He alone is to go to the villages, and he is to be very careful not to consort with women, or sleep in the village, but to go to a church or monastery for the night.[379]

Regulating business (n. 11): "There shall be no business-affairs of buying and selling in the monasteries, except only for that {. . .} which is sufficient for their needs, without greediness" (p. 29); also see n. 25,[380] against making money on the harvest. Against ownership: read (copy) {n.} 12.[381] {It is also} against going out to engage in lawsuits (15).[382] Visits, even with relatives, are

376. Vööbus, *Documents*, 22.

377. Vööbus, *Documents*, 24–50.

378. Vööbus, *Documents*, 27.

379. Vööbus, *Documents*, 27 (nn. 2, 3).

380. Vööbus, *Documents*, 33.

381. Vööbus, *Documents*, 30: "No one of those brothers who are in the monasteries shall possess anything, privately for himself besides that which belongs to the community of brothers and is under the authority of the *risdaira*."

382. Vööbus, *Documents*, 30.

restricted (forbidden outside {the} monastery) (13).[383] Monks who are sick must stay in {the} monastery and bear the sickness there, not seeking treatment outside.[384] Monks must not offer their work as an excuse for missing the office (16).[385] Parish work in the villages is provided for, by trustworthy monks (21).[386] Laypeople {are} not to be brought in for funerals (24).[387] Other special matters: receiving monks from other monasteries {is} not {allowed} without permission of his superior (26).[388] Restriction on hermit life: {it is} only for the brother "who has given proof regarding works during a long period of time" (18).[389] Caution {should be exercised} in relations with heretics (n. 48 ff.).[390]

Anonymous Canons:[391] "which are necessary for the monks"[392] include the following—"A monk who knows Psalms shall sing; that one who has learning, shall speak at the time of prayer in the church, or—let him write, so that he may not be condemned with that one who hid his talent in the ground" (n. 1; p. 71); cf. n. 14: "It is right for the monks to clothe zeal in doctrine for the Church their mother and teach the mystery of faith . . . . They shall not become as a soil that (produces) no fruits in order that they shall not receive a curse and cleansing of the sons of fire, as the Apostle says" (p. 74); n. 23: Penance for a monk who beats his brother {is} three months' fast.[393] {There are} canons against owning too much farm land and livestock, against engaging in business (nn. 2, 3, 10, 17).[394] *Beardless boys shall not be received as monks or dwell in* {*the*}

383. Vööbus, *Documents*, 30.
384. Vööbus, *Documents*, 30 (n. 14).
385. Vööbus, *Documents*, 30.
386. Vööbus, *Documents*, 31.
387. Vööbus, *Documents*, 32.
388. Vööbus, *Documents*, 33.
389. Vööbus, *Documents*, 31.
390. Vööbus, *Documents*, 48 (nn. 48-51).
391. Vööbus, *Documents*, 69–77.
392. Vööbus, *Documents*, 71 (title).
393. Vööbus, *Documents*, 76.
394. Vööbus, *Documents*, 71, 73, 75.

monastery (p. 72).[395] *"It is not lawful for a monk to make for himself brothers and sisters from the cross instead of bodily brothers"* (n. 7; p. 72). Monk priests are not to serve in parishes unless there is a special need (n. 11; p. 73). Love of the poor, and especially strangers {is paramount}. (Read [copy] n. 13; p. 73–74.[396])

Philoxenos: In the *Rules* of Vööbus (p. 53–54) is a "Rule" of Philoxenos—i.e., a letter on zeal. It is principally concerned with the monk's duty to bear witness to the truth (of faith above all) and not be silent out of human respect, or in order to remain in favor with those in power. To fail to testify to the truth because one has received gifts from the powerful is to be like Judas who sold the Lord (n. 1). A monk who allows himself to be influenced by human favor "does not know God" (n. 2). "A monk who is frightened before (worldly) power and ceases from zeal is not conscious of the Messiah" (n. 3). "A monk who puts on sackcloth but becomes silent about the truth has the leprosy of Giezi for his garment" (n. 5). Neither ascetic mortification nor mystical graces of prayer can exempt a monk from bearing witness to the truth and thus facing persecution.

Philoxenos of Mabbug (5th–6th century)

Introduction

1. *Mar Philoxenos*—{the} Monophysite bishop of Mabbug, {is} honored as a saint and doctor of the Church by the Jacobites, Copts and Ethiopians (18th February or 16th August). Mabbug (Hierapolis, today Mambidj) {is located} between Antioch and the Euphrates. {He was} born in Persia, studied at Edessa, {and} became bishop {in} 485 (elevated by {the} Monophysite Patriarch

395. Vööbus, *Documents*, n. 5.

396. "It is right for monks that they shall clothe themselves with mercy and pity of atonement towards the poor and needy, and especially towards the strangers who live among them, in order that the Messiah shall confess goodness from them that 'I was a stranger and you have gathered me,' and again 'forget not love of the strangers.'"

of Antioch). {He was} exiled {in} 519 (because of Monophysitism) {and} died {in} 523 at Gangres.

Works—Exegetical—on {the} Gospels (not published). Theological—*De Trinitate; De Inhumanatione Unigeniti; De Uno ex Trinitate Incarnato et Passo;*[397] and other works, mostly controversy against Nestorianism (listed in *DTC* 1517-1520).[398] Ascetical—*De Institutione Morum* (English by Budge [London, 1894][399]—compare material in *Sources Chrétiennes*[400]): *On {the} Parable of {the} Ten Talents* (not edited); other opuscules not edited; *Letter on Monastic Life* (French translation in *Orient Syrien*, 1961–1962).[401]

The importance of Philoxenos according to Hausherr (*RAM* 1933,[402] p. 175) is that he combined the Syrian tradition of Aphraat and Ephrem with the Greco-Egyptian philosophical thought of Evagrius and Origen. His homilies, preached or *read* to monastic audiences, are free of Monophysitism. His Monophysitism depended on the fact that he took nature and person to be the same, though frequently saying Christ was both God and Man. He was closer to {the} Council of Chalcedon than to the Monophysites condemned by the Council (E. Lemoine, introduction to *Homilies of Philoxenos*, Sources Chrétiennes 44, p. 16). He was so opposed to Nestorianism that he feared the term "two natures." "The homilies reveal to us . . . a Philoxenos anxious to gather the teachings of tradition, but a Philoxenos who came out of the desert

397. *On The Trinity; On the Incarnation of the Only-Begotten; On One of the Trinity Who Became Incarnate and Suffered.*

398. E. Tisserant, "Philoxène de Mabboug," *DTC*, 12, cols. 1509-32.

399. E. A. Wallis Budge, *The Discourses of Philoxenus Bishop of Mabbôgh, A.D. 485–519*, 2 vols. (London: Asher, 1893, 1894); this edition includes the Syriac text as well as an English translation.

400. Philoxène de Mabboug, *Homélies*, trans. Eugène Lemoine, SC 44 (Paris: Éditions du Cerf, 1956).

401. This letter is now considered to have been written not by Philoxenos but by the later Syriac writer Joseph Hazzaya (8th c.): see Joseph Hazzaya, *Lettre sur les Trois Étapes de la Vie Monastique*, ed. and trans. Paul Harb and François Graffin, *Patrologia Orientalis*, vol. 202 (Brepols: Turnhout, 1992).

402. Irénée Hausherr, "Contemplation et Saintété: Une Remarquable Mise en Point par Philoxène de Mabboug," *Revue d'Ascetique et de Mystique*, 14 (1933), 171–95.

and for whom *the witnesses of tradition are the wise men, the saints of the desert, rather than the bishops. . . .* [For him] the bishops baptize but do not preach the Gospel to the baptized. *They make good citizens out of them at the most, leading them to practise the justice of the world but not the justice of Christ: the Gospel is taught and lived only in the desert*" (*id.*, p. 16).[403]

2. *Homilies and Doctrine.* Note the long general title to manuscript collections of his homilies. Note on *titles*: usually the copyist of an important work tends to improvise a long title which is a summary of the whole contents. For instance, the important *Letter* 11 of Philoxenos to another abbot has this title in one ms.: "Letter which Mar Philoxenos sent to one of his friends, an archimandrite: on the beginnings after one has left the world, on obedience in the monastery, on staying in the cell, silence and solitude, struggles and revelations, the tribulations and joys which come to those who live in silence. The letter is divided into three chapters according to the three stages. *Understand!*"[404] {Another:} "Treatise on the teaching of Rules which were written by the Blessed Mar Philoxenos, bishop of Mabbug, by which he makes known, first the general order of *discipline* by which one begins in the state of *disciple* of Christ, then by what *laws and rules* one advances until he reaches that *spiritual love* from which is born that *perfection that makes us like unto Christ*, as the Apostle Paul has said" (p. 9).[405] The title is a condensation of an entire theology of the spiritual life. Note the Latin abbreviates this as *De Institutione Morum*[406] (n.b. *tradition*). "*Mores*" {are} not only customs, habits but especially "rules which monks make for themselves" (p. 11). This is a teaching of Rules, especially the spirit of rules. *The letter of rules is learned from others* by the words of teachers. The *Spirit of rules, which is liberty, is taught by God* Himself, and is learned in the heart.

403. Emphasis, here and in subsequent quotations, added by Merton.

404. "Lettre sur la Vie Monastique," 318.

405. Philoxène, *Homélies* (unless otherwise noted, subsequent unattributed page numbers in the text are to this work).

406. *On Instruction in the Rules.*

Examples:

1) On *Faith*—What is important *above all is the reason for believing*, not the truth believed only. One may believe the truths of faith for various reasons. But if when a man teaches the word of God one hears God Himself teaching, then one immediately believes because he hears God.

2) On *Eating*—The Rule prescribes what to eat, when to fast, etc.:

a) In {the} monastery—the Spirit may show one to eat less than {the} Rule allows, to combat self-indulgence;

b) Outside {the} monastery—the Spirit may lead one to eat things not permitted by {the} Rule, to be all things to all men.

The world is under the law of constraint. The Church (formed perfectly only in the desert) *lives by God's own life and by His Justice and is under no merely exterior law.*

3. *Literary Genre*: MEMRA—These are not homilies in the Western sense {but} a particular literary genre in Syrian monasticism: *the discourse written to be read aloud to a community of monks or a gathering of hermits*: "The very special genre of the spiritual reading, a genre in use only in religious communities; when he wrote these [homilies] it was with the intention of reading them himself to the monks" (Lemoine, p. 13), but they were then edited for (private) readers.

4. *The Introductory Sermon*—{this is the} basis of all the Sermons:

1) The foundation of the monastic life (discipleship) is learning Christ *in the heart* (by deep assimilation and experience) and not only "in the ear."[407]

2) In the monastic life, when one overcomes the passions of the world one is in danger merely of passing over to other passions, proper to monks (vanity, pride, etc.) and thus simply conquering one set of desires by another.

407. Lemoine, Introduction, 17.

3) The only solution to this is to pass over entirely to a supernatural life in the death and resurrection of Christ.

5. *The Collection* is incomplete:

a) There are six sermons on the state of the *disciple* (beginner, novice): two on faith, two on simplicity, two on the fear of God;

b) {These are} followed by six sermons on those *advancing* to perfection; two on renunciation of the world, two on the fight against gluttony, two on the fight against fornication.

In each pair, the first sermon tends to be a discussion of the *letter*, the material and external aspect of the subject, the second its spiritual and interior fulfillment. For instance, on *renunciation*, the first sermon shows the Christian as *not of this world by baptism, and living by almsgiving and detachment from material things*; the second shows the *mature* Christian, who *has left the world altogether* and thus become *fully aware of who he is*. In the world, the Christian is living and holy but only like a foetus in the womb. Born out of the world by monastic renunciation, he becomes fully aware of himself as a person in Christ. He is able *consciously* to live his Christian discipleship. In the first sermon of each pair he tends to reproduce commonly accepted ideas (v.g. from Aphraat); in the second he is deeper and more original. Note: we do not have the third series, on perfection and contemplation. ({For a} Bibliography, see *RAM*: Hausherr on Philoxenos—1933 [vol. 14], p. 171–195; *DTC*: Tisserant on Philoxenos—vol. 12.)

Division of {the} Spiritual Life—What are the *three divisions* in Philoxenos? They correspond in general to the familiar beginners, progressives, perfect; or the three degrees of Pseudo-Denys: purgation, illumination, union;[408] or those of Origen—Evagrius: *praxis* (*ascesis*), *theoria physica*, *theologia*;[409] or St. Bernard:

408. Pseudo-Dionysius, *Ecclesiastical Hierarchy* 5.I.3, 7; 6.III.5-6; *Celestial Hierarchy* 3.2; 7.2-3; 10.1: see Bernard McGinn, *The Foundations of Mysticism: Origins to the Fifth Century—The Presence of God: A History of Western Christian Mysticism*, vol. 1 (New York: Crossroad, 1991), 172–73.

409. See Lossky, *Vision de Dieu*, 48 (Origen), 87 (Evagrius).

slaves, faithful servants (hired servants—mercenaries), sons.[410] Philoxenos uses the Biblical (Pauline) division, as does William of St. Thierry:[411] *somatikoi* (animal man) fight against sins; *psychikoi* (rational man) fight against thoughts and demons; *pneumatikoi* (spiritual man) {have} reception of spiritual gifts.[412] This division is specifically *Syrian* and not Greek. (Discuss the various implications of these divisions.) However note that Philoxenos wrote a commentary on the *Centuries* of "Blessed Mar Evagrios."[413] Note too that for Philoxenos the first degree equals ascesis in the cenobitic life (after {the} passage over the Red Sea—entering {the} monastery); the second degree equals passage to {the} solitary life in the cell (crossing the Jordan, entering {the} Promised Land and fighting the "seven nations"); the third degree equals attaining {the} height of contemplation in solitude.

Homily 1. The foundations of the spiritual life.

{The} basic idea {is} *order* in the spiritual life. Discipline {involves} *starting at the beginning and going on from there*. Prelude: {the} importance of starting, of *recognizing the need to work*, and not merely of being a "hearer of the word" who does nothing.[414] He who simply reads the word without responding in his actions is like a dead man over whom a thousand trumpets are blown. He does not move. So failure to respond to the word of God in action is a sign that the will is dead. In apprenticeship and education, the master begins by having the pupil carry out the smallest tasks. Wrestlers and fighters are first taught the basic position

410. See *On Loving God*, cc. 36–38 (*Treatises* II, 127-30).

411. See William of St. Thierry, *Golden Epistle* (*A Letter to the Brethren at Mont Dieu*), trans. Theodore Berkeley, ocso, CF 12 (Kalamazoo, MI: Cistercian Publications, 1976), 25 (1:12).

412. See Graffin's introduction to "Lettre sur la Vie Monastique," 319–21.

413. See Graffin's introduction to "Lettre sur la Vie Monastique," which cites an expanded opening to the letter in one manuscript in which this lost commentary is mentioned; note once again that this letter is now attributed to Joseph Hazzaya, so that even if the opening section is authentic it does not provide evidence for Philoxenos' authorship of such a commentary.

414. Philoxène, *Homélies*, 28.

which sets them "on guard,"[415] then the first hold; after that they wrestle. In a palace, the new courtiers are taught by the old ones how to walk, how to conduct themselves and speak before the king, etc.

{The} basis of the spiritual life {is the} struggle against the passions. The novice must learn *how the passions of the body work*, what temptations to expect, how to confront them, and then he will later learn the more difficult combat against the *passions of the soul* (cf. Cassian).[416] This means also learning *what passions arise as a result of our good works*. Certain passions are born of fasting, others of psalmody, vigils, etc.

> We must know what passion is born in the soul from fasting of the body, from continency, from psalmody in choir, from prayer in silence, from renunciation of property, austerity of clothing . . . what passion awakens in us when our rule is better than that of our brother, what passions come to us from the science of thought, what passion we fall into when we have overcome the love of the stomach for food, what other awakens against us when we have finally triumphed in the war against fornication; what passion is born in us from obedience to bishops, and what from obedience towards all; and what are the thoughts that are in us when we rebel against obedience; and by what teaching thoughts of indocility to the masters are overcome; by what thought

415. Philoxène, *Homélies*, 33.

416. The distinction between fleshly and spiritual passions is found in *Conference* 5, c. 4 (*PL* 49, cols. 611A-614B), where it is said that to expel carnal passions both bodily discipline and mental effort are needed, while spiritual passions require the remedy of a simple heart. This distinction is based on the teaching of Evagrius, who writes in the *Praktikos*, c. 35: "The passions of the soul are occasioned by men. Those of the body come from the body. Now the passions of the body are cut off by continence and those of the soul by spiritual love" (25). In his note on this passage, Bamberger writes, "Vainglory is an example of a 'passion of the soul'; pride, *acedia*, avarice and probably anger are also in this category. This emphasis on spiritual love as the remedy for these passions is a highly significant indication of the relations between *apatheia* and *agape*. Purification of passions supposes love. Love fully flowers only when the passions are put in order" (25, n. 42).

> we escape from the presumption of our own knowledge; . . . etc.[417]

This will then be a study of great psychological subtlety. He will also play one passion against the other. For the beginner it is important to: concentrate on special commandments important for them; obey their masters without paying attention to the faults of these latter; learn how to profit from the good works they do; how to conduct themselves in the cells of their brethren; the measure of fasting—fasting of body, fasting of soul, fasting of spirit; how to overcome antipathies to other monks; how to fight distractions in the time of silence and *how to keep alive in the soul the passion for God and the desire for pure prayer*; how to recognize by experience the harm done by unnecessary human contacts, conversations, etc. Only if he knows these things can the beginner advance with confidence in the way of his vocation.

HENCE THE FIRST RULE OF ALL FOR THE BEGINNER IS TO RECOGNIZE THAT HE IS A DISCIPLE, THAT HE DOES NOT KNOW THESE THINGS, AND THAT HE MUST LEARN. Beginners must be prepared to receive the knowledge of these things from masters, just as the apprentice receives his training from his master. Further reasons: *this knowledge is a new kind*, a supernatural knowledge. Hence it has to be received through someone appointed by God. And *if one is attached to his own natural knowledge, he cannot receive the supernatural knowledge.* He becomes detached from his own knowledge and judgement by tears of repentance and humility. "It is only then that he will approach the banquet hall of the divine mysteries clad in the spiritual garments that are required if he is to enter."[418] Better to begin his discipleship in childhood so as to grow up with good habits, says Philoxenos.

Duty of the Master: he must "consider himself as a tutor to whom are entrusted the children of a heavenly king, having a King for Father, a king for brother, a queen for mother. And just as those who educate the children of a worldly king apply them-

417. Philoxène, *Homélies*, 35.
418. Philoxène, *Homélies*, 38.

selves with infinite care to form them and strive through the children to please the parents . . . so the master must be greatly attentive to his disciples and to their care and their progress."[419] We are all physicians entrusted with the health of one another. *The remedy for every illness is found in the word of God*. In the word of God we seek the proper remedy, the contrary to the sickness: i.e., faith, against doubt, etc. ({Here} follows what is practically a list of instruments of good works—see this list, page 40–41 and note elements of definiteness, clarity, simplicity, so that the atmosphere of the spiritual life is *not confused and ambiguous*.) {The} resumé of all these works {is that} *death of the physical desire is necessary before spiritual desire is born in the soul*. {The} principle {is that} wherever there is a sickness there is a natural remedy near at hand. Our remedies are within reach, but we have to know our sicknesses and desire the remedies. Hence his sermons will progress in order, taking the remedies in their proper order: first: two homilies on faith; then, two homilies on simplicity; fear of God; renunciation of the world; gluttony; fornication.

Vocation: There is an interesting analysis of {the} vocation to the monastic life in the beginning of *Letter* 11, of which many excerpts are printed serially in the magazine *Orient Syrien* for 1961 and 1962.[420] (Note {that} Philoxenos insists that true Christian perfection is not possible in the world. A man in the world can be justified but cannot attain to full perfection which implies a deeply mystical life for Philoxenos. Those with riches can have the "memory of God" in the sense of memory *of words about God* but not a true [mystical] awareness of God.[421]) The passage with which we are concerned is in 1961, pp. 330, 331.

419. Philoxène, *Homélies*, 39.

420. "Lettre sur la Vie Monastique."

421. This is apparently a reference (not an exact quotation) not to "Lettre sur la Vie Monastique" but to a passage from *Homily* 8 (222–23), or more precisely to Lemoine's discussion of the passage in his introduction to *Homilies* 8 and 9 "'. . . celui qui a la richesse ne pense pas à Dieu; et si le souvenir de Dieu se lève en lui, ce n'est pas continuellement; car il n'est pas possible qu'il pense à Dieu quand il pense à ses biens; et s'il croit se souvenir de Dieu, c'est par un souvenir d'emprunt et non véritable' (n. 224). Souvenir d'emprunt, souvenir emprunté à

1) *A natural element*. Vocation to the monastic life is not without certain "natural seeds" for good, sown in our nature by God, and which immediately germinate where there is good will.

2) *An angelic intervention*. Where the "natural seeds of good"[422] germinate, immediately the angel guardian begins his work in the soul. *He awakens the fear of the Lord, fear of judgement, desire for heaven*. This results in *alternating hope and fear*, the result no longer of nature but of supernatural intervention. The angel then "awakens another impulse which *plunges the soul further into trouble* [anguish]: he drives the soul to penance, that is to say he represents to the soul all the faults it has committed; the more it sees its failures the more the world becomes, for it, an object of contempt, along with all its desires and passions."[423] Note {the} danger of "spiritualities" that seek simply to prevent trouble from arising, "peace of soul" at any price.

3) *Response of the natural seeds*. At this there is a reaction on the part of the natural good of the soul. It is strengthened and begins to develop. "The more the fire from these natural seeds [sparks] inflames the powers of the soul, the more the action of the guardian angel is strengthened, and the more the angel reassures the soul about the resurrection of the dead: also he fortifies in the soul the memory of the alternating fear of hell and desire of heaven."[424]

4) It is from this memory, awareness, that is born *the desire to leave the world*. This in turn further *consumes all remains of love*

---

la parole des autres, des prédicateurs, ou même des Livres Saints. Souvenir véritable, conversation personnelle de l'âme avec Dieu. C'est la distinction si chère à Philoxène" (214). ("'. . . one who is rich does not think of God, and if the recollection of God does arise in him it is not continual, for it is impossible for him to think of God while he is thinking of his possessions; and if he believes he is remembering God, it is by a borrowed memory, not a genuine one.' A borrowed memory is one taken from the words of others, from preachers, or even Holy Books. A genuine memory comes from personal encounter of the soul with God. This is a crucial distinction for Philoxenos.")

422. "Lettre sur la Vie Monastique," 330 (#6).

423. "Lettre sur la Vie Monastique," 330 (#7).

424. "Lettre sur la Vie Monastique," 330 (#7).

for the world, and for possessions, so that now the angel drives man to give away his goods to the poor, *to forget his own needs and put away care for the body*, meditating on such Scripture texts as Matt. 19:21, 16:24, 6:34, 6:24, which are quoted. "By these texts the angel guardian, as with fire, enkindles man with love and affection for God his creator. Then, wishing to strip him entirely of possessions, he suggests to him the idea of going out into the desert and living there with the animals, reminding him of the many men who out of love for Our Lord went out in the desert and lived upon grasses and plants of the field."[425] *Without these desires* of perfection and total renunciation it is not possible for men to break away and liberate themselves from the world. But with these desires, leaving the world becomes a relatively easy matter: "Just as fire eats up straw and reduces it to nothing; *so these impulsions loose all the bonds of the world and the soul is freed* so that the world and all its goods appear only as a dungeon of darkness" (332). At this point, the devil begins to offer his arguments, as we have seen or shall see elsewhere (especially fear). Meanwhile, pursuing the subject of the "natural seeds of good," we might examine Philoxenos' teaching on *simplicity*.

Philoxenos on Simplicity—The necessary connection {is shown} between *simplicity and faith* (*Homilies* 4-5). *Homily* 4 discusses:

1) What is simplicity?
2) *True simplicity is acquired only in the desert.*
3) Only simplicity can please God.

Man is made *simple by nature*. He comes simple from the hand of God. *Society endows him with craftiness and duplicity*. If a man were to remain in the desert, untouched by social influences, he would remain simple; and the *characteristic of simplicity is that it attributes nothing to itself* but sees all as coming from God. Even in monasteries perfect simplicity is not always found (*Hom*. 5). Ruse and craftiness exist in an atmosphere of "dealing, of buying

425. "Lettre sur la Vie Monastique," 331 (#9).

and selling, of trading,"[426] *the adjustment of mutual advantage.* Hence even in {the} monastery words may be spoken with the intention to mislead or to deceive. With this there may be a tendency to mock true simplicity. But the simple monk should not be ashamed of his childlikeness and his guilelessness. For the simple are essential to the Kingdom of God.

Nature of Simplicity

a) Unity: single-mindedness. "*It hears the word of God without judging it and receives it without questioning it.*"[427] Abraham heard the word of God, held it at once as completely true, and obeyed without afterthought. "*Abraham ran toward the word of God as a child to his Father*, and all things became contemptible in his eyes as soon as he had heard God's word" (4.75).[428] "*The Apostles did not require a long instruction: they needed only to hear the word of faith. Since their faith was alive, as soon as it received the living voice it obeyed the voice of life; they ran at once after Christ and made no delay to follow Him; by this it was evident that they were disciples even before they were called.*"[429] Simple faith *does not require arguments*—but as the healthy eye responds directly to light, so it responds directly to the living word of God (cf. St. Anselm, *Proslogion*[430]). This implies a mind *free from the tyranny of social prejudice and bad habits of thought acquired through conformism in the world.* "*The Apostles obeyed like living*

426. Philoxène, *Homélies*, 130.

427. Philoxène, *Homélies*, 93.

428. Philoxène, *Homélies*, 94 (the enumeration refers to the pagination of the Syriac ms. used as copy text by Budge).

429. Philoxène, *Homélies*, 95.

430. See Anselm, *Proslogion*, c. 14: "If I have not found you, what is this light and truth that I have found? How did I understand all this, except by the light and the truth? How could I understand anything at all about you, except by your light and your truth? So if I see the light and the truth I have seen you"; and c. 16: "In truth, Lord, this is that light inaccessible in which you dwell. Nothing can pierce through it to see you there. I cannot look directly into it, it is too great for me. But whatever I see, I see through it, like a weak eye that sees what it does by the light of the sun, though it cannot look at the sun itself" (*The Prayers and Meditations of Saint Anselm*, trans. Benedicta Ward, SLG [New York: Penguin, 1973], 255, 257).

men and went forth unburdened because nothing in the world impeded them with its weight. Nothing can bind and impede the soul that is aware of God: it is open and ready, so that the light of the divine voice, whenever it appears, finds the soul ready and receptive" (4.79).[431]

Readiness: Zacchaeus "hoped to see Jesus and become his disciple even before he was called."[432] *He had already believed the report of others.* This is simplicity (cf. Homily of St. Gregory {the} Great on Zacchaeus[433]). The temptation of Adam: *the simplicity of obedience is divided into "two wills"*[434] by temptation—this duplicity puts Adam in a position where he presumes to *judge the divine command*. But in this case he *did not show real autonomy—he obeyed the deceit of the enemy*, not the simplicity of the divine will. {This is an} erroneous concept of liberty—*the presumption that liberty consists in judging reality and deciding not to conform to it!* The Apostles {were} deliberately chosen for their simplicity—to confound the wise of the world. (Read 1 Cor. 1:20 ff.[435])

Simplicity of Adam and Eve before the Fall: (They knew nothing of "worldly affairs"[436]—which were simply irrelevant to their state.) God was always with them, taking them wherever they went.

431. Philoxène, *Homélies*, 97.

432. Philoxène, *Homélies*, 97.

433. There is no homily on Zacchaeus, nor extended discussion of Zacchaeus, in Gregory's *Forty Gospel Homilies*, nor in his *Homilies on Ezechiel*; Merton is perhaps recalling his brief comments on Zacchaeus in the *Moralia on Job*, 27:79 (*PL* 76, cols. 444-\45).

434. Philoxène, *Homélies*, 98 (the text reads "deux pensées" ["two thoughts"], though the context relates it to willing: "il voulut et ne voulut pas").

435. "Where is the 'wise man'? Where is the scribe? Where is the disputant of this world? Has not God turned to foolishness the 'wisdom' of this world? For since, in God's wisdom, the world did not come to know God by 'wisdom,' it pleased God, by the foolishness of our preaching, to save those who believe. For the Jews ask for signs, and the Greeks look for 'wisdom'; but we, for our part, preach a crucified Christ—to the Jews indeed a stumbling block and to the Gentiles foolishness, but to those who are called, both Jews and Greeks, Christ, the power of God and the wisdom of God. For the foolishness of God is wiser than men, and the weakness of God is stronger than men" (1 Cor. 1:21-25).

436. Philoxène, *Homélies*, 100.

> And He showed them everything from near at hand like a man. *And they received no thought about Him in their Spirit. They never asked: Where does He live who shows us these things*? How long has He existed? *And if He created all else, was He also created*? And we, why has He created us? Why has He placed us in this Paradise? Why has He given us this Law? All these things were far from their minds, because *simplicity does not think such things, but is completely absorbed in listening to what it hears, and all its thought is mingled with the word of him who speaks*, as is the little child absorbed in the one who speaks to him. So, then, God put simplicity into the first leaders of our race, and it was to simplicity that he gave the first commandment (4.84).[437]

Later, Philoxenos adds, in another connection: "God has chosen ignorant ones who do not imagine, when they have learned His word, that it is *their* word, but they know Him who has spoken and give thanks to Him . . ." (4.105).[438]

> At our birth, simplicity is at work in us before craftiness. . . . When children grow in the world they learn deceit by acting and growing. If someone were to take a year-old child and go forth and bring him up in the desert where there is no occupation of men and no use of the things of this world, and where he will see absolutely nothing of the activity of men, the child can maintain himself in all the simplicity of nature even when he has attained to the age of man, and he can quite easily perceive divine visions and spiritual thoughts and can promptly become a receptacle that will accept the divine wisdom (4.85).[439]

NOTE—compare here the idea of man's natural simplicity in Chinese thought (Mencius).[440]

437. Philoxène, *Homélies*, 100-101.

438. Philoxène, *Homélies*, 117.

439. Philoxène, *Homélies*, 101-102.

440. See Merton's translation of the "Ox Mountain Parable" of Meng Tzu (Mencius) at the end of his essay "Classic Chinese Thought," in Thomas Merton, *Mystics and Zen Masters* (New York: Farrar, Straus and Giroux, 1967), 65–68 (also

"If deceit and wickedness are acquired by education in the world, it is certain that *simplicity and innocence are acquired by training and occupation in silence, and that the more one dwells in silence, the simpler one becomes*" (4.91).[441] Texts from the Psalms on simplicity are quoted and commented {on} (4.91-92).[442] He does not even hesitate to call *Jacob* an example of simplicity—because he obeyed his mother in tricking Isaac! (4.97)[443] (which in fact is not far from the mind of the Yahwist; Jacob did what he was told and the Lord took care of everything for him). "*Thou therefore, O disciple, remain in the purity of thy spirit. It is for the Lord to know how He will guide thy life and He will deal with thee as is best for thee*" (4.101).[444] Note {the} special aspect of "purity of heart."[445] In all things and in all trials the essential {thing} is to remain with one's gaze towards God in trust and simplicity, not concerned with plans of our own.

Hope {is seen} as the stabilizing power of simplicity. "Remain simple with regard to all that you hear, and let those who talk about you not change you and not make you become as they are. For the adversary brings all this about in order to turn your spirit away from its meekness, to disturb and trouble your purity of heart, to make your simplicity deceitful, *so that you will become like those who fight against you, that you may be filled with anger as they are and become a vessel of wrath like unto them*, putting on the

---

published in a limited edition by Stamperia del Santuccio in 1960); in his introduction to the text Merton emphasizes the Chinese Confucian sage's belief in the basic goodness of humanity, one's "right mind," which has been perverted but could be restored by a humane process of education, just as the "night spirit," the "pervasive and mysterious influence of unconscious nature," can restore the abused mountain of the parable. See also his comments on the text in *Conjectures of a Guilty Bystander* (Garden City, NY: Doubleday, 1966), 123, where he concludes, "Without the night spirit, the dawn breath, silence, passivity, rest, man's nature cannot be itself. In its barrenness it is no longer *natura*: nothing grows from it, nothing is born of it any more."

441. Philoxène, *Homélies*, 106.

442. Philoxène, *Homélies*, 106-108.

443. Philoxène, *Homélies*, 110-11.

444. Philoxène, *Homélies*, 114.

445. The literal expression is "purity of [your] spirit," as in the passage just quoted.

garment of iniquity" (4.102).[446] "Simplicity is the vessel which receives the revelations of God" (4.112).[447] Simplicity in Philoxenos has the same function as Purity of Heart in Cassian.

Philoxenos: Letter to a Converted Jew (*Orient Syrien*, 1961, p. 41 ff.)[448]—This is a letter of encouragement and advice to a converted Jew who is seeking union with God in the monastic life. {Its} theme of the full *development of the New Man in silence and solitude* {is} characteristic of Philoxenos. Christ leads the Christian into solitude to defend him and lead him to *full maturity and to the experience of God and spiritual joy*.

1. *Introduction*: "You have begun well—you are following the way of knowledge and thus we may hope you will attain to wisdom."[449]

2. *The Two Ways—Asceticism* and *Knowledge*. *ʿAmlè*—corporal *asceticism*—{consists in} *the works that are necessary for true knowledge, which is not acquired from words* or books. "*Words beget nothing but words and if one sets out to find Christ by words, one finds only words before him*" (p. 44). "*But if one seeks knowledge by labors and austerities then this knowledge in person appears* before him and lets herself be touched by him and leads him to ascend her highest steps" (44).

Steps—(a) detachment from pleasure to attain to *virtue*; (b) *detachment from* {*the*} *world to attain to knowledge*. Silence is the way to this. {Note the} *Importance of silence—selio*[450]—as the way to knowledge. It is *silence* that marks the transition from active asceticism to inner detachment and spiritual knowledge. "*If you love silence then I know that you have experienced Christ Himself*. If one does not understand the word of the wise man, one does not love to live with him, and *if one has not first experienced the power of Christ, one does not love the silence that brings us close to Him*."[451]

446. Philoxène, *Homélies*, 115.

447. Philoxène, *Homélies*, 122.

448. "Une Lettre Inédite de Philoxène de Mabboug à un Juif Converti Engagé dans la Vie Parfaite," ed. and trans. M. Albert, *L'Orient Syrien*, 6 (1961), 41–50.

449. "Lettre à un Juif," 43 (#2) (paraphrased and condensed).

450. "Lettre à un Juif," 42.

451. "Lettre à un Juif," 45 (#6).

Two reasons for choosing silence:

a) One may live with a Master because one *experiences* the power of his word and one may choose silence because one has purity of heart and experiences God.

b) Or one can follow a Master because of his reputation, and one can love silence because one has been told it is good.

"Material silence introduces us into spiritual silence and spiritual silence raises man to life in God; but if man ceases to live in silence he will have no converse with God. Hence, as long as the mind has not silenced all the trepidations and agitation of the world it will not even begin to stammer a little conversation with God" (45). {He emphasizes} the importance of interior silence—calming down before trying seriously to pray. *The New Man is a "man of silence"*—{note the} relationship of silence and joy. But again there are two levels: by grace (of the Sacrament) one puts on the new man but does not experience this silence; *by the practice of joy one experiences the silence of the Spirit* (46). This means getting rid of *all* the old man by renunciation, and putting on *all* the new man, made in the likeness of God. If one does not completely renew himself in Christ, the old man becomes merely "the tomb in which the new man is buried" (46{-47}). (Conflicts of monastic life {are} due to this!) If he becomes a contemplative, the Jew, {a} member of the people who saw God in the flesh, will be a true Israelite seeing Him also in spirit (47). "I have the firm conviction that if someone of that race comes to be converted he will be more greatly loved by the Master of Election and there will awaken in him a greater power to experience the gifts of Christ" (47). *Asceticism is perfected in silence*—purity of body rejects desires but does not see God—but purity of heart rejects inmost thoughts of flesh and does see God. {One should desire} *to have Christ always by one's side*. He is the perfect model. The spiritual man must see himself with Christ on one side and Satan on {the} other, and he must rely always on the power of Christ (49).

Philoxenos: Letter to a Novice (*Orient Syrien*, 1961, p. 245 f.)[452]—*There is hope for progress* when the novice has:

1) "taken root in the earth of doctrine."[453]

2) been "consoled by the hope that gives strength."[454] This is hope in God, not in one's own powers—it is based on *a remembrance of the life one led in the world when abandoned to his own ideas, and gratitude for the grace that called one out of the world*—{an} *awareness that this grace puts us in debt and we must pay our debt to Christ*, by fidelity to the knowledge He has given us of his love.

Perseverance: The novice must put into his monastic life all the zeal and energy with which he formerly followed the things of the world. Perseverance is based on a "taste" for the things of God. "*Receive the taste for Christ who has called you; this sense of taste is in the understanding*; taste the chalice in secret; each thing is tasted in its proper place, and through those things which are related to it. The bodily senses taste the desires of the world, while the understanding of the soul tastes the sweetness of Christ" (246). Remembering Lot's wife, the novice must not look back. ({Is this} demythologizing? {Note the} existential situation here! [cf. Luke 17:20-36]).

Sonship—The Novice should not work as a *slave* or a *mercenary* but as a *son*.[455]

Other aids {include}: *constant thought of* {*the*} *presence of God; not associating with dissolute monks; strict discipline, austerity; readiness to carry out humiliating* tasks in the interests of the monastery, motivated by the humility with which Christ rendered services to his disciples; prayer: awareness of the mysteries of Christ, *especially the crucifixion*; psalmody: "*If you put your heart in the psalm you will learn, and if you enclose your mind in the verses of your office you will fill up what is wanting in the Passion*" (248); obedience even

452. "Lettre Inédite de Philoxène de Mabboug à l'Un de ses Disciples," ed. and trans. M. Albert, *L'Orient Syrien*, 6 (1961), 243–54.

453. "Lettre à l'Un de ses Disciples," 245 (#2).

454. "Lettre à l'Un de ses Disciples," 245 (#2).

455. "Lettre à l'Un de ses Disciples," 247 (#7).

to one's juniors, when occasion offers; silence: not seeking to hear news; never mocking anyone; not undertaking great things without being proficient in little things; not multiplying ascetic practices beyond one's strength.

Stability: "Do not move from one monastery to another even if you think you are prevented from doing works of mortification [where you are]. Rather apply yourself to confronting the difficulties of the place where you are."[456]

Reading {is essential}.

Courage and humility {are developed} in overcoming our actual faults. "There is nothing greater in this world for us than to show, on the occasion of some fault, great or small, heroic strength of soul, and not allow ourselves to be downcast" (253). Comment. {Note the} use of faults to face {the} truth.

Control of thoughts {is crucial}.

{Note the} *supreme importance of humility and obedience for beginners*. Without humility and obedience the ascetic life has no foundations. See *Letter on Monastic Life* (*Orient Syrien*, 1961, 337): "The first virtue which must be possessed by those who receive the habit (*eskimo*) must be humility, from which is born *obedience, which is a fruit of the spirit . . . and from which all good actions are born*."[457] Then {he} quotes: "He humbled himself . . . obedient unto death" (Phil. 2:8). As the disobedience of Adam brought into the world all evils, "so true obedience prepares, for him who possesses it, all the consolations and delights of the Spirit" (337). The qualities of obedience are then described. "It does not consist in a man doing what he pleases . . . *but in cutting away all his own will and doing the will of him to whom he has surrendered himself once for all*, even if this is displeasing by reason of the carnal desires still in himself. *If you do what you like, and do not do what is hard to you, you prove that you are not obedient and that you serve your own will*."[458] Josue and Caleb are given as models of obedience (*Numbers*

456. "Lettre à l'Un de ses Disciples," 252 (#27).
457. "Lettre sur la Vie Monastique," 337 (#23).
458. "Lettre sur la Vie Monastique," 337 (#24).

13), while all the others, disobedient, perished in the desert. So the cenobite who wishes to go and live in a cell (symbolized by the "promised land") must first prove himself perfectly obedient in community. On the other hand stubborn disobedience is the root of all vices. This is described in relation to *Exodus* 32 (p. 338, 339). Fixing one's eyes on the "serpent" of the obedient Christ (Numbers 14) saves one from the serpent of calumny and unjust reproach, so often met in the desert (p. 340). So too for all other trials. "By His crucifixion Jesus is nearer to you than the brazen serpent was to the Jews for He dwells in your heart, and in the secret recesses of your soul there shines the radiance of His glorious visage" (341).

Vocation to the Desert. *Homily* 9. Christ going out into the desert is the model of monastic renunciation. The monk, like Christ, goes into the desert to engage in combat with the spiritual enemy. *He must not take anything of the world with him. He leaves the world in the "Jordan" or the "Red Sea" on his way into the desert.* The Holy Spirit accompanies those who go out into the desert, but only if they rely on *no other source of strength.* "The disciples who abandon the company of the world are at once aided by the Spirit, and when they have despised human help they win celestial assistance; as soon as they reject bodily strength, spiritual strength is given to them at once."[459] (Here the world is considered as an end in itself, a closed system in which individual survival is cared for.)

Jesus before and after baptism: Before baptism Jesus is subject to the Law. *After it, He has no law but the Spirit and the will of His Father.* "Man is born from one world into another when he passes *from the rule of the world to the rule of Christ*, and from being the master of possessions to the renunciation that God asks of him. When a man is in the world he is subject to a rule that demands that he do all those things of the world; when he is gone out after Jesus it is demanded of him that he fulfill the spiritual law, *according to the order of the place into which he is come.*"[460] This last

459. Philoxène, *Homélies*, 245-46.

460. Philoxène, *Homélies*, 246.

phrase refers not to a written or traditional set of rules, but to the mode of life dictated by the very nature of the desert. Really going out of the world means giving away all one's goods to the poor and "coming forth naked as one came forth from the womb."[461] He insists that going out into the desert is really a new birth. This throws much light on the traditional doctrine of religious profession as a second baptism. It is in so far as it is a death and a resurrection to a new life. A mere change of worldly habits into other worldly habits will not suffice. ({Note the} ambiguity of Philoxenos' concept: Christian life "in the world" for him is insufficient. Is this the Biblical concept?) The new life {entails} "*renouncing one's own thoughts, errors and ignorance.*"[462] What is this ignorance?

The child in the womb of the world. Though baptized and "saved" the Christian in the world lives only in the same way that a child in the womb lives. *He is alive, but he cannot make use of his senses.* Hence he is blind and helpless, spiritually. "The man who is shut up in the rule of the world like a child in the womb, *has his discernment buried in the obscurity of cares* . . . and human preoccupations; he cannot taste the riches of the rule of Christ and he does not see Spiritual things . . ."[463] (cf. Heidegger![464]). "The spiritual foetus, having accomplished all the justice of the law in the world, as though in the womb, goes forth from the world as by a new birth, . . . he begins a new growth and becomes perfect . . . not in the body of justice which is in the world *but in the spiritual person* who will reach the fullness of Christ."[465] Note the well-developed concept of spiritual maturity here. Good

461. Philoxène, *Homélies*, 247.

462. Philoxène, *Homélies*, 246.

463. Philoxène, *Homélies*, 247.

464. See *Climate of Monastic Prayer*, 34 (*Contemplative Prayer*, 24): "After all, some of the basic themes of the existentialism of Heidegger, laying stress as they do on the ineluctable fact of death, on man's need for authenticity, and on a kind of spiritual liberation, can remind us that the climate in which monastic prayer flourished is not altogether absent from our modern world. Quite the contrary."

465. Philoxène, *Homélies*, 248-49.

works in the world by no means constitute perfection. They are only the life and growth of the foetus in the womb of ignorance. "The foetus cannot become a man in the womb and man cannot become perfect in the world. No matter how the foetus in the womb develops, he cannot develop beyond the limits of the womb that encloses him: the justice of the Christian is confined to the limits of the womb of the world in which he is enclosed."[466]

The trauma of spiritual birth. We are born to spiritual life in the world by the sacrament and by faith: that is to say by "hearing" only, by being told of the mystery of Christ and of our participation in Christ. But now we must actually experience in our lives the sufferings and death of Christ. "*Now the time has come to will to leave the old man and to experience the fact that we leave him, by our labors and our weariness, and not just by the hearing of faith,* by experience, by sufferings and tears, by love for God and pure prayers, by continual petitions, by wonder and contemplation of God's majesty, and by the rapid progress of the hidden man toward the Lord."[467] The true maturity of the Christian is in that knowledge of God that is granted only in the desert. The justification of the Christian by faith and baptism is *real* but it is not a matter of experience, only of hearsay. He must experience *the new life that comes from liberation from the passions and desires.* Error and ignorance are closely associated with desire. *They are born in the "service of desire" and "when the heart is hardened in delights."*[468] In order to live serving one's desires one must maintain a false concept of the meaning of life, centered on the self.

Balance: What balance is to be maintained? Man is made up of body and soul. But according to Philoxenos, *it would be an error to say that we must therefore treat the body and the soul on an equal basis.* Hence the "measure" or "golden mean" of natural virtue is not enough. One must first bring the body into complete submission to the soul, and this means *giving it less than it might rea-*

466. Philoxène, *Homélies*, 249-50.
467. Philoxène, *Homélies*, 251-52.
468. Philoxène, *Homélies*, 253.

sonably require. He will treat this in a later Homily (10-11: Against Gluttony). To live even reasonably in the world, while amassing riches (even though one does so without injustice) is a life of weariness, frustration (cf. Ecclesiastes). "*What fatigue is more painful than to be wearied when one seeks to rest?* The way of human riches is a way without end in the world. The further one advances, the further one must go. It has no end but death. If you accumulate riches in order to rest, even your rest becomes weariness, and if even the delights of the world are heavy labors and burdens, what shall we call its labor? {. . .} Those who seek the good things of the world bear heavy burdens. They wear themselves out seeking loss" etc.[469] But "*the true rich man is not he who has many things but he who has need of nothing* . . ."[470] "The more the rich man enriches himself the more he is poor . . . The rich man is charmed by the love of what does not exist."[471] This theme of the weariness of the good things of life, seen to be burdensome, is familiar (cf. Gregory of Nyssa, *Commentary on Ecclesiastes*[472]). Thus, though a man may be rich and still be a "just man," he cannot attain to the perfection and the knowledge of God that are possible only in renunciation.

The Jordan. "Christ at the Jordan ended the road of the law and began the road of perfection which he showed by His passion to those who love Him . . . The Jordan was for Him the

469. Philoxène, *Homélies*, 254.

470. Philoxène, *Homélies*, 255.

471. Philoxène, *Homélies*, 255.

472. See the section "The Cycle of Desire" (*Commentary on Ecclesiastes*, Homily 1 [*PG* 44, cols. 624B-625D]) in *From Glory to Glory: Texts from Gregory of Nyssa's Mystical Writings*, ed. Jean Daniélou, SJ, trans. Herbert Musurillo, SJ (New York: Charles Scribner's Sons, 1961), 84–87, particularly the following: "But man, in his lack of wisdom, does not penetrate the phenomena to see what is truly to be admired, and admires instead what he sees. Now since the sense function is only temporary and shortlived, we learn from the profound words of our text (Eccles. I.2) that he who sees thus sees nothing. . . . What does the soul get out of all the toil of life in those men who live only for the superficial? In what is life to be found? Of all the things that appear to be good, how many of them endure?" (84–85).

passage from one world to the other, from the world of the body to the world of the Spirit."[473] After the Jordan,

a) Jesus fulfills the will of no one but the Father;

b) He takes with Him nothing of the world, no law of the world, no human rule or measure. "He went out alone with no one to help Him and without company, without friends to care for Him, without precious things, without riches, without possessions, without clothes, without ornaments; nothing of the world went forth with him but only Himself in the company of the Holy Spirit. Model thyself thus on the going out of thy master; go out also having with thee nothing of the world and the Holy Spirit will go with thee."[474]

c) One of the chief reasons for going forth without burdens is that the world pursues us into the desert and seeks to win us back. *If we have anything in us belonging to the world, the world has a claim on us*. "Cast off the burdens of the world in order to fight the world."[475] What this means especially is not only the physical renunciation implicit in our going forth, but especially the renunciation of worldly thoughts and desires, the renunciation of the *fundamental error* which is in the service of desires, and which centers on care of the self and its protection. Our cares will be left in the "Red Sea" like the Egyptians if we are generous and knowing in our renunciation. "Wash thyself in the waters of knowledge rather than in the Jordan and having washed, go forth in the Rule of the Spirit."[476] {Note the} long development of the comparison of the Egyptians in the Red Sea (p. 258 etc.). "*Before they came to the Red Sea the Israelites worked for the Egyptians. After the Red Sea they worked for God alone*" (p. 258). There are then two baptisms: the second leads into the desert.

473. Philoxène, *Homélies*, 256-57 (compressed).

474. Philoxène, *Homélies*, 257.

475. Philoxène, *Homélies*, 257-58.

476. Philoxène, *Homélies*, 258.

The Desert Life:

> Having come up out of the sea the Israelites received another law and were given another food, they slaked their thirst with other waters, obeyed other commandments and other laws, received celestial revelations, heard the voice of God speaking with them near at hand etc. . . . They had passed over into a world that was exempt from all the customs of the world. When you came out of the world you passed through a sea of afflictions and you were in fear and in sufferings. . . . The disciple does not taste joy all at once. . . . He fears afflictions, he is tormented by thoughts, he regrets having left the world. . . . The demons surround him like the Egyptians and darken his mind with cares, preoccupations, etc. etc. so that he cannot receive the light of the knowledge of Christ.[477]

The temptation of "thoughts" when one has just entered the desert (see page 259 ff. in detail):

a) Regret for having left a life that was after all virtuous, reasonable, just, etc. To have riches, administer them rightly and help the poor—this is a good life. Why desire to be a better man than Abraham or Job? A merciful rich man is a godlike man, a father of orphans, etc.

b) Fasting and penance would be all the more meritorious in the world because food would be right there, one could have it, one would have {the} merit of resisting, etc.

c) You could pray in the world, in your house, or in church, and you could bring many others to pray with you.

d) {There is} fear of sickness and death in the desert. The devils make the novice fear that fasts will ruin him and kill him. There are no medicines. Or if you use medicines you will be ridiculed by the other solitaries (261). The way is long; how can you stand it? You will never see your friends and relatives again. You may have to depend on the alms of others and thus you may be led to flatter those on whom you depend. All these and many

477. Philoxène, *Homélies*, 258-59.

other ideas produce "the chagrin of thoughts,"[478] sorrow, acedia, joylessness: "The joy of the world is far away and the joy of Christ is not yours because you have not yet reached it. Your soul is filled with fear because it is dark and deprived of the light of knowledge . . . and it is from knowledge that joy is born in the soul, just as in the world joy is born of the light of the sun."[479]

Prayer the Remedy. One must cry out to the Lord in prayer as did Moses on the mountain. Forgetting thoughts, concentrate on prayer—let the cry of anguish go up to God from the depths of our heart, thoughts or no thoughts, and then the sea will be parted and we will go through. "Then the light of salvation [like the pillar of fire] will go before you and the darkness will be behind you between you and the Egyptians."[480]

This theme is developed in the *Letter on Monastic Life* (*Orient Syrien*, 1961, 334–35). The Israelites, hearing they were to leave Egypt, were at first filled with joy and hope. Pharaoh (the devil) filled them with thoughts of fear and despair, and made them "labor harder."[481] The Angel of the Lord suggests fear of judgement—Moses knows they *must* go. Giving away one's property, one passes the Red Sea and is no longer pursued by {the} Egyptians. "Just as the pillar of fire between the Israelites and the Egyptians shed light on the Israelites and covered the Egyptians with darkness, so the Angel Guardian sheds light on the intelligence, covering the Prince of Evil and all his suggestions with darkness. For the more the soul is illumined by going out of the world, the more the thoughts of self-love disappear" (p. 335{-36}).

{Note the} metaphor of the Cloud: it is important on which side of the Cloud one finds himself. If {one is} behind the Cloud with the enemy, then {there is} danger, anguish—if beyond the Cloud, in the light, then joy and confidence.

478. Philoxène, *Homélies*, 262.

479. Philoxène, *Homélies*, 262.

480. Philoxène, *Homélies*, 264 (paraphrased and compressed).

481. "Lettre sur la Vie Monastique," 334 (#16).

> The black cloud is scattered, serene brightness rises upon your soul, you have passed dry shod over the sea of afflictions . . . you walk with confidence in a terrible place, you pass over the deeps that you never crossed before, you go where nature cannot pass, you escape the yoke of servitude, you ascend into the place of liberty, you leave Egypt with all its misery, the desert, filled with heavenly blessings, receives you, you have been conceived and born into a new world, the world of the spiritual rule. . . . Now you turn toward the holy mountain of God and you walk forward in a place where you never were before. . . . There you merit to see what is above the world, to eat the manna which your fathers never ate, to drink the sweet and pleasant water that flows for you from the rock which is Christ, to be in the cloud of light, to be illuminated by the pillar of fire of the spirit . . . and to come each day closer to the mountain of Sion which is the dwelling of the hidden essence, and to be associated in the knowledge of the angels . . .[482]

Here we might quote an important passage on contemplation in a letter of Philoxenos to Patricius of Edessa[483] (commented on by Hausherr in *RAM*, 1933; see p. 186):

> If the intellect looks within upon the interior man, *where there are no diverse objects to be seized in varying similitudes* but *where Christ is all in all* it is clear that the intellect receives *simple contemplation* [an Evagrian term, distinct from the highest contemplation or "theology"]. There is nothing that so delights the soul, giving it "*parrhesia*" in prayer [*parrhesia* = free speech = perfect trust]. For this is the *proper food of our nature* and when the intellect is in the realm of true knowledge it has no need to ask questions for just as the eye asks no questions and [directly] perceives the light of the sun, so the eye of the soul does not search but sees [directly] the light of the spirit. So too the mystical contemplation which

482. Philoxène, *Homélies*, 265-66.

483. This letter has been published in its entirety as *La Lettre à Patricius de Philoxène de Mabboug*, ed. and trans. René Lavenant, SJ, *Patrologia Orientalis*, 30.5 (Paris: Firmin-Didot, 1963).

> you, O man of God, desire *is revealed to the intellect after the soul recovers its health*. But to seek to learn it by study and inspection of such mysteries is mere folly.[484]

Hence the importance of *ascetic life* to restore health of soul and purity of heart, and above all *charity* without which there is no true contemplation.

Conditions of Perseverance in the Desert: This is a life of pure praise, the life of the Kingdom of God, not of man.

> Here is nothing but tranquillity and spiritual repose, all the inhabitants sing out the Trisagion in praise of the Holy Essence. . . . All you know is that you have joy, but you know not how to explain whence that joy comes. Instead of conversation with men you have conversation with Jesus Christ, and you sustain your labors without weariness because the awareness of Christ does not allow you to feel them and the ravishment of your mind in God makes you unable to feel bodily things. . . . Here as in the ark of the testament, in your spiritual understanding, are deposited the spiritual signs of divine knowledge, not in symbol but in truth because *knowledge comes to meet knowledge without intermediary*.[485]

"Here is no altar of gold on which incense is offered but the altar of the Spirit where all good and reasonable thoughts go up . . ."[486]

Important: all the signs, symbols, rites etc. that were used collectively by the People of God are here realized in the *spiritual person*. The worship of the spiritual person in solitude is then the fulfillment of all these signs in collective worship. The sacrifice offered to God here is more pleasing than that of outward liturgy: "Here is the living table which is Christ Himself. . . . Here the high priest Himself, Christ, consecrates before His Father living and reasonable substances . . ."[487] The condition of remaining in

484. "Contemplation et Saintété," 186–87 (nn. 22–23).
485. Philoxène, *Homélies*, 266-67.
486. Philoxène, *Homélies*, 267.
487. Philoxène, *Homélies*, 267.

this kingdom is then "to work legitimately in this place according to the justice of the place,"[488] that is to say in the spirit, in contemplation, and not according to the rule of the world, in outward works and signs. One must get rid both of "bodily rules" and of "dead thoughts."[489] One must live by the spiritual rule, *conversatio nostra in coelis* (quoted here).[490] One must not only fulfill the *external actions* of the desert life (solitude, silence, etc.), but one must think the thoughts of the spiritual world in which one now dwells. This calls for unequivocal renunciation of the world in all thoughts. One must not remain linked to the world even by the smallest thoughts and desires (here he uses the famous image of the bird held by a thread). Note—like St. John of the Cross,[491] Philoxenos also mistrusts *visions* and other extraordinary psychological experiences. "St. Paul says that all that the tongue can represent of contemplation in the region of bodily beings is nothing but *a phantom of the thoughts of the mind* and not an effect of grace. Consequently you must remember this and be on your guard against the phantasies of deep thoughts [unconscious images]. For the solitaries, with more subtle minds, seeking vain glory and avid for novelties, run into this kind of temptation" (from the *Letter to Patricius*, *RAM* [1933], p. 192). The inordinate desire of contemplative experiences is therefore reproved.

The Kingdom of Heaven: true science comes when one is no longer "bound" by the ignorance which imagines that the things of the world are definitively real.[492] This means in fact freedom

488. Philoxène, *Homélies*, 267.

489. Philoxène, *Homélies*, 268.

490. Philoxène, *Homélies*, 268, quoting Phil 3:20-21 (generally translated "our citizenship is in heaven" or the like in contemporary English versions, but the word "*conversatio*" carries the connotations of "rule" or "way of life"); Merton has translated the French ("Notre règle est dans les cieux") back into the Latin.

491. See *Ascent*, II.11 (Peers, I:96-103), in which John teaches that even visions coming from God are not to be desired; II.19 (140–48), in which he points out that even authentic visions can be easily misinterpreted, and II.24 (175–80), which warns that the devil can reproduce visions, and counsels detachment from visions of created substances.

492. Philoxène, *Homélies*, 270-71.

from cares and anxieties about the things of the world. The knowledge that comes to one who is free from care is twofold:

1) He perceives "the spiritual rule"[493] as a beginner;

2) As a progressive and perfect man he sees and dwells in the Kingdom of God.

The Kingdom of Heaven (enjoyed even on earth by the wise) is freedom from all care, because free of illusion. Philoxenos says: "A spiritual master has said [who? he does not tell us], 'The Kingdom of Heaven is a soul without passions, having knowledge of that which is.'"[494] The passions bring care because they bring *fear of loss*—hence also mistrust, anxiety. When one has forsaken care about worldly things and about one's own life on earth, then there is no room for anxiety. All is joy and hope. This joy is a foretaste of the joy of heaven itself. The Kingdom of Heaven on earth then consists in a beginning of the future life by the foretaste which is given us in: perfect trust; Eucharistic union with Christ, foreshadowing perfect union with His Person in Heaven; union with the Holy Spirit in faith, presaging the perfectly known union with Him in Heaven.

Hence it becomes important to study the "rule of perfection"[495] which is the way to the "Kingdom of Heaven." He mentions living examples of the rule of perfection: John the Baptist is the model of solitaries. He never sinned. He possessed the Holy Spirit from his mother's womb. "He received the Spirit even in the womb and grew up out of the world so that by these means he might possess the purity of the first man before he transgressed the commandment, and by this purity of soul he received the knowledge of the divine mysteries."[496] The rule of perfection is then the solitary life, in freedom, and far from men, avoiding all human conversation. {This is} the complete renunciation de-

493. Philoxène, *Homélies*, 271.
494. Philoxène, *Homélies*, 272.
495. Philoxène, *Homélies*, 274.
496. Philoxène, *Homélies*, 275-76.

manded by Christ in Luke 14:26 and Luke 9:60. Commenting on this latter passage ("Let the dead bury the dead"), Philoxenos paraphrases it: "It is not necessary for you to observe the law because I have observed it and have loosed it. It is not necessary to serve your natural parents because I have served them for all. Hence the yoke of the law of nature is lifted off you and you are left free to yourself in such manner that the world cannot oblige you to serve it, since it is dead to you and you are dead to it. One does not serve corpses. . . . Let the corpses bury each other."[497] {On} not looking back (Luke 9:61), {he has Christ say}: "I have come to divide a man against his father. . . . I brought the sword and you want to go and salute your relatives? . . . You run to sew up with your foolishness the rent that I have torn in the world. . . . I have torn this mantle of agreement because it was entirely woven in errors, and in its place I have woven the mantle of heavenly salvation."[498] Hence the need of perfect interior detachment in thought, to accord with the exterior signs of detachment, the monastic habit, tonsure, etc.

Philoxenos on Gluttony (*Homilies* 10-11): Note on fasting: {This is} an essential monastic observance and mortification. "Fight, my sons. Do not pay attention to the crowd that eats, drinks and sleeps and has no compunction . . . . He who fills his heart with bread and water gives the key of his house to thieves" (Pseudo-Macarius).[499] The *exceptional* fasts of the great saints are *not a norm*. They set a certain *tone*. Monastic fasting in

497. Philoxène, *Homélies*, 278.

498. Philoxène, *Homélies*, 279.

499. Merton, or possibly whatever source he used for this quotation, is mistaken in attributing it to Pseudo-Macarius (whom Merton discusses in *Cassian and the Fathers*, 81–88). The second saying in this quotation, though it is not found in Greek or Latin collections, is found as an apothegm of St. Macarius the Great (or "the Egyptian") in two Coptic sources, *The Sayings of Saint Macarius of Egypt* (n. 28) and *The Virtues of Saint Macarius of Egypt* (n. 45): see *Saint Macarius the Spiritbearer: Coptic Texts Relating to Saint Macarius the Great*, trans. Tim Vivian (Crestwood, NY: St. Vladimir's Seminary Press, 2004), 72, 120; the first saying is found in section 51 of *Virtues* (124).

the *Rules* (Pachomius,[500] Benedict,[501] etc.) is proportionate to the fasting of the faithful. {It} consists in *one meal a day at None*—of bread and simple vegetables like lentils, chickpeas, etc. And {it includes} a principle of *never eating to satiety*. Beyond that, *discretion* is praised, and the devil is the one who incites to excessive fasting. Evagrius teaches—the worst error would be to make a passion out of what is supposed to heal the passions (i.e. to make asceticism itself a passion or obsession).[502]

Homily 10 {is} a fierce attack on the love of eating and drinking—and a masterpiece of writing, but very long! "This corrupt and abominable passion is the door to all ills . . . all guilty actions enter by this door . . . . It is the most abominable of all the passions. It loads upon the body a second body—the body of desire, and this weighs the body down, inclining it easily upon the path down to hell. . . . ."[503] Why is gluttony the source of all evil? Because it darkens the heart, prevents meditation, makes us forget Christ, and when we fail to meditate we are ready to do any evil. "*The beginning of all good is the awareness of God.*"[504] Love of food destroys that awareness. *Ergo*. ({N.B. it is a} question of *consciousness*.) "The intelligence is weighed down with sleep. Thoughts are drowned by bodily humours. The fire of nature is extinguished by excess. The eye of the soul which should be open to knowledge is blocked up. . . . There are two bodies to carry:

500. See above, page 103, and below, pages 318–19.

501. See *Rule*, c. 41 (McCann, 99), which fixes the mealtime at the ninth hour from September 14 through the beginning of Lent (and on Wednesdays and Fridays from Pentecost through the summer); during Lent the meal is to be in the evening, while during Paschaltide and on other days during the summer it is at noon, with a light supper in the evening.

502. In the *Praktikos* (c. 15), Evagrius provides defenses against the eight passionate thoughts, but warns that "all these practices are to be engaged in according to due measure and at the appropriate times. What is untimely done, or done without measure, endures but a short time. And what is short-lived is more harmful than profitable" (*Praktikos; Chapters on Prayer,* 20).

503. Philoxène, *Homélies*, 321–22.

504. Philoxène, *Homélies*, 321.

the body itself and the body of foods"[505] (alienation). "Love of food destroys courage, destroys reputation, *deprives one of 'lightness' and freedom of action to perform good works.*"[506] Hence it darkens the sense of justice and deadens compassion. "A cow when it is full walks away from the feeding trough and lies down. The glutton, having filled his gut at the table of his cravings, does not consent to look upon another person with the eye of mercy and does not grant a share of his own goods to another who is in need, for, in total subjection to his own desire, *he believes there is no one in so great need as he is himself.* . . . And it is true that no one is in so great need as he who is the slave of his desire, for the more he grants to his desire, the greater is his craving."[507] It prevents one from learning, because it confuses the mind. It closes the door to the birth of words in him who must speak and teach. It deadens faith, makes one skeptical of the Scriptures and of {the} victories of saints.

Continual Temperance—"lightens, purifies. The weight of nature is diminished. The soul is full of light and joy—the body easily obeys the will—the *soul is free*—it is able to do what it likes, unimpeded by the body."[508] This dualistic view of man may be a bit crude but what he says is essentially correct in practice. His treatment of gluttony seems to refer to cenobites, because he speaks of the glutton looking at his neighbor's portion and grumbling because his neighbor has more (p. 328). He speaks of the glutton being furious because he is mocked by his companions. When someone calls him a pig, "he does not see that the insult is not in the word but in himself. *He is an insult to himself*" (337). Good psychology! *The soul of the glutton is dead*—because it has lost the power of self-movement. "*It is no longer moved by those things which are proper to itself—v.g. by knowledge. It is moved by the*

505. Philoxène, *Homélies*, 322 (condensed).

506. Philoxène, *Homélies*, 322-23 (condensed and paraphrased).

507. Philoxène, *Homélies*, 326.

508. Philoxène, *Homélies*, 325 (paraphrased).

desires of the body"[509] which are alien to it. Here we re-encounter one of the great themes of Philoxenos: *freedom & alienation*.

The glutton "destroys by this refusal of temperance the beautiful work of God" ({380}).[510] "He destroys the beautiful creature of God, his body, and throws down the building which the architect had set up" (380).[511] "He corrupts the noble members which God created by His grace to serve His Will" (381).[512] "You are the beautiful image of your Creator; why do you draw over yourself the image of an animal?"[513] "You have been made a god by the God of Truth, and you have made a god of your belly" (382).[514] "You have been made the reasonable instrument of His praises, but you cut the strings of your harp" (382).[515]

The Will of the Glutton. "You are the master of creation by the will of your Creator; why have you made yourself the servant of your belly by the will of your liberty?" (382).[516] "The sicknesses of the glutton come from will not from nature, and even if they germinate in the nature of the body, yet the will is their cause and they are born in him by his liberty, through intemperance" (383).[517]

Satirical Portrait of the Glutton. Like Climacus[518] and other monastic authors, Philoxenos excels as a writer in portraying gluttony (384 ff.):

> The childhood of the glutton is hateful, his adolescence ridiculous, his old age contemptible. His childhood is undisciplined, his adolescence lustful, his old age voluptuous. His childhood is full of play and amusements, his adolescence

509. Philoxène, *Homélies*, 336 (paraphrased).
510. Philoxène, *Homélies*, 341 (typescript reads "379").
511. Philoxène, *Homélies*, 341.
512. Philoxène, *Homélies*, 342.
513. Philoxène, *Homélies*, 342.
514. Philoxène, *Homélies*, 343.
515. Philoxène, *Homélies*, 343.
516. Philoxène, *Homélies*, 343.
517. Philoxène, *Homélies*, 344.
518. See step 14, "On the Clamorous yet Wicked Master—the Stomach," in St. John Climacus, *The Ladder of Divine Ascent*, trans. Archimandrite Lazarus Moore (New York: Harper & Brothers, 1959), 140–45.

> with adulteries and fornications, his old age with overeating and vain conversations. He not only hates to do good, but even to hear about it. . . . If someone speaks of the victories of the saints he is instantly overcome by yawning and the desire to sleep, and he shows the death of his soul by signs such as the stretching of his limbs and the whole attitude of his body. If he can get away, he goes, if not he falls asleep where he is. The soul of the glutton is like a dog . . . for as the dog sleeps while men converse together [since the conversation of men has no meaning in his ears] and wakes up at the sound of the table being set and at the sight of food, so the glutton, . . . etc. He runs to the table like a cow to the manger. . . . The feet of Abraham when he ran to the flock, moved by the love of God, to get a calf for the angels, were not as light as the glutton's feet as he runs toward one who invites him to dinner. Two eggs are dearer to him than the Old and New Testaments. . . . His prayer is short, his dinner is long. The glutton [who is now pictured as a monk] preaches discretion, advises against fasting and prayer, praises "hidden virtues" and considers all zeal excessive. He can quote Scripture in favor of his doctrine, viz. "It is not what enters the stomach that defiles a man . . ." (Mt. 15:11), but he does not relish the word of the Cross, or commands like Mt. 16:24. But he likes this: "The belly is for foods and foods for the belly" (1 Cor. 6:13). "Let not him who eats not, judge him who eats" (Rom. 14:3). He rejoices in these statements and gives them a magnificent welcome—without understanding their meaning. The fool![519]

Exhortation. Then follows a long exhortation to courage in abstinence and fasting, especially in order to attain *true spiritual liberty* by control of the passions. If we do not gain the mastery over our stomach we cannot conquer any of the other passions. This is a basic principle of ancient monastic tradition.[520] Food *as*

519. Philoxène, *Homélies*, 344-45, 347, 348, 350-51, 351-52.

520. See Cassian, *Instituta*, Book 5 (*PL* 49, col. 204), and Merton's commentary in *Cassian and the Fathers*: "Cassian *begins with fasting*. Start with control of the belly—the earliest, most obvious and most elementary passion. The passion of infancy! Today we have lost a real sense of the importance of fasting. If we do

such creates a veil over the spiritual intelligence; hence, says Philoxenos, we should confine our use of it to strict necessity. Even in the plainest and simplest foods the ascetic should fear gluttony.

The full stomach makes pure prayer impossible and the belly stuffed by

> intemperance prevents attentive psalmody. . . . The sleep of the eater is long, his dreams are agitated, his visions troubled, his desires frequently flow forth in emissions. His sleep is not healthy rest but burial under a crushing weight. When he rises for psalmody in the night, he is not really "up" . . . he falls against the walls, he grabs for the posts to support himself, he hangs over the stalls and rests his weight on them, or rather suspends on them the heavy bag full of food which is his body. . . . He is like a dead body among the living. He does not know what psalm is being chanted. He flies into a rage if someone tries to wake him up. . . . He may even sleep so soundly on his feet that he falls and crashes to the floor throwing the whole office into confusion . . . (369–370).

Homily 11 {takes} a more positive approach. The "ulcer"[521] of gluttony having been cleansed, the doctor now puts on the wound a soothing and healing dressing. The death of gluttony is now followed by the resurrection—the "taste"[522] of the good things of heaven. The hideousness of greed is replaced by the beauty of the new man. Abstinence is situated in the context of "cultivation of the person."[523] The ascetic renounces the world of affairs, and instead of owning and administering property and giving alms, he now cultivates his own person, developing the "talent" entrusted to him. "Having renounced all and having delivered his own person from the world he has now undertaken to cultivate the field of his own person. He plows his field, sows

---

not know how to fast, according to our strength, we will lack a realistic spiritual life right from the start" (157).

521. Philoxène, *Homélies*, 374-75.

522. Philoxène, *Homélies*, 375.

523. Philoxène, *Homélies*, 376.

it. . . . He no longer sows alien fields . . . but the reasonable field of his own person. . . . The first rule for cultivating this field is fasting and abstinence. Without this, the goods of the person are feebly cultivated and they do not grow strong, their power being weakened and diminished."[524]

Bios Angelikos—We glorify Christ by freely striving to live as "new men" with the grace He has given us. If He wished, He could have instantly established us in sinless perfection: "He did not do this, but He taught us to resemble angels, and then left it to our free wills to strive after their resemblance. He desired that we ourselves, by the power of our own freedom, should divest ourselves of the old bodily man and put on newness of life in the likeness of the angels."[525]

Freedom—consists in not serving a master alien to ourselves, but living autonomously. But desire is an alien master. "Take your food like a free man. Do not take food for the sake of another, but for yourself. Serve yourself, and not desire. You would be a fool to take food out of your own mouth and put it in the mouth of another—especially if this other is a mortal enemy! Desire has no force of its own, but it gains strength from you in order to keep you in subjection. Do not therefore give him strength by which he will overcome you! It is by your will alone that this enemy lives or dies!"[526] This means "exchanging spiritual for bodily food, desire for desire, table for table, sustenance for sustenance, fruit for fruit and dish for dish."[527] We have two stomachs. When we close the one to bodily food we open the other to the food of the spirit. We must remember always the heavenly banquet in order to have strength to resist earthly desires. Even the argument that we have a natural need for food is to be regarded as a temptation, since in fact it leads quickly to eating out of mere desire. We need a special gift to recognize what is real necessity and not mere self-gratification. The "normal hunger" envisaged by Philoxenos

524. Philoxène, *Homélies*, 376.
525. Philoxène, *Homélies*, 377.
526. Philoxène, *Homélies*, 382-83 (condensed).
527. Philoxène, *Homélies*, 377.

seems to come rather close to starvation. Hunger is "normal" when the strength of the members is about to give out, and they will not respond until we have some nourishment. Even then, one must be careful not to eat with desire, or sin will mix itself in with even natural eating. "Obviously," he says, it is not "natural hunger"[528] that we feel in the early morning, or even at the middle of the day. This is just greed. The weakness that comes on toward evening is the sign of a "natural" need for a little food. One should then break one's fast. Before that, hunger should be resisted as a pure temptation of passion.

He admits various degrees of *natural need*:

1) The need to keep fit, in good condition;

2) The need to build up one's strength, and recover a state of normal health;

3) The need barely to keep oneself alive. Only this third need is admissible for monks, in his mind. People in the world may legitimately seek to keep themselves in a state of perfect health, and eat accordingly.

Battle with gluttony.

1) First realize that the joy of victory will not be felt during the struggle, but only after true abstinence has been acquired. "If in the battle you are anguished and covered with sweat, realize that this is how it is supposed to be. It is good for your purpose."[529]

2) Realize also the full shame of defeat. "You are signed with grace to combat the spiritual principalities and powers, and how much more ought you to overcome the body."[530]

3) Dash the first movements of desire against the rock of Christ (a classic comparison in monastic literature: cf. *RB*[531]) (Ps. 137:9).

4) Resort to prayer and *despise* the solicitations of the belly.

528. Philoxène, *Homélies*, 379.

529. Philoxène, *Homélies*, 386.

530. Philoxène, *Homélies*, 386.

531. See the Prologue: ". . . who graspeth his evil suggestions as they arise and dasheth them to pieces on the rock that is Christ" (McCann, 11; the image is an adaptation of Ps. 136 [137]:9).

5) Trust God. "The hand of Christ is with you in the battle. His right hand grasps your right hand and his powerful arm sustains your feeble strength."[532]

6) Do not fight specific foods (meat, etc.) but *desire* itself. Realize that abstinence from foods not proper to monks is due to shame and does not constitute a real victory. "It is better for you to eat meat without desire, than lentils with desire."[533]

7) "Do not be led only by laws that are outside you. Let your law be discretion: if you feel desire in yourself, recognize that you are a slave and that the law [of self-denial] is necessary for you."[534] "If the movement of hunger comes from nature, moderate it, and if it comes from desire, uproot it."[535]

8) "Become without passion and eat as the angels ate with Abraham and as all the just of the Old Testament ate, and you will not be blamed."[536]

9) There is an intimate connection between greed and fornication. The next two homilies are devoted to lust. The main thing is to overcome impure desires. This is not possible unless we first overcome our greed.

Combat Against Fornication: Without going into details, we can observe that here we find the opposite of what was said in the homilies on simplicity. The main thing is *not to identify oneself* with the thought of fornication.

1) As man lost his simplicity by standing back from God's will and passing objective judgement on it, so he recovers purity by standing back from the desire of the flesh and viewing and judging it objectively, not identifying with it. But this is difficult, and one's spirit must first be free. If one is caught by the sensation of pleasure and held by it, this objectivity no longer exists. However, when "observing" the lust of the flesh one must by contrast begin to long for the purity of the spirit.

532. Philoxène, *Homélies*, 388-89.
533. Philoxène, *Homélies*, 389-90.
534. Philoxène, *Homélies*, 391.
535. Philoxène, *Homélies*, 391.
536. Philoxène, *Homélies*, 399-400.

2) However, this mere "analyzing" objectivity is of small worth by itself. The power of the flesh must be overcome by the power of the Holy Spirit and by divine knowledge. The process must be completed by *identifying ourselves with the Holy Spirit* (which in fact is not up to us, but is His gift; but by obedience we fit ourselves to receive this gift). If we do not overcome fornication by the power of the Spirit, but only by natural analysis, fornication will once again triumph.[537]

3) Basic principle: we do not go into the desert merely to overcome one passion by another, but to overcome all passion in the power of the Spirit.

Appendix to Philoxenos on Gluttony—Ascetic texts from St. Pachomius (see Resch, *Doctrine Ascétique des Maitres Égyptiens* [Paris, 1931], p. 226 ff.[538])

1) On Fasting. "Brother, the Lord has said: I came down from heaven not to do my own will but the will of Him who sent me. Listen to us, for I see that you are exposed to the traps of the enemy and in large measure deprived of the fruit of your labor. Obey the rule therefore, and when it calls you to eat, do not remain without food but go with your brothers, eat the bread that is given you with moderation and eat the cooked portion that is given. Do not satisfy all your hunger especially if your body is strong; but if your body is weak do not exhaust it. Govern yourself against the powers of your body until you have overcome the demon of vanity for he is pressing hard upon you"[539] (from the *Life of Pachomius*, 58; *PO* 4[540]).

2) To this same passage the Latin life of Pachomius in {the} *Acta Sanctorum* adds: "In addition I would not have you make long prayers in private: the prayer in common is enough until such time as you have overcome the demon of vanity who is

537. See Philoxène, *Homélies*, 478-80, 539-41.

538. P. Resch, *La Doctrine Ascétique des Premiers Maitres Égyptiens du Quatrième Siècle* (Paris: Beauchesne, 1931).

539. Resch, 226.

540. 485–87.

laying traps for you in everything that you do."[541] In both these texts: the common life and unostentatious following of the Rule are presented as basic in monastic asceticism.

3) Jobs in the monastery are very effective for penance according to St. Pachomius. "He desired that the brother who had been given some responsible work should profit by the troubles attached to his job and obtain the reward from the Lord for these troubles: this reward is the pardon of sin, because our Father knew that a job in the monastery carried out in the fear of the Lord, with faith, with application to the demands of the job, would earn a reward equal to fasting, vigils and long prayers for the glory of God. Secondly he wanted [all to be willing to take jobs] in order that no one would be overburdened, in order to give rest to those who had previously exercised the job and to give them respite from it" (Resch, p. 226–227, from Amélineau[542]).

4) Small services in the community are referred to as "adorations" because they give great glory to God.

> Those who seem to do only small "adorations" [services] in the community, services which are not worthy of honor, but who are found to be more perfect in the law of the Lord by their modesty and their obedience, these will be preferred to those who mortify themselves greatly but not in accordance with the worship prescribed by St. Paul where he says, "For God's love, serve one another." . . . Hence it is that those who are least in cenobitism and do not give themselves to great practices and numerous and excessive ascetic mortifications . . . who are perfect in the law of Christ because of their patience, who live in all submissiveness according to God, these will be preferred in God's eyes as elect before the anchorites (Resch, p. 227).[543]

On pp. 232 and 233 of the same book Resch takes issue with Butler's thesis that the monks of Egypt were always encouraged to

541. Resch, 226 (the reference is to *Acta Sanctorum*, 43).

542. É. Amélineau, ed., *Vie de Pakhôme*, texte arabe et traduction, *Annales du Musée Guimet*, 17 (Paris: ADMG, 1889), 375.

543. Resch, quoting Amélineau, 191–92.

outdo one another in ascetic exploits and to become "great athletes of penance."[544] He shows that they tended rather to excel in obedience, humility and modesty, at least in the Pachomian system.

Philoxenos: Homily 12—On Fornication

Why does the natural desire (of marriage) persist in the ascetic? For his advantage, to teach him the power of spiritual love.

> *The disciple needs to experience the force and heat of the desire of the Spirit by experiencing the heat of natural desire.* When the fire of lawlessness is kindled in their members, they can also experience the burning fire that Jesus has placed in them. Then instead of unnatural pleasure [fornication, being lawless, is "unnatural" for Philoxenos, but marriage is "natural"] *they experience the joys of our true nature*. Instead of the movements [of lust] which end as soon as they have begun, the disciple tastes the *joy of living movement which begins with a desire to see the beauty of Christ* and remains without end in the soul purified to be its worthy habitation (p. 443).

Hence, the thing to do is to make good use of temptation in order to grow spiritually by it, and not be ruined by it. At the same time, one who has experienced the joys and light of the spirit has greater cause for sorrow and shame if he allows himself to compromise with impure thoughts. But this can teach them the need for vigilance in thoughts, and make them realize that *the avoidance of lustful actions is not enough*. If one finds himself thinking of bodily beauty, he must realize that this is because he does not see the beauty of God. "*It is for lack of beauty that you desire beauty*."[545] *One must acquire a standard of comparison, and then judge.* If desire overcomes us, it is because we are cowardly and ungenerous, says Philoxenos (452). This is because desire would not have real force against us unless we allowed it to grow strong

544. Butler, *Lausiac History*, 1:237.
545. Philoxène, *Homélies*, 447.

and blind us (at least unconsciously). We must "teach the soul to live solitary in the house of the body,"[546] that is to say, {to become} aware of itself as not identified completely with the body and its desires. ({Is there a} danger of dualism and {a} split {between body and soul here}?)

Virginity of Spirit: "Though dwelling in the body the [pure] soul does not participate in its passions. *It does not unite the mystery of its love with that which does not deserve love, but living apart and solitary, in admiration at the greatness of God's glory, it dwells in a house of silence . . .*"[547] "A solitary mind is that which, living in the body, is a stranger and remote from all its desires and pleasures, and is with itself . . . etc."[548] When the soul is "solitary" in the body it can summon to itself all the natural energies and use them against the passions (or withdraw their use from the passions, rather).

The Allies of Desire—The body alone has not strength to overcome the soul. But it entices to itself the energies of the soul by pleasures of eating and drinking; all pleasure and recreation—"play"; fine clothes; conversation turning upon pleasures, desires, lusts; contemplating faces, bodies; daydreams; memories. *To fight desire, "take away fuel and the flames will go out"* (456). He advises "fury" against even small inclinations to the above. (Note: exaggerated effort and agitation do more harm than good. Peaceful, positive, turning away is more effective.) He admits anger is an evil, but use passion to fight passion in the beginning, he says. {He points out the} special danger of supposedly "spiritual friendships."[549]

Three Kinds of Fornication:

1) of Body;
2) of Mind (lustful desires and thoughts, consented to);

546. Philoxène, *Homélies*, 453 (the text says that it is through the reading of the sacred books that one receives the power to make the soul live solitary etc.).

547. Philoxène, *Homélies*, 454.

548. Philoxène, *Homélies*, 454.

549. Philoxène, *Homélies*, 457-58.

3) of Spirit (consent to false doctrines and submission to demons of untruth).

Three Kinds of "*Commercium*":[550]

1) of Body—legitimate marriage;
2) of Mind—study and meditation of {the} nature of things and {the} meaning of events;
3) of Spirit—contemplation of spiritual realities.

Importance of awareness of God's presence: in order to yield to sinful desires, the soul seeks darkness and oblivion of God. If one is aware of God, he cannot surrender to sin. Hence, keep the light of awareness burning, and you will not yield to temptation.

> Only the light of God's presence can restrain the soul from sins of the flesh; thus it must always preserve this light in itself, that it may continually shine there. The soul must not let the memory of God depart, but must be held by the pleasure of converse with Him. As long as the soul converses with Him it will not abase itself to converse with its desire. As long as the light of God shines in the soul, the darkness does not enter, as into its own house, into this place of light. As long as the desire of the soul is mingled with the desire of the Holy Spirit, it does not mingle its thoughts with the desire of the flesh (p. 464).

However, it is clear that the body may independently have desires which the soul does not accept. Union of the soul with God in charity does not exclude all bodily feelings. On the contrary, the combat of the monk consists in keeping the soul detached, untouched, even though desires may rage. "Therefore let desire work in your body, not for your defeat but for victory . . . let not its movement blind the eye of your understanding but act as an eyesalve to cleanse the eye of your thoughts."[551] Philoxenos recommends that we try *to draw spiritual profit from inevitable desires,*

550. Philoxène, *Homélies*, 461-62; Merton translates the French "commerce" (exchange, intercourse) into its Latin equivalent.
551. Philoxène, *Homélies*, 468.

studying them objectively, without panic, trying to learn the causes. Thus, according to Philoxenos, the monk even permits the heat of desire to grow, in order to observe how it works. But this, we may add, is dangerous. For instance he suggests that the ascetic ought to be able to *arouse impure desires and quiet them again by an act of will.* Philoxenos supposes that the intelligence will remain cool, objective and detached and not be blinded by desire itself. But precisely the danger is that while the mind imagines itself cool and detached, it has perhaps already been blinded and deceived. "If you have confidence in the power of the mind do not be alarmed by the movement of desire in your members; it is the occasion of much good for you, if you have knowledge and can draw profit from this trial instead of loss."[552] He admits this will not work as long as "the thought is seized by the sweetness of the desire."[553] It must be entirely untouched. The condition of *"drawing profit" is that one should struggle manfully to make one's desire of God greater and more fervent than is the ardor of lust in the body.*

Later, Philoxenos himself admits that if the mind is not sure of remaining free from desire, it should take flight from the combat and not try to gain knowledge by calmly observing the rise of passion. The practice requires a cool, objective power to observe without being affected by what one sees. This is not to be recommended as a tactic, especially for beginners. One can easily be misled by false confidence, and if it works one may still be confirmed in pride. Philoxenos recognizes this himself. A victory based on vainglory is of no value. Victory must come from God (p. 473). The real remedy is trust in grace, not in "the power of the mind."[554] However there is no harm in remaining calm and objective and not giving in to useless fears. *Fasting* remains supremely important, because an abundance of food is like oil on the flames (of lust).

552. Philoxène, *Homélies*, 465.

553. Philoxène, *Homélies*, 466 (this is a paraphrase).

554. Philoxenos speaks of the power of the mind ("l'âme se sert de sa puissance"), when detached from desire, working together with the grace of the Spirit (Philoxène, *Homélies*, 478).

Other Aids

1) Bodily sickness, the danger of death, etc. can be used profitably, as God allows and sends these to help cleanse the body of its alien desires. "When the body takes account of the afflictions that are ever near, and the continual sufferings which accompany life, it will extinguish the desire that stimulates its members; that is, the fire that is kindled in all the members like flame in kindling wood, fanned by intemperance, will go out and grow cold."[555]

2) Fasting. He repeats—too much food and drink is like pouring oil on the fire (of lust), but fasting and abstinence are like water. They put out the flames.

3) Avoiding persons and situations that lead to trouble.

4) Fervor in reading and in the love of spiritual things.

Conclusions:

1) To understand this treatment of fornication in which the ascetic combats it not only by flight but *by direct attack*, the usual outlook of Philoxenos must be remembered. "All teaching that comes from outside us accumulates in us through the medium of words. But the doctrine that we acquire by overcoming passion establishes wisdom in us by the experience of the fact itself. Such knowledge is worthy of confidence and is truly certain. And when the soul finds this wisdom, this is more pleasing to it than that which comes from outside because it is of our own household, and by it the soul rests in itself, its joy coming from within itself and not from the outside."[556] "Therefore observe [your passions] with the discernment of knowledge, understand and distinguish between your person and your passion, so that you may make haste to seek the purity of your person."[557]

2) Overcoming passion by passion is only a beginning. It is not real victory but only "containment"[558] of passion. Here the

555. Philoxène, *Homélies*, 467.
556. Philoxène, *Homélies*, 469.
557. Philoxène, *Homélies*, 470.
558. Philoxène, *Homélies*, 473.

desire of self-knowledge is regarded merely as a passion and its victories are not secure. The other passion may come back and win. *True victory comes from the love of the Holy Spirit overcoming the lust of the body*. This is the "divine triumph,"[559] the only true victory. The great thing is then not to gain knowledge by experiment with passion but to surrender completely to the Holy Spirit, to be led by Him, so that all our actions are spiritualized.

Appendix I. Abbot Mark

Appendix 1. Abbot Mark. *From the Philokalia*.[560]

1. Abbot Mark. Is this the same as "Mark the Mourner" in Palladius, II.l?[561] "Macarius said, 'At the time when I was administering the holy offering I took good heed unto Mark the Mourner. And I never gave it to him, but an angel did so from the altar; I saw, however, the palm of the hand of the angel who gave it to him.' Now this Mark was a young man, and he could repeat by heart the New and Old Testaments; he was meek beyond measure, and both in body and in thought he was purer than many" (Budge—*Paradise of Fathers* vol. 1, p. 197).[562]
Note—in *DTC*,[563] E. Amann writes on Mark the Hermit:

a) A "corpus" of works attributed to him is attested by Photius[564] and appears in printed collections of {the} Greek Fathers.

b) {He} is probably *not* an Egyptian or a monk of Egypt, and *not* the Mark mentioned by Palladius.

c) Probably {he} *is* a Mark who was a cenobite in Galatia and afterwards a hermit in Palestine.

559. Philoxène, *Homélies*, 473.

560. *Early Fathers from the Philokalia*, ed. and trans. E. Kadloubovsky and G. E. H. Palmer (London: Faber and Faber, 1954), 57–93.

561. This is according to the text and numbering in the Syriac version translated in *Paradise of the Fathers*; it is c. 18:25 in the Greek (see Meyer, 65–66).

562. The text in Budge begins, "Macarius the priest told us the following story, . . ."

563. E. Amann, "Marc l'Ermite," *DTC*, 9, cols. 1964-68.

564. Under the name of Mark the Monk (Amann, col. 1964).

d) Dogmatic and Ascetic works are attributed to him. We are concerned here only with {the} ascetic works:

1) *De Lege Spirituali*—{These are} aphorisms on ascetic life, {with an} emphasis on *grace*.

2) *De Paenitentia*—{This focuses on the} necessity of penance for all. Penance {is} essentially a matter of interior contrition rather than of external works. {There is an} emphasis on interior mortification by custody of {the} heart and acceptance of ordinary trials of everyday life.

3) *De Baptismo*—Baptism implants in us a seed of perfection which has to be cultivated by virtuous life and self-denial.

4) *Ad Nicolaum*—which we will discuss in more detail.

5) *Disputatio cum Causidico*—{This is} a debate with a lawyer, on {the} value of ascetic life. {The} lawyer is annoyed at Mark who has said that the life of the law courts endangers one's soul.

6) *Consultatio intellectus cum {sui ipsius} anima*[565]—{This is a} soliloquy on sources of evil in our life: not Adam, not Satan or others; but only ourselves.

7) *De Jejunio*[566]

(spurious—Maxims on *Temperance*).

2. *Epistle to Nicholas* (*Writings from the Philokalia*, p. 60[567]):

a) The importance of "knowledge and reason" in the quest for perfect love of Christ {is stressed}. This means zeal and energy, but also *direction* of others. Read (copy): p. 60: "For a self-reliant man . . . these labours useless and vain."[568] {Note the} danger of self-confidence and self-will in asceticism.

565. *Consultation of the Intellect with its Own Soul.*

566. *On Fasting.*

567. This selection from *Early Fathers* (60–62) includes ##10, 22–24.

568. "For a self-reliant man, walking without the knowledge and guidance of the Gospels, often stumbles and falls into many pitfalls and nets of the evil one, frequently goes astray and is subject to many calamities, not knowing where he will arrive in the end. Many have gone through great feats of self-mortification and endured much labour and sweat for the sake of God; but their self-will, lack of good judgement and the fact that they did not deem it necessary to seek salutary advice from their brethren, made these labours useless and vain."

b) The Spiritual Way. The monk must seek to walk the spiritual way, which is the way of the Gospels, and the aim of direction is to provide the humble and zealous monk with "your own lamp of mental light and spiritual knowledge so that you may walk without stumbling in the deepest night of this age *and have your steps ordered by the Lord*"[569] (cf. Ps. 118). The true light is then the light of God by which He Himself guides us securely.

c) The "inner work" {is} "to practice the most perfect Gospel commandments with ardent faith and become a participant in the passion of Christ through desire and prayer"[570] (cf. *Rule* of St. Benedict, Prologue[571]). But this requires diligent self-custody and holy fear.

d) The Three Giants—the "three mental *aliens*"[572] (comment). If these are defeated, all the rest of the passions are overcome: *Ignorance*; *Forgetfulness*; *Laziness*—{this last} strengthens and consolidates the work of the other two (also called "indifference"[573]). To attack other passions without attacking these is completely useless. But few really know these three, and even fewer come to grips with them. They are to be fought with {by}:

1) "memory of the good":[574] "memory of God's word"[575] ({vs.} forgetfulness). "Reflecting on whatever things are true, . . . etc."[576]

569. *Early Fathers*, 60, which reads ". . . knowledge, that . . ."; emphasis added.

570. *Early Fathers*, 60.

571. "we shall run with unspeakable sweetness of love in the way of God's commandments; so that, never abandoning his rule but persevering in his teaching in the monastery until death, we shall share by patience in the sufferings of Christ, that we may deserve to be partakers also of his kingdom" (McCann, 13).

572. *Early Fathers*, 62, which reads ". . . these three giants of mental aliens . . ."

573. *Early Fathers*, 61.

574. *Early Fathers*, 61.

575. *Early Fathers*, 62, which reads ". . . memory of the words of God . . ."

576. *Early Fathers*, 62: "reflecting on 'whatsoever things are true, whatsoever things are honest, whatsoever things are just, whatsoever things are pure, whatsoever things are lovely, whatsoever things are of good report; if there be any virtue, and if there be any praise' (Phil. iv. 8), you will chase away wicked forgetfulness; . . ."

(Phil. 4:8); cf. Symeon the New Theologian: "There is no protection against [agitation of mind produced by Satan] except through constant remembrance of God; in other words, if the memory of God, engraved in the heart by the power of the cross, strengthens the mind in its steadfastness. To this end lead all the efforts of mental struggle" (*Writings from* {*the*} *Philokalia*, p. 31; quoted by Nicephorus).[577]

2) "Enlightened [heavenly] Knowledge by which the soul is kept in sobriety"[578] ({vs.} Ignorance).

3) "lively zeal,"[579] {which is} "ready for every good action"[580] ({vs.} Laziness).

4) Without grace the above are unavailing. Grace unites these three in a "tripartite alliance"[581] and then the "three giants" are totally defeated.

The idea of the Three Giants as developed by Gregory of Sinai—14th cent. (d. 1360).[582] (Gregory of Sinai was influential in reviving Hesychasm on Athos.) The Three Giants fight with {the} three powers of the soul. *Prince of the Abyss*—wars on those who practice prayer of the *heart*. "He sends the lust-loving Giant of *Forgetfulness*," {which} stirs up {the} "turbulent sea" of passion, causing forgetfulness of God (*Writings from* {*the*} *Philokalia*, p. 67). *Prince of this World*—{he is} "in charge of warfare against the excitable part"[583] (*epithumia*—energy for action) {and} attacks those who follow active virtue—with *laziness*. *Prince of High Places*—

577. Nicephorus the Solitary, "A Most Profitable Discourse on Sobriety and the Guarding of the Heart," in *Writings from the Philokalia on Prayer of the Heart*, ed. and trans. E. Kadloubovsky and G. E. H. Palmer (London: Faber and Faber, 1951), 30–31.

578. *Early Fathers*, 61, which reads ". . . enlightened knowledge, by which a soul kept in sobriety chases away the darkness of ignorance, . . ."

579. *Early Fathers*, 61.

580. *Early Fathers*, 62.

581. *Early Fathers*, 62.

582. St. Gregory of Sinai, "Texts on Commandments and Dogmas," n. 122 (*Writings from the Philokalia*, 66–67); this reference is found in *Early Fathers*, 62 n.

583. *Writings from the Philokalia*, 67.

attacks the *mind* of those exercised in contemplation with *Prelest*[584] (illusory visions) or darkness and phantoms, "vague fantastic images of spirits and their metamorphoses . . . phantoms of lightning and thunder, tempests and earthquakes" (p. 67).

Appendix 2. Notes on Palestinian Monasticism: *Treatment of Breakdown by St. Theodosius* (5th–6th cent.)

Palestinian Monasticism: St. Theodosius {was} Abbot of Deir Dosi between Jerusalem and Bethlehem. (See the article "Erreurs de Spiritualité et Troubles Psychiques" by P. Canivet, SJ in *Recherches de Science Religieuse* [1962], p. 161 ff.).[585] *Theodosius* {was} born in Cappadocia. In {the} mid-5th century {he} went to Jerusalem to visit {the} holy places and stayed as {a} hermit. {He} visited St. Symeon Stylites on the way. In Jerusalem {he was} directed by Longinus, a Cappadocian hermit living in the town of David. {He} joins a community of *Spoudaei* in {the} desert, under a pious woman, Hikelia. When elected Higoumenos he flees into {the} desert—{later he} founds Deir Dosi. {In} 493—he is archimandrite of the cenobites in Jerusalem. {In} 529—{he} dies at {the} age of 105.

Treatment of mentally sick monks—a special feature of Deir Dosi.

1) Text—*from {the} Life of Theodosius* by *Theodore of Petra*:

a) Some ascetics in {the} desert, due to immoderate asceticism, no longer had a "spirit to preside over their thoughts" because their "combat" was not "according to Christ."[586] Having believed themselves to be responsible for their good works,

584. The translators retain the Russian term, which they define, following Bishop Ignatiy Brianchaninov, as "the corruption of human nature through the acceptance by man of mirages mistaken for truth," and they add, "we are all in prelest" (*Writings from the Philokalia*, 22, n. 8).

585. Pierre Canivet, SJ, "Erreurs de Spiritualité et Troubles Psychiques à Propos d'un Passage de la Vie de S. Théodose par Théodore de Pétra," *Recherches de Science Religieuse*, 50 (1962), 161–205.

586. Canivet, "Erreurs," 167.

pierced by the sword of exaltation, they were delivered to Satan for the punishment of their flesh and for their spiritual salvation. Source of {the} trouble {is} θερμοτης—the "overheated" ascetic mind. {The} natural fire runs away with the ascetic, out of control {due to an} inordinate trust in one's own natural spirits, {a} failure to follow direction or to acquire proper formation. {This} leads to exhaustion of {one's} natural strength, without grace (true asceticism, {based on} love of God, takes one beyond {the} limits of nature). {There is} "forgetfulness" of the Lord's word, "Without me you can do nothing!"[587] Errors of judgement are therefore punished, by "dereliction."[588] They become "twisted up" (στρεβλούμενοι).[589]

b) Theodosius, with Gospel compassion, received them into a place of rest (ἡσυχίας τόπον). Their "hesychasterion" is a "monastery within a monastery"[590] with its own liturgy, etc. He received them *"joyously, as a Father"*[591]—{he} wanted everything peaceful.

c) He visits, consoles and directs them, telling them to accept their trial in good spirits and in gratitude as a purification. "He helped some to get rid of their inconquerable fatigue [neurasthenia]."[592] "To others he gave courage to stand firm against their terrors."[593] *He does not treat them like madmen.*

d) His therapy {is} based on faith in {the} Fatherhood of God (Hebrews 12:3-8).[594] Evil has a providential place in God's plan. "He believed that in such cases it is better to be patient than to want to get rid of one's trouble, for the first way brings impassibility whereas the second proves that one lacks courage. For this reason he did not struggle to cure the illness but gave the sick man counsels to hold fast with generosity, offering to God the

587. Canivet, "Erreurs," 167.
588. Canivet, "Erreurs," 187–88.
589. Canivet, "Erreurs," 191–92.
590. Canivet, "Erreurs," 167.
591. Canivet, "Erreurs," 167.
592. Canivet, "Erreurs," 169.
593. Canivet, "Erreurs," 169.
594. Canivet, "Erreurs," 189.

humble thoughts that arise from our situation" (169). Canivet remarks[595] that if Theodosius had exhorted them to get rid of their troubles he would have severely stirred up the "heat" which was causing them. In urging them to accept reality he was permitting the "*nous*" to resume control of their "ardor" and restore equilibrium. {Note} *Eucharistia*—thanksgiving—{was seen as} an essential part of treatment.[596] *Contrast* the strong-arm approach generally used (*Historia Lausiaca*, 25).[597]

Appendix 3. Palestinian Monasticism—John the Hesychast

John the Hesychast. His life {was written} by Cyril of Scythopolis (see Festugière, *Les Moines d'Orient*, vol. III, 3). {He was} born in Armenia, 8 January, 484, of Christian parents. After {the} death of his parents he builds a church in honor of Mary and founds a cenobium. {He lives an} ascetic life—especially concentrated on fasting and humility. "A full stomach is not capable of vigils or temperance and vanity leaves one no rest" (p. 14). {He undertakes the} formation of others—{he is} not excessively demanding but still enough to challenge them and urge them on: "watering [the garden of their souls] with divine grace he brought them to bear fruit in conformity with their vocation" (p. 14). At 28 he is named Bishop of Colonia. {He} continued to live as an ascetic, not washing, fearing to see his own naked body. (This is a weakness, not strength, as Festugière remarks [p. 15, note].) {He} strove for purity of heart, "purifying himself unceasingly of all evil thoughts and all swelling of pride which is

595. Canivet, "Erreurs," 203.

596. Canivet, "Erreurs," 204.

597. In this chapter, the arrogant monk Valens, who has a vision of the Antichrist, whom he adores, mistaking him for the Lord, is bound and put in chains for a year, which (along with the prayers of his brethren) cures him (Meyer, 85). However, see also chapter 53, in which the monk Abramius is "smitten in his mind with troublesome self-conceit" and claims to have been ordained a priest by Christ himself; the fathers cure him by taking him out of the desert and bringing him "to a less ascetic and less exacting way of life," through which he is able to become aware of his own weakness (Meyer, 133–34).

contrary to the knowledge of God" (p. 15). After nine years as bishop he flees to Palestine, lives in a hospice for {the} aged poor, concealing his identity. {He} follows a miraculous light to {the} monastery of St. Sabas, "a community of 150 anchorites who all lived in great poverty as to the goods of the body but in great abundance of spiritual gifts" (p. 17). St. Sabas receives him as a simple postulant and servant, carrying water and helping masons to build {the} guest house; also cooking. {He} became guestmaster {while} continuing as cook. After a year as guestmaster he is allowed a solitary cell. "As the flower comes before the fruit, the cenobitic life precedes that of the anchorite" (p. 18).

His regime as {a} solitary: {He spends} five days a week as {a} recluse, Saturday and Sunday at {the} common liturgy in church. Taken to be ordained {a} priest in Jerusalem, he finally reveals to {the} archbishop that he is a bishop. St. Sabas is crestfallen, thinking John is for a secret reason unworthy of ordination. He is told in {a} vision of John's secret. *In his fiftieth year he retires to the desert of Rouba*, fleeing from unrest in {the} monastery, a "Sanhedrin of disorder" (p. 21). {He} lives in a cave, seeing no man. "He had but one desire: to converse with God in silence, to purify the eye of his soul by long ascetic exercises, to see with face unveiled the glory of the Lord" (p. 21). He gets a disciple who wants to go back to {the} Laura for Easter to get a decent meal. John refuses {and} urges trust in God and patience and renunciation of the "broad way" in order to follow faithfully the "narrow way." The disciple tries to go to {the} Laura, is lost, {and} returns half-starved to find a benefactor has provided John with "white fresh bread, wine and oil, fresh cheese and eggs and a pot of honey" (p. 23). John refuses {an} invitation to return to {the} Laura and life in safety while Saracens are ravaging the country. "If God ceases to have a care for me, what need have I to live longer?" (p. 24). God sent a lion to be his bodyguard. When the lion came and lay down beside him "he was a little frightened."[598] In the fifty-sixth year of his age he is brought back to {the} Laura by St. Sabas, as an act

598. *Les Moines d'Orient*, 4:24 (c. 13).

of humility, and lives as a recluse. St. Sabas dies {in} 531 {and} warns John in {a} vision of troubles to come upon {the} monastery. {John performs} miracles—including a fig tree growing from the rock *inside* his cell (p. 32). {He} eats three figs from this tree and prepares for his death. He is *still living* at 104, after 47 years as {a} recluse, following his six years in the desert. "He is very old but his face shines brightly, his soul burns, filled with divine grace, and even the little ones pray God to give him ever more and more strength and bring him to the end of his course in peace" (p. 34).

Appendix 4. {The} Ethiopian Church and Monasticism

1) Ethiopia {is} converted by Syrians who were captured by pirates while returning by ships from India (*DS*, 1453[599]—Rufinus, *Hist. Eccles.* I.9; *PL* 21[600]). One of these, St. Frumentius, {is} consecrated by Athanasius about 328, hence {the} connection with {the} Church of Alexandria. {He is called} "Father of Peace," "Revealer of Light."[601] {They} accept {the} Bible according to {the} Coptic canon (excluding Machabees, including some Apocrypha such as {the} Ascension of Isaias, Henoch, Jubilees).[602] {There is} much influence of {the} Greek Fathers, Basil, Gregories, Chrysostom, etc. {The Church becomes} *Monophysite*—especially under influence of "The Nine Saints"[603]—or Syrian Monophysites who fled to Ethiopia in {the} sixth century: {they believe in} a unification or fusion of two natures in Christ; but His human body is truly flesh and passible; His human soul came by traducianism from {the} soul of Mary.

2) *Liturgy*. {The} language—Ge'ez—equals classical Ethiopian. Texts {include} seventeen anaphorae. Note {the} Eucharistic Hymns, especially by St. Yared (6th cent.)—{in} three musical

599. Bernard Velat, "Éthiopie," *DS*, 4:1453-77.

600. Cols. 478-80.

601. Velat, "Éthiopie," col. 1453.

602. Velat, "Éthiopie," col. 1454.

603. Velat, "Éthiopie," col. 1454.

modes, etc. Architecture—churches {are} influenced by Syrian architecture: {they are} rectangular; {the} sanctuary {is} enclosed after {the} Middle Ages; {the} *Tabot*, {a} wooden block, {was used} for {the} altar—specially consecrated and venerated (cf. altar stone); {they eventually have} *circular churches* (modern).[604]

3) *Monachism*—{There are} early translations of {the} *Rule* of St. Pachomius, *Vita Antonii, Vita Pauli*. Monks evangelized pagan regions—{they have a} great influence in society even today. {There were} some double monasteries.

4) *Dabtara*—{these were} a special class of cantors and poets attached to every church—specialists in Liturgy and chant, composers of hymns; {they} sing with drums and other instruments, dancing (B. Velat, "Chantres, Poètes . . . Les Dabtara Éthiopiens," *Cahiers Coptes*, n. 5, 1954).[605]

Ethiopian Monachism (E. Cerulli, in *Il Monachesimo Orientale, Orientalia Christiana Analecta*, 153).[606]

1) {The} *locale* {was} mountains and woods, {with a} grove on top of {a} hill or mountain, around {the} monastery. *Dabr*—mountain—{is the common name for} monastery. "A monastery without trees is like a Master without a beard" (p. 259).

2) *Organization*—Ethiopian monasteries recognize as their head the Abbot of *Dabra Libanos*, {a} big monastery north of Addis Ababa—always an Ethiopian (nominated by {the} Negus[607]). (Secular clergy {served} under {a} Metropolitan approved by {the} Patriarch of Alexandria.) *Nuns*—often {lived} adjacent to monasteries of men and {were} controlled by {the} Abbot (262-263).

3) *Novitiate*—may last 9 or 10 years. Orders: some receive diaconate—but are not professed; only a few are priests {who} also may be non-professed; professed and priests are called "the holy ones," {and} have {a} voice in {the} council (264).

604. Velat, "Éthiopie," cols. 1456-57.

605. B. Velat, "Chantres, Poètes, Professeurs: Les Dabtara Éthiopiens," *Cahiers Coptes*, 5 (1954), 21–29.

606. Enrico Cerulli, "Il Monachismo Etiopico edi Suoi Ordinamenti," *Il Monachesimo Orientale, Orientalia Christiana Analecta*, 153 (1958), 259–78.

607. I.e., the emperor of Ethiopia.

4) {The} *Rule* {was that} *of St. Pachomius, with original Ethiopic adjustments and additions*—cf. St. Anthony *idem*—in unpublished mss. (late) (265); or particular rules and customs of houses, statutes voted in Chapter, etc.; strict asceticism has prevailed and impresses travellers down the ages (265–266) (standing on one leg; burial for certain periods; chains; silence); work: Batra Maryam, founder of Zage monastery, {wrote}: "Work and do not be idle"; they grew coffee (268); {they} take turns in menial service, etc.; {they are} not allowed to eat outside {the} monastery (Zage).

5) *Devotions*—{there is} opposition to {a} cult of relics, but veneration of tombs of holy monks, {and a} desire to be buried near them (p. 274); {the} preeminence of {the} monastery of Dabra Libanos {is} due to {the} fact that bodies of two great monastic saints were translated there to be venerated (St. Takaa Hayamot, and St. Philip) (274).

6) *Diffusion*—Ethiopian monasteries were founded:

a) along {the} pilgrimage route to Jerusalem;
b) in Palestine and Syria;
c) even one at Rome (277–278).

Appendix 5. Prayer of Cyrillonas

Cyrillonas {was} a Syrian poet, {at the} end of {the} fourth century, from {the} region of Edessa, {who} writes of the anguish of the Church in the Barbarian invasions.[608] The Huns were already attacking the Eastern confines of the Empire. {In} his poem on the Church in Supplication, in time of war, "Supplication and Parrhesia,"[609] the Church with all her children, "*Apostles and Martyrs*

608. Cyrillonas (also written as Qurilona) has been identified with Absamya, a nephew of St. Ephrem, who is mentioned in Syriac sources as author of hymns on the invasion of the Huns. See the Introduction by Dominique Cerbelaud, OP, to his translation of the works of Cyrillonas: *L'Agneau Véritable: Hymnes, Cantiques et Homélies* (Chevetogne: Éditions de Chevetogne, 1973), 8.

609. The hymn, or verse homily, is the fourth of six in the ordering of the Syriac manuscript, with the title "The Plague: Hymns on the Locust and on the Chastisement, and on the Invasion of the Huns": see *L'Agneau Véritable*, 72–87;

and Friends of the King" (virgins and monks?), appears before God's throne in sorrow to supplicate for the world. *She reminds God that He made man out of love, that He is merciful* and compassionate, that He forgives the sinner. She begs Him not to strike man with such force.[610]

> "Look not, O Lord, upon those who anger Thee,
> Look rather on those who seek to appease Thee."

There are still many in the world who are loyal to God, who are concerned only with truth. These are, above all, the monks.

> "Monasteries have been planted and within their walls
> Live men of strong and fully mature [perfect] hearts.
> Look! In the clefts of the rock dwell the hermits
> and in the wilderness the doughty worshippers, men of
> reconciliation.
> Seest thou them not, out on the lonely mountains
> On the far islands, the heroes of Thy choice?"

But there are also the laypeople and praise goes up to Him from palace and field. *Like Jerome,*[611] *Cyrillonas evokes the picture of the peasant singing psalms at work. Sailors at sea send up prayers to Him from their ships.* His word has gone out into the land of idols:

Merton's excerpts are from cc. 15–17, the final sections of the text; his source for the excerpts has not been located.

610. For a description of the Hunnic invasion of 395, around the time the hymn is thought to have been written, see Otto Maenchen-Helfen, *The World of the Huns: Studies in Their History and Culture* (Berkeley: University of California Press, 1973), 51–59, which quotes from this hymn of Cyrillonas.

611. See Jerome, *Epistola* 46 (*PL* 22, col. 491): *"Quocumque te verteris, arator stivam tenens, alleluia decantat. Sudans messor Psalmis se avocat, et curva attondens vitem falce vinitor, aliquid Davidicum canit."* ("Wherever you turn, the farmer holding the plow is singing an alleluia. The sweating reaper is occupying himself with psalms, and the vinedresser trimming the vine with curved pruning hook is singing something from David.")

"Persia has heard Thy word,
Thy Gospel flowers in the land of the Assyrian, Thomas has taught India
And Peter has preached in Rome. . . . Thy Cross today rules over the Emperors
and Thy love penetrates the hearts of royal women . . ."

"Behold, Thy life-giving Body dwells in the midst of the Church
And the Chalice of Thy own Blood protects Thy Bride
Thus all Nature and all she has brought forth
As a feast full of glory to Thee, one single cry for mercy."

The whole earth then becomes a cry for peace. War is recognized as a punishment for sin, well-deserved, but which can be remitted if men will repent. Here is the prayer of all things to God:

"Let not, O Lord, the sword of Thy wrath swing.
Our strength is too weak to stand the blows of God.
Put an end to the war that rages beneath us [like a stormy sea].
Give to earth the salvation and fullness of Peace!"

And he appeals to the Incarnation:

"Thy Birth in the Flesh was an act of love for Thy Church.
May it even now become, for Thy Creation, a birth of mercy."

Note this theology has many affinities with that of St. Irenaeus.[612]

612. Merton is apparently referring to Irenaeus' doctrine of the recapitulation of all things in Christ, the Second Adam, whose Incarnation and Redemption penetrate and permeate the entire creation.

APPENDIX A

TEXTUAL NOTES

Readings adopted from mimeograph

3–44 PROLOGUE . . . (Chadwick, p. 7).] *typescript missing*

44 f)] e)

45–68 What is the objective? . . . *postulatio* and *gratiarum actio.*] *typescript missing*

68 "To teach . . . praying.'"] Copy: Western Asceticism p 229, c. 31, paragraph 1.

72 PACHOMIAN CENOBITISM] (start a new page for this) *added in upper margin*

88 *Ostiarii . . . PL* 103, col. 481).] Here read from the (Pachomian) *Regula Orientalis*, cap. 26. PL 103–481 (please copy this short chapter (Latin)) *interlined above and joined to* read *by an arrow*

91 as worthless] was worthless

113 *De cibis . . . conceditur?*] *missing in typescript*

119 "During . . . gate."] Read (copy)—bottom p. 428 'During the first Sabbaton . . .'

"Let not . . . them . . ."] middle 429 'let not any man acquire . . .'

120 SHENOUTE] Please spell *SHENOUTE* throughout not *Schenouti*

121 and Ladeuze] et Ladeuze

133–34 "Come to me, . . . series). READ (copy) p. 15 (*St. Basil Ascetical Works* F of C) "Come to me all you that labor. . . . make haste to embrace the cross bearing life of the monks . . . . . . down to . . . the life of lowliness and recollection."

134–35 Does it not . . . (p. 17).] READ (copy) p. 17 "Does it not seem to you that the Gospel applies to married persons also . . . . down to . . . . bottom of the page "before your eyes".

135 With much . . . (p. 19).] Read (copy) p. 19 line 8 to end of that paragraph.

136 The vice . . . (pp. 24–25).] Read (copy) p. 24 begin line 6 from bottom "The vice of gluttony is wont to display . . . . on to p. 25 end of first par.

139 (from . . . works).] *missing in typescript*

174 are sung] and sung

191–208 **The Spiritual** . . . to God" (612).] *no typescript*

213–14 The influence . . . spiritual life.] [Copy History p. VIII (vol.1) paragraph 2 The influence . . .]

214 Vööbus, *History* . . . areas."] [Copy Voobus p VIII last par IX first par]

215–16 "There is only . . . p. 10] Insert quote from Doctrina Addai. Voobus vol I. p. 10. bottom

271 8]7
9]8
10]9

Additions and alterations

44 1.] *added in left margin*
he was advanced] he *interlined with a caret*

45 Another Christian . . . this!)] *added on line*
(Greek)] *interlined with a caret*
(*Praktike*)] *added on line*

47 4. In either . . . *Conf.* 8).] *opposite page*

69 (cf. Gospel . . . Easter)] *added on line*
They arise . . . grace.] *added on line*
"pure prayer."] *added on line after cancelled* prayer

70 1.] *added in left margin*
Cf. St. Ambrose . . . col. 125).] *opposite page*

71 2.] *added in left margin*

72 Hence this . . . Savior.] *added in lower margin*

73 The *Vita* . . . material.] *added on line*
(the only complete one)] *added on line*
Theodore was . . . disciple.] *added on line*

73–74 Unfortunately . . . tradition.] *opposite page*

74 The *Latin* . . . Boon, osb] *inserted with a caret*
But this . . . grace.] *added in lower margin*

75 see also . . . 308 ff.] *added on line*
plus texts from Lefort.] *added on line*
He was considered . . . to Pachomius.] *opposite page*
The atmosphere . . . different.] *added on line*
75–76 Note that . . . actualité."] *opposite page*
75 some] *interlined above cancelled* a lot of
conventional and even] *inserted with an arrow*
76 We must not . . . p. 1)] *opposite page*
76–77 Note the . . . *Daniel*.] *added on line*
77 However the . . . is patience.] *opposite page*
as though in] *followed by cancelled* exile
78–79 In St. Jerome's . . . *tendentes*" (col. 461)] *opposite page*
79 and a common . . . precepts.] *added on line*
contemplative union] contemplative *interlined with a caret*
Purity of heart . . . distracting thoughts.] *opposite page*
rather than] *followed by cancelled* from
lofty] *added on line*
80 However, within . . . life" (col. 462).] *opposite page*
great] *inserted with a caret*
servants] *interlined above cancelled* disciples
whom] *interlined above cancelled* which
serve] *interlined above cancelled* contemplate
1] *added on line*
2. He is . . . fear of the Lord.] *opposite page*
3.] *added on line*
We must . . . His Law.] *added on line*
including] *interlined above cancelled* and especially with
82 N.B., the idea . . . Benedict!] *added on line*
Hence . . . common life.] *added on line*
83 See below . . . judged.] *added on line*
It is a common . . . efforts.] *added on line*
(see above)] *added on line*
in the beginning of the *Catechesis*] *interlined with a caret*
elsewhere] *added on line*
84 He is not . . . defaced image.] *added on line*
85 documentation on] *interlined above cancelled* a consideration of
actual problem] *followed by cancelled* of rather widespread homosexuality in one of the Egyptian cenobia of Upper Egypt
of Upper Egypt] *added on line*

85–86 The problem of chastity . . . strict and chaste.] *opposite page to replace cancelled* We do not know the historical background. It seems at any rate that while sexual offenses are alluded to clearly, general way, the real problem was one of the formation of private cliques, in which monastic discipline was rather seriously relaxed, and a widespread "epidemic" of at least sentimental and worldly attachments was noted [*sic:* only hinted at in a very *x'd out and replaced by* alluded to clearly *without repeating* in a very]

85 (and *highly exaggerated*)] *interlined with a caret*

86 very strict] *preceded by cancelled* in general

chaste.] *followed by cancelled* Note—the question of sodomy arose even in the familiar documents known before recent discoveries v.g. in the *Life* of Pachomius. The *Homily of Orsiesius* is then no isolated document. But this does not mean that vice was rampant in the cenobia.

Orsiesius'] *interlined above cancelled* the

the danger of] *interlined above cancelled* general prevalence of

sin, as a] sin *followed by cancelled* that is about this

the chief . . . *danger* of sin] *added on line after cancelled* the problem seems to be not really sexual, but one of discipline.

admitted] *followed by cancelled* as very real

It is to be . . . *temptations.*] *opposite page*

"sick friendship."] *followed by cancelled* However, once Pachomius expelled from the monastery a young boy who was a problem—he first burned all the boy's clothes, his sleeping mat and utensils, then sent him away.

Orsiesius describes] *interlined above cancelled* After describing

ornaments,] *followed by cancelled* as well as a kind of lascivious gait.

the friendship] *added in lower margin to replace cancelled* those

87 Note: the enemies . . . general scandal.] *added in lower margin*

In effect . . . p. 283).] *written on reverse side of page*

89 *Note*: when . . . St. Benedict).] *opposite page*

subtly] *interlined with a caret*

91 (Here—discuss . . . contrast.)] *added on line*

94	However, Pachomius . . . p. 323.)] *opposite page*
	docility] *followed by cancelled* of heart
95	(Comment . . . *conversatio.*)] *added on line*
96	pursuit] *added in left margin before cancelled* entity
	or that . . . group] *added on line*
	relation of . . . Church] *added in lower margin*
97	cf. *Vita* . . . 259] *added on line*
	Offices were . . . early monasticism)] *opposite page to replace* Some offices—all in church—compline in the "houses" *added in right margin and cancelled*
97–98	Superiors participate . . . "order."] *opposite page*
97	singing . . . permitted] *interlined with a caret*
98	community cannot] community *interlined above cancelled* monastery
	characteristic] *preceded by cancelled* great
99	Did monks . . . pp. 298–299] *added on line after cancelled* Many differences were expected and tolerated, perhaps encouraged (for instance meals. Monks ate at different times, some fasting until vespers, etc.)
99–100	business . . . food, etc.] *opposite page*
100	The heads . . . meet.] *opposite page*
	The Holy . . . *all.*] *added on line*
	In commanding, . . . *Rule.*] *added on line*
101	However, . . . them, etc.] *opposite page*
101–102	Everything is . . . cf. St. Benedict] *opposite page*
103–104	Egyptian custom . . . 12 psalms.] *opposite page*
104	office] *followed by cancelled* each
	psalm] *interlined with a caret*
	and supper] *interlined below*
105	*Pachomian Foundations.* . . . alone] *opposite page*
106–107	See *Vita* . . . Judgement.] *opposite page*
107	Note: there . . . death (346).] *opposite page*
109	begins] *followed by cancelled* mon *interlined above cancelled* (cenobitic)
110	However, see . . . (col. 254).] *opposite page*
111	chapter 44 . . . to Arius.] *opposite page*
113	cf. chapter 49 . . . decline (268).] *opposite page*
114	"Doctrine"] *preceded by cancelled* "Rule" or
	wrong to . . . St. Pachomius.] *interlined*
119	Father] *followed by cancelled* Pachomius

time . . . view of] *interlined above illegible cancellation*

120 And yet . . . furnace.] *opposite page*

Bgoue] *followed by cancelled* an un

121–22 We must . . . . conditions of the poor.] *opposite page*

122 Those who . . . expelled.] *opposite page*

123 *in Latin*] *interlined below and marked for insertion*

though not] *followed by cancelled* with *and uncancelled* a

completely] *altered from* complete

rejecting] *added in right margin followed by cancelled* rejection

124 much confusion . . . names] *added on line*

124–25 and supports . . . Eustathians] *added on line following cancelled* against ascetic doctrine and practice

125 by the more radical Eustathians] *added on line following cancelled for all* by Eustathius.

more radical] *preceded by cancelled* extremists

TOTALLY] *added in right margin*

from the ordinary . . . community life] *added on line*

125–26 *example,* . . . p. 61–62.] *opposite page*

126 these texts] *interlined above cancelled* them

(monastic)] *interlined with a caret*

Such is . . . OSB.] *added on line*

They are . . . know it.] *added on line to replace cancelled* The ascetic doctrine which Basil preached in the east for all Christians was read in the west *as a strictly monastic doctrine for monks above all.*

127 a group] a *added on line*

128 which involved . . . un-Christian.] *added on line*

strictly speaking] *interlined above cancelled* a

though tradition . . . such.] *added on line*

If by monastic . . . monks."] *opposite page, replacing cancelled* Basil did not found monasteries, but rather Christian communities separate from the world, not however seeking a more perfect way than that of the ordinary faithful. These communities were, in his mind, "ordinary faithful," but great emphasis was laid on the encouragement of celibacy, chastity, poverty etc.

These communities] *added in left margin replacing* These

"exaggerated"] *quotation marks added*

129 The ordinary . . . *world.*] *added on line*

in these . . . to St. Basil.] interlined
A.] *added in left margin*
(Contrast . . . Bernard.)] *added on line*
130 is regarded . . . *Rules.*] *added on line before cancelled* Note, Dom Amand assumes that Basil's asceticism is essentially "monastic" and writes a book on this subject. With the qualifications we have made above, we can certainly accept this if we understand that
"monastic" ideas] *quotation marks added*
though to Gregory] *interlined with a caret*
(the "business of the city")] *interlined with a caret*
program] *followed by cancelled* (acc. to Amand)
131 to get free . . . teachings;] *opposite page, replacing cancelled* To live without—[p 48]
liberating] *preceded by cancelled* freedom
"Preparation of the heart"] *interlined*
Solitude tames the passions.] *added on line*
131–32 Hence Basil . . . *splendor.*] *opposite page*
131 Basil and his companions] *interlined above cancelled* they
132 *Prayer* is . . . pleases God.] *opposite page*
which could . . . of Christians.] *interlined with a caret*
133 vigils: . . . midnight.] *interlined*
further . . . *"the Christian."*] *opposite page*
B.] *added in left margin*
134 emphasis on . . . call.] *interlined*
Old Testament] *interlined above cancelled* OT
who] *added on line*
135 Note the . . . Catharism, etc.] *interlined*
Spiritual Father] *interlined above cancelled* man
136 his thought] *interlined above cancelled* him
137 (one of . . . tradition)] *added on line*
(not by St. Basil)] *added on line*
"Basilian"] *interlined with a caret*
indications . . . Lérins.] *added on line*
138 question] *interlined above cancelled* dismiss
(cf. *soli Deo placere*)] *added on line*
139 and also: . . . *alienum"*] *interlined*
140 (cf. . . . St. Benedict).] *added on line*
141 N.B.: *Pax . . . truth.*] *interlined*

142 and true sense of community] *added on line*
144 importance of *puritas*] *added on line*
importance of *sapientia* and *vigilantia*] *added on line*
full implications of *sapienter*)] *added on line*
(examine . . . this).] *added on line*
145 *"RULES" (The Asceticon*)] *added on line*
(Gribomont . . . *Asceticon*"))] *added on line*
abbot] *interlined above cancelled* monk
"as it is . . . Cappadocia."] *quotation marks added on line*
(Note: the earlier . . . thought.)] *added on line*
146 instruction . . . together.] *added on line*
quae] *interlined below cancelled qaue*
150 One must . . . in solitude.] *added on line*
151 Other points . . . Q. 18] *opposite page*
152 The monks . . . town.] *added in left margin*
asceticism] *interlined above cancelled* exegesis
153 threatened] *interlined above cancelled* attacked
of women] *interlined with a caret*
relative of St. Paulinus] *interlined with an arrow for placement*
154–55 "Now as concerning . . . *alienum*)] *opposite page*
155 death] *interlined above cancelled* birth
158 However, they . . . gate.] *added in left margin*
159 Mass on . . . Sebaste] *added in left margin*
Poets tell us] *interlined above cancelled* Virgil
161 This is . . . studies.] *opposite page*
and hear] *interlined with a caret*
164 monk in Gaul] monk *interlined above cancelled* man
The community . . . p. 42)] *opposite page*
166 Hence he must . . . *amabis*] *opposite page*
169 and detractor] *interlined*
Bishop] *preceded by cancelled* his
(Pilgrim . . . devotion.)] *interlined*
agrum] rum *interlined above cancelled* er
First theory: "Sylvia"] *added in left margin*
Second theory: "Aetheria"] *added in left margin*
Second] *altered from* First
theory] *followed by cancelled* rectified
(Aetheria)] *added on line*
170 Third theory: "Eucheria"] *added in left margin*

Third] *altered from* Second
She used the official imperial relay system (*cursus publicus*)] *added on line*
Revue Bénédictine] *added in left margin to replace* RB
This letter . . . anything.] *added on line*
(But did . . . missing.)] *added on line*
(quite likely)] *added on line*
171 passed through] *preceded by cancelled* just
some time] *interlined below with indication of placement*
Fourth theory: "Egeria"] *added in left margin*
Fourth] *altered from* Third
Eiheria] *followed by added and cancelled* Egeria
Here—sample . . . p. 202] *added in upper margin*
172 She is . . . p. 146)] *added on line*
She travels . . . translation] *opposite page*
1)] *added in left margin*
She is . . . at Haran] *added on line*
2)] *added in left margin*
3)] *added in left margin*
subordinated to . . . sites.] *added on line after cancelled* somewhat indirect.
4)] *added in left margin*
at Jerusalem] *added on line*
173 Other traits . . . colloquial.] *opposite page*
Often there . . . purpose.] *added in left margin*
by an *oratio* . . . reading.] *added on line*
174 The True Cross] *added in left margin before cancelled* It
(Monks are . . . entirety.)] *added on line*
175 They are . . . Spirit.] *interlined with a caret*
176 There had been . . . microfilm.] *opposite page*
177 (Comment on connection with *RB*.)] *added on line*
180 King Abgar V, . . . time.)] *opposite page*
181–82 To understand . . . 296).] *opposite page*
183 who live] who *interlined above cancelled* which
to the shrine of St. Thecla,] *followed by cancelled* and
184–85 *Egkrateia* (see *DS*) . . . sweet voice."] *opposite page*
186 *Jerome on the "Remoboth."*] *added in left margin*
189 devote] *preceded by cancelled* abandon them
psalms with melodies] *preceded by cancelled* song

190 *Augustine*] *followed by cancelled* (not in monastic

213 **SYRIAN . . . introduction:**] PRIMITIVE MONACHISM Part II *cancelled above*
and PERSIAN] *interlined with a caret*
those of Vööbus] *added in left margin before cancelled* that
and Festugière] *added in left margin*
see Vööbus: . . . *Chrétienne*] *opposite page*
(see . . . Part I)] *added on line*
Pre-Benedictine] *preceded by cancelled* Primitive Monasti
Syrian Monasticism] *interlined with a caret above cancelled* It
History] *interlined below* Vööbus intro.

215 explained] *added on line after cancelled* vouched for
(Zoroaster)] *added on line*

217 (see below—Marcionites)] *added on line*

217–18 *Marcionites*: . . . an initiation)] *typed on opposite page*

218 Did he . . . *Remoboth*?] *added on line*

219 the *basic* . . . terminology.] *opposite page*

220 Comment: mere . . . anthropology.] *added on line*

221 (Contrast Aphraat.)] *added on line*
fulserunt."] *followed by cancelled* cf. oriental lumen of Wm St Thierry
Was he a monk?] *added on line*
a cave] a *interlined with a caret before* cave *altered from* caves
(*Boskoi*)] *added on line*

222 James of Nisibis is described . . . Pauline.] *opposite page*
in Syrian . . . compunction."] *added on line*

223 Mysticism] *added in left margin*
Here comment . . . *agape*.] *opposite page*
Later when . . . *speculari*."] *opposite page*

224 A hymn, . . . by it."] *added on line*
One of . . . praise him.] *opposite page*
(contrast {the} Gospel)] *added in left margin*

225 cenobitic] *interlined above cancelled* active
He lived in . . . recluse.] *added on line*
Comment.] *added on line*

227 *corde suo*] *suo interlined with a caret*

229 a*groikia*] *added in left margin*

229–30 Monks . . . *hypacthrioi*.] *opposite page*

231 *apatheia*] *added in left margin*

232 in the sense that . . . married] *added on line*

cf. exegesis of Origen] *opposite page*

233 as opposed . . . beardless"] *added on line*

234 (See this . . . marriage!)] *added on line*

"Instruments of Good Works"] *added on line*

use of . . . *thesis*] *interlined*

236 contrast "dove] *added in left margin*

237 being, not doing] *added on line*

238 of the same sex] *added on line*

eschatological] *interlined*

239 "solitaries" . . . world] *interlined above cancelled* monks

240 cf. n. 18: . . . *spiritual"*] *opposite page*

241 Prayer] *added in left margin*

242 (d. 373)] *added on line*

I. *Life*] *added on line*

special . . . his works] *interlined*

his "graciousness" (τὸ χαρίεν)] *added in right margin*

Carmina . . . and Vologesius] *interlined*

Did he . . . legends] *interlined*

Rather . . . sense.] *interlined above cancelled* He may have done so intermittently *and followed by cancelled* (see below)

243 The Syrian . . . Shepherd" (*id.* {591-}592)] *opposite page*

Armenian] *preceded by cancelled* Syrian

in . . . January 28] *interlined below with arrow for placement*

243–44 Vööbus tends . . . thesis.] *interlined*

244 Hence Vööbus . . . 1959] *opposite page*

1. Church] *added in left margin*

probably] *interlined with a caret*

knew . . . (Vööbus)] *added on line*

in Ephrem.] *interlined below before cancelled* Does it later merge into distinction between cenobites and hermits?

by nature] *followed by cancelled* (but he does not see nature in this sense).

2.] *added in left margin*

245 Note however . . . *monks.*] *interlined*

245–46 In *Memra 2* . . . angelic vision.] *opposite page*

246 Cf. *Commentary* . . . *suo."*] *added above insert with arrow for placement*

247 theology of . . . love] *added on line*

Cf. *Memra 2*: . . . thanks!"] *interlined with arrow for placement*

to eat] to *interlined with a caret above cancelled* the

This idea . . . *occultis*] *opposite page*

Memra 5, . . . eating] *opposite page*

247–48 (cf. monastic silence?)] *added on line*

248 (for instance . . . 32:1-13)] *added in lower margin*

Wine] *altered from* wine *preceded by cancelled* But

249 Cf. *Memra* 9 . . . *est*.] *opposite page*

(cf. St. Ammonas . . . Fathers")] *added on line*

250 implications for monastic silence!] *interlined below with arrow for placement*

Why is this?] *interlined*

4.] *added in left margin*

Faith comes . . . to silence.] *added on line*

251 5.] *added in left margin*

De Fide, 4] 4 *added on line*

252 virginity of spirit] *added in left margin*

253 St. John . . . XXXV] *added in left margin*

6.] *added in left margin*

(Compare . . . point)] *interlined*

(Note . . . sake)] *added on line*

254 Virginity makes . . . worldly cares.] *opposite page*

254–55 for in them . . . attachment] *added on line*

255 Ephrem is stressing] Ephrem *interlined below cancelled* He

since it . . . not God] *interlined with a caret*

256 Note: in the . . . Aniane.] *opposite page*

256–57 *More points . . . regret!*)] *opposite page*

257 Five of . . . p. 58)] *opposite page followed by cancelled* Question —in what way does a mature person still place himself in dependence on another man? Discuss.

258 This comparison . . . stability.] *added on line*

See for instance . . . *Ep*. 176] *opposite page*

(meaning of *glory*)] *interlined*

259 viewpoint.] *followed by cancelled*—perhaps not by Ephrem (?)—a bit conventional.

IV.] *added in left margin*

Hymn 1] *interlined in left margin*

"I will . . . support."] *quotation marks added*

260 "sons of God"] *quotation marks added*
This division . . . Philoxenos] *interlined*
261 The cosmos . . . "place."] *interlined*
Each one . . . key.] *added in right margin*
(Implied . . . door.")] *interlined*
Their life was *truth.*] *added on line*
(in contemplation)] *added on line*
262 "Blessed . . . life."] *quotation marks added*
Those who lived . . . not Greek!] *opposite page*
as a reward] *interlined with arrow for placement*
263 clothe you!] you *interlined above cancelled* thee.
At sight of] *preceded by cancelled* Upon this place
have come] *preceded by cancelled* come to your end!
Ephrem himself] Ephrem *interlined above cancelled* Then he
sold] *preceded by cancelled* exchanged it
264 and contrast] *interlined with a caret*
not "in existence"] existence" *interlined above cancelled* being"
world in existence] existence *interlined above cancelled* being
measuring] *preceded by cancelled* functioning
entity] *interlined above cancelled* being
in {the} image] *interlined above cancelled* like
the "spiritual . . . of prayer] *added on line*
265 accuse] *followed by cancelled* themselves
266 note . . . profane] *added on line*
passage in the book] *interlined above cancelled* book
act] *preceded by cancelled* action for my
luminous] *interlined with a caret*
267 FINALE: . . . bounty."] *opposite page*
Number 23 is attributed] *preceded by cancelled* N. 22 in this Collectio is attributed to Ephrem, as we have seen above.
intrinsic interest (historical)] *added on line preceded by cancelled* value
It refers . . . lauras.] *interlined*
especially . . . journey] *added on line*
(cf. Gospel . . . Pentecost)] *added on line*
268 (n.b. *our* . . . town, etc.)] *interlined with arrow for placement*
269 good manners . . . self-control] *interlined*
270 (N.B. . . . usages)] *interlined*

272 example of Christ] *added in left margin*
272–73 Note: the "debate" . . . by all.] *opposite page*
virginal] *interlined with a caret*
274 *in saecula. Amen.*] *followed by cancelled page marked* Do not copy: *Latin Texts of Ephrem in High Middle Ages*. 1) Smaragdus. Diadema 87-88. PL. 102.680-681. 2) Alcuin—see PL. 101.606-607 "prayers" of Ephrem. 3) *Liber Scintillarum*. (about 700) 8 references from Sermo Asceticus. XV.28. XL.36-40. XLIII.10-11. XLV.36. certainly from Greek "Ephrem." Abs. from Greek E. I.52 VI.29-30. III.66-67. Attrib to Ephrem but questionable. XXII.10-13. XVIII.86 (Gregory? Caesarius?) Probably *not* Ephrem—Dicta Ephremi or Pseudo August. ad Fratres in eremo. PL. 40.1347-1348. l. 13.
Texts attributed to E. on friendship come from Isidore of Seville LXIIII.46, 48, 50, 51 + "Quelques sondages dans le florilege de Defensor revelent un Ephrem Latin très proche encore de ses sources et plus fidele parfois que ne sont les manuscripts Grecs paléographiquement beaucoup plus tardifs. Par son [ ] il demeure ainsi un temoin de premier ordre pour l'histoire de la tradition textuelle ephremienne.
275 SYRIAN MONASTIC RULES] *preceded by Manichaeism*—III Cent. Mani—dualism. Liberation of divine element imprisoned in matter. Signaculum oris—no meat or wine {Signaculum} manus—no killing {Signaculum} sinus—no sexual union extends west to Spain—in *Priscillianism* then to France *Catharism* also strengthened from Balkans—*Bogomils*
Voobus—Syrian Monasticism.
Ephrem—small, perpetually sad, bald + beardless. V. S in E. p. 46. [ ], vigils' in solitude. S in E. 53. Ephrem (Commem. 1st Sat of Lent. Orient. [ ]) (See *Or. Syr* 1959 249 f. 1958—341 f.) d. June 9th 373. Biographical writings + Sources Testament—Sugita—'confessions' self castigations for sinfulness (one genuine) in Syriac + one in Greek.) (Biography—spurious) (Encomium—attrib. to Greg. Nyssa—not his) Sources. Palladius. Sozomen.

Life—Syrian—ignored Greek but was in contact with Basil did not go to Egypt. + was not in contact with Basil though this is said. 'historical Ephrem quite different from the Ephrem of hagiography'. Vol 2—p 84, 89. Became a monk in his youth (as opp. to other confused traditions) Vol. 2—p. 85. active in teaching (school of Nisibis) Was ordained deacon. Last ten years of life was *not* making contacts as above 'He lived in his cell in the mountains of Edessa but his seculusion was not absolute. He kept contact with the needs of the Christian community of Edessa . . .' vol 2 p. 90. (taught hymns to nuns of Edessa) organized relief work in famine. wrote against heresy. Beck—E grew up at Nisibis in atmosphere of primitive ascetes but knew of monachism growing up along Persian frontier. Only came in contact with mon. in last 10 years of his life. The higher ideal—not only to live in celibacy (ascetes) but in isolation from all men.—some take vow never to *see* men. + *Asceticism* 1) Mon. life—a way of repentance in the desert. 'typus eremitis—ut diligerent desertum liberans omnes.' A city of refuge to which Jesus himself fled John 11:54 'civitas longinqua, vicina deserti, in societate solitudinis et vicinitate pacis plena. [ ] over the mountains.—place of judgement + renewal—+ of health. Flight from the world which is on fire. Christ dwells wholly in His disciples.' 1a) *queama* The "covenant community" (virgins, fasters, watchers) (also used for groups of Gk philosophers)—overcomes fate" + the determinism supposed to be manifested by the stars. Testata est virginitas non esse fatum. despexerunt fatum jejunantes, qui perduraverunt in jejuniis suis. The 'continentes' (qadisse) contradict planet Venus. View of nature—as a fund or capital—Natura est pecunia pro bonis et malis. Si quis ordinat eam augetur per eam Si quis autem perturbat eam mereatur omnes jacturas. Hence two degrees—avoiding sin (married life) living above nature itself (jejunare a natura)—virgin life) 2) hermit ideal.—more familiar to him knows solitaries + small groups, not cenobia. Loneliness + tranquillity—

praises dying alone. Companionship of angels in solitude. 3) Poverty and asceticism—pushed to the limit. Fast as much as you can endure—boskoi avoiding sleep, danger of dreams dirt—rags 'Your dirtiness that has become your clothing weaves for you a garment of glory." Contempt for nature. Continuous struggle to subjugate the body. Death to natural existence by mon. vocation. 'everyone that bends his neck + serves in this institution is regarded as dead' vol 2: p 97. 4) Suffering —Hallmark of mon life. monk = *one who is afflicted* 'If you are truly His, put on His suffering' 'Jesus first tasted bitterness + showed us that no one can be His disciple in Name only, but through suffering.' 'Jesus died to the world in order that no one should live to the world, + He existed in a crucified body in order that no one should walk sensually by it." Vol 2. p 98

Ephrem 2. Monks glory is 'only in the Cross.' Purpose of monasticism. 'To seek for the glory of the Cross, to seek for the shame of the Cross, to love the riches of the cross and to carry the pain of the Cross' vol 2. p 99. note. Hence mon. life is a true *physical* martyrdom, but hidden. 'Your members are martyrs of hiddenness which along with (visible) martyrs are *worthy of their suffering*.' Vol 2. p 100 'Their appearance is consumed by their fastings'—mortification should *disfigure* the body vol 2 p 100. Ephrem's hermit ideal. Quia viderunt mundum gaudii, ipsi dilexerunt tristitiam Et quia in mundo viderunt delicias ipsi pascunt in radicibus Quia viderunt in mundo gloriationem ipsi dilexerunt humilitatem Quia in mundo viderunt cupiditates sibi eligerunt jejunium parcum etc. (Beck Or Syr 1958 294–295.)

Monk—called to abjection + poverty like Lazarus in parable. Called to share in the Cross of Christ by renunciation of the world. Virginity—one must not rely on external protection—enclosure. But on *truth*. (our Lord talking to Samaritan woman)—virginity *the essential mortification of the monk prayer*—must be audacious and constant. (Chanannite woman.) but humble (like that of publican) *works*—necessity for real action, not just words. not "Lord Lord" but to do His will. esp. accepting humiliation, poverty + rebuff.—*charity*. *Word of God*—immense treasure. inexhaustible fountain. Bible has nourishment for all needs. Tree of life, rock in desert. *Perseverance* in reading, grace maybe only after repeated efforts + *Conclusions*—nb. differences from Benedictine + Basilian trad: suppleness. solitude—pastoral work.—*not emphasizing organization*. *Pre-monastic*. Emphasis on interior—purity of heart, truth, self-mastery love as essentials of monk. St Ephrem—Moine et Pasteur—(306-373) Dom Louis Leloir. TVM 89 ff. (1) Difficulty of finding the truth amid idealizations of E. + legends. Difficulty of establishing genuine works among the many ascribed to him. Dom Beck in DS. is reliable. *Life*—born Nisibis abt 306. son of a pagan priest + Xtian mother—brought up secretly as Xtian? Legend. Left Nisibis in 363 when Persians invaded—went to Edessa for last 10 years of his life. *He founded the School of Nisibis* + another at Edessa. A choirmaster—writer of hymns,—apostolic—mon. life—defender of orthodoxy agst Arians. (2) *Carmina Nisibena*. a) heir of 3 monk bishops—James—severity. Babu—firmness (a genuine ideal) x *Vologesius*—gentle + friendly—το χαρειν—graciousness alertness to reality of times + needs. wisdom. monk (ascete) at all times—holy in body + soul b) *Monastic ideas*: (1) *praises hermit life*. gives *agraphon*. "Where there is one alone there I am with him.' said, E. claims "to remove all motive of sorrow from those who are alone, for Christ is our joy and He is with us." The hermit is "one who weeps." emphasis on compunction. The shepherds, alone in fields, were first called to the crib. (2) Also praises combination of monasticism + pastoral life. (monks = *ascetes*.) (3) Is in reality pre-monastic—(Beck) rejoices when mon. movement gets in full swing near Edessa at end of his life. (3) *Other hymns*—praises *silence*—but as correlative to right speech "day + night"—praises *virginity*—as equivalent to martyrdom—but not selfish—must flower in charity *fruitfulness* in souls—tends to separate clearly *lay* life + *mon.* life Laypeople—salvation Monks—perfection. as opp Chrysost.

Vööbus argues] *interlined with a caret*

says Vööbus] *interlined with a caret*

276 Immaturity . . . problem.] *opposite page*

277 importance of . . . remembered.] *added in lower margin*

Fifth Century] *added on line*

278 Caution . . . heretics (n. 48 ff.)] *added in lower margin*

278–79 *Anonymous Canons* . . . p. 73–74)] *added on lower part of page and marked* (put this last part first) *for transposition before Philoxenos*: In the *Rules*

278 cf. n. 14: "It . . . fast.] *opposite page*

279 and doctor . . . August)] *interlined*

born . . . Edessa] *added in left margin*

280 Works . . . and Origen.] *opposite page*

who came out] *preceded by cancelled* for whom

281 Note on . . . *Understand!*"] *opposite page*

(n.b. *tradition*)] *added in right margin*

282 not the truth believed only] *added on line*

teaches] *preceded by cancelled* preaches

283 In each pair] *preceded by cancelled* These groups are generally

283–84 Division . . . in solitude.] *opposite page*

284 slaves] *preceded by cancelled* servants

reception] *preceded by cancelled* fight against

285 (cf. Cassian)] *added on line*

286 learn] *added on line*

Beginners] *interlined above cancelled* They

287 see this . . . *ambiguous*] *opposite page*

41] *interlined with a caret*

fornication] *followed by cancelled* (this is as far as he goes in this volume.)

Note . . . awareness of God.] *opposite page*

288 Note . . . price] *added on line*

289 (especially fear)] *added on line*

Meanwhile . . . *simplicity*.] *added in lower margin*

290 (cf. St. Anselm, *Proslogion*)] *added in right margin*

291 *the light*] *preceded by cancelled when*

292 NOTE—compare . . . (Mencius).] *opposite page*

293 *thy life*] *thy written above cancelled your*

Note . . . heart."] *added on line*

294 lets herself] *preceded by cancelled* leads him to ascend

live with him] live *interlined above cancelled* himself (French however has *avec lui*—but is this correct?)

296 demythologizing? . . . 17:20-36] *interlined*

297 works of mortification] *preceded by cancelled* penance

Comment . . . truth] *added on line*

298 radiance] *preceded by cancelled* glory

(Here the world . . . cared for.)] *interlined*

299 ambiguity . . . concept?] *added on line*

(cf. Heidegger!)] *added on line*

301 cf. Ecclesiastes] *added in left margin*

burdens] *followed by cancelled* without knowing it,

304 This theme . . . p. 335] *opposite page*

thoughts of fear] *preceded by cancelled* increasing

Prince of Evil] *followed by cancelled* with

305–306 Here we might . . . true contemplation.] *opposite page*

305 in a letter of Philoxenos] *interlined with a caret*

306 Trisagion] *preceded by cancelled* praise of the adorable Thrice Holy One

how to] *interlined with a caret*

307 Note—like . . . reproved.] *added in lower margin*

308 Baptist is] is *interlined with a caret*

309 sew up] *followed by cancelled* the tear

309–310 Note on fasting . . . obsession] *opposite page*

310 Evagrius . . . obsession] *marked with arrow for insertion*

Why is . . . *consciousness*.] *opposite page*

311 "A cow . . . craving."] *opposite page*

He speaks . . . psychology!] *opposite page*

312 of God"] *followed by cancelled* p. 341

set up"] *followed by cancelled* 341

been made a god] made *followed by cancelled* by God

nature] *preceded by cancelled* body

313 eats not] *interlined above cancelled* fasts

315 fasting and] *interlined with a caret*

Freedom . . . dies!"] *opposite page*

316 He admits] *preceded by illegible cancelled word*

spiritual] *interlined with a caret*
much more] *preceded by cancelled* should you
321 solitary mind] mind *interlined above cancelled* thought
322 nature] *preceded by cancelled* truth
"Therefore let . . . thoughts."] *opposite page*
movement] *preceded by cancelled* blind
323 For instance . . . *of will.*] *opposite page*
desire in] *interlined with a caret*
He admits . . . untouched.] *opposite page*
He admits] *interlined with a caret*
Later . . . one sees.] *opposite page*
A victory . . . (p. 473).] *added on line*
324 experience] *added in left margin to replace cancelled* truth
person] *interlined above cancelled* self
325–26 Note—in *DTC* . . . *Temperance*)] *opposite page*
327 lamp] *preceded by cancelled* light of
328 cf. Symeon . . . Nicephorus] *opposite page*
330 Source of . . . στρεβλούμενοι] *opposite page*
Evil has . . . plan.] *added on line*
hold fast] *followed by cancelled* in his difficulties
331 Canivet . . . treatment.] *opposite page*
332 archbishop] *interlined above cancelled* St. Sabas
333 He is *still living*] *added in left margin before cancelled* He died
hence . . . Alexandria] *added in right margin*
334 Ababa] *followed by cancelled* like head of secular clergy
335 St. Philip] St. *interlined below and marked for insertion*

APPENDIX B

TABLE OF CORRESPONDENCES:
Pre-Benedictine Monasticism—Lectures and Taped Conferences

Date	Page #	Opening Words	TMC CD #	Published Tape Title & #
2/3/63	3	The *Rule*	45–1	
2/17/63	13	2. *St. Martin*	45–2	
2/24/63	19	*Channels of*	45–3	
3/3/63	22	*Apothegmata*	45–4	*The Desert of God* (Credence 3017) *Life and Prophecy—The Monk: Prophet to Modern Man* (EPB I:9B)
3/17/63	29	c) *The peacemakers,*	48–1	
3/24/63	34	Hence the essence	48–3	
4/21/63	45	Abbot Nesteros begins	55–1	*Prayer and Active Life* (Credence 2072)
4/28/63	47	Chapter 4	55–2	*Prayer and Active Life* (Credence 2072)
5/12/63	52	{The prime} example	55–3	*Renunciation and Contemplation* (Credence 2073)
5/19/63	56	*Puritas Cordis*:	55–4	*Renunciation and Contemplation* (Credence 2073)

5/23/63	69	PRAYER WITHOUT FORMS	57–1	*Renunciation and Contemplation* (Credence 2073) *Life and Prayer: The Jesus Prayer— The Person of Christ in Prayer* (EPB I:3A)
6/2/63	72	**PACHOMIAN CENOBITISM**	57–2	
6/16/63	74	The *Latin* Pachomian	57–3	
6/23/63	81	{B.} *The Monastic Life*	57–4	
6/30/63	82	See the *Catechesis* 2	62–1	*Love and Hope* 2A&B (EPB III:5)
7/14/63	89	Taking off the secular	62–2	*Life and Afterlife* 2A (EPB III:4)
7/21/63	93	He lives in the *koinonia,*	62–3	
7/28/63	99	*Poverty*	62–4	
8/11/63	101	*Discretion*:	65–3	
8/18/63	107	*Vita Pachomii*	66–1	
8/25/63	123	**SAINT BASIL**	66–4	*Community and the Christian Life* (Credence 2456)
9/29/63	133	*Letter* 22	67–4	
10/20/63	132	*Silence* plays	75–4	
11/17/63	151	**ROMAN MONASTICISM**	76–1	
12/1/63	162	*Some Monastic Ideas*	76–3	
1/6/64	169	*THE PILGRIMAGE*	90–4	
1/12/64	174	*To sum up*	99–2	
2/2/64	176	*Monasticism in*	99–4	
2/16/64	191	**THE SPIRITUAL DOCTRINE**	100–1	
2/23/64	195	3. *Letter to Solitaries*	100–2	
3/15/64	198	c) *The fruits of health*	100–4	
3/22/64	201	With the "joy of God,"	101–1	
6/21/64	210	*Monastic Chronology*	106–3	
6/28/64	218	*Thesis of* {*the*} *Egyptian*	106–4	
7/12/64	221	I. *James of Nisibis*	120–1	
7/19/64	222	II. *Julian Saba*	120–4	

7/26/64	224	b) prayer	121–2	
8/9/64	231	seeking *symmetry*	122–3	
8/16/64	232	{Note} his exegesis	123–1	
8/23/64	233	*Constant Prayer*	123–4	*Prayer: Search for Inner Rest* A (Credence 2262)
8/30/64	238	Prepare yourselves,	124–3	
9/20/64	242	**St. Ephrem**	126–1	
10/11/64	248	To preserve temperance	126–4	
10/18/64	249	3—*The World*:	128–3	
10/25/64	250	3) God reveals Himself	129–1	*Life and Prayer: The Desert Source—St. Ephrem on Prayer* (EPB I:1a)
11/29/64	254	See *Collectio Monastica*	132–4	
12/13/64	257	St. Ephrem III.	135–3	*Life and Afterlife* 1A (EPB III:3)
12/20/64	257	the fountain of water	136–1	*The Door of Paradise* A (Credence 2914)
1/3/65	259	1. The height of Paradise:	136–3	*The Door of Paradise* B (Credence 2914)
2/14/65	262	9. The ark	138–4	
2/21/65	267	Ephrem: more texts	139–2	
3/7/65	271	*Seven Hymns on Virginity*	141–1	
3/14/65	275	**Syrian Monastic Rules**	141–3	
3/21/65	280	Ascetical—	142–1	
4/11/65	284	Homily 1.	142–4	
4/25/65	285	basis of the spiritual life	144–2	
5/9/65	287	*Vocation*:	145–1	*The Contemplative Call* A (Credence 2915)
5/16/65	289	*on Simplicity*	145–4	
5/27/65	291	*Readiness*:	147–4	

6/7/65	292	At our birth,	148–3	
6/20/65	294	*Letter to a Converted Jew*	149–1	
6/27/65	296	*Letter to a Novice*	149–3	*The Contemplative Call* B (Credence 2915)
7/18/65	296	demythologizing?	151–3	
7/25/65	296	*Sonship*—	152–2	*Surrender to God* A (Credence 2904)
8/8/65	320	*Homily* 12—	153–1	*The Contemplative Call* B (Credence 2915)
8/15/65	298	Vocation to the Desert.	153–4	

- "EPB" refers to tapes published by Electronic Paperbacks (Chappaqua, NY: 1972 [first series], 1983 [third series]).
- "Credence" refers to tapes published by Credence Communications (Kansas City, MO: 1987–).

APPENDIX C

FOR FURTHER READING

A. Other Writings by Merton on Topics Treated in *Pre-Benedictine Monasticism*

Anthony

"St. Anthony." *Cassian and the Fathers: Initiation into the Monastic Tradition.* MW1. Kalamazoo, MI: Cistercian, 2005: 31–39.

Rufinus

"Macarius and the Pony." *Collected Poems.* New York: New Directions, 1977: 317–18.

"Macarius the Younger." *Collected Poems*: 319–21.

Cassian

"The Testimony of Tradition." Chapter 2 of *Bread in the Wilderness.* New York: New Directions, 1953: 16–24.

"Puritas Cordis [Purity of Heart]." Part 1, Chapter 1 of *The Silent Life.* New York: Farrar, Straus and Cudahy, 1957: 1–20.

"The Humanity of Christ in Monastic Prayer." *The Monastic Journey*, ed. Brother Patrick Hart. Kansas City: Sheed, Andrews and McMeel, 1977; 87–106, especially 90–94.

"Lectures on Cassian." *Cassian and the Fathers*: 97–259.

Pachomius

"St. Pachomius and the Cenobites." *Cassian and the Fathers*: 39–45.

Basil

"St. Basil." *Cassian and the Fathers*: 45–51.

Jerome

"Virginity and Humanism in the Western Fathers." *Mystics and Zen Masters.* New York: Farrar, Straus and Giroux, 1967: 113–27.

"Two Desert Fathers: I. St. Jerome; II. St. Paul the Hermit." *Collected Poems*: 165–69.

"Palestinian Monasticism: St. Hilarion—St. Jerome." *Cassian and the Fathers*: 60–69.

Egeria

"From Pilgrimage to Crusade." *Mystics and Zen Masters*: 91–112.

Philoxenos

"Rain and the Rhinoceros." *Raids on the Unspeakable*. New York: New Directions, 1966: 9–23.

B. Significant Writings by Other Authors on Topics Treated in *Pre-Benedictine Monasticism*

General Studies

Bouyer, Louis. *The Spirituality of the New Testament and the Fathers*. Trans. Mary P. Ryan. The History of Christian Spirituality, vol. 1. New York: Seabury, 1963.

Brock, Sebastian. *The Syriac Fathers on Prayer and the Spiritual Life*. CS 101. Kalamazoo, MI: Cistercian Publications, 1987.

Burton-Christie, Douglas. *The Word in the Desert: Scripture and the Quest for Holiness in Early Christian Monasticism*. New York: Oxford University Press, 1993.

Dunn, Marilyn. *The Emergence of Monasticism: From the Desert Fathers to the Early Middle Ages*. Oxford: Blackwell, 2000.

Goehring, James E. *Ascetics, Society, and the Desert: Studies in Early Egyptian Monasticism*. Harrisburg, PA: Trinity Press, 1999.

Harmless, William, SJ. *Desert Christians: An Introduction to the Literature of Early Monasticism*. New York: Oxford University Press, 2004.

Jones, Cheslyn, Geoffrey Wainwright, and Edward Yarnold, eds. *The Study of Spirituality*. New York: Oxford University Press, 1986.

Kannengiesser, Charles. *Early Christian Spirituality*. Philadelphia: Fortress, 1986.

Louth, Andrew. *The Origins of the Christian Mystical Tradition from Plato to Denys*. Oxford: Oxford University Press, 1981.

Luckman, Harriet A., and Linda Kulzer, OSB, eds. *Purity of Heart in Early Ascetic and Monastic Literature*. Collegeville, MN: Liturgical Press, 1999.

McGinn, Bernard, John Meyendorff, and Jean Leclercq, eds. *Christian Spirituality: Origins to the Twelfth Century*. World Spirituality: An Encyclopedic History of the Religious Quest, vol. 16. New York: Crossroad, 1988.

McGinn, Bernard. *The Foundations of Mysticism: Origins to the Fifth Century*. The Presence of God: A History of Western Christian Mysticism, vol. 1. New York: Crossroad, 1992.

Spidlík, Tomás. *The Spirituality of the Christian East: A Systematic Handbook*. Trans. Anthony P. Gythiel. CS 79. Kalamazoo: Cistercian Publications, 1986.

Vööbus, A. *A History of Asceticism in the Syrian Orient*. 3 vols. CSCO 184, 197, 500. Louvain: 1958, 1960, 1988.

Williams, Rowan. *The Wound of Knowledge: Christian Spirituality from the New Testament to St. John of the Cross*. London: Darton, Longman and Todd, 1979.

Paulinus of Nola

The Letters of Paulinus of Nola, trans. P. G. Walsh. 2 vols. ACW 35-36. Westminster, MD: Newman Press, 1966, 1967.

The Poems of St. Paulinus of Nola, trans. P. G. Walsh. ACW 40. New York: Newman Press, 1975.

* * * * *

Green, R. P. H. *The Poetry of Paulinus of Nola*. Brussels: Latomus, 1971.

Lienhard, Joseph T. *Paulinus of Nola and Early Western Monasticism*. Köln: P. Hanstein, 1977.

Trout, Dennis E. *Paulinus of Nola: Life, Letters, and Poems*. Berkeley: University of California Press, 1999.

Martin of Tours

Sulpicius Severus. *Life of Martin of Tours*. In *Early Christian Lives*, trans. Carolinne White. New York: Penguin, 1998.

* * * * *

Donaldson, Christopher. *Martin of Tours: Parish Priest, Mystic and Exorcist*. London; Routledge & Kegan Paul, 1980.

Stancliffe, Clare. *St. Martin and His Hagiographer: History and Miracle in Sulpicius Severus*. Oxford: Clarendon Press, 1983.

Anthony

The Letters of St. Antony the Great. Trans. Derwas J. Chitty. Fairacres, Oxford: SLG Press, 1975.

Athanasius. *The Life of Antony and the Letter to Marcellinus*. Trans. Robert C. Gregg. Classics of Western Spirituality. New York: Paulist, 1980.

Athanasius. *The Life of Antony*, trans. Tim Vivian and Apostolos N. Athanassakis. CS 202. Kalamazoo, MI: Cistercian Publications, 2003.

* * * * *

Brakke, David. *Athanasius and the Politics of Asceticism*. Oxford: Clarendon Press, 1995.

Rubenson, Samuel. *The Letters of St. Antony: Monasticism and the Making of a Saint*. Minneapolis: Fortress, 1995.

Rufinus

The Lives of the Desert Fathers. Trans. Norman Russell. Introduction by Benedicta Ward. CS 34. Kalamazoo: Cistercian Publications, 1981.

* * * * *

Frank, Georgia. *The Memory of the Eyes: Pilgrims to Living Saints in Christian Late Antiquity*. Berkeley: University of California Press, 2000.

Murphy, Francis X. *Rufinus of Aquileia*. Washington, DC: Catholic University of America Press, 1945.

Cassian

The Conferences. Trans. Boniface Ramsey. ACW 57. New York: Paulist, 1997.

Conferences. Trans. Colm Luibheid. Classics of Western Spirituality. New York: Paulist, 1985 (*Conferences* 1–3, 9–11, 14–15, 18).

The Institutes. Trans. Boniface Ramsey. ACW 58. New York: Paulist, 2000.

The Monastic Institutes. Trans. Jerome Bertram. London: St. Austin Press, 1999.

* * * * *

Chadwick, Owen. *John Cassian: A Study in Primitive Monasticism*. Cambridge: Cambridge University Press, 1950; 2nd ed. 1968.

Driver, Steven D. *John Cassian and the Reading of Egyptian Monastic Culture*. New York: Routledge, 2002.

Funk, Mary Margaret. *Thoughts Matter: The Practice of the Spiritual Life*. New York: Continuum, 1997.

Rousseau, Philip. *Ascetics, Authority, and the Church in the Age of Jerome and Cassian*. Oxford: Oxford University Press, 1978.

Stewart, Columba. *Cassian the Monk*. New York: Oxford University Press, 1998.

Pachomius

Pachomian Koinonia: The Lives, Rules, and Other Writings of Saint Pachomius and His Disciples. I: The Life of Saint Pachomius and His Disciples; II: Rule; III: Other Writings. Trans. Armand Veilleux. CS 45–47. Kalamazoo: Cistercian Publications, 1980–1982.

* * * * *

Rousseau, Philip. *Pachomius: The Making of a Community in Fourth-Century Egypt*. Berkeley: University of California Press, 1985.

Shenoute

Besa, *The Life of Shenoute*, trans. David N. Bell. CS 73. Kalamazoo, MI: Cistercian Publications, 1983.

* * * * *

Emmel, Stephen. *Shenoute's Literary Corpus*. Corpus Scriptorum Christianorum Orientalium, vols. 599–600. Louvain: Peeters, 2004.

Krawiec, Rebecca. *Shenoute and the Women of the White Monastery: Egyptian Monasticism in Late Antiquity*. New York: Oxford University Press, 2002.

Basil

Ascetical Works, trans. Sister M. Monica Wagner, CSC. FC 9. Washington: Catholic University of America Press, 1950.

Exegetic Homilies, trans. Sr. Agnes Clare Way, CDP. FC 46. Washington, DC: Catholic University of America Press, 1963.

Gateway to Paradise: Basil the Great, ed. Oliver Davies, trans. Tim Witherow. Brooklyn, NY: New City Press, 1991.

Letters, trans. Sr. Agnes Clare Way, CDP. FC 13, 28. New York: Fathers of the Church, 1951, 1955.

On the Holy Spirit, trans. David Anderson. Crestwood, NY: St. Vladimir's Seminary Press, 1980.

The Fathers Speak: St. Basil the Great, St. Gregory of Nazianzus, St. Gregory of Nyssa: Selected Letters and Life-Records, trans. Georges A. Barrois. Crestwood, NY: St. Vladimir's Seminary Press, 1986.

* * * * *

Fedwick, Paul J., ed. *Basil of Caesarea: Christian, Humanist, Ascetic*. 2 vols. Toronto: Pontifical Institute of Medieval Studies, 1981.

Fedwick, Paul. *The Church and the Charisma of Leadership in Basil of Caesarea*. Toronto: Pontifical Institute of Mediaeval Studies, 1979.

Holmes, Augustine. *A Life Pleasing to God: The Spirituality of the Rules of St. Basil*. CS 189. Kalamazoo, MI: Cistercian Publications, 2000.

Meredith, Anthony. *The Cappadocians*. Crestwood, NY: St. Vladimir's Seminary Press, 1995.

Rousseau, Philip. *Basil of Caesarea*. Berkeley: University of California Press, 1994.

Melania the Younger

Handmaids of the Lord: Contemporary Descriptions of Feminine Asceticism in the First Six Christian Centuries, ed. and trans. Joan M. Peterson. CS 143. Kalamazoo, MI: Cistercian Publications, 1996.

The Life of Melania the Younger, trans. Elizabeth A. Clark. New York: E. Mellen Press, 1984.

Jerome

St. Jerome, *Dogmatic and Polemical Works*, trans. John Hritzu. FC 53. Washington, DC: Catholic University of America Press, 1965.

Letters of St. Jerome, vol. 1, trans. Charles C. Mierow, ed. Thomas Comerford Lawlor. ACW 33. Westminster, MD: Newman Press, 1963.

* * * * *

Kelly, J. N. D. *Jerome: His Life, Writings and Controversies*. New York: Harper & Row, 1975.

Rebenich, Stefan. *Jerome*. New York: Routledge, 2002.

Egeria

Egeria: Diary of a Pilgrimage, trans. George E. Gingras. ACW 38. New York: Newman Press, 1970.

Ammonas

The Letters of Ammonas, Successor of Saint Anthony, trans. Derwas J. Chitty and Sebastian Brock. Oxford: SLG, 1979.

Theodoret of Cyrrhus

Theodoret of Cyrrhus, *A History of the Monks of Syria*, trans. R. M. Price. CS 88. Kalamazoo, MI: Cistercian Publications, 1985.

* * * * *

Urbainczyk, Theresa. *Theodoret of Cyrrhus: The Bishop and the Holy Man*. Ann Arbor: University of Michigan Press, 2002.

Aphraat

Murray, Robert. *Symbols of Church and Kingdom: A Study in Early Syriac Tradition*. New York: Cambridge University Press, 1975.

Ephrem

The Harp of the Spirit: Eighteen Poems of Saint Ephrem, trans. Sebastian Brock. 2nd ed. London: Fellowship of St. Alban and St. Sergius, 1983.

Hymns, trans. Kathleen E. McVey. New York: Paulist, 1989.

Hymns on Paradise, trans. Sebastian Brock. Crestwood, NY: St. Vladimir's Seminary Press, 1998.

Selected Prose Works, trans. Edward G. Mathews, Jr. and Joseph P. Amar, ed. Kathleen McVey. FC 91. Washington, DC: Catholic University of America Press, 1994.

* * * * *

Brock, Sebastian. *The Luminous Eye: The Spiritual World Vision of Saint Ephrem*. CS 124. Kalamazoo, MI: Cistercian Publications, 1992.

Griffith, Sidney. *Faith Adoring the Mystery: Reading the Bible with St. Ephraem the Syrian*. Milwaukee: Marquette University Press, 1997.

Philoxenos

Chesnut [Bondi], Roberta C. *Three Monophysite Christologies: Severus of Antioch, Philoxenus of Mabbug, and Jacob of Sarug*. Oxford: Oxford University Press, 1976.

ACKNOWLEGEMENTS

Cistercian Publications gratefully acknowledges permission to cite the following works:

The Journals of Thomas Merton: *Turning Towards the World* and *Dancing in the Waters of Life*. Reprinted with the permission of HarperCollins Publishers.

The Correspondence of Thomas Merton: *Hidden Ground of Love* and *The School of Charity*. Quoted with permission of Farrar, Straus & Giroux, New York.

The Rule of Benedict in Latin and English (1952). Reproduced by kind permission of The Continuum International Publishing Group.

Monica Wagner, trans. *Saint Basil: Ascetical Works,* Fathers of the Church, 9. Used with permission: The Catholic University of America Press, Washington, D.C.

Owen Chadwick, trans. *Western Asceticism,* Library of Christian Classics volume 12. Published by Westminster John Knox Press, Louisville, Kentucky.

Arthur Vööbus, *History of Asceticism in the Syrian Orient. A Contribution to the History of Culture in the Near East,* Corpus Scriptorium Christianorum Orientalium, 184. Published by Peeters Publishers, Leuven, for the Secretariat du CSCO, Louvain.

INDEX

Texts in English translation:

- Monastic insights from the desert, and from christian monks and nuns East and West
- Cistercian homilies and treatises from the formative twelfth and thirteenth centuries

Studies of the monastic tradition:

- Its history, customs, architecture, liturgy, and influence, from desert beginnings through the Middle Ages and into the present day
- Reflections on prayer and the christian vocation by contemporary contemplatives
- Audio and video resources on monasticism as well as books published abroad and not readily available in North America

All books are available singly or by series standing order. Standing order customers automatically receive new titles as they appear at a 25% discount from the list price

Series:

- Cistercian Fathers
- Monastic Wisdom
- Cistercian Studies
- Cistercian Liturgy

Editorial Offices

Cistercian Publications • WMU Station
1903 West Michigan Avenue • Kalamazoo, MI 49008-5415 USA
tel 269 387 8920 fax 269 387 8390
e-mail cistpub@wmich.edu

Customer Service—North America: USA and Canada

Cistercian Publications at Liturgical Press
Saint John's Abbey • Collegeville, MN 56321-7500 USA
tel 800 436 8431 fax 320 363 3299
e-mail sales@litpress.org

Customer Service—Europe: UK, Ireland, and Europe

Cistercian Publications at Columba Book Service
55A Spruce Avenue • Stillorgan Industrial Park
Blackrock, Co. Dublin, Ireland
tel 353 1 294 2560 fax 353 1 294 2564
e-mail sales@columba.ie

To explore the range of titles offered by Cistercian Publications, please request our free complete catalogue from one of the customer service offices or visit our website at **www.cistercianpublications.org**